FUNDAMENTALS OF DATA STRUCTURES

[Using Python and C++]

Anuradha A. Puntambekar

M.E. (Computer)

Formerly Assistant Professor in

P.E.S. Modern College of Engineering,

Pune

TECHNICAL PUBLICATIONS

SINCE 1993

An Up-Thrust for Knowledge

FUNDAMENTALS OF DATA STRUCTURES

First Edition : December 2020

Published by :

TECHNICAL PUBLICATIONS
SINCE 1993 An Up-Thrust for Knowledge

Amit Residency, Office No.1, 412, Shaniwar Peth, Pune - 411030, M.S. INDIA
Ph.: +91-020-24495496/97, Email : sales@technicalpublications.org
Website : www.technicalpublications.org

ISBN 978-93-332-2379-9

9789333223799

PREFACE

The importance of **Fundamentals of Data Structures** is well known in various engineering fields. Overwhelming response to my books on various subjects inspired me to write this book. The book is structured to cover the key aspects of the subject **Fundamentals of Data Structures.**

The book uses plain, lucid language to explain fundamentals of this subject. The book provides logical method of explaining various complicated concepts and stepwise methods to explain the important topics. Each chapter is well supported with necessary illustrations, practical examples and solved problems. All the chapters in the book are arranged in a proper sequence that permits each topic to build upon earlier studies. All care has been taken to make students comfortable in understanding the basic concepts of the subject.

Representative questions have been added at the end of each section to help the students in picking important points from that section.

The book not only covers the entire scope of the subject but explains the philosophy of the subject. This makes the understanding of this subject more clear and makes it more interesting. The book will be very useful not only to the students but also to the subject teachers. The students have to omit nothing and possibly have to cover nothing more.

I wish to express my profound thanks to all those who helped in making this book a reality. Much needed moral support and encouragement is provided on numerous occasions by my whole family. I wish to thank the **Publisher** and the entire team of **Technical Publications** who have taken immense pain to get this book in time with quality printing.

Any suggestion for the improvement of the book will be acknowledged and well appreciated.

Author

A. A. Puntambekar

Dedicated to God.

SYLLABUS

Unit I Introduction to Algorithm and Data Structures

Introduction : From Problem to Program (Problem, Solution, Algorithm, Data Structure and Program). Data Structures : Data, Information, Knowledge, and Data structure, Abstract Data Types (ADT), Data Structure Classification (Linear and Non-linear, Static and Dynamic, Persistent and Ephemeral data structures).

Algorithms : Problem Solving, Introduction to algorithm, Characteristics of algorithm, Algorithm design tools : Pseudo-code and flowchart. **Complexity of algorithm** : Space complexity, Time complexity, Asymptotic notation - Big-O, Theta and Omega, Finding complexity using step count method, Analysis of programming constructs-Linear, Quadratic, Cubic, Logarithmic.

Algorithmic Strategies : Introduction to algorithm design strategies - Divide and Conquer, and Greedy strategy. **(Chapter - 1)**

Unit II Linear Data Structure using Sequential Organization

Concept of Sequential Organization, Overview of Array, Array as an Abstract Data Type, Operations on Array, Merging of two arrays, Storage Representation and their Address Calculation : Row major and Column Major, Multidimensional Arrays : Two-dimensional arrays, n-dimensional arrays. Concept of Ordered List, **Single Variable Polynomial** : Representation using arrays, Polynomial as array of structure, Polynomial addition, Polynomial multiplication. **Sparse Matrix** : Sparse matrix representation using array, Sparse matrix addition, Transpose of sparse matrix- Simple and Fast Transpose, Time and Space tradeoff. **(Chapter - 2)**

Unit III Searching and Sorting

Searching : Search Techniques-Sequential Search/Linear Search, Variant of Sequential Search- Sentinel Search, Binary Search, Fibonacci Search, and Indexed Sequential Search. **Sorting** : Types of Sorting-Internal and External Sorting, General Sort Concepts-Sort Order, Stability, Efficiency, and Number of Passes, Comparison Based Sorting Methods-Bubble Sort, Insertion Sort, Selection Sort, Quick Sort, Shell Sort, Non-comparison Based Sorting Methods-Radix Sort, Counting Sort, and Bucket Sort, Comparison of All Sorting Methods and their complexities. **(Chapter - 3)**

Unit IV Linked List

Introduction to Static and Dynamic Memory Allocation, **Linked List** : Introduction of Linked Lists, Realization of linked list using dynamic memory management operations, Linked List as ADT, **Types of Linked List** : singly linked, linear and Circular Linked Lists, Doubly Linked List, Doubly Circular Linked List, Primitive Operations on Linked List-Create, Traverse, Search, Insert, Delete, Sort, Concatenate. Polynomial Manipulations-Polynomial addition. Generalized Linked List (GLL) concept, Representation of Polynomial using GLL. **(Chapter - 4)**

Unit V Stack

Basic concept, stack Abstract Data Type, Representation of Stacks Using Sequential Organization, stack operations, Multiple Stacks, Applications of Stack- Expression Evaluation and Conversion, Polish notation and expression conversion, Need for prefix and postfix expressions, Postfix expression evaluation, Linked Stack and Operations. **Recursion** - concept, variants of recursion - direct, indirect, tail and tree, Backtracking algorithmic strategy, use of stack in backtracking. **(Chapter - 5)**

Unit VI Queue

Basic concept, Queue as Abstract Data Type, Representation of Queue using Sequential organization, Queue Operations, Circular Queue and its advantages, Multi-queues, Linked Queue and Operations. **Deque**-Basic concept, types (Input restricted and Output restricted), Priority Queue- Basic concept, types(Ascending and Descending). **(Chapter - 6)**

TABLE OF CONTENTS

Unit - I

Unit - II

Chapter - 2 Linear Data Structure using Sequential Organization (2 - 1) to (2 - 66)

Unit - III

Part II : Sorting

Unit - IV

Chapter - 4 Linked List (4 - 1) to (4 - 86)

Unit - V

Unit - VI

Unit - I

1 Introduction to Algorithm and Data Structures

Syllabus

Introduction : *From Problem to Program (Problem, Solution, Algorithm, Data Structure and Program). Data Structures : Data, Information, Knowledge, and Data structure, Abstract Data Types (ADT), Data Structure Classification (Linear and Non-linear, Static and Dynamic, Persistent and Ephemeral data structures).*

Algorithms : *Problem Solving, Introduction to algorithm, Characteristics of algorithm, Algorithm design tools : Pseudo-code and flowchart.* ***Complexity of algorithm :*** *Space complexity, Time complexity, Asymptotic notation- Big-O, Theta and Omega, Finding complexity using step count method, Analysis of programming constructs-Linear, Quadratic, Cubic, Logarithmic.*

Algorithmic Strategies : *Introduction to algorithm design strategies - Divide and Conquer, and Greedy strategy.*

Contents

Part I : Introduction to Data Structures

1.1 From Problem to Data Structure (Problem, Logic, Algorithm, and Data Structure)

- Problem can be solved using series of actions. The steps that are followed in order to solve the problem are collectively called as **algorithm.**
- There are some problems for which the direct solution does not exist. For building the solution to such problems some reasoning is required. This reasoning is usually based on knowledge and prior experience. Hence the process of trial and error is followed to solve the given problem. This process is called **logic building** for particular solution.
- For example – For displaying the list of numbers in reverse direction, we should read and display the last element of the list, then last but one and so on.
- In computer science, when we want to solve any problem, then we need Data, the **data structure** that will arrange the data in some specific manner and the algorithm which will handle this data structure in some **systematic manner**.
- Data structure is the means by which we can **model the problem**.
- For example - Arrays - It contains integer elements(data) which are arranged in sequential organization (data structure) and then algorithms such as - addition of all elements, or for sorting the elements in specific manner are applied on this data structure.
- Thus Data structure is used for arranging the data and algorithm is used to solve the problem by systematic execution of each step.

1.2 Data Structures : Data, Information, Knowledge, and Data Structure

Data : Data refers to raw data or unprocessed data.

Information : Information is data that has been processed in such a way that it will become meaningful to the person who receives it. The information has structure and context.

Knowledge : Knowledge is basically something which person knows. Knowledge requires a person to understand what information is, based on their experience and knowledge base

Data structure : A data structure is a particular way of organizing data in a computer so that it can be used effectively.

For example – Consider set of elements which can be stored in array data structure. The representation of array containing set of elements is as follows –

0	1	2	3	4
10	20	30	40	50

Any element in above array can be referred by an index. For instance the element 40 can be accessed as array[3].

Difference between Data and Information

Sr. No.	Data	Information
1.	Data is in raw form.	Information is processed form of data.
2.	Data may or may not be meaningful.	Information is always meaningful.
3.	Data may not be in some specific order.	Information generally follows specific ordering.
4.	For example - each Student's marks in exam is one piece of data.	For example - The average score of a class is information that can be derived from given data.

1.3 Abstract Data Types (ADT)

SPPU : Dec.-10, 11, May-10, 11, 12, 13, 19, Marks 6

The abstract data type is a triple of D - Set of domains, F - Set of functions, A - axioms in which only what is to be done is mentioned but how is to be done is not mentioned.

In ADT, all the implementation details are hidden. In short

ADT = Type + Function names + Behavior of each function

We will discuss in further chapters how the ADT can be written

1.3.1 Realization of ADT

The abstract datatype consists of following things

1. Data used along with its data type.
2. Declaration of functions which specify only the purpose. That means "What is to be done" in particular function has to be mentioned but "how is to be done" must be hidden.
3. Behavior of function can be specified with the help of data and functions together.

Thus ADT allows programmer to hide the implementation details. Hence it is called **abstract**. For example : If we want to write ADT for a set of integers, then we will use following method

AbstractDataType Set {

Instances : Set is a collection of integer type of elements.

Preconditions : none

Operations :

1. **Store ( ) :** This operation is for storing the integer element in a set.
2. **Retrieve ( ) :** This operation is for retrieving the desired element from the given set.
3. **Display ( ) :** This operation is for displaying the contents of set.

}

There is a specific method using which an ADT can be written. We begin with keyword **AbstractDataType** which is then followed by name of the data structure for which we want to write an ADT. In above given example we have taken **Set** data structure.

- Then inside a pair of curly brackets ADT must be written.
- We must first write **instances** in which the basic idea about the corresponding data structure must be given. Generally in this section definition of corresponding data structure is given.
- Using **Preconditions** or **Postconditions** we can mention specific conditions that must be satisfied before or after execution of corresponding function.
- Then a listing of all the required operations must be given. In this section, we must specify the purpose of the function. We can also specify the data types of these functions.

1.3.2 ADT for Arrays

AbstractDataType Array
{
Instances : An array A of some size, index i and total number of elements in the array n.
Operations :
Store () – This operation stores the desired elements at each successive location.
display () – This operation displays the elements of the array.
}

Review Questions

1. *Explain what is abstract data type ?* **SPPU : Dec.-10, Marks 4**
2. *What is ADT ? Write ADT for an arrays.* **SPPU : May-10,11, Dec.-11, Marks 6, May-12, Marks 4**

3. *Explain following terminologies : i) Data type ii) Data structure iii) Abstract data type.* **SPPU : May-13, Marks 6**

4. *Define (1) ADT (2) Data Structure.* **SPPU : May-19, Marks 2**

1.4 Data Structure Classification

SPPU : May-17, Dec.-18, 19, Marks 4

The data structures can be divided into two basic types primitive data structure and non primitive data structure. The Fig. 1.4.1. shows various types of data structures.

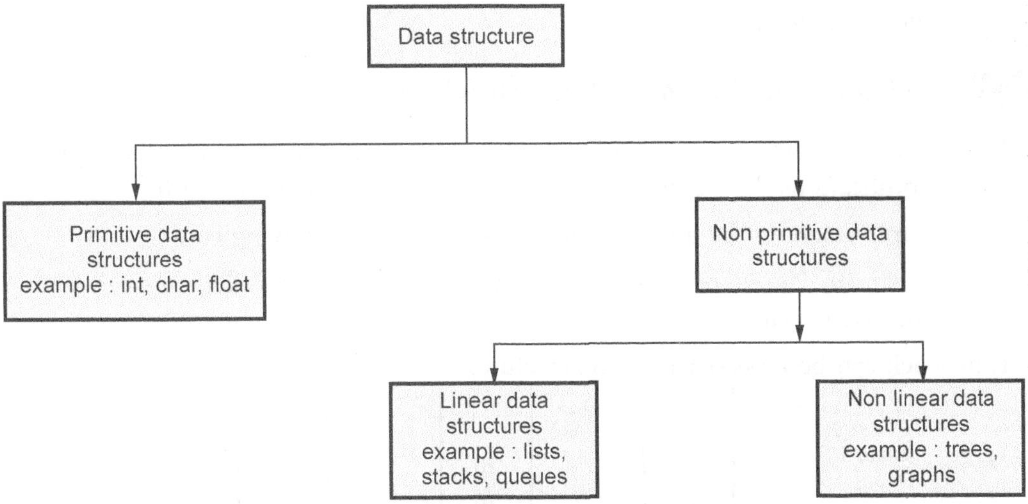

Fig. 1.4.1 Classification of data structure

1.4.1 Linear and Non linear Data Structure

Linear data structures are the data structures in which data is arranged in a list or in a straight sequence.

For example : arrays, list.

Non linear data structures are the data structures in which data may be arranged in hierarchical manner.

For example : trees, graphs.

1.4.2 Static and Dynamic Data Structure

The static data structures are data structures having fixed size memory utilization. One has to allocate the size of this data structure before using it.

For example (Static Data Structure) :

Arrays in C is a static data structure. We first allocate the size of the arrays before its actual use. Sometimes what ever size we have allocated for the arrays may get wasted or we may require larger than the one which is existing. Thus the data structure is static in nature.

The dynamic data structure is a data structure in which one can allocate the memory as per his requirement. If one does not want to use some block of memory, he can deallocate it.

For example (Dynamic Data Structure (Dynamic)) :

Linked list, the linked list is a collection of many nodes. Each node consists of data and pointer to next node. In linked list user can create as much nodes (memory) as he wants, he can dellocate the memory which cannot be utilized further.

The advantage of dynamic data structure over the static data structure is that there is no wastage of memory.

1.4.3 Persistent and Ephimeral Data Structure

The persistent data structures are the data structures which retain their previous state and modifications can be done by performing certain operations on it.

For example stack can be a persistent data structure in following case

If we push 10, 20, 30 onto it and by performing pop operation we can gain its previous state. That means -

Thus stack can be a persistent data structure.

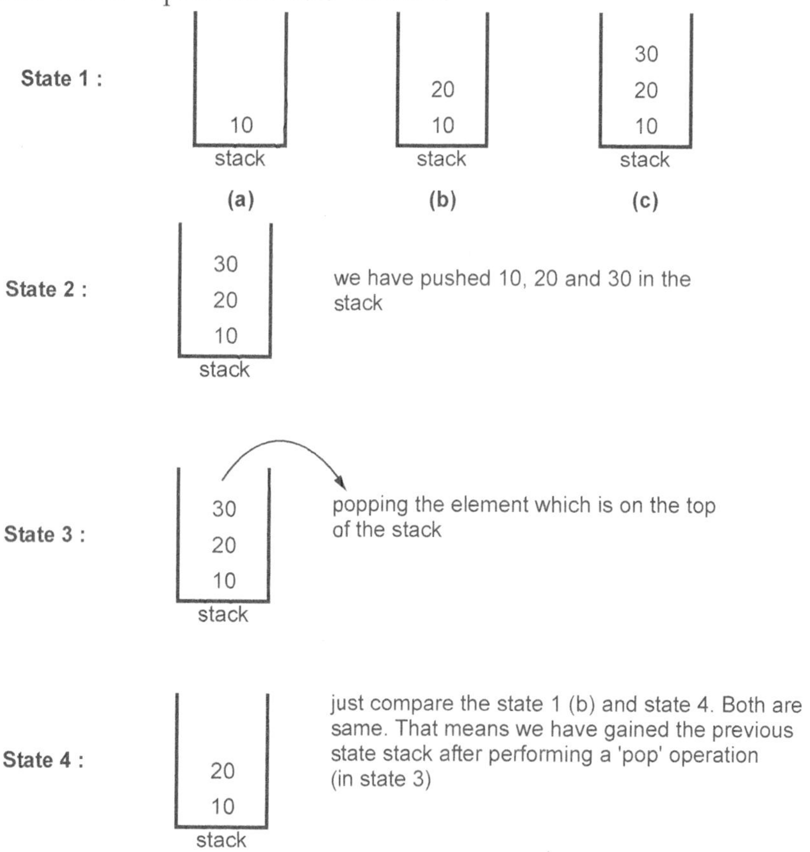

The ephemeral data structures are the data structures in which we cannot retain its previous state.

For example Queues

State 1 : In queues elements are inserted by one end and deleted by other end. Let us insert 10, 20, 30 in the queue.

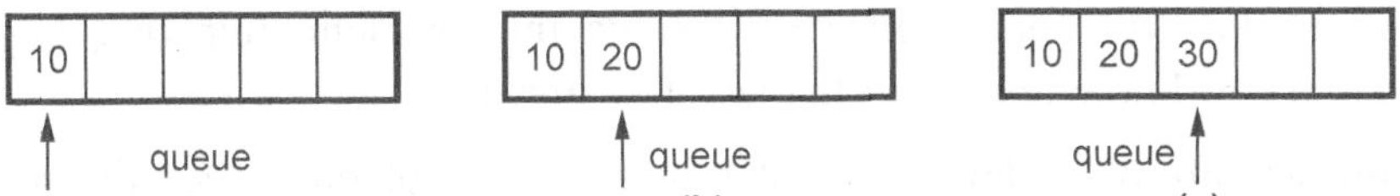

(a) (b) (c)

State 2 : Now if we delete the element, we can delete it only by other end. That means 10 can be deleted. And queue will be -

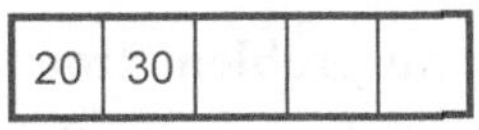

Now this state is not matching with any of the previous states. That means we can not retain the previous state of the data structure even after performing certain operations. Such a data structure is called ephemeral data structure.

Review Questions

1. *Differentiate between linear and non linear data structure with example.* **SPPU : May-17, Marks 3**
2. *Explain static and dynamic data structures with examples* **SPPU : Dec.-18, Marks 4**
3. *Write short note on Linear and Non-Linear data structure with example* **SPPU : Dec.-19, Marks 4**

Part II : Introduction to Algorithms

1.5 Problem Solving

SPPU : Dec.-09, 10, May-10, 11, Marks 12

Problem solving is based on the decisions that are taken. Following are the **six steps of problem solving** -

1. **Identify the problem :** Identifying the problem is the first step in solving the problem. Problem identification is very essential before solving any problem.
2. **Understand the problem** : Before solving any problem it is important to understand it. There are three aspects based on which the problem can be understood.

- **Knowledgebase** : While solving the problem the knowledgebase can be related to **a person or a machine**. If the problem is to be solved for the person then it is necessary to know **what the person knows**. If the problem is to be solved for the machine then its **instruction set** must be known. Along with this the problem solver can make use of his/her own instruction set.
- **Subject** : Before solving the problem the subject on which the problem is based must be known. For instance : To solve the problem involving Laplace, it is necessary to know about the Laplace transform.
- **Communication** : For understanding the problem, the developer must communicate **with the client**.

3. **Identify the alternative ways to solve the problem** : The alternative way to solve the problem must be known to the developer. These alternatives can be decided by **communicating** with the customer.
4. **Select the best way to solve the problem from list of alternative solutions** : For selecting the best way to solve the problem, the merits and demerits of each problem must be analysed. The criteria to evaluate each problem must be predefined.
5. **List the instructions using the selected solution** : Based on the knowledgebase(created/used in step 2) the step by step instructions are listed out. Each and every instruction must be understood by the person or the machine involved in the problem solving process.
6. **Evaluate the solution** : When the solution is evaluated then - i) check whether the solution is correct or not ii) check whether it satisfies the requirements of the customer or not.

Example 1.5.1 *An admission charge for the cinemax theatre varies according to the age of the person. Complete the six problem solving steps to calculate the ticket charge given the age of the person. The charges are as follows :*

i) Over 55 : ₹ 50.00 *ii) 21-54 : ₹ 75.00*

iii) 13-20 : ₹ 50.00 *iv) 3-12 : ₹ 25.00* *v) Under 3 : free*

(Hint: No need to draw flowchart) **SPPU : Dec.-09, Marks 12**

Solution : Step 1 : Identify the problem : What are the charges for the person for the cine ticket?

Step 2 : Understand the problem : Here the age of the person must be known so that the charge for the ticket can be calculated.

Step 3 : Identify alternatives : No alternative is possible for this problem.

Step 4 : Select the best way to solve the problem : The only way to solve this problem is to calculate ticket charge based on the age of the person.

Step 5 : Prepare the list of selected solutions :

i. Enter the age of the person.

ii. If age>55 charge for the ticket is ₹ 50.00

iii. If age>=21 and <=54 charge for the ticket is ₹ 75.00

iv. If age>=13 and <=20 charge for the ticket is ₹ 50.00

v. If age>=3 and <=12 charge for the ticket is ₹ 25.00

vi. If age <=3 charge for the ticket is ₹ 00.00

vii. Print charge

Step 6 : Evaluate Solution : The charge for the ticket should be according to the age of the person.

Review Questions

1. *State a reason why each of the six problem solving steps is important in developing the best solution for a problem. Give one reason for each step.* **SPPU : May-10, Marks 8**
2. *Consider any one problem and solve that problem using six steps of problem solving. Explain each step in detail.* **SPPU : Dec.-10, Marks 8**
3. *Describe the six steps in problem solving with example.* **SPPU : May-11, Marks 8**

1.6 Difficulties in Problem Solving

SPPU : Dec.-10, May-16, Marks 4

Various difficulties in solving the problem are -

- People do **not know** how to solve particular problem.
- Many times people get **afraid of** taking decisions
- While following the problem solving steps people complete one or two **steps inadequately**.
- People do **not define** the problem statements correctly.
- They do not generate the **sufficient list of alternatives.** Sometimes good alternatives might get eliminated. Sometimes the merits and demerits of the alternatives is defined hastily.
- The **sequence of solution** is not defined **logically,** or the focus of the design is sometimes on **detailed work** before the framework solution.

- When solving the problems on **computer** then **writing the instructions** for the computer is most crucial task. With **lack of knowledgebase** one can not write the proper instruction set for the computers.

Review Questions

1. *State and explain any four difficulties with problem solving* **SPPU : Dec.-10, Marks 4**
2. *What are the difficulties in problem solving ? Explain any four steps in problem solving with suitable example.* **SPPU : May-16, Marks 4**

1.7 Introduction to Algorithm **SPPU : Dec.-16, May-18, 19, Marks 4**

Definition of Algorithm : An algorithm is a finite set of instructions for performing a particular task. The instructions are nothing but the statements in simple English language.

Example : Let us take a very simple example of an algorithm which adds the two numbers and store the result in a third variable.

Step 1 : Start.

Step 2 : Read the first number is variable 'a'

Step 3 : Read the second number in variable 'b'

Step 4 : Perform the addition of both the numbers i.e. and store the result in variable 'c'.

Step 5 : Print the value of 'c' as a result of addition.

Step 6 : Stop.

1.7.1 Characteristics of Algorithm

1. Each algorithm is supplied with **zero or more inputs.**
2. Each algorithm must **produce** at least one **output**
3. Each algorithm should have **definiteness** i.e. each instruction must be **clear and unambiguous.**
4. Each algorithm should have **finiteness** i.e. if we trace out the instructions of an algorithm, then for all cases the algorithm will terminate after finite number of steps.

Each algorithm should have **effectiveness** i.e. every instruction must be sufficiently basic that it can in principal be carried out by a person using only pencil and paper. Moreover each instruction of an algorithm must also be feasible.

Review Questions

1. *Define algorithm and its characteristics.* **SPPU : Dec.-16, Marks 4, May-19, Marks 2**
2. *Define and explain following terms – (i) Data (ii) Data structure (iii) Algorithm.* **SPPU : May-18, Marks 3**

1.8 Algorithm Design Tools

There are various ways by which we can specify an algorithm.

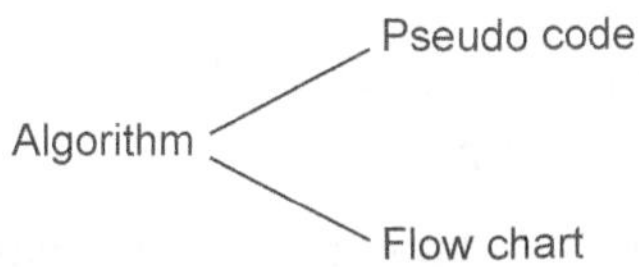

Let us discuss these techniques

1.8.1 Pseudocode

SPPU : May-10, 11, Dec.-10, Marks 8

- **Definition :** Pseudo code is nothing but an informal way of writing a program. It is a combination of algorithm written in simple English and some programming language.
- In pseudo code, there is no restriction of following the syntax of the programming language.
- Pseudo codes cannot be compiled. It is just a previous step of developing a code for given algorithm.
- Even sometimes by examining the pseudo code one can decide which language has to select for implementation.

The algorithm is broadly divided into two sections. (Refer Fig. 1.8.1)

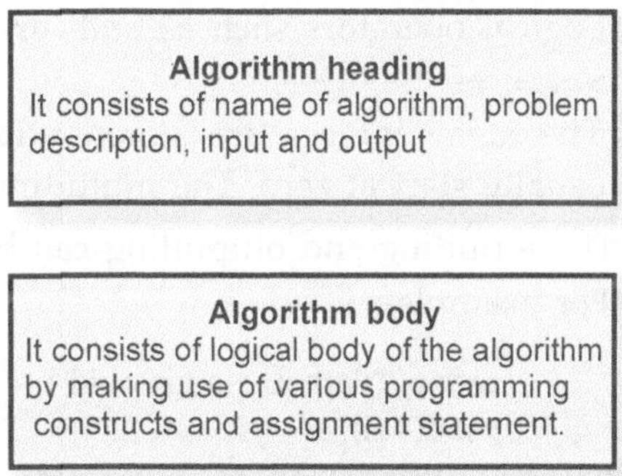

Fig. 1.8.1 Structure of algorithm

Let us understand some rules for writing the algorithm.

1. Algorithm is a procedure consisting of heading and body. The heading consists of keyword **Algorithm** and name of the algorithm and parameter list. The syntax is

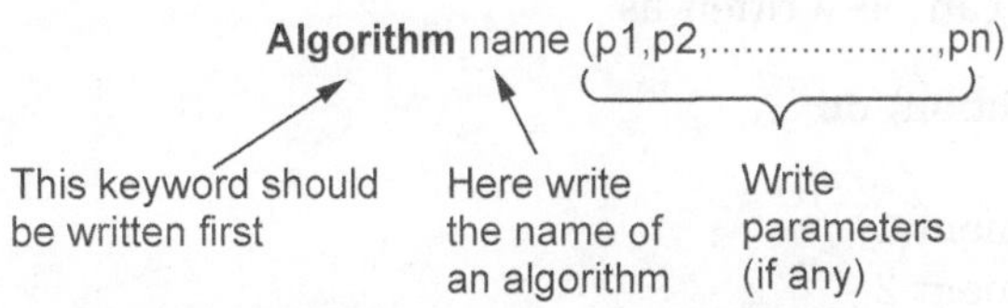

2. Then in the heading section we should write following things :

```
//Problem Description :
//Input :
//Output :
```

3. Then body of an algorithm is written, in which various programming constructs like if, for, while or some assignment statements may be written.
4. The compound statements should be enclosed within { and } brackets.
5. Single line comments are written using // as beginning of comment.
6. The **identifier** should begin by letter and not by digit. An identifier can be a combination of alphanumeric string.

   It is not necessary to write data types explicitly for identifiers. It will be represented by the context itself. Basic data types used are integer, float, char, Boolean and so on. The pointer type is also used to point memory location. The compound data type such as structure or record can also be used.
7. Using assignment operator ← an assignment statement can be given.

   For instance :

```
Variable ← expression
```

8. There are other types of operators such as Boolean operators such as true or false. Logical operators such as **and, or, not**. And relational operators such as <, <=, >, >=, =, ≠
9. The array indices are stored with in square brackets '[' ']'. The index of array usually start at zero. The multidimensional arrays can also be used in algorithm.
10. The inputting and outputting can be done using **read** and **write**.

    For example :

```
write("This message will be displayed on console");
read(val);
```

11. The conditional statements such as if-then or if-then-else are written in following form :

```
if (condition) then statement
if (condition) then statement else statement
```

    If the **if-then** statement is of compound type then { and } should be used for enclosing block.
12. **while** statement can be written as :

```
while (condition) do
{
        statement 1
        statement 2
```

```
            :
            :
        statement n
    }
```

While the condition is true the block enclosed with { } gets executed otherwise statement after } will be executed.

13. The general form for writing for loop is :

```
    for variable ← value1 to valuen do
    {
        statement 1
        statement 2
            :
            :
        statement n
    }
```

Here **value$_1$** is initialization condition and **value$_n$** is a terminating condition.

Sometime a keyword **step** is used to denote increament or decreament the value of variable for example

```
for i←1 to n step 1  ◄──  Here variable i is
{                          incremented by 1
    Write (i)              at each iteration
}
```

14. The **repeat - until** statement can be written as :

```
    repeat
        statement 1
        statement 2
            :
            :
        statement n
    until (condition)
```

15. The **break** statement is used to exit from inner loop. The **return** statement is used to return control from one point to another. Generally used while exiting from function.

    Note that statements in an algorithm executes in sequential order i.e. in the same order as they appear-one after the other.

A sub-algorithm is complete and independently defined algorithmic module. This module is actually called by some main algorithm or some another sub-algorithm.

There are two types of sub-algorithms -

1. Function sub-algorithm
2. Procedure sub-algorithm

Example of function sub-algorithm

```
Function sum(a,b:integer):integer
{
 //body of function
 //return statement
}
```

Example of Procedure sub-algorithm

```
Procedure sum(a,b:integer):integer
{
 //body of procedure
}
```

The **difference between function** sub-algorithm **and procedure** sub-algorithm is that, the function can return only one value where as the procedure can return more than one value.

Examples of Pseudo Code

Example 1.8.1 *Write an pseudo code to count the sum of n numbers.*

Solution :

```
Algorithm sum (1, n)
//Problem Description: This algorithm is for finding the
//sum of given n numbers
//Input: 1 to n numbers
//Output: The sum of n numbers
    result ← 0
    for i ← 1 to n do i ← i+1
        result ← result+i
return result
```

Example 1.8.2 *Write a pseudo code to check whether given number is even or odd.*

Solution :

```
Algorithm eventest (val)
//Problem Description: This algorithm test whether given
//number is even or odd
//Input: the number to be tested i.e. val
//Output: Appropriate messages indicating even or oddness
if (val%2=0) then
        write ("Given number is even")
else
        write("Given number is odd")
```

Example 1.8.3 *Write a pseudo code for sorting the elements.*

Solution :

```
Algorithm sort (a,n)
//Problem Description: sorting the elements in ascending order
//Input:An array a in which the elements are stored and n
//is total number of elements in the array
//Output: The sorted array
for i ← 1 to n do
for j ← i+1 to n – 1 do
{
 if(a[i]>a[j]) then
 {
            temp ← a[i]
            a[i] ← a[j]
            a[j] ← temp
 }
}
write ("List is sorted")
```

Example 1.8.4 *Write a pseudo code to find factorial of n number. (n!)*

Solution :

```
Algorithm fact (n)
//Problem Description: This algorithm finds the factorial
//of given number n
//Input: The number n of which the factorial is to be
//calculated.
//Output:factorial value of given n number.
if(n ← 1) then
            return 1
else
            return n*fact(n – 1)
```

Example 1.8.5 *Write a pseudo code to perform multiplication of two matrices.*

Solution :

```
Algorithm Mul(A,B,n)
//Problem Description:This algorithm is for computing
//multiplication of two matrices
//Input:The two matrices A,B and order of them as n
//Output:The multiplication result will be in matrix C
for i ← 1 to n do
  for j ← 1 to n do
    C[i,j] ← 0
            for k ← 1 to n do
      C[i,j] ← C[i,j]+A[i,k]B[k,j]
```

1.8.2 Flowchart

- Flowcharts are the graphical representation of the algorithms.
- The algorithms and flowcharts are the final steps in organizing the solutions.
- Using the algorithms and flowcharts the programmers can find out the bugs in the programming logic and then can go for coding.
- Flowcharts can show errors in the logic and set of data can be easily tested using flowcharts.

Symbols used in Flowchart

Description	Symbol
Flow lines are used to indicate the flow of data. The arrow heads are important for flowlines. The flowlines are also used to connect the different blocks in the flowchart.	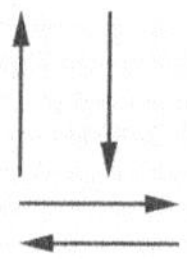 Flowline
These are termination symbols. The start of the flowchart is represented by the **name of the module** in the ellipse and the end of the flowchart is represented by the keywords End or Stop or Exit	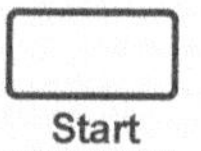 Start  End/Stop/Exit
The rectangle indicates the processing. It includes calculations, opening and closing files and so on.	 Processing
The parallelogram indicates input and output.	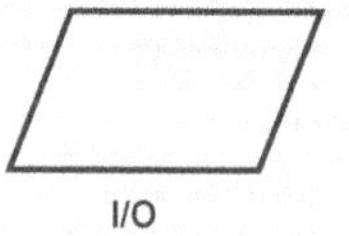 I/O
The diamond indicates the decision. It has one entrance and two exits. One exit indicates the true and other indicates the false.	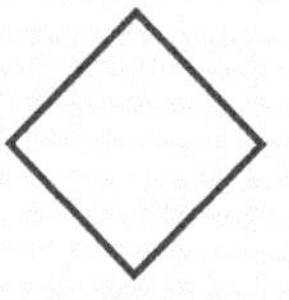 Decision
The process module has only one entrance and one exit.	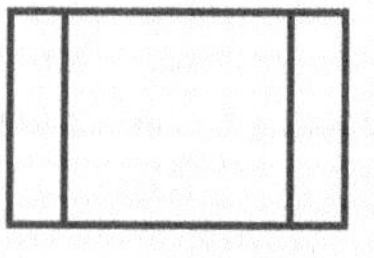 Process Module

This polygon indicates the loop A indicates the starting of the counter S indicates the step by which the counter is incremented or decremented. B indicates the ending value of the counter Using the counter the number of times the looping instruction gets executed.	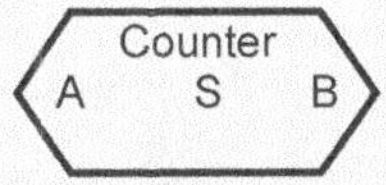
The on-page connector connects the two different sections on the same page. A letter is written inside the circle. The off-page connector connects the two different sections on the different pages. The page numbers are used in off-page connector. These two symbols should be used as little as possible because then the readability of the flowchart may get affected.	 On page connector  Off page connector

Example 1.8.6 *What do you mean by flow chart ? Give the meaning of each symbol used in flowchart. Draw flowchart to compute the sum of elements from a given integer array*

SPPU : May-10, Marks 8

Solution : Refer section 1.8.2 for flowchart and symbols used in it.

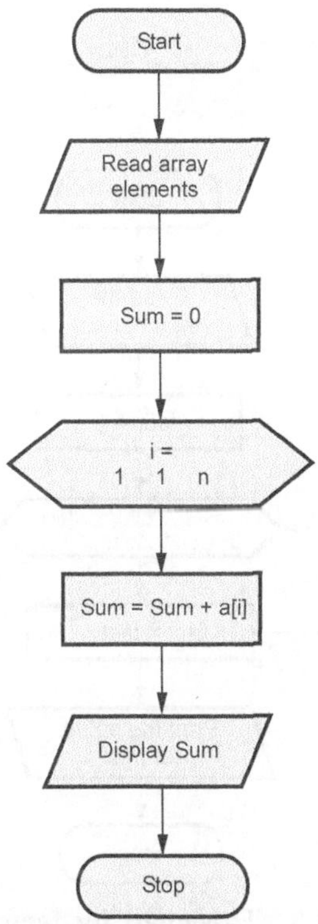

Fig. 1.8.2

Example 1.8.7 *Design and explain an algorithm to find the sum of the digits of an integer number.* **SPPU : Dec.-10, Marks 6**

Solution :

```
Read N
Remainder=0
Sum=0
Repeat
  Remainder=N mod 10
  Sum=Sum+remainder
   N=N/10
Until N<0
Display Sum
End
```

Example 1.8.8 *What is a difference between flowchart and algorithm ? Convert the algorithm for computing factorial of given number into flowchart.* **SPPU : May-11, Marks 8**

Solution : Algorithm is a set of instructions written in natural language or pseudo code and flowchart is a graphical representation of an **algorithm**.

```
Read N
Set i and F to 1
While i<=N
   F=F * i
   Increase the value of i by 1
Display F
End
```

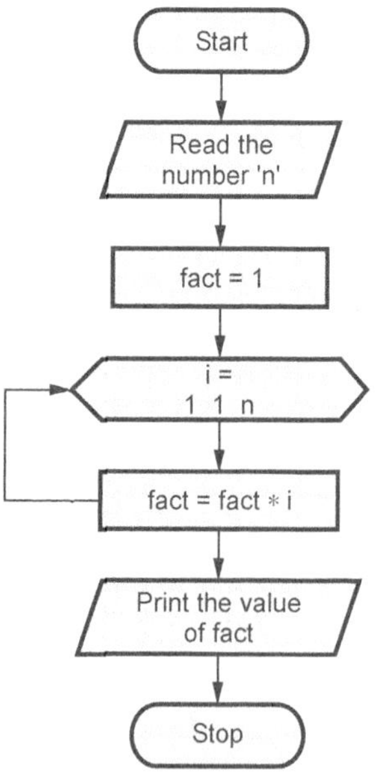

Fig. 1.8.3 Flowchart for factorial

1.9 Step Count Method

Definition : The frequency count is a count that denotes how many times particular statement is executed.

For Example : Consider following code for counting the frequency count

```
void fun()
{
 int a;
 a=10; ............................................1
 printf("%d",a); ...................................1
}
```

The frequency count of above program is **2.**

1.10 Complexity of Algorithm **SPPU : Dec.-09, 10, 11, 19, May-12, 13, Marks 8**

1.10.1 Space Complexity

The space complexity can be defined as amount of memory required by an algorithm to run.

To compute the space complexity we use two factors : **constant and instance characteristics**. The space requirement S(p) can be given as

$$S(p) = C + Sp$$

where **C** is a constant i.e. fixed part and it denotes the space of inputs and outputs. This space is an amount of space taken by instruction, variables and identifiers. And **Sp** is a space dependent upon instance characteristics. This is a variable part whose space requirement depends on particular problem instance.

There are two types of components that contribute to the space complexity - Fixed part and variable part.

The **fixed part** includes space for

- Instructions
- Variables
- Array size
- Space for constants

The **variable part** includes space for

- The variables whose size is dependent upon the particular problem instance being solved. The control statements (such as for, do, while, choice) are used to solve such instances.
- Recursion stack for handling recursive call.

Consider an example of algorithm to compute the space complexity.

Example 1.10.1 *Compute the space needed by the following algorithms justify your answer.*

```
Algorithm Sum(a,n)
{
    s : = 0.0 ;
        For i : = 1 to n do
            s : = s + a[i] ;
            return s
}
```

In the given code we require space for

```
s : = 0       ←      O(1)
    For i : = 1 to n     ←      O(n)
        s : = s + a[i] ; ← O(n)
        returns ;            ← O(1)
```

Hence the space complexity of given algorithm can be denoted in terms of big-oh notation. It is **O(n).** We will discuss big oh notation concept in section 1.11.

1.10.2 Time Complexity

The amount of time required by an algorithm to execute is called the time complexity of that algorithm.

For determining the time complexity of particular algorithm following steps are carried out -

1. Identify the basic operation of the algorithm
2. Obtain the frequency count for this basic operation.
3. Consider the order of magnitude of the frequency count and express it in terms of big oh notation.

Example 1.10.2 *Write an algorithm to find smallest element in a array of integers and analyze its time complexity* **SPPU : May-13, Marks 8**

Solution :

```
Algorithm MinValue(int a[n])
{
    min_element=a[0];
    for(i=0;i<n;i++)
    {
        if (a[i]<min_element) then
            min_element=a[i];
    }
    Write(min_element);
}
```

We will first obtain the frequency count for the above code

By neglecting the constant terms and by considering the order of magnitude we can express the frequency count in terms of Omega notation as O(n). Hence the frequency count of above code is O(n).

Statement	Frequency Count
min_element=a[0]	1
for(i=0;i<n;i++)	n+1
if (a[i]<min_element) then	n
Write(min_element);	1
Total	2n+3

Review Questions

1. *What is space complexity of an algorithm? Explain its importance with example.* **SPPU : Dec.-10, Marks 4**
2. *What do you mean by frequency count and its importance in analysis of an algorithm* **SPPU : Dec.-09,10, May-12,13, Marks 6**
3. *What is time complexity? How is time complexity of an algorithm computed ?* **SPPU : Dec.-11, Marks 6**
4. *What is complexity of algorithm ? Explain with an example.* **SPPU : Dec.-19, Marks 3**

1.11 Asymptotic Notations

SPPU : Dec.-09, 10, 11, 16, 17, 19, May-10, 12, 13, 18, 19, Marks 8

To choose the best algorithm, we need to check efficiency of each algorithm. The efficiency can be measured by computing time complexity of each algorithm. Asymptotic notation is a shorthand way to represent the time complexity.

Using asymptotic notations we can give time complexity as "fastest possible", "slowest possible" or "average time".

Various notations such as Ω, Θ and O used are called **asymptotic notations**.

1.11.1 Big oh Notation

The **Big oh** notation is denoted by 'O'. It is a method of representing the **upper bound of** algorithm's running time. Using big oh notation we can give longest amount of time taken by the algorithm to complete.

Definition

Let f(n) and g(n) be two non-negative functions.

Let n_0 and constant c are two integers such that n_0 denotes some value of input and $n > n_0$. Similarly c is some constant such that $c > 0$. We can write

$$f(n) \leq c*g(n)$$

then f(n) is big oh of g(n). It is also denoted as $f(n) \in O(g(n))$. In other words f(n) is less than g(n) if g(n) is multiple of some constant c.

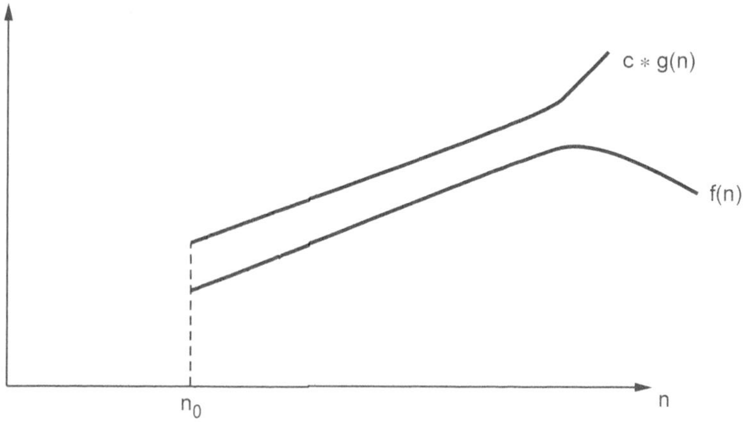

$f(n) \in O(g(n))$

Fig. 1.11.1 Big oh notation

Example : Consider function f(n) = 2n + 2 and $g(n) = n^2$. Then we have to find some constant c, so that $f(n) \leq c * g(n)$. As F(n) = 2n + 2 and $g(n) = n^2$ then we find c for n = 1 then

$$f(n) = 2n+2$$
$$= 2(1) + 2$$
$$f(n) = 4$$

and $$g(n) = n^2$$
$$= (1)^2$$
$$g(n) = 1$$

i.e. $$f(n) > g(n)$$

If n = 2 then,

$$f(n) = 2(2) + 2$$
$$= 6$$
$$g(n) = (2)^2$$
$$g(n) = 4$$

i.e. $$f(n) > g(n)$$

If n = 3 then,

$$f(n) = 2(3) + 2$$
$$= 8$$

$$g(n) = (3)^2$$

$$g(n) = 9$$

i.e. $f(n) < g(n)$ is true.

Hence we can conclude that for $n > 2$, we obtain

$$f(n) < g(n)$$

Thus always **upper bound** of existing time is obtained by big oh notation.

1.11.2 Omega Notation

Omega notation is denoted by 'Ω'. This notation is used to represent the **lower bound** of algorithm's running time. Using omega notation we can denote shortest amount of time taken by algorithm.

Definition

A function f(n) is said to be in Ω (g(n)) if f(n) is bounded below by some positive constant multiple of g(n) such that

$$f(n) \geq c * g(n)$$

For all $n \geq n_0$

It is denoted as $f(n) \in \Omega(g(n))$. Following graph illustrates the curve for Ω notation.

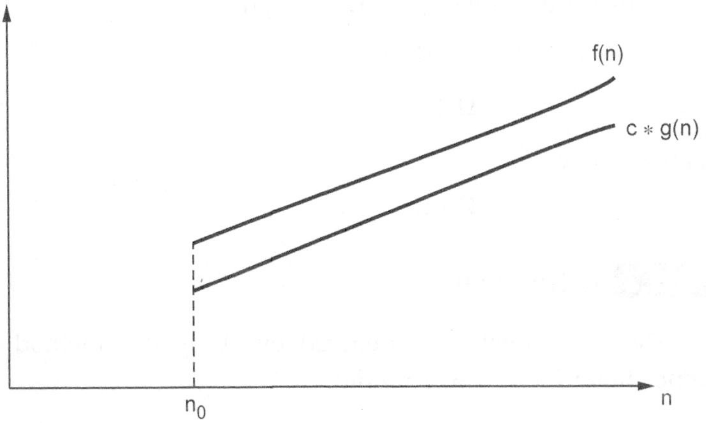

Fig. 1.11.2 Omega notation $f(n) \in \Omega(g(n))$

Example :

Consider $f(n) = 2n^2 + 5$ and $g(n) = 7n$

Then if $n = 0$

$$f(n) = 2(0)^2 + 5$$

$$= 5$$

$$g(n) = 7(0)$$

$$= 0 \quad \text{i.e. } f(n) > g(n)$$

But if $n = 1$

$$f(n) = 2(1)^2 + 5$$

$$= 7$$

$$g(n) = 7(1)$$

$$7 \text{ i.e. } f(n) = g(n)$$

If n = 3 then,

$$f(n) = 2(3)^2 + 5$$

$$= 18 + 5$$

$$= 23$$

$$g(n) = 7(3)$$

$$= 21$$

i.e. $f(n) > g(n)$

Thus for n > 3 we get $f(n) > c * g(n)$.

It can be represented as

$$2n^2 + 5 \in \Omega(n)$$

Similarly any

$$n^3 \in \Omega(n)^2$$

1.11.3 Θ Notation

The theta notation is denoted by Θ. By this method the running time **is between upper bound and lower bound**.

Definition

Let f(n) and g(n) be two non negative functions. There are two positive constants namely c_1 and c_2 such that

$$c_1 \leq g(n) \leq c_2 \, g(n)$$

Then we can say that

$$f(n) \in \Theta(g(n))$$

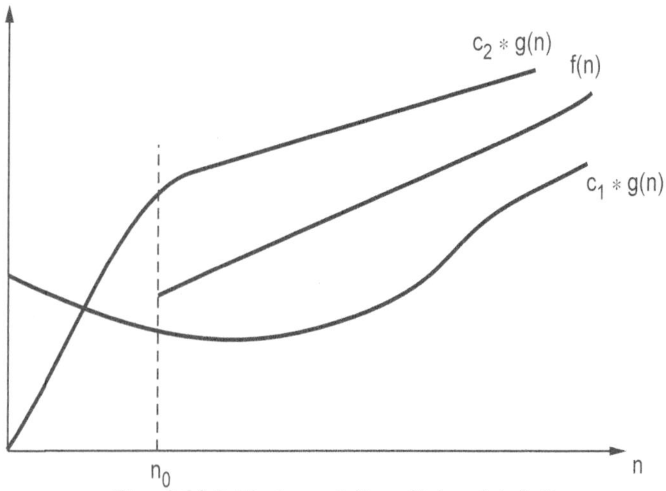

Fig. 1.11.3 Theta notation f(n) ∈ Θ (g(n))

Example :

If f(n) = 2n + 8 and g(n) = 7n.

where $n \geq 2$

Similarly $f(n) = 2n + 8$

$g(n) = 7n$

i.e. $5n < 2n + 8 < 7n$ For $n \geq 2$

Here $c_1 = 5$ and $c_2 = 7$ with $n_0 = 2$.

The theta notation is more precise with both big oh and omega notation.

Some Examples of Asymptotic Order

1) $\log_2 n$ is f(n) then

$\log_2 n \in O(n)$ $\because$ $\log_2 n \leq O(n)$, the order of growth of $\log_2 n$ is slower than n.

$\log_2 n \in O(n^2)$ $\because$ $\log_2 n \leq O(n^2)$, the order of growth of $\log_2 n$ is slower than n^2 as well.

But

$\log_2 n \notin \Omega(n)$ $\because$ $\log_2 n \leq \Omega(n)$ and if a certain function F(n) is belonging to $\Omega(n)$ it should satisfy the condition $F(n) \geq c * g(n)$

Similarly $\log_2 n \notin \Omega(n^2)$ or $\Omega(n^3)$

2) Let $f(n) = n(n-1)/2$

Then

$n(n-1)/2 \notin O(n)$ $\because$ $f(n) > O(n)$ we get $f(n) = n(n-1)/2 = \frac{n^2 - 1}{2}$

i.e. maximum order is n^2 which is $> O(n)$.

Hence $F(n) \notin O(n)$

But $n(n-1)/2 \in O(n^2)$ As $f(n) \leq O(n^2)$

and $n(n-1)/2 \in O(n^3)$

Similarly,

$n(n-1)/2 \in \Omega(n)$ $\because$ $f(n) \geq \Omega(n)$

$n(n-1)/2 \in \Omega(n^2)$ $\because$ $f(n) \geq \Omega(n^2)$

$n(n-1)/2 \notin \Omega(n^3)$ $\because$ $f(n) > \Omega(n^3)$

1.11.4 Properties of Order of Growth

1. If $f_1(n)$ is order of $g_1(n)$ and $f_2(n)$ is order of $g_2(n)$, then $f_1(n) + f_2(n) \in O(\max(g_1(n), g_2(n)))$.

2. Polynomials of degree $m \in \Theta(n^m)$.

   That means maximum degree is considered from the polynomial.

   For example : $a_1n^3 + a_2n^2 + a_3n + c$ has the order of growth $\Theta(n^3)$.

3. $O(1) < O(\log n) < O(n) < O(n^2) < O(2^n)$.

4. Exponential functions a^n have different orders of growth for different values of a.

Key Points

i) O(g(n)) is a class of functions F(n) that grows less fast than g(n), that means F(n) possess the time complexity which is always lesser than the time complexities that g(n) have.

ii) Θ (g(n)) is a class of functions F(n) that grows at same rate as g(n).

iii) Ω(g(n)) is a class of functions F(n) that grows faster than or atleast as fast as g(n). That means F(n) is greater than Ω(g(n).

Example 1.11.1 *Analyze time complexity of the following code segments :*

i)
```
for (i = 1 ; i <= n ; i++)
   for (j = 1 ; j <= m ; j++)
      for (k = 1 ; k <= p ; k++)
         x = x + 1 ;
```

ii)
```
i = 1
while (i <= n)
{ x++ ;
  i++;
}
```

iii)
```
int process (int no)
{
      if (no <= 0)
            return (0) ;
      else
            return (no + process (no - 1));
      }
```

SPPU : Dec.-10, Marks 8

Solution : i) $O(n^3)$ ii) O(n) iii) O(n)

1.11.5 How to Choose the Best Algorithm ?

If we have two algorithms that perform same task and the first one has a computing time of $O(n)$ and the second of $O(n^2)$, then we will usually prefer the first one.

The reason for this is that as n increases the time required for the execution of second algorithm will get far more than the time required for the execution of first.

n	$\log_2 n$	$n\log_2 n$	n^2	n^3	2^n
1	0	0	1	1	2
2	1	2	4	8	4
4	2	8	16	64	16
8	3	24	64	512	256
16	4	64	256	4096	65536
32	5	160	1024	32768	2147483648

We will study various values for computing function for the constant values. The graph given below will indicate the rate of growth of common computing time functions.

Notice how the times $O(n)$ and $O(n \log n)$ grow much more slowly than the others. For large data sets algorithms with a complexity greater than $O(n \log n)$ are often impractical. The very slow algorithm will be the one having time complexity 2^n.

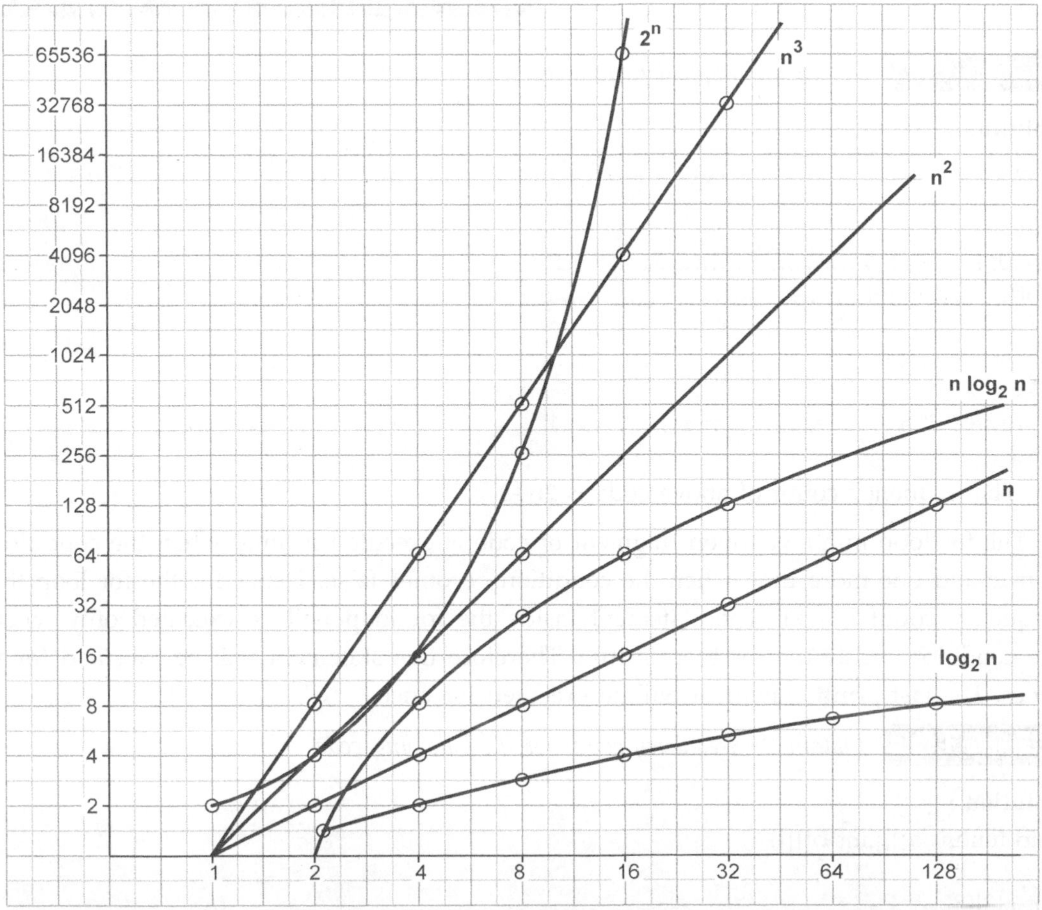

Fig. 1.11.4 Rate of growth of common computing time function

Review Questions

1. *Explain different asymptotic notation*

   SPPU : Dec.-09, May-12, Marks 4, May-13, Marks 6

2. *With respect to algorithm analysis, explain the following terms :*

   i) Omega notation ii) Theta notation iii) Big oh notation

   SPPU : May-10, Dec.-11, Marks 6

3. *Explain asymptotic notations Big O, Theta and Omega with one example each.*
SPPU : Dec.-16, 17, May-18, Marks 6, Dec.-19, Marks 3

4. *What is complexity analysis of an algorithm ? Explain the notations used in complexity analysis.* **SPPU : May-19, Marks 6**

1.12 Analysis of Programming Constructs

SPPU : May-10, 13, 14, Dec.-11, 13, Marks 8

Example 1.12.1 *Obtain the frequency count for the following code*

Solution :

```
void fun()
{
 int a;
 a=0; ...............................................1
 for(i=0;i<n;i++) ..................................n+1
  {
     a  = a+i; .......................................n
  }
  printf("%d",a); .....................................1
}
```

The frequency count of above code is **2n+3**

The for loop in above given fragment of code is executed n times when the condition is true and one more time when the condition becomes false. Hence for the for loop the frequency count is n+1. The statement inside the for loop will be executed only when the condition inside the for loop is true. Therefore this statement will be executed for n times. The last printf statement will be executed for once.

Example 1.12.2 *Obtain the frequency count for the following code*

Solution :

```
void fun(int a[][],int b[][])
{
 int c[3][3];
 for(i=0;i<m;i++) ...................................m+1
 {
   for(j=0;j<n;j++) ..................................m(n+1)
   {
     c[i][j]=a[i][j]+b[i][j]; ..........................m.n
   }
 }
```

The frequency count =(m+1)+m(n+1)+mn=2m+2mn+1=**2m(1+n)+1**

Example 1.12.3 *Obtain the frequency count for the following code*

```
for(i=1;i<=n;i++)
{
  for(j=1;j<=n;j++)
  {
    c[i][j]=0;
    for(k=1;k<=n;k++)
      c[i][j]=c[i][j]+a[i][k]*b[k][j];
  }
}
```

SPPU : May-13, Marks 8; Dec.-13, Marks 3

Solution : After counting the frequency count, the constant terms can be neglected and only the order of magnitude is considered. The time complexity is denoted in terms of algorithmic notations. The Big oh notation is a most commonly used algorithmic notation. For the above frequency count all the constant terms are neglected and only the order of magnitude of the polynomial is considered. Hence the time complexity for the above code can be $O(n^3)$. The higher order is the polynomial is always considered.

Statement	Frequency Count
for(i=1;i<=n;i++)	n+1
for(j=1;j<=n;j++)	n.(n+1)
c[i][j]=0;	n.(n)
for(k=1;k<=n;k++)	n.n(n+1)
c[i][j]=c[i][j]+a[i][k]*b[k][j];	n.n.n
Total	**$2n^3+3n^2+2n+1$**

Example 1.12.4 ***Obtain the frequency count for the following code*** *i=1;*

```
do
{
  a++;
  if(i==5)
    break;
  i++;
}while(i<=n)
```

Solution :

Statement	Frequency Count
i=1;	1
a++;	5
if(i==5)	5
break;	1
i++;	5
while(i<=n)	5
Total	**22**

Example 1.12.5 *Obtain the frequency count for the following code*

```
m=n/2;
for(i=0;i+m<m;i++)
{
  a++;
  k++;
}
```

Solution :

Statement	Frequency Count
m=n/2	1
for(i=0;i+m<m;i++)	(n/2)+1
a++;	n/2
k++;	n/2
Total	**(3n/2)+2**

If we consider only the degree of the polynomial for this code then the time complexity in terms of Big-oh notation can be specified as **O(n/2)**.

Example 1.12.6 *Find the frequency count (F.C.) of the given code :*

Explain each step.

```
double IterPow(double X, int N)
{
double Result = 1;
while (N > 0)
{
Result = Result *X;
N--;
}
return Result;
}
```

SPPU : May-10, Marks 6

Solution :

Statement	Frequency Count
double Result=1	1
while(N>0)	N+1
Result=Result*X	N
N--	N
return Result	1
Total	**3N+3**

Example 1.12.7 *What is frequency count of a statement ? Analyze time complexity of the following code :*

i)
```
for(i = 1; i <= n; i++)
for(j = 1; j <= m; j++)
for(k = 1; k <= p; k++)
sum = sum + i;
```
ii)
```
i = n;
while(i ≥ 1)
  {i--;}
```

SPPU : Dec.-11, Marks 6, May-14, Marks 3

Solution : i)

Statement	Frequency Count
for(i=1;i<=n;i++)	n+1
for(j=1;j<=m;j++)	n(m+1)
for(k=1;k<=p;k++)	n.m.(p+1)
sum=sum+i	n.m.p
Total	2(n+nm+nmp)+1

ii)

Statement	Frequency Count
i=n	1
while(i>=1)	n+1
i– –	n
Total	2(n+1)

Example 1.12.8 *Determine the frequency counts for all the statements in the following program segment*

```
i=10;
for(i=10;i<=n;i++)
  for(j=1;j<i;j++)
   x=x+1;
```

SPPU : May-13, Marks 6

Solution : Assume (n–10+2)=m. Then the total frequency count is -

Statement	Frequency Count
i=10;	1
for(i=10;i<=n;i++)	m (we assume the count of execution is m)
for(j=1;j<i;j++)	m((m+1)/2)
x=x+1;	m(m)

The outer loop will execute for m times. The inner loop is dependant upon the outer loop. Hence it will be (m+1)/2. Hence overall frequency count is $(1+m+m^2)(m(m+1)/2)$

If we consider only the order of magnitude of this code then overall time complexity in terms of big oh notation is $O(n^2)$.

If an algorithm takes time O(logn) then it is faster than any other algorithm, for larger value of n. Similarly O(nlogn) is better than $O(n^2)$. Various computing time can be O(1), O(logn), O(n),O(nlogn), $O(n^2)$, $O(n^3)$ and $O(2^n)$.

1.13 Recurrence Relation

SPPU : Dec.-18, Marks 2

- **Definition :**

  The recurrence equation is an equation that defines a sequences resursively. It is normally in following form :

$$T(n) = T(n-1) + n \text{ for } n > 0 \quad (1)$$

Recurrence relation

$$T(0) = 0 \quad (2)$$

Initial condition

- The recurrence equation can have infinite number of sequence.
- The **general solution** to the recursive function specifies some formula.
- **For example :** consider a recurrence relation

$$T(n) = 2T(n-1) + 1 \quad \text{for } n > 1$$

$$T(1) = 1$$

By solving this relation we will get $T(n) = 2^n - 1$ where $n > 1$.

Review Question

1. *What is recurrence relation ? Explain with example.* **SPPU : Dec.-18, Marks 2**

1.14 Solving Recurrence Relation

The recurrence relation can be solved by following methods -

1. **Substitution method** 2. **Master's method.**

Let us discuss methods with suitable examples -

1.14.1 Substitution Method

The substitution method is a kind of method in which a guess for the solution is made

There are two types of substitutions -

- Forward substitution
- Backward substitution

Forward Substitution Method - This method makes use of an initial condition in the initial term and value for the next term is generated. This process is continued until some formula is guessed. Thus in this kind of substitution method, we use recurrence equations to generate the few terms.

For example -

Consider a recurrence relation

$$T(n) = T(n-1) + n$$

With initial condition T(0) = 0.

Let,

$$T(n) = T(n-1) + n \qquad \text{... (1.14.1)}$$

If n = 1 then

$$T(1) = T(0) + 1$$

$$= 0 + 1 \qquad \because \text{Initial condition}$$

$$\therefore \quad \mathbf{T(1) = 1} \qquad \text{... (1.14.2)}$$

If n = 2, then

$$T(2) = T(1) + 2$$

$$= 1 + 2 \qquad \because \text{equation (1.14.2)}$$

$$\therefore \quad \mathbf{T(2) = 3} \qquad \text{... (1.14.3)}$$

If n = 3 then

$$T(3) = T(2) + 3$$

$$= 3 + 3 \qquad \because \text{equation (1.14.4)}$$

$$\therefore \quad \mathbf{T(3) = 6} \qquad \text{... (1.14.5)}$$

By observing above generated equations we can derive a formula

$$T(n) = \frac{n(n+1)}{2} = \frac{n^2}{2} + \frac{n}{2}$$

We can also denote T(n) in terms of big oh notation as follows -

$$T(n) = O(n^2)$$

But, in practice, it is difficult to guess the pattern from forward substitution. Hence this method is not very often used.

Backward Substitution : In this method backward values are substituted recursively in order to derive some formula.

For example - Consider, a recurrence relation

$$T(n) = T(n-1) + n \qquad \text{... (1.14.6)}$$

With initial condition T(0) = 0

$$T(n-1) = T(n-1-1) + (n-1) \quad \ldots (1.14.7)$$

Putting equation (1.14.7) in equation (1.14.6) we get

$$T(n) = T(n-2) + (n-1) + n \quad \ldots (1.14.8)$$

Let

$$T(n-2) = T(n-2-1) + (n-2) \quad \ldots (1.14.9)$$

Putting equation (1.14.9) in equation (1.14.8) we get.

$$T(n) = T(n-3) + (n-2) + (n-1) + n$$

$$\vdots$$

$$= T(n-k) + (n-k+1) + (n-k+2) + \ldots + n$$

if k = n then

$$T(n) = T(0) + 1 + 2 + \ldots n$$

$$T(n) = 0 + 1 + 2 + \ldots + n \quad \because T(0) = 0$$

$$T(n) = \frac{n(n+1)}{2} = \frac{n^2}{2} + \frac{n}{2}$$

Again we can denote T(n) in terms of big oh notation as

$$\mathbf{T(n) \in O(n^2)}$$

Example 1.14.1 *Solve the following recurrence relation T(n) = T(n – 1) + 1 with T(0) = 0 as initial condition. Also find big oh notation.*

Solution : Let,

$$T(n) = T(n-1) + 1$$

By backward substitution,

$$T(n-1) = T(n-2) + 1$$

$$\therefore \quad T(n) = T(n-1) + 1$$

$$= (T(n-2) + 1) + 1$$

$$\mathbf{T(n) = T(n-2) + 2}$$

Again $T(n-2) = T(n-2-1) + 1$

$$= T(n-3) + 1$$

$$\therefore \quad T(n) = T(n-2) + 2$$

$$= (T(n-3) + 1) + 2$$

$$T(n) = T(n-3) + 3$$

$$\vdots$$

$$T(n) = T(n-k) + k \qquad \dots (1)$$

If k = n then equation (1) becomes

$$T(n) = T(0) + n$$

$$= 0 + n \qquad \because T(0) = 0$$

$$T(n) = n$$

∴ We can denote T(n) in terms of big oh notation as

$$\mathbf{T(n) = O(n)}$$

Example 1.14.2 *Solve the following recurrence :*

T(1) = 1

$T(n) = 4T(n/3) + n^2$ for $x \geq 2$

Solution :

$$T(n) = 4T\left(\frac{n}{3}\right) + n^2 \qquad T\left(\frac{n}{3}\right) = 4T\left(\frac{n}{9}\right) + \left(\frac{n}{3}\right)^2$$

$$= 4\left[4 \cdot T\left(\frac{n}{3^2}\right) + \frac{n^2}{3^2}\right] + n^2$$

$$= 4^2 T\left(\frac{n}{3^2}\right) + 4 \cdot \frac{n^2}{3^2} + n^2$$

$$= 4^2 T\left(\frac{n}{3^2}\right) + \frac{13n^2}{3^2}$$

$$= 16 \cdot T\left(\frac{n}{9}\right) + \frac{13n^2}{9} \qquad \because T\left(\frac{n}{9}\right) = 4T\left(\frac{n}{27}\right) + \left(\frac{n}{9}\right)^2$$

$$= 16\left[4 \cdot T\left(\frac{n}{27}\right) + \frac{n^2}{81}\right] + \frac{13n^2}{9} \qquad \because T\left(\frac{n}{9}\right) = 4T\left(\frac{n}{27}\right) + \frac{n^2}{81}$$

$$= 64T\left(\frac{n}{27}\right) + 16 \cdot \frac{n^2}{81} + \frac{13n^2}{9}$$

$$= 64T\left(\frac{n}{27}\right) + \frac{133n^2}{81}$$

$$= 4^3 T\left(\frac{n}{3^3}\right) + 133 \cdot \left(\frac{n}{3^2}\right)^2$$

$$\vdots$$

$$= 4^k T\left(\frac{n}{3^k}\right) + C\left(\frac{n}{3^{k-1}}\right)^2 \qquad \because\ 133 + C_1 = C$$

Now if we assume $\frac{n}{3^k} = 1$ then $n = 3^k$ and $k = \log_3 n$

$$= 4^k T(1) + C\left(\frac{n}{3^{k-1}}\right)^2 \qquad \because \frac{n}{3^k} = 1$$

Purposely we kept constant term in terms of n.

$$= 4^k \cdot 1 + \frac{C}{(3^{k-1})^2} \cdot n^2 \qquad \because T(1) = 1$$

$$= 4^k + C_1 \cdot n^2 \qquad \because\ C_1 = \frac{C}{(3^{k-1})^2}$$

$$= 4 \log_3 n + C_1 n^2$$

$$= n \log_3 4 + C_1 n^2 \qquad \because\ a \log_b n = n \log_b a$$

$$= n^{1.26} + C \cdot n^2$$

$$\mathbf{T(n)} \approx \mathbf{\Theta(n^2)}$$

Example 1.14.3 *Solve the following recurrence relations -*

i) $T(n) = 2T\left(\frac{n}{2}\right) + C$ $\quad T(1) = 1$ $\qquad$ *ii)* $T(n) = T\left(\frac{n}{3}\right) + C$ $\quad T(1) = 1$

Solution : i) Let

$$T(n) = 2T\left(\frac{n}{2}\right) + C$$

$$= 2\left(2T\left(\frac{n}{4}\right) + C\right) + C$$

$$= 4T\left(\frac{n}{4}\right) + 3C$$

$$= 4\left(2T\left(\frac{n}{8}\right) + C\right) + 3C$$

$$= 8T\left(\frac{n}{8}\right) + 7C$$

$$= 2^3 T\left(\frac{n}{n^3}\right) + (2^3 - 1)\, C$$

$$\vdots$$

$$T(n) = 2^k T\left(\frac{n}{2^k}\right) + (2^k - 1)\, C$$

If we $2^k = n$ then

$$T(n) = nT\left(\frac{n}{n}\right) + (n - 1)\, C$$

$$= nT(1) + (n - 1)\, C$$

$$\mathbf{T(n) = n + (n - 1)\, C} \qquad \because T(1) = 1$$

ii) Let,

$$T(n) = T\left(\frac{n}{3}\right) + C$$

$$= \left(T\left(\frac{n}{9}\right) + C\right) + C$$

$$= T\left(\frac{n}{9}\right) + 2C$$

$$= \left[T\left(\frac{n}{27}\right) + C\right] + 2C$$

$$= T\left(\frac{n}{27}\right) + 3C$$

$$\vdots$$

$$= T\left(\frac{n}{3^k}\right) + kC$$

If we put $3^k = n$ then

$$= T\left(\frac{n}{n}\right) + \log_3 n \cdot C$$

$$= T(1) + \log_3 n \cdot C$$

$$\mathbf{T(n) = C \cdot \log_3 n + 1} \qquad \because T(1) = 1$$

Example 1.14.4 *Solve the recurrence relation by iteration :*
$T(n) = T(n-1) + n^4$.

Solution : Let

$$T(n) = T(n-1) + n^4$$

By backward substitution method,

$$T(n) = [T(n-2) + (n-1)^4] + n^4 \qquad \because T(n-1) = T(n-2) + (n-1)^4$$

$$= T(n-2) + (n-1)^4 + n^4$$

$$= [T(n-3) + (n-2)^4] + (n-1)^4 + n^4$$

$$= T(n-3) + (n-2)^4 + (n-1)^4 + n^4$$

$$= [T(n-4) + (n-3)^4] + (n-2)^4 + (n-1)^4 + n^4$$

$$= T(n-4) + (n-3)^4 + (n-2)^4 + (n-1)^4 + n^4$$

$$\vdots$$

$$= T(n-k) + (n-k+1)^4 + (n-k+2)^4 + (n-k+3)^4 + \ldots n^4$$

If k = n then

$$= T(n-n) + (n-n+1)^4 \ (n-n+2)^4 + (n-n+3)^4 + \cdots + n^4$$

$$= T(0) + 1^4 + 2^4 + 3^4 + \ldots + n^4$$

$$= T(0) + \sum_{i=1}^{n} n^4$$

$$= T(0) + n(n^4) \qquad \because \sum_{i=1}^{n} n^4 = n^4 \cdot \sum_{i=1}^{n} 1 = n^4 \cdot n$$

$$= 0 + n^5 \qquad \because \text{Assume } T(0) = 0 \text{ as initial condition}$$

$$\therefore \quad \mathbf{T(n) \approx \theta(n^5)}$$

Example 1.14.5 *Consider the following code :*

```
int sum (int a [ ], n)
{
        count = count + 1 ;
        if (n < = 0)
        {
                count = count + 1 ;
                return 0 ;
}
else
{
        count = count + 1
        return sum (a, n – 1)+a[n] ;
    }
}
```

Write the recursive formula for the above code and solve this recurrence relation.

Solution : In the above code the following statement gets executed at least twice

count = count + 1

In the else part, there is a recursive call to the function **sum,** by changing the value of n by n – 1, each time.

Hence the recursive formula for above code will be

$$T(n) = T(n-1) + 2$$

T(n – 1): For recursive call to function sum in else part.

2: For count statement

$$T(0) = 2$$

We can solve this recurrence relation using backward substitution. It will be

$$= [T(n-2) + 2] + 2$$

$$\therefore \quad = T(n-2)+2(2)$$

$$= [T(n-3) + 2]+ 2(2)$$

$$\therefore \quad T(n-2) = T(n-3) + 3 \cdot (2)$$

$$\vdots$$

$$T(n) = T(n-n) + n \cdot (2)$$

$$= T(0) + 2n$$

$$= 2 + 2 \cdot n \qquad \because T(0) = 2$$

$$\mathbf{T(n) = 2(n+1)}$$

We can denote the time complexity in the form of big oh notation as **O(n).**

1.14.2 Master's Method

We can solve recurrence relation using a formula denoted by Master's method.

$$T(n) = aT(n/b) + F(n) \qquad \text{where } n \geq d \text{ and } d \text{ is some constant.}$$

Then the Master theorem can be stated for efficiency analysis as -

If F(n) is $\Theta(n^d)$ where $d \geq 0$ in the recurrence relation then,

1. $T(n) = \Theta(n^d)$ if $a < b^d$
2. $T(n) = \Theta(n^d \log n)$ if $a = b$
3. $T(n) = \Theta(n^{\log_b a})$ if $a > b^d$

Let us understand the Master theorem with some examples :

Example 1.14.6 *Solve the following recurrence relation $T(n) = 4T(n/2) + n$*

Solution : We will map this equation with

$$T(n) = aT(n/b) + f(n)$$

Now f(n) is n i.e. n^1. Hence d = 1.

a = 4 and b = 2 and

$a > b^d$ i.e. $4 > 2^1$

$$\therefore \quad T(n) = \Theta(n^{\log_b a})$$

$$= \Theta(n^{\log_2 4})$$

$$= \Theta(n^2) \qquad \because \log_2 4 = 2$$

Hence time complexity is $\Theta(n^2)$.

For quick and easy calculations of logarithmic values to base 2 following table can be memorized.

m	k
1	0
2	1
4	2
8	3
16	4
32	5
64	6
128	7
256	8
512	9
1024	10

Another variation of Master theorem is

For $T(n) = aT(n/b) + f(n) \quad \text{if } n \geq d$

1. If f(n) is $O(n^{\log_b a - \varepsilon})$, then

   $T(n) = \Theta(n^{\log_b a})$

2. If f(n) is $\Theta(n^{\log_b a} \log^k n)$, then

   $T(n) = \Theta(n^{\log_b a} \log^{k+1} n)$

3. If f(n) is $\Omega(n^{\log_b a + \varepsilon})$, then

   T(n) is $= \Theta(f(n))$

Example 1.14.7 *Solve the following recurrence relation. $T(n) = 2T(n/2) + n \log n$*

Solution :

Here $f(n) = n \log n$

$a = 2, \; b = 2$

$\log_2 2 = 1$

According to case 2 given in above Master theorem

$$f(n) = \Theta(n^{\log_2 2} \log^1 n) \quad \text{i.e.} \quad k = 1$$

Then $$T(n) = \Theta(n^{\log_b a} \log^{k+1} n)$$

$$= \Theta(n^{\log_2 2} \log^2 n)$$

$$= \Theta(n^1 \log^2 n)$$

$\therefore$ $$T(n) = \Theta(n \log^2 n)$$

Example 1.14.8 *Solve the following recurrence relation $T(n) = 8T(n/2) + n^2$*

Solution :

Here $$f(n) = n^2$$

$a = 8$ and $b = 2$

$\therefore$ $$\log_2 8 = 3$$

Then according to case 1 of above given Master theorem

$$f(n) = O(n^{\log_b a - \varepsilon})$$

$$= O(n^{\log_2 8 - \varepsilon})$$

$= O(n^{3-\varepsilon})$. If we put $\varepsilon = 1$ then $O(n^3 - 1) = O(n^2) = f(n)$

Then $$T(n) = \Theta(n^{\log_b a})$$

$\therefore$ $$T(n) = \Theta(n^{\log_2 8})$$

$$T(n) = \Theta(n^3)$$

Example 1.14.9 *Solve the following recurrence relation $T(n) = 9T(n/3) + n^3$*

Solution :

Here $a = 9$, $b = 3$ and $f(n) = n^3$

And $\log_3 9 = 2$

According to case 3 in above Master theorem

As $f(n)$ is $= \Omega(n^{\log_3 9 + \varepsilon})$

i.e. $\Omega(n^{2+\varepsilon})$ and we have $f(n) = n^3$.

Then to have $f(n) = \Omega(n)$. We must put $\varepsilon = 1$.

Then $T(n) = \Theta(f(n))$

Then $T(n) = \Theta(f(n))$

$T(n) = \Theta(n^3)$

Example 1.14.10 *Solve the following recurrence relation. $T(n) = T(n/2) + 1$*

Solution : Here a = 1 and b = 2.

and $\log_2 1 = 0$

Now we will analyze f(n) which is = 1.

We assume $f(n) = 2^k$

when k = 0 then $f(n) = 2^0 = 1$.

That means according to case 2 of above given Master theorem.

$$f(n) = \Theta(n^{\log_b a} \log^k n)$$

$$= \Theta(n^{\log_2 1} \log^0 n)$$

$$= \Theta(n^0 \cdot 1)$$

$$= \Theta(1) \qquad \because n^0 = 1$$

$$\therefore \text{ We get } T(n) = \Theta(n^{\log_b a} \log^{k+1} n)$$

$$= \Theta(n^{\log_2 1} \log^{0+1} n)$$

$$= \Theta(n^0 \cdot \log^1 n)$$

$$T(n) = \Theta(\log n) \qquad \because n^0 = 1$$

Example 1.14.11 *Find the complexity of the following recurrence relation. $T(n) = 9T(n/3) + n$*

Solution : Let $T(n) = 9T(n/3) + n$

$$\begin{matrix} \downarrow & \downarrow & \downarrow \\ a & b & f(n) \end{matrix}$$

$\therefore$ We get a = 9, b = 3 and f(n) = n.

$$n^{\log_b a} = n^{\log_3 9} = n^2$$

Now $f(n) = n$

i.e. $T(n) = f(n) = \Theta(n^{\log_b a - \varepsilon}) = \Theta(n^{2-\varepsilon})$

When $\varepsilon = 1$. That means case 1 is applicable. According to case 1, the time complexity of such equations is

$$T(n) = \Theta(n^{\log_b a})$$

$$= \Theta(n^{\log_3 9})$$

$$T(n) = \Theta(n^2)$$

Hence the complexity of given recurrence relation is $\Theta(n^2)$.

Example 1.14.12 *Solve recurrence relation $T(n) = k \cdot T(n/k) + n^2$ when $T(1) = 1$, and k is any constant.*

Solution : Let,

$T(n) = k \cdot T\left(\frac{n}{k}\right) + n^2$ be a recurrence relation. Let us use substiturion method

If we assume k = 2 then the equation becomes

$$T(n) = 2T\left(\frac{n}{2}\right) + n^2 \qquad T\left(\frac{n}{2}\right) = 2T\left(\frac{n}{4}\right) + \left(\frac{n}{2}\right)^2$$

$$= 2\left[2 \cdot T\left(\frac{n}{4}\right) + \frac{n^2}{4}\right] + n^2$$

$$= 4T\left(\frac{n}{4}\right) + \frac{n^2}{2} + n^2$$

$$= 4T\left(\frac{n}{4}\right) + \frac{3n^2}{2} \qquad T\left(\frac{n}{4}\right) = 2T\left(\frac{n}{8}\right) + \left(\frac{n}{4}\right)^2$$

$$= 4\left[2 \cdot T\left(\frac{n}{8}\right) + \frac{n^2}{16}\right] + \frac{3n^2}{2}$$

$$= 8T\left(\frac{n}{8}\right) + \frac{n^2}{4} + \frac{3n^2}{2}$$

$$= 8T\left(\frac{n}{8}\right) + \frac{7n^2}{4}$$

$$= 2^k T\left(\frac{n}{2^k}\right) + \frac{2^k - 1}{2^{k-1}} n^2$$

$$= 2^k T\left(\frac{n}{2^k}\right) + Cn^2 \qquad \because \frac{2^k - 1}{2^{k-1}} = C = \text{Constant}$$

If we put $\frac{n}{2^k} = 1$ then $2^k = n$ and $k = \log_2 n$

$$= nT(1) + Cn^2$$

$$= n + Cn^2 \qquad \because T(1) = 1$$

$$T(n) = \Theta(n)^2$$

Alternate Method

We can solve the given recurrence relation using Master's theorem also.

$$T(n) = k \cdot T\left(\frac{n}{k}\right) + n^2$$

$$\downarrow \quad \downarrow \quad \downarrow$$

$$a \quad b \quad f(n)$$

By Master's theorem $n^{\log_b a} = n^{\log_k k} = n^1$

For $T(n) = f(n)$ we need

$$T(n) = n^{\log_k k + \varepsilon} \qquad \text{Applying case 3}$$

$$= n^{1+1} \qquad \text{when } \varepsilon = 1$$

$$= f(n) \text{ i.e. } n^2$$

$$\therefore \quad T(n) = \Theta(f(n))$$

$$\mathbf{T(n) = \Theta(n^2)}$$

1.15 Best, Worst and Average Case Analysis

If an algorithm takes minimum amount of time to run to completion for a specific set of input then it is called **best case** time complexity.

For example : While searching a particular element by using sequential search we get the desired element at first place itself then it is called best case time complexity.

If an algorithm takes maximum amount of time to run to completion for a specific set of input then it is called **worst case** time complexity.

For example : While searching an element by using linear searching method if desired element is placed at the end of the list then we get worst time complexity.

The time complexity that we get for certain set of inputs is as a average same. Then for corresponding input such a time complexity is called **average case** time complexity.

Consider the following algorithm

```
Algorithm Seq_search(X[0 ... n – 1 ],key)
// Problem Description: This algorithm is for searching the
//key element from an array X[0...n – 1] sequentially.
//Input: An array X[0...n – 1] and search key
//Output: Returns the index of X where key value is present
for i ← 0 to n – 1 do
 if(X[i] =key)then
 return i
```

Best case time complexity

Best case time complexity is a time complexity when an algorithm runs for short time. In above searching algorithm the element **key** is searched from the list of **n** elements. If the **key** element is present at first location in the list(X[0...n–1]) then algorithm runs for a very short time and thereby we will get the best case time complexity. We can denote the best case time complexity as

$$C_{best} = 1$$

Worst case time complexity

Worst case time complexity is a time complexity when algorithm runs for a longest time. In above searching algorithm the element **key** is searched from the list of **n** elements. If the **key** element is present at n^{th} location then clearly the algorithm will run for longest time and thereby we will get the worst case time complexity. We can denote the worst case time complexity as

$$C_{worst} = n$$

The algorithm guarantees that for any instance of input which is of size n, the running time will not exceed $C_{worst}(n)$. Hence the worst case time complexity gives important information about the efficiency of algorithm.

Average case time complexity

This type of complexity gives information about the behaviour of an algorithm on specific or random input. Let us understand some terminologies that are required for computing average case time complexity.

Let the algorithm is for sequential search and

P be a probability of getting successful search.

n is the total number of elements in the list.

The first match of the element will occur at i^{th} location. Hence probability of occurring first match is P/n for every i^{th} element.

The probability of getting unsuccessful search is (1 – P).

Now, we can find average case time complexity $C_{avg}(n)$ as -

$$C_{avg}(n) = \text{Probability of successful search (for elements 1 to n in the list)} + \text{Probability of unsuccessful search}$$

$$C_{avg}(n) = \left[1 \cdot \frac{P}{n} + 2 \cdot \frac{P}{n} + \ldots + i \cdot \frac{P}{n}\right] + n \cdot (1-P)$$

There may be n elements at which chances of 'not getting element' are possible. Hence n.(1 – P)

$$= \frac{P}{n}[1+2+\ldots+i\ldots n] + n(1-P)$$

$$= \frac{P}{n}\frac{n(n+1)}{2} + n(1-P)$$

$$C_{avg}(n) = \frac{P(n+1)}{2} + n(1-P)$$

Thus we can obtain the general formula for computing average case time complexity.

Suppose if P = 0 that means there is no successful search i.e. we have scanned the entire list of n elements and still we do not found the desired element in the list then in such a situation,

$$C_{avg}(n) = 0(n+1)/2 + n(1-0)$$

$$C_{avg}(n) = n$$

Thus the average case running time complexity becomes equal to n.

Suppose if P = 1 i.e. we get a successful search then

$$C_{avg}(n) = 1(n+1)/2 + n(1-1)$$

$$C_{avg}(n) = (n+1)/2$$

That means the algorithm scans about half of the elements from the list.

For calculating average case time complexity we have to consider probability of getting success of the operation. And any operation in the algorithm is heavily dependent on input elements. Thus computing average case time complexity is difficult than computing worst case and best case time complexities.

1.16 Introduction to Algorithm Design Strategies

SPPU : May-17, 18, Dec.-17, 19, Marks 6

Algorithm design strategy is a general approach by which many problems can be solved algorithmically. These problems may belong to different areas of computing. Algorithmic strategies are also called as **algorithmic techniques** or **algorithmic paradigm**.

- Various algorithm techniques are-
  - **Brute Force :** This is a straightforward technique with naive approach.
  - **Divide-and-Conquer :** The problem is divided into smaller instances.
  - **Greedy Technique :** To solve the problem locally optimal decisions are made.
  - **Backtracking :** In this method, we start with one possible move out from many moves out and if the solution is not possible through the selected move then we backtrack for another move.

1.16.1 Divide and Conquer

- In divide and conquer method, a given problem is,
  1) Divided into smaller sub problems.
  2) These sub problems are solved independently.
  3) If necessary, the solutions of the sub problems are combined to get a solution to the original problem.
- If the sub problems are large enough, then divide and conquer is reapplied.

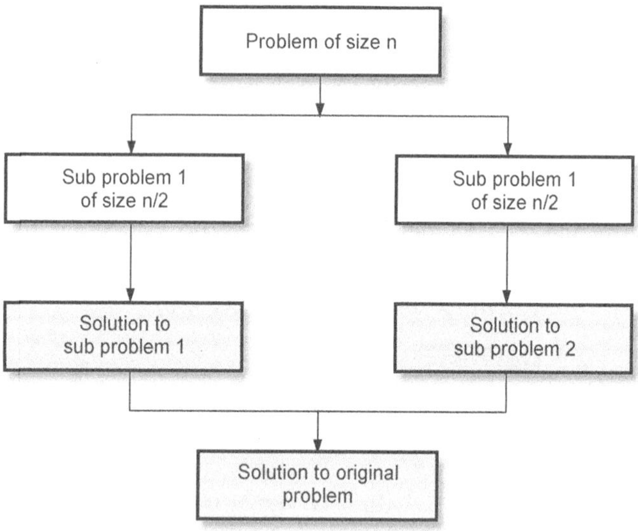

Fig. 1.16.1 Divide and conquer technique

The divide and conquer technique is as shown in Fig. 1.16.1.

The generated sub problems are usually of same type as the original problem. Hence sometimes recursive algorithms are used in divide and conquer strategy.

1.16.1.1 Merge Sort

The merge sort is a sorting algorithm that uses the divide and conquer strategy. In this method division is dynamically carried out.

Merge sort on an input array with n elements consists of three steps:

Divide : partition array into two sub lists s1 and s2 with n/2 elements each.

Conquer : Then sort sub list s1 and sub list s2.

Combine : merge s1 and s2 into a unique sorted group.

Consider the elements as

70, 20, 30, 40, 10, 50, 60

Now we will split this list into two sublists.

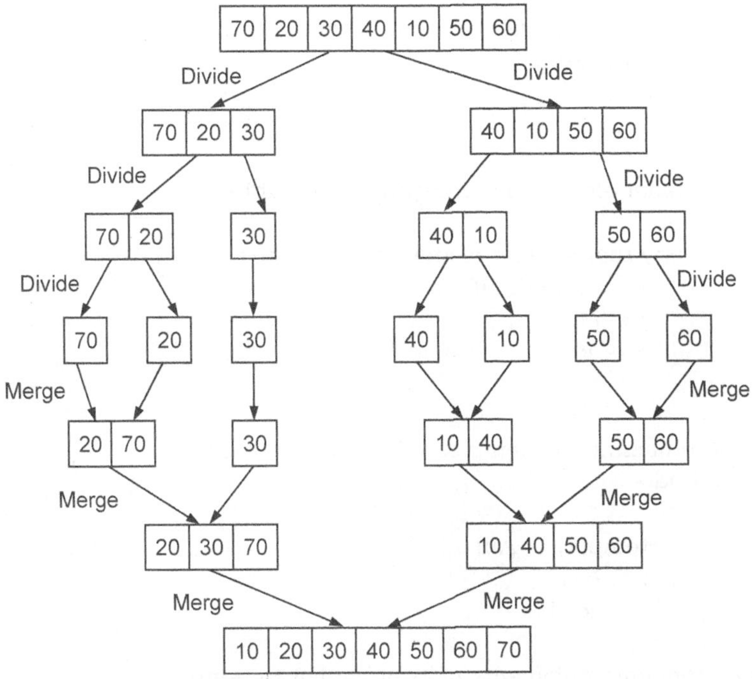

Fig. 1.16.2

Pseudo Code

```
Algorithm MergeSort(int A[0...n-1],low,high)
//Problem Description: This algorithm is for sorting the
//elements using merge sort
//Input: Array A of unsorted elements, low as beginning
//pointer of array A and high as end pointer of array A
//Output: Sorted array A[0...n-1]
        if(low < high)then
        {
            mid ← low+high)/2            //split the list at mid
            MergeSort(A,low,mid)         //first sublist
            MergeSort(A,mid+1,high) //second sublist
            Combine(A,low,mid,high) //merging of two sublists
        }
Algorithm Combine(A[0...n-1],low, mid, high)
{
        k ← low;  //k as index for array temp
        i ← low;          //i as index for left sublist of array A
```

```
    j ← mid+1 //j as index for right sublist of array A
    while(i <= mid and j <= high)do
    {
  if(A[i]<=A[j])then
//if smaller element is present in left sublist
    {
        //copy that smaller element to temp array
        temp[k] ← A[i]
        i ← i+1
        k ← k+1
    }
    else //smaller element is present in right sublist
    {
        //copy that smaller element to temp array
            temp[k] ← A[j]
            j ← j+1
            k ← k+1
        }
    }
    //copy remaining elements of left sublist to temp
  while(i<=mid)do
    {
            temp[k] ← A[i]
            i ← i+1
            k ← k+1
    }
    //copy remaining elements of right sublist to temp
    while(j<=high)do
    {
        temp[k] ← A[j]
        j ← j+1
        k ← k+1
    }
```

Logic Explanation

To understand above algorithm consider a list of elements as

70	20	30	40	10	50	60
0	1	2	3	4	5	6
↑			↑			↑
low			mid			high

Then we will first make two sublists as

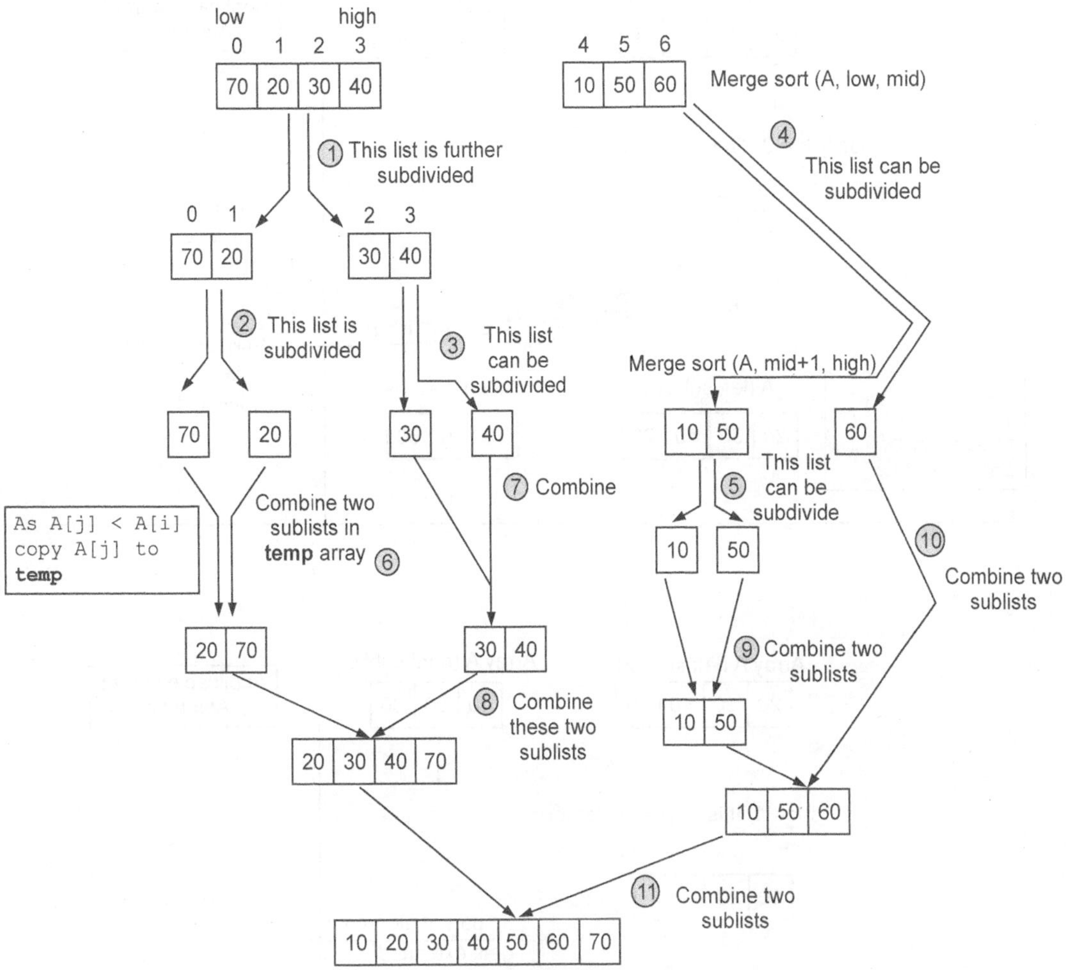

Fig. 1.16.3

Let us see the **combine** operation more closely with the help of some example.

Consider that at some instance we have got two sublits 20, 30, 40, 70 and 10, 50, 60, then

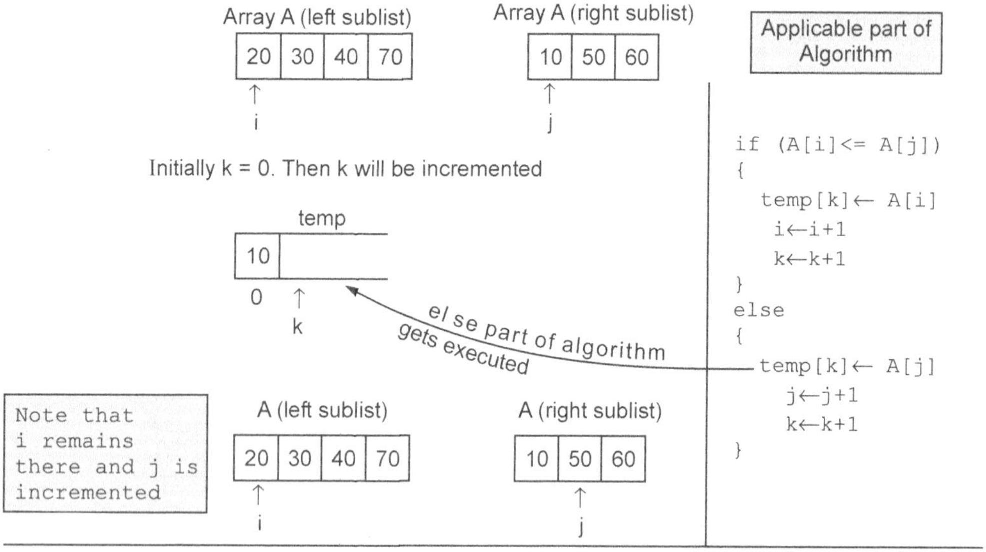
Array A (left sublist)
20 30 40 70
i
Array A (right sublist)
10 50 60
j
Applicable part of Algorithm
Initially k = 0. Then k will be incremented
temp
10
0
k
else part of algorithm gets executed
if (A[i]<= A[j])
{
temp[k]← A[i]
i←i+1
k←k+1
}
else
{
temp[k]← A[j]
j←j+1
k←k+1
}
Note that i remains there and j is incremented
A (left sublist)
20 30 40 70
i
A (right sublist)
10 50 60
j

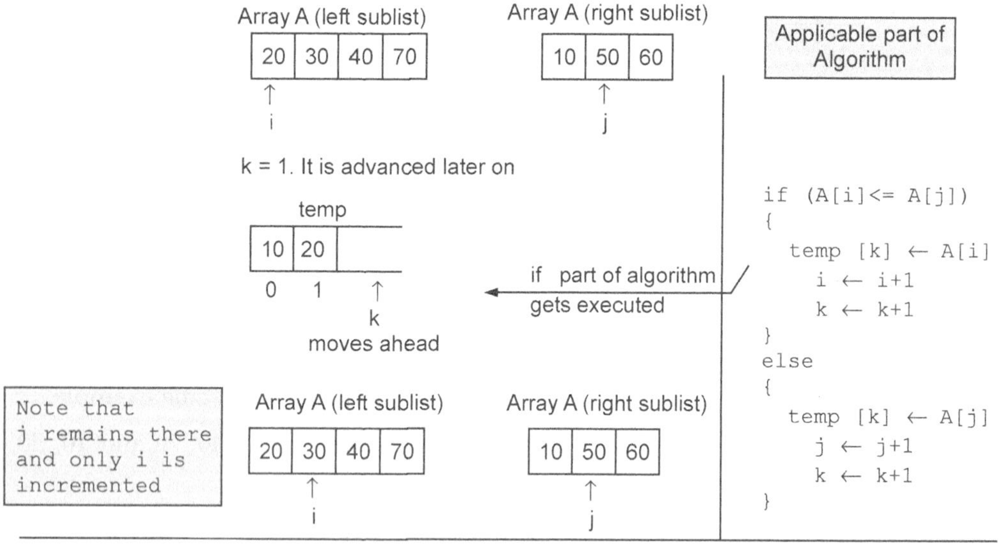
Array A (left sublist)
20 30 40 70
i
Array A (right sublist)
10 50 60
j
Applicable part of Algorithm
k = 1. It is advanced later on
temp
10 20
0 1
k
moves ahead
if part of algorithm gets executed
if (A[i]<= A[j])
{
temp [k] ← A[i]
i ← i+1
k ← k+1
}
else
{
temp [k] ← A[j]
j ← j+1
k ← k+1
}
Note that j remains there and only i is incremented
Array A (left sublist)
20 30 40 70
i
Array A (right sublist)
10 50 60
j

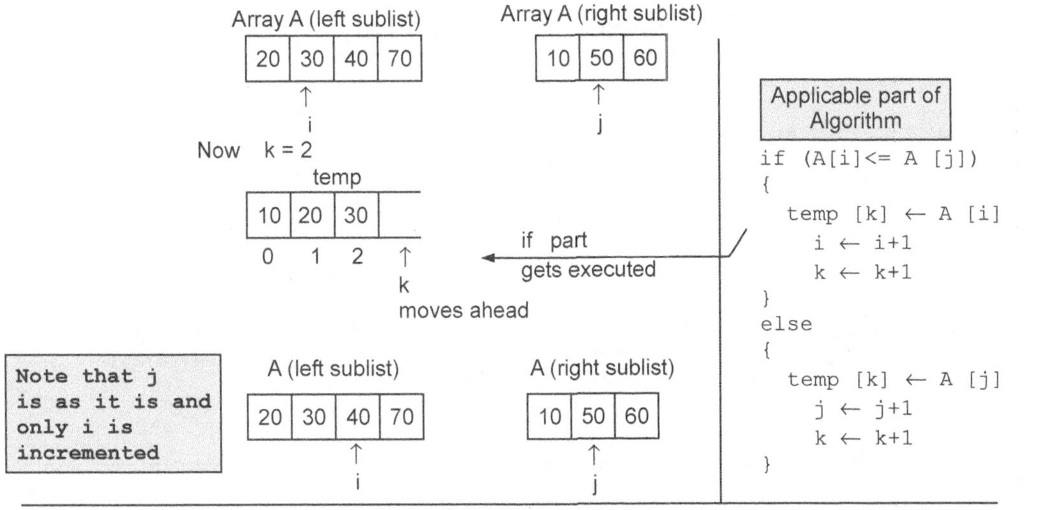

Array A (left sublist)
20 30 40 70
i
Array A (right sublist)
10 50 60
j
Now k = 2
temp
10 20 30
0 1 2
k
moves ahead
if part
gets executed
Applicable part of Algorithm
if (A[i]<= A [j])
{
temp [k] ← A [i]
i ← i+1
k ← k+1
}
else
{
temp [k] ← A [j]
j ← j+1
k ← k+1
}
Note that j is as it is and only i is incremented
A (left sublist)
20 30 40 70
i
A (right sublist)
10 50 60
j

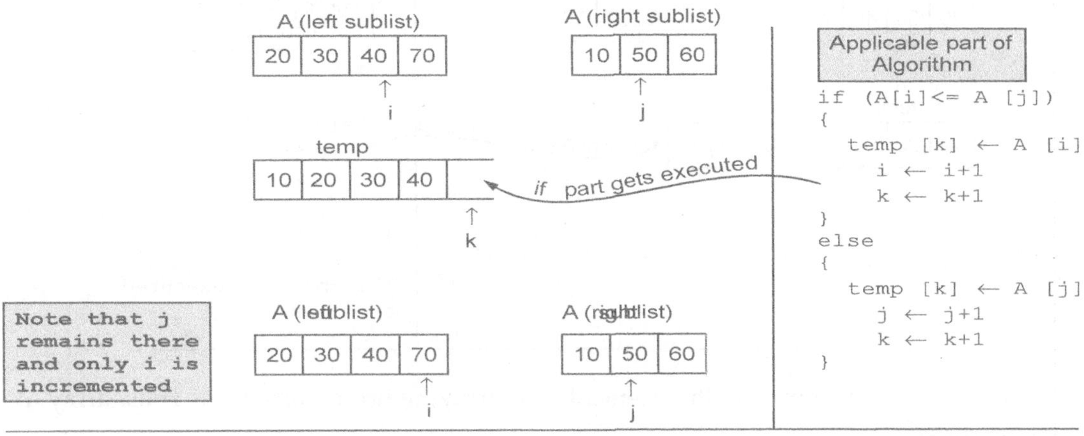

A (left sublist)
20 30 40 70
i
A (right sublist)
10 50 60
j
temp
10 20 30 40
k
if part gets executed
Applicable part of Algorithm
if (A[i]<= A [j])
{
temp [k] ← A [i]
i ← i+1
k ← k+1
}
else
{
temp [k] ← A [j]
j ← j+1
k ← k+1
}
Note that j remains there and only i is incremented
20 30 40 70
i
10 50 60
j

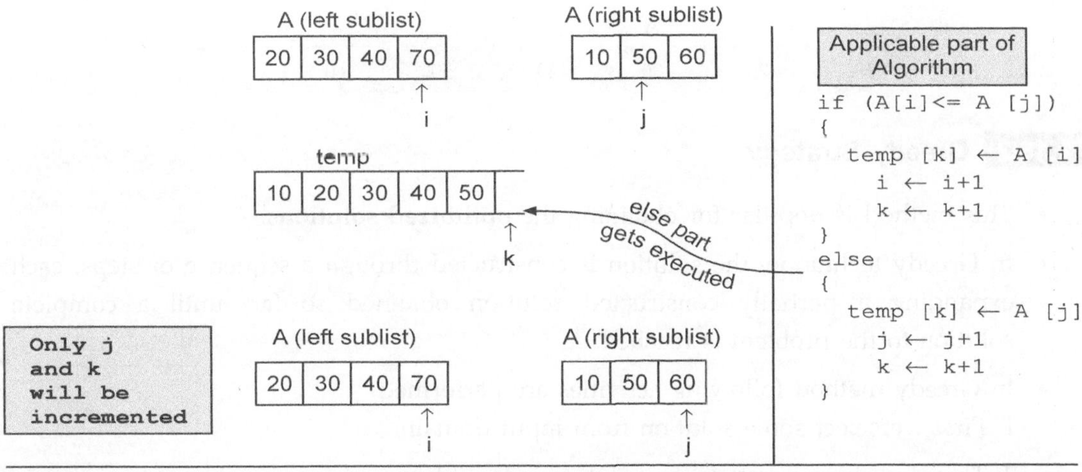

A (left sublist)
20 30 40 70
i
A (right sublist)
10 50 60
j
temp
10 20 30 40 50
k
else part
gets executed
Applicable part of Algorithm
if (A[i]<= A [j])
{
temp [k] ← A [i]
i ← i+1
k ← k+1
}
else
{
temp [k] ← A [j]
j ← j+1
k ← k+1
}
Only j and k will be incremented
A (left sublist)
20 30 40 70
i
A (right sublist)
10 50 60
j

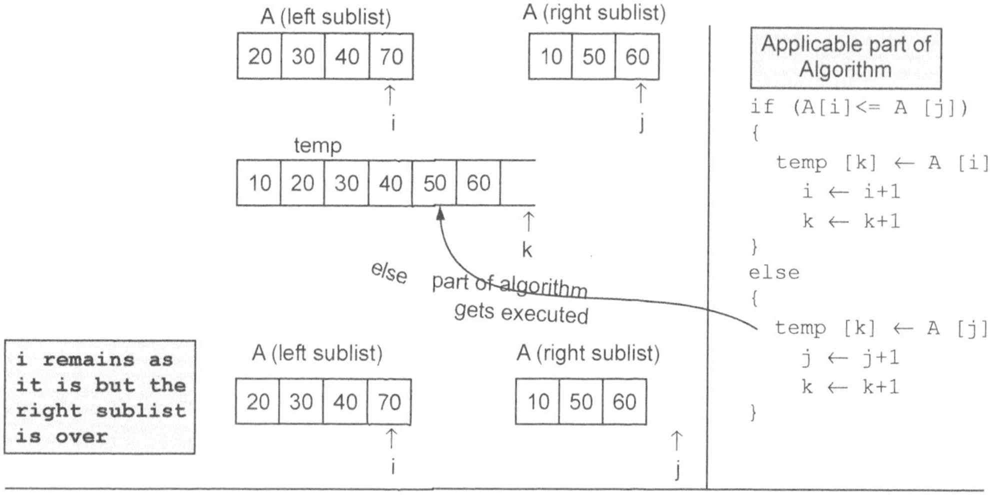

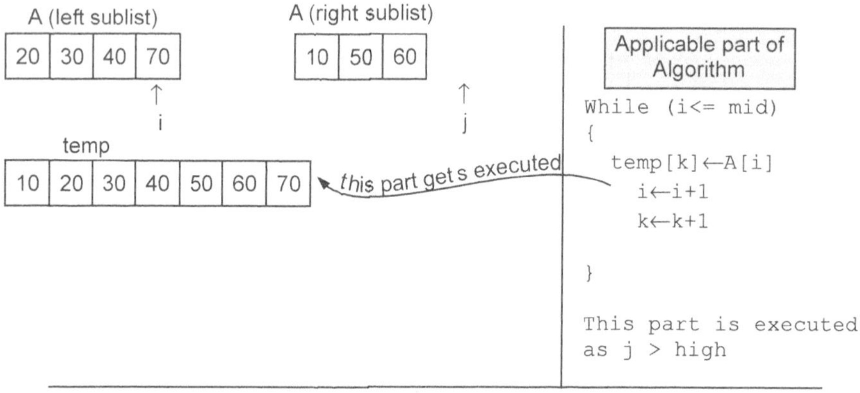

Finally we will copy all the elements of array **temp** to array **A.** Thus array **A** contains sorted list.

A

10	20	30	40	50	60	70

1.16.2 Greedy Strategy

- This method is popular for obtaining the **optimized solutions.**
- In Greedy technique, the solution is constructed through a sequence of steps, each expanding a partially constructed solution obtained so far, until a complete solution to the problem is reached.
- In Greedy method following activities are performed.
  1. First we select some solution from input domain.
  2. Then we check whether the solution is feasible or not.

3. From the set of feasible solutions, particular solution that satisfies or nearly satisfies the objective of the function. Such a solution is called optimal solution.

4. As Greedy method works in stages. At each stage only one input is considered at each time. Based on this input it is decided whether particular input gives the optimal solution or not.

1.16.2.1 Example of Greedy Method

- Dijkstra's Algorithm is a popular algorithm for finding shortest path using Greedy method. This algorithm is called **single source shortest path** algorithm.
- In this algorithm, for a given vertex called source the shortest path to all other vertices is obtained.
- In this algorithm the main focus is not to find only one single path but to find the shortest paths from any vertex to all other remaining vertices.
- This algorithm applicable to graphs with non-negative weights only.

Consider a weighted connected graph as given below.

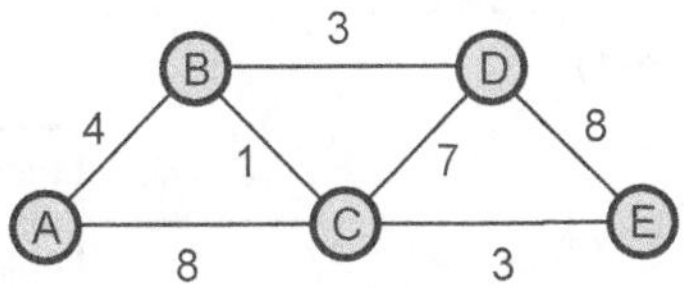

Now we will consider each vertex as a source and will find the shortest distance from this vertex to every other remaining vertex. Let us start with vertex A.

Source vertex	Distance with other vertices		Path shown in graph
A	**A-B,** A-C, A-D, A-E	**path = 4** path = 8 path = ∞ path = ∞	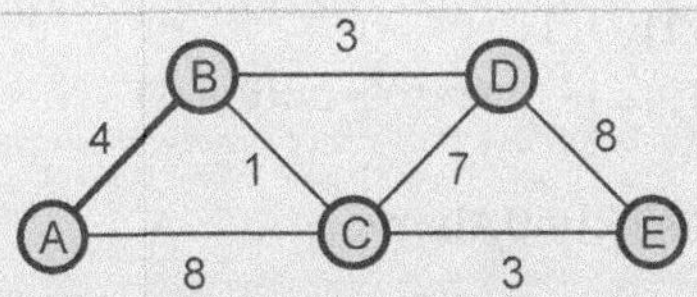
B	**B-C,** B-D, B-E	**path = 4 + 1** path = 4 + 3 path = ∞	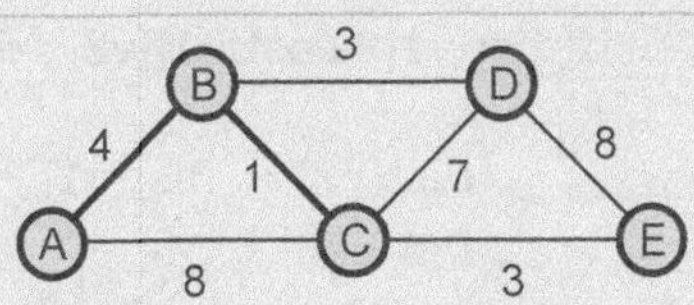
C	C-D, **C-E,**	path = 5 + 7 = 12 **path = 5 + 3 = 8**	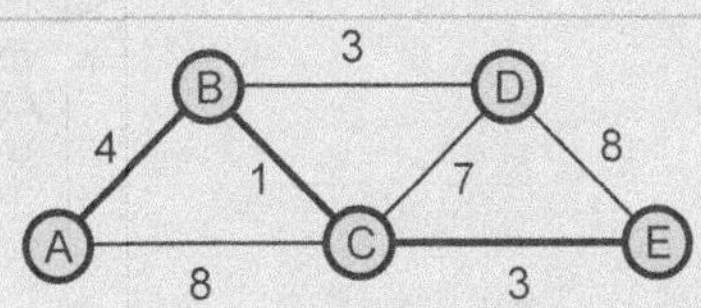
D	D-E,	path = 7 + 8 = 15	

But we have one shortest distance obtained from A to E and that is A - B - C - E with path length = 4 + 1 + 3 = 8. Similarly other shortest paths can be obtained by choosing appropriate source and destination.

Pseudo Code

```
Algorithm Dijkstra(int cost[1...n,1...n],int source,int dist[])

for i ← 0 to tot_nodes
{
        dist[i] ← cost[source,i]//initially put the
        s[i] ← 0 //distance from source vertex to i
        //i is varied for each vertex
        path[i] ← source//all the sources are put in path
}
    s[source] ← 1          <-- Start from each source node
for(i ← 1 to tot_nodes)
{
        min_dist ← infinity;
        v1 ← -1//reset previous value of v1
        for(j ← 0 to tot_nodes-1)
        {
             if(s[j]=0)then
             {
                 if(dist[j]<min_dist)then      <-- Finding minimum distance from
                 {                                 selected source node.That is :
                  min_dist ← dist[j]               source-j represents min_dist. edge
                  v1 ← j
                 }
             }
        }
        s[v1] ← 1
        for(v2 ← 0 to tot_nodes-1)
        {
         if(s[v2]=0)then
         {
             if(dist[v1]+cost[v1][v2]<dist[v2])then
             {
                 dist[v2] ← dist[v1]+cost[v1][v2]
                 path[v2] ← v1     <-- v1 is next selected destination
             }                         vertex with shortest distance.
         }                             All such vertices are
        }                              accumulated in array
    }                                      path[ ]
}
```

Review Questions

1. *Explain divide and conquer strategy with example. Also comment on the time analysis.*
SPPU : May-17, 18, Marks 6
2. *Explain the greedy strategy with suitable example. Comment on its time complexity.*
SPPU : Dec.-17, Marks 6
3. *What is divide and conquer strategy ?* **SPPU : Dec.-19, Marks 3**

❑❑❑

Notes

Unit - II

2 Linear Data Structure using Sequential Organization

Syllabus

Concept *of Sequential Organization, Overview of Array, Array as an Abstract Data Type, Operations on Array, Merging of two arrays, Storage Representation and their Address Calculation : Row major and Column Major, Multidimensional Arrays : Two-dimensional arrays, n-dimensional arrays. Concept of Ordered List,* ***Single Variable Polynomial :*** *Representation using arrays, Polynomial as array of structure, Polynomial addition, Polynomial multiplication.* ***Sparse Matrix :*** *Sparse matrix representation using array, Sparse matrix addition, Transpose of sparse matrix- Simple and Fast Transpose, Time and Space tradeoff.*

Contents

2.1 Concept of Sequential Organization

Arrays is refered as the **sequential organization** that means the data in arrays is stored in some sequence.

For example : If we want to store names of all the students in a class we can make use of an array to store the names in **sequential** form.

Defintion of Arrays : Array is a set of consecutive memory locations which contains similar data elements.

Array is basically a **set of pair-index and the value.**

Syntax

data_type name_of_array [size] ;

For example, int a [10]; double b[10] [10];

Here 'a' is the name of the array inside the square bracket size of the array is given. This array is of integer type i.e. all the elements are of integer type in array 'a'.

Advantages of sequential organization of data structure

1. Elements can be retrieved or stored very efficiently in sequential organization with the help of index or memory location.
2. All the elements are stored at continuous memory locations. Hence searching of element from sequential organization is easy.

Disadvantages of sequential organization of data structure

1. Insertion and deletion of elements becomes complicated due to sequential nature.
2. For storing the data large continuous free block of memory is required.
3. Memory fragmentation occurs if we remove the elements randomly.

2.2 Array as an Abstract Data Type

The abstract data type is written with the help of instances and operations.

We make use of the reserved word **AbstractDataType** while writing an ADT.

AbstractDataType Array

{

Instances : An array A of some size, index i and total number of elements in the array n.

Operations :

1. Create () – This operation creates an array.

2. **Insert()** - This operation is for inserting the element in an array
3. **Delete()** - This operation is for deleting the elements from the array. Only logical deletion of the element is possible.
4. **display ()** – This operation displays the elements of the array.

}

2.3 Array Overview

Definition: Array is a collection of similar type of elements.

The arrays can be one dimensional, two dimensional, or multidimensional.

One dimensional array :

The one dimensional array 'a' is declared as int a[10];

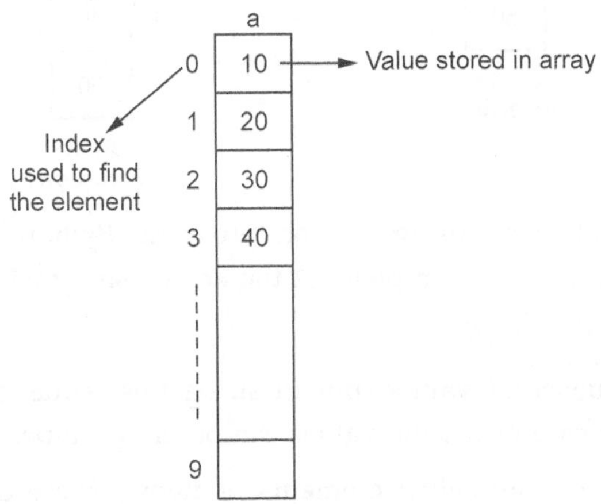

Two dimensional array :

If we declare a two dimensional array as

int a[10] [3];

Then it will look like this -

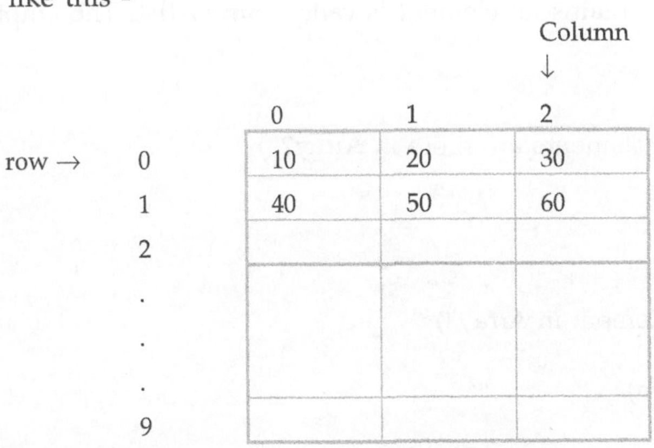

The two dimensional array should be in row-column form.

2.4 Operations on Array

(1) Insertion of Element in Array

- Inserting an element in an array is complex activity because we have to shift the elements ahead in order to create a space for new element.
- That means after inserting an element array size gets incremented by one.

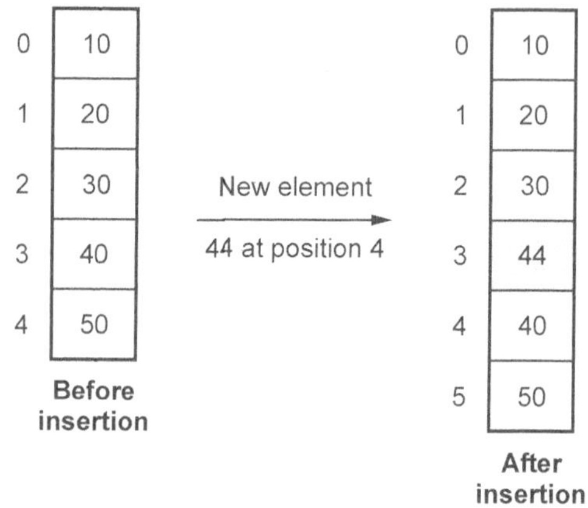

- We can implement array using Python program. Python does not support the concept of array, but we can implement the array using **List**
- List is a sequence of values.
- String is also sequence of values. But in string this sequence is of characters. On the other hand, in case of list the values can be of any type.
- The values in the list are called **elements** or **items**. These elements are separated by commas and enclosed within the square bracket.

For example

```
[10,20,30,40]   # list of integers
['aaa','bbb','ccc'] #list of strings
```

- The list that contains no element is called **empty list**. The empty list is represented by [].

Python Program

```
print("\nHow many elements are there in Array?")
n = int(input())
array = []
i=0
for i in range(n):
    print("\n Enter element in Array")
    item = int(input())
    array.append(item)
```

```
print("Enter the location where you want to insert an element")
position = int(input())

print("Enter the value to insert")
value = int(input())
array=array[:position]+[value]+array[position:]
print("Resultant array is\n")
print(array)
```

Output

```
How many elements are there in Array?
5

 Enter element in Array
10

 Enter element in Array
20

 Enter element in Array
30

 Enter element in Array
40

 Enter element in Array
50
Enter the location where you want to insert an element
4
Enter the value to insert
44
Resultant array is

[10, 20, 30, 40, 44, 50]
>>>
```

Logic Explanation

For insertion of any element in the array, we can make use of list slicing technique. Here is an illustration.

Suppose the array is as follows -

0	1	2	3	4
10	20	30	40	50

array

Position = 4

Element to be inserted = 44

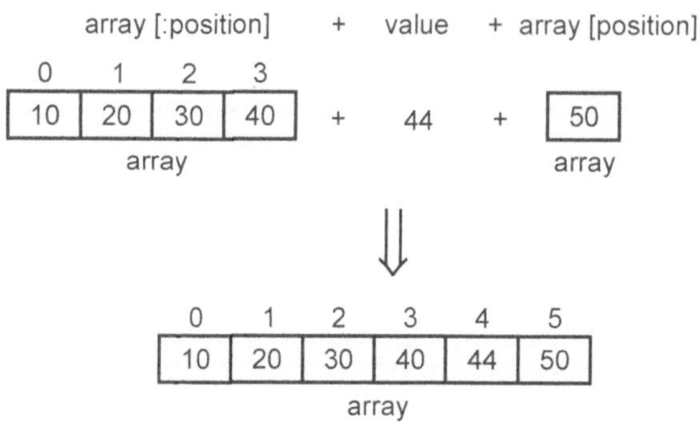

C++ Code

```
#include <iostream>
using namespace std;
int main()
{
    int array[100], position, i, n, value;
    cout<<"\n How many elements are there in array";
    cin>>n;
    cout<<"Enter the elements\n";
    for (i = 0; i < n; i++)
        cin>>array[i];
    cout<<"\n Enter the location where you wish to insert an element: ";
    cin>> position;
    cout<<"\n Enter the value to insert: ";
    cin>>value;
    for (i = n - 1; i >= position - 1; i--)//creating space by shifting the element down
        array[i + 1] = array[i];
    array[position - 1] = value;//at the desired space inserting the element
    printf("Resultant array is\n");
    for (i = 0; i <= n; i++)
        cout<<"\n"<< array[i]);
    return 0;
}
```

(2) Traversing List

- The loop is used in list for traversing purpose. The **for** loop is used to traverse the list elements.

Syntax

```
for VARIABLE in LIST :
    BODY
```

Example

```
>>> a=['a','b','c','d','e'] # List a is created
>>> for i in a:
print(i)
will result into
a
b
c
d
e
>>>
```

- We can traverse the list using **range()** function. Using range() function we can access each element of the list using index of a list.
- If we want to increment each element of the list by one, then we must pass index as argument to for loop. This can be done using range() function as follows -

```
>>> a=[10,20,30,40]
>>> for i in range(len(a)):
a[i]=a[i]+1   #incremented each number by one
>>> a
[11, 21, 31, 41]
>>>
```

(3) Deleting an element from array

- Deleting an element from array is complex activity because have to shift the elements to previous position.
- That means after deleting an element size gets decremented by one.

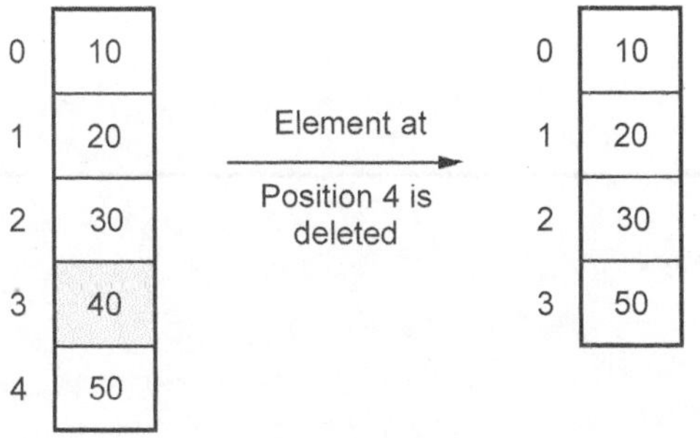

Python Program

```
print("\nHow many elements are there in Array?")
n = int(input())
array = []
i=0
```

```
for i in range(n):
    print("\n Enter element in Array")
    item = int(input())
    array.append(item)

print("Enter the index from where you want to delete an element")
position = int(input())
array=array[:position]+array[position+1:]
print("Resultant array is\n")
print(array)
```

Output

```
How many elements are there in Array?
5

 Enter element in Array
10

 Enter element in Array
20

 Enter element in Array
30

 Enter element in Array
40

 Enter element in Array
50
Enter the index from where you want to delete an element
2
Resultant array is

[10, 20, 40, 50]
>>> |
```

Logic Explanation :

Suppose array is

0	1	2	3	4
10	20	30	40	50

Position = 2. That meants we want to delete an element 30, then

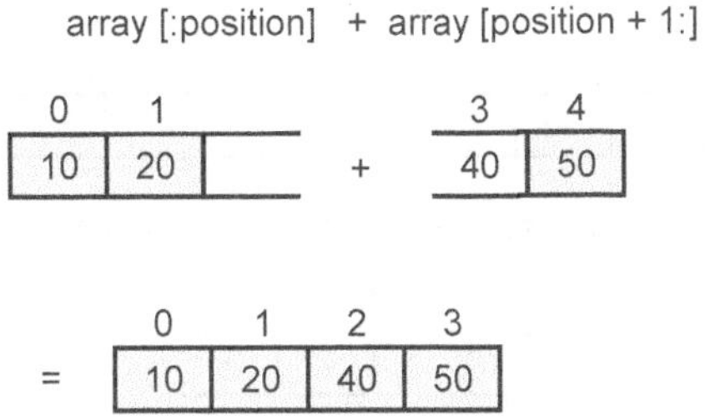

C++ Code

```
#include <iostream>
using namespace std;
int main()
{
        int array[100], position, i, n;
        cout<<"\n How many elements are there in array ";
        cin>>n;
        cout<<"\nEnter the elements:\n";
        for (i = 0; i < n; i++)
                cin>>array[i];
        cout<<"\n Enter the location of the element which is to be deleted ";
        cin>>position;
        if (position >= n + 1)
                cout<<"Element can not be deleted\n";
        else
        {
                for (i = position - 1; i < n - 1; i++)
                        array[i] = array[i + 1];
                cout<<"\nArray is\n";
                for (i = 0; i < n - 1; i++)
                        cout<<"\n"<< array[i]);
        }
        return 0;
}
```

2.5 Merging of Two Arrays

Merging of two arrays result into a single array in which elements are arranged in sorted order.

For example - consider two arrays as follows

Step 1 :

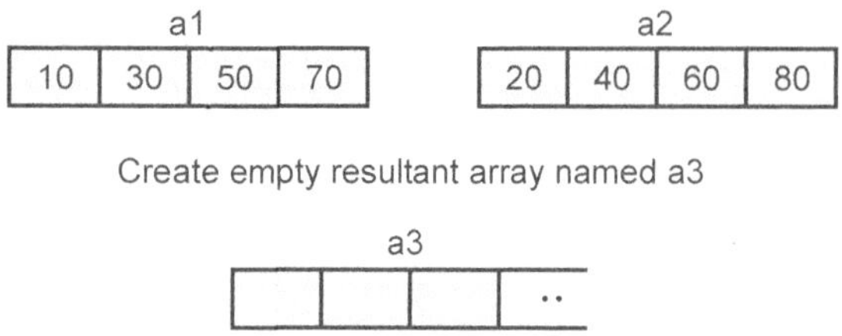

Step 2 :

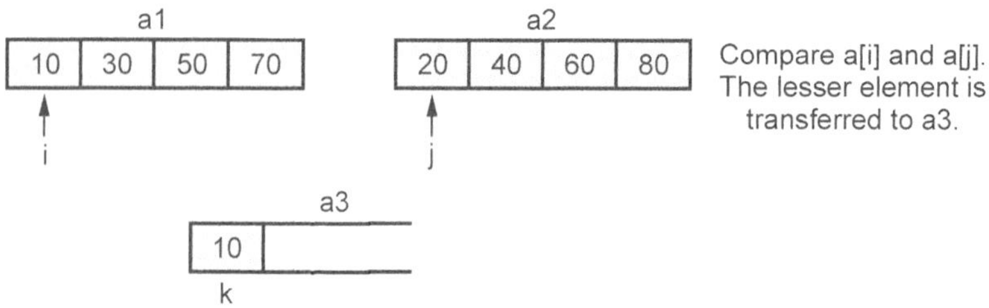

As a1[i] < a2[j], transfer element a1[i]to a3[k]. Then increment i and k pointer

Step 3 :

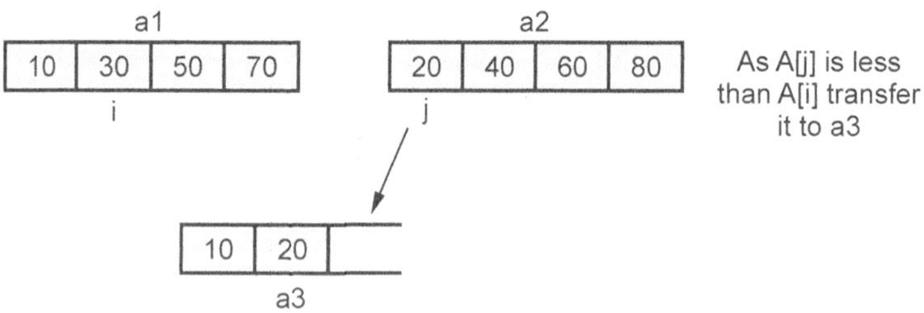

As a2[j] is transferred to a3 array increment j and k pointer.

Step 4 :

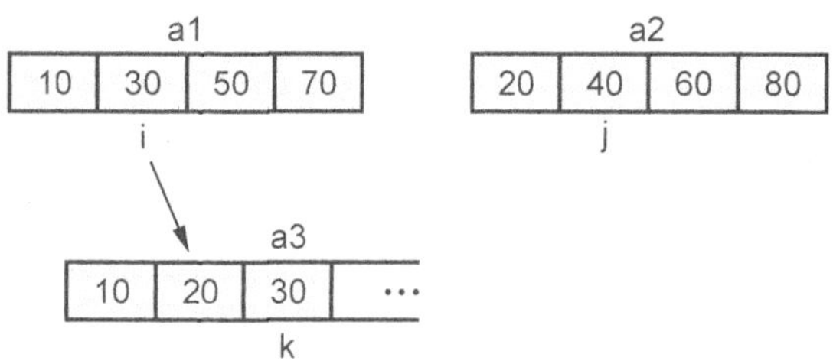

Increment i and k pointers. In this way we can transfer the elements from two arrays a1 and a2 to get merged array a3.

Finally we get

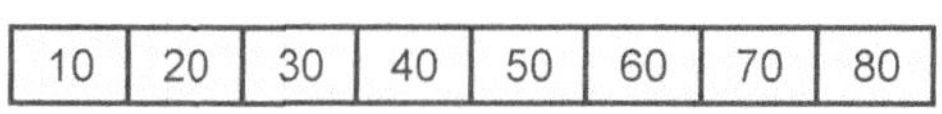

Python Program

```
def mergeArr(a1,a2,n,m):
    a3 = [None]*(n+m)
    i = 0
    j = 0
    k = 0
    #traverse both arrays
    #if element of first array is less then store it in third array
    #if element of second array is less then store it in third array
    while i < n and j < m:
        if a1[i] < a2[j]:
            a3[k] = a1[i]
            k = k + 1
            i = i + 1
        else:
            a3[k] = a2[j]
            k = k + 1
            j = j + 1
    #if elements of first array are remaining
    #then transfer them to third array
    while i < n:
        a3[k] = a1[i]
        k = k + 1
        i = i + 1

    #if elements of second array are remaining
    #then transfer them to third array
    while j < m:
        a3[k] = a2[j]
        k = k + 1
        j = j + 1

    #display the resultant merged array
    print("Merged Array is ...")
    for i in range (n+m):
        print(str(a3[i]), end = " ")
```

#Driver Code

```
a1 = []
n = int(input("Enter total number of elements in first array:"))
for i in range(0,n):
    item = int(input("Enter the element: "))
    a1.append(item)

a2 = []
m = int(input("Enter total number of elements in second array:"))
for i in range(0,m):
    item = int(input("Enter the element: "))
```

```
    a2.append(item)

mergeArr(a1,a2,n,m)
```

Output

```
Enter total number of elements in first array:4
Enter the element: 10
Enter the element: 30
Enter the element: 50
Enter the element: 70
Enter total number of elements in second array:4
Enter the element: 20
Enter the element: 40
Enter the element: 60
Enter the element: 80
Merged Array is ...
10 20 30 40 50 60 70 80
>>>
```

2.6 Storage Representation and their Address Calculation

SPPU : Dec.-06, 09, 16, 18, Marks 6

The array can be represented using **i) Row Major ii) Column Major Representation.**

Row Major Representation

If the elements are stored in **rowwise manner** then it is called row major representation.

For example : If we want to store elements

10 20 30 40 50 60 then in a two dimensional array

The ⇒ elements will be stored horizontally

	0	1	2
0	10	20	30
1	40	50	60
.			
.			
.			
9			

To access any element in two dimensional array we must specify both its row number and column number. That is why we need two variables which act as row index and column index.

Column Major Representation

If elements are stored in **column wise manner** then it is called column major representation.

For example : If we want to store elements

10 20 30 40 50 60 then the elements will be filled up by columnwise manner as follows (consider array a[3] [2]). Here 3 represents number of rows and 2 represents number of columns.

	0	1
0	10	40
1	20	50
2	30	60

Each element is occupied at successive locations if the element is of integer type then 2 bytes of memory will be allocated, if it is of floating type then 4 bytes of memory will be allocated and so on.

For example :

```
int a [3] [2]  =  { {10, 20 }
                    {30, 40}
                    {50, 60} }
```

Then in row major matrix

a[0][0]	a[0][1]	a[1][0]	a[1][1]	a[2][0]	a[2][1]	
10	20	30	40	50	60	...
100	102	104	106	108	110	

And in column major matrix

a[0][0]	a[1][0]	a[2][0]	a[0][1]	a[1][1]	a[2][1]	
10	30	50	20	40	60	...
100	102	104	106	108	110	

Here each element occupies 2 bytes of memory base address will be 100.

Address calculation for any element will be as follows

In row major matrix, the element a[i] [j] will be at

base address + (row_index * total number of columns + column_index)

* element_size.

In column major matrix, the element at a[i] [j] will be at

base address + (column_index * total number of rows + row_index) * element.

In C normally the row major representation is used.

Example 2.6.1 *Consider integer array int arr[3][4] declared in 'C' program. If the base address is 1050, find the address of the element arr[2][3] with row major and column major representation of array.* **SPPU : Dec.-06, Marks 6**

Solution : Row Major Representation

The element a[i][j] will be at

a[i][j]=base address+(row_index*total number of columns + column_index)

*element_size

= (base address+(i*col_size+j)*element_size)

when i=2 and j=3, element_size=int occupies 2 bytes of memory hence it is 2

total number of columns=4,

a[2][3] = 1050+(2*4+3)*2

= 1050+22

a[2][3] = 1072

Column Major Representation

The element a[i][j] will be at

a[i][j] = base address+(col_index*total number of

rows+row_index)*element_size

= (base address+(j*row_size+i)*element_size)

when i=2 and j=3 ,element_size=int occupies 2 bytes of memory hence it is 2

total number of rows=3

a[2][3] = 1050+(3*3+2)*2

= 1050+22

a[2][3] = 1072

Example 2.6.2 *Consider integer array int arr[4][5] declared in 'C' program. If the base address is 1020, find the address of the element arr[3][4] with row major and column major representation of array.* **SPPU : Dec.-09, Marks 6**

Solution : Row Major Representation

The element a[i][j] will be at

a[i][j] = base address+(row_index*total number of columns + col_index)*element_size

= (base address+(i*col_size+j)*element_size)

when i=3 and j=4 ,element_size=int occupies 2 bytes of memory hence it is 2

total number of columns=5

a[3][4] = 1020+(3*5+4)*2

= 1020+38

a[3][4] = 1058

Column Major Representation

The element a[i][j] will be at

a[i][j] = base address+(col_index*total number of rows+row_index)*element_size

= (base address+(j*row_size+i)*element_size)

when i=3 and j=4, element_size=int occupies 2 bytes of memory hence it is 2

total number of rows = 4

a[3][4] = 1020+(4*4+3)*2

= 1020+38

a[3][4] = 1058

Review Questions

1. *Derive address calculation formula for one dimensional array with one example.* **SPPU : Dec.-16, Marks 6**
2. *Explain two dimensional arrays with row and column major implementation. Explain address calculation in both cases with example* **SPPU : Dec.-18, Marks 6**

2.7 Multidimensional Arrays

Multidimensional array is an array having more than one dimension. Popularly, two and three dimensional arrays are used.

2.7.1 Two Dimensional Array

The two dimensional array is used to represent the matrix.

Various operations that can be performed on matrix are –

(1) Matrix Addition (2) Matrix Multiplication and (3) Transpose of Matrix

Let us discuss the implementation of various matrix operations

Example 2.7.1 *Write a python program for representation two dimensional matrix.*

Solution :

```
# This program stores and displays the elements of two dimensional Array
row_num = int(input("Input number of rows: "))
col_num = int(input("Input number of columns: "))
arr = [[0 for col in range(col_num)] for row in range(row_num)]

for row in range(row_num):
    for col in range(col_num):
        item = int(input("Enter the element: "))
        arr[row][col]= item

print(arr)
```

Output

```
Python 3.7.3 Shell
File Edit Shell Debug Options Window Help

Input number of rows: 3
Input number of columns: 3
Enter the element: 10
Enter the element: 20
Enter the element: 30
Enter the element: 40
Enter the element: 50
Enter the element: 60
Enter the element: 70
Enter the element: 80
Enter the element: 90
[[10, 20, 30], [40, 50, 60], [70, 80, 90]]
>>> |
                                                    Ln: 17 Col: 4
```

C++ Code

```
// This program stores and displays the elements of two dimensional Array
cout<<"\nInput number of rows: ";
cin>>row_num;
cout<<"\nInput number of columns: ";
cin>>col_num;
```

```
int arr[row_num][col_num];
for (row=0;row<row_num;row++)
{
   for (col=0;col<col_num;col++)
   {
      cout<<"Enter the element: ";
      cin>>arr[row][col];
    }
}
for (row=0;row<row_num;row++)
{
   for (col=0;col<col_num;col++)
   {
      cout<<"\t"arr[row][col];
   }
   cout<<"\n";
}
```

(1) Addition of Two Matrices

Consider matrix A and B as follows –

Matrix A

1	2	3
4	5	6
7	8	9

Matrix B

1	1	1
2	2	2
3	3	3

Addition of Matrices is

2	3	4
6	7	8
10	11	12

Example 2.7.2 *Write a python program for performing addition of two matrices*

Solution :

```
def add_matrix(arr1,arr2):
   result = [[arr1[i][j] + arr2[i][j]  for j in range(len(arr1[0]))] for i in range(len(arr1))]

   print("The Addition of Two Matrices...")
   print(result)
row_num = int(input("Input number of rows: "))
col_num = int(input("Input number of columns: "))
arr1 = [[0 for col in range(col_num)] for row in range(row_num)]
for row in range(row_num):
   for col in range(col_num):
      item = int(input("Enter the elements in first matrix: "))
      arr1[row][col]= item
```

```
print("The first matrix is...")
print(arr1)

arr2 = [[0 for col in range(col_num)] for row in range(row_num)]
for row in range(row_num):
    for col in range(col_num):
        item = int(input("Enter the elements in second matrix: "))
        arr2[row][col]= item

print("The second matrix is...")
print(arr2)

#Driver Code
add_matrix(arr1,arr2,)
```

Output

```
Input number of rows: 3
Input number of columns: 3
Enter the elements in first matrix: 1
Enter the elements in first matrix: 2
Enter the elements in first matrix: 3
Enter the elements in first matrix: 4
Enter the elements in first matrix: 5
Enter the elements in first matrix: 6
Enter the elements in first matrix: 7
Enter the elements in first matrix: 8
Enter the elements in first matrix: 9
The first matrix is...
[[1, 2, 3], [4, 5, 6], [7, 8, 9]]
Enter the elements in second matrix: 1
Enter the elements in second matrix: 1
Enter the elements in second matrix: 1
Enter the elements in second matrix: 2
Enter the elements in second matrix: 2
Enter the elements in second matrix: 2
Enter the elements in second matrix: 3
Enter the elements in second matrix: 3
Enter the elements in second matrix: 3
The second matrix is...
[[1, 1, 1], [2, 2, 2], [3, 3, 3]]
The Addition of Two Matrices...
[[2, 3, 4], [6, 7, 8], [10, 11, 12]]
>>>
```

(2) Matrix Multiplication

Consider matrix A

1	2	3
4	5	6
7	8	9

Consider matrix B

1	1	1
2	2	2
3	3	4

The resultant matrix is

14	14	17
32	32	38
50	50	59

Example 2.7.3 *Write a python program to implement matrix multiplication operation.*

Solution :

```
    A    =    [[1,2,3],
              [4,5,6],
              [7,8,9]]


    B    =    [[1,1,1],
              [2,2,2],
              [3,3,4]]


    result=   [[0,0,0],
              [0,0,0],
              [0,0,0]]


print("Matrix A is ...")
print(A)

print("Matrix B is ...")
print(B)

# iterate through rows of X
for i in range(len(A)):
  for j in range(len(B[0])):
    for k in range(len(B)):
      result[i][j] += A[i][k] * B[k][j]

print("Matrix Multiplication is ...")
for r in result:
  print(r)
```

Output

```
Matrix A is ...
[[1, 2, 3], [4, 5, 6], [7, 8, 9]]
Matrix B is ...
[[1, 1, 1], [2, 2, 2], [3, 3, 4]]
```

```
Matrix Multiplication is ...
[14, 14, 17]
[32, 32, 38]
[50, 50, 59]
>>>
```

(3) Transpose of Matrix

Consider matrix A

1	2	3
4	5	6
7	8	9

Transposed matrix

1	4	7
2	5	8
3	6	9

Example 2.7.4 *Write a Python program for performing transpose of matrix.*

Solution :

```
    A    =    [[1,2,3],
               [4,5,6],
               [7,8,9]]

    result=   [[0,0,0],
               [0,0,0],
               [0,0,0]]

print("Original Matrix is...")
print(A)

# iterate through rows
for i in range(len(A)):
   for j in range(len(A[0])):
      result[j][i] = A[i][j]

print("Transposed Matrix is ...")
for r in result:
   print(r)
```

Output

```
Original Matrix is...
[[1, 2, 3], [4, 5, 6], [7, 8, 9]]
Transposed Matrix is ...
[1, 4, 7]
[2, 5, 8]
[3, 6, 9]
>>>
```

2.7.2 Three Dimensional Array

The multidimensional array is similar to the two dimensional array with multiple dimensions for example Here is 3-D array

a [3] [2] [3] = { {{1, 2, 3}, {4, 5, 6}},
{{7, 8, 9}, {10, 11, 12}},
{{13, 14, 15} {16, 17, 18}}
}

(a [3] → dimension; [2] → rows; [3] → column)

We can represent it graphically as

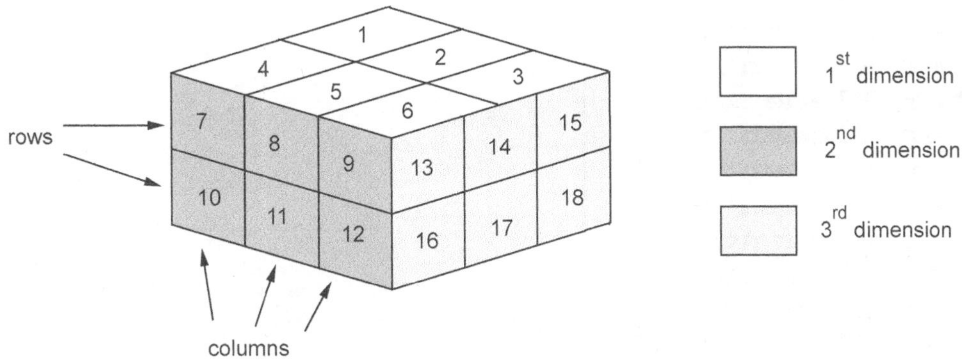

Python Program

```
row_num = int(input("Input number of rows: "))
col_num = int(input("Input number of columns: "))
dim_num = int(input("Input number of dimensions: "))
arr1 =[]#creating an empty list
for dim in range(dim_num):
    arr1.append([])
    for row in range(row_num):
        arr1[dim].append([])
        for col in range(col_num):
            item = int(input("Enter Element: "))
            arr1[dim][row].append(item)

print("\n Elements in 3D Array are...")
for dim in range(dim_num):
    for row in range(row_num):
        for col in range(col_num):
            print(arr1[dim][row][col],end =" ")
        print()
    print("——————————")
```

Output

```
Input number of rows: 2
Input number of columns: 3
Input number of dimensions: 3
Enter Element: 1
Enter Element: 2
Enter Element: 3
Enter Element: 4
Enter Element: 5
Enter Element: 6
Enter Element: 7
Enter Element: 8
Enter Element: 9
Enter Element: 10
Enter Element: 11
Enter Element: 12
Enter Element: 13
Enter Element: 14
Enter Element: 15
Enter Element: 16
Enter Element: 17
Enter Element: 18

 Elements in 3D Array are...
1  2  3
4  5  6
-------------
7  8  9
10  11  12
-------------
13  14  15
16  17  18
-------------
>>> |
```

C++ Code

```
/*
    This program is for storing and retrieving the elements in a 3-D array
*/
# include<iostream>
using namespace std;
int main()
```

```
{
	int a[3][2][3]
	int i,j,k;
	cout<<"\n Enter the elements";
	for (i=0; i<3; i++)
	{
		for(j=0; j<2; j++)
		{
			for(k=0; k<3; k++)
			{
				cin>>a[i][j][k];
			}
		}
	}
	cout<<"\n Printing the elements \n";
	for(i=0; i<3; i++)
	{
		for (j=0; j<2; j++)
		{
			for(k=0; k<3; k++)
			{
				cout<<"\t"<<a[i][j][k];
			}
			cout<<"\n";
		}
		cout<<"\n--------------------------------";
	}
	return 0;
}
```

2.8 Concept of Ordered List

Ordered list is nothing but a set of elements. Such a list sometimes called as linear list.

For example

1. List of one digit numbers

   (0, 1, 2, 3, 4, 5, 6, 7, 8, 9)

2. Days in a week.

   (Sunday, Monday, Tuesday, Wednesday, Thursday, Friday, Saturday)

With this concept in mind let us formally define the ordered list.

Definition : An ordered list is set of elements where set may be empty or it can be written as a collection of elements such as (a1, a2, a3 .... an).

Operations on ordered list

Following operations can be possible on an ordered list.

1. Display of list
2. Searching a particular element from the list
3. Insertion of any element in the list
4. Deletion of any element from the list

Ordered List can be implemented using the List data structure in Python.

Various operations on List are possible using following methods

2.8.1 Ordered List Methods

(1) append

The append method adds the element at the end of the list. For example

```
>>> a=[10,20,30]
>>> a.append(40)   #adding element 40 at the end
>>> a
[10, 20, 30, 40]
>>> b=['A','B','C']
>>> b.append('D')   #adding element D at the end
>>> b
['A', 'B', 'C', 'D']
>>>
```

(2) extend

The extend function takes the list as an argument and appends this list at the end of old list. For example

```
>>> a=[10,20,30]
>>> b=['a','b','c']
>>> a.extend(b)
>>> a
[10, 20, 30, 'a', 'b', 'c']
>>>
```

(3) sort

The sort method arranges the elements in increasing order. For example

```
>>> a=['x','z','u','v','y','w']
>>> a.sort()
>>> a
['u', 'v', 'w', 'x', 'y', 'z']
>>>
```

The methods append, extend and sort does not return any value. These methods simply modify the list. These are void methods.

(4) Insert

This method allows us to insert the data at desired position in the list. The syntax is **insert(index,element)**

For example -

```
>>> a=[10,20,40]
>>> a.insert(2,30)
>>> print(a)
[10, 20, 30, 40]
>>>
```

(5) Delete

The deletion of any element from the list is carried out using various functions like **pop, remove, del**.

If we know the index of the element to be deleted then just pass that index as an argument to **pop** function.

For example

```
>>> a=['u','v','w','x','y','z']
>>> val=a.pop(1)  #the element at index 1 is v, it is deleted
>>> a
['u', 'w', 'x', 'y', 'z']        #list after deletion
>>> val        #deleted element is present in variable val
'v'
>>>
```

If we do not provide any argument to the pop function then the last element of the list will be deleted.

For example -

```
>>> a =['u','v','w','x','y','z']
>>> val=a.pop()
>>> a
['u', 'v', 'w', 'x', 'y']
>>> val
'z'
>>>
```

If we know the value of the element to be deleted then the **remove** function is used. That means the parameter passed to the remove function is the actual value that is to be removed from the list. Unlike, **pop** function the **remove** function does not return any value. The execution of **remove** function is shown by following screenshot.

```
>>> a=['a','b','c','d','e']
>>> a.remove('c')
>>> a
['a', 'b', 'd', 'e']
>>>
```

In python, it is possible to remove more than one element at a time using **del** function.

For example

```
>>> a=['a','b','c','d','e']
>>> del a[2:4]
>>> a
['a', 'b', 'e']
>>>
```

2.8.2 Built in Functions

- There are various built in functions in python for supporting the list operations. Following table shows these functions

Built-in function	Purpose
all()	If all the elements of the list are true or if the list is empty then this function returns true.
any()	If the list contains any element true or if the list is empty then this function returns true.
len()	This function returns the length of the string.
max()	This function returns maximum element present in the list.
min()	This function returns minimum element present in the list.
sum()	This function returns the sum of all the elements in the list.
sorted()	This function returns a list which is sorted one.

For example - Following screenshot of python shell represents execution of various built in functions –

```
Python 3.7.3 Shell
File Edit Shell Debug Options Window Help

>>> myList=[10,20,30,40,50]
>>> print("The length of List is: ",len(myList))
The length of List is:  5
>>> print("The maximum of List is: ",max(myList))
The maximum of List is:  50
>>> print("The minimum of List is: ",min(myList))
The minimum of List is:  10
>>> print("The sum of all the elements of the list is: ",sum(myList))
The sum of all the elements of the list is:  150
>>>
                                                          Ln: 12 Col: 4
```

2.8.3 List Comprehension

- List comprehension is an elegant way to create and define new lists using existing lists.
- This is mainly useful to make new list where each element is obtained **by applying some operations to each member** of another sequence.

Syntax

```
List=[expression for item in the list]
```

Example 2.8.1 *Write a python program to create a list of even numbers from 0 to 10.*

Solution :

```
even = [] #creating empty list
for i in range(11):
  if i % 2 ==0:
    even.append(i)
print("Even Numbers List: ",even)
    even = [] #creating empty list
for i in range(11):
  if i % 2 ==0:
    even.append(i)
print("Even Numbers List: ",even)
```

Output

```
Even Numbers List:  [0, 2, 4, 6, 8, 10]
```

Program explanation : In above program,

1) We have created an empty list first.
2) Then using the range of numbers from 0 to 11 we append the empty list with even numbers. The even number is test using the if condition. i.e. if I %2= =0. If so then that even number is appended in the list.
3) Finally the comprehended list will be displayed using print statement.

Example 2.8.2 *Write a python program to combine and print two lists using list comprehension.*

Solution :

```
print([(x,y)for x in['a','b'] for y in ['b','d'] if x!=y])
```

Output

```
[('a', 'b'), ('a', 'd'), ('b', 'd')]
```

2.9 Single Variable Polynomial

SPPU : May-17, 18, Marks 3

Definition : Polynomial is the sum of terms where each term consists of variable, **coefficient** and **exponent.**

Various operations on polynomial are – addition, subtraction, multiplication and evaluation.

2.9.1 Representation

For representing a single variable polynomial one can make use of one dimensional array. In single dimensional array the index of an array will act as the exponent and the coefficient can be stored at that particular index which can be represented as follows :

For e.g. : $3x^4 + 5x^3 + 7x^2 + 10x - 19$

This polynomial can be stored in single dimensional array.

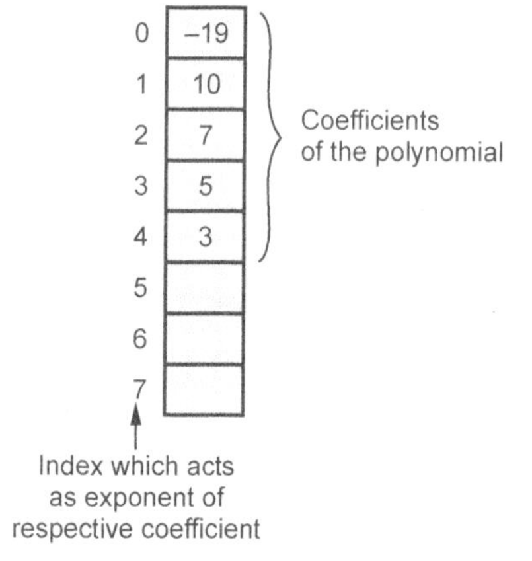

Fig. 2.9.1 Polynomial representation

2.9.2 Polynomial Addition

Algorithm :

Assume that the two polynomials say A and B and the resultant polynomial storing the addition result is stored in one large array.

1. Set a pointer i to point to the first term in a polynomial A.

2. Set a pointer j to point to first term in a polynomial B.
3. Set a pointer k to point to the first position in array C.
4. Read the number of terms of A polynomial in variable t1 and read the number of terms of B polynomial in variable t^2.
5. While i < t1 and j < t2 then

{ if exponent at i^{th} position of A poly is equal to the exponent at j^{th} position of polynomial B then

Add the coefficients at that position from both the polynomial and store the result in C arrays coefficient field at position k copy the exponent either pointed by i or j at position k in C array.

Increment i, j and k to point to the next position in the array A, B and C.

}

else

{

if the exponent position i is greater than the exponent at position j in polynomial B then

{

copy the coefficient at position i from A polynomial into coefficient field at position k of array C copy the exponent pointed by i into the exponent field at position k in array C.

Increment i, k pointers.

}

else

{

Copy the coefficient at position j of B polynomial into coefficient field at position k in C array.

Copy the exponent pointed by j into exponent field at position k in C array.

Increment j and k pointers to point to the next position in array B and C.

}

}

6. While i < t1

{

Copy the coefficient at position i of into the

coefficient field at position k in C.

Copy the exponent pointed by i into the exponent field

at position k in C array.

Increment i and k to point to the next position in

arrays A and C.

}

7. While j < t2

{

Copy the coefficient at position j of B into the coefficient field at position k in C.

Copy the exponent pointed by j into exponent field at

position k in C.

Increment j, k to point to the next position in B and

C arrays.

8. Display the complete array C as the addition of two given polynomials.

9. Stop.

Logic of Addition of two polynomials

Let us take polynomial A and B as follows :

$3x^3 + 2x^2 + x + 1$

$5x^3 + 7x$

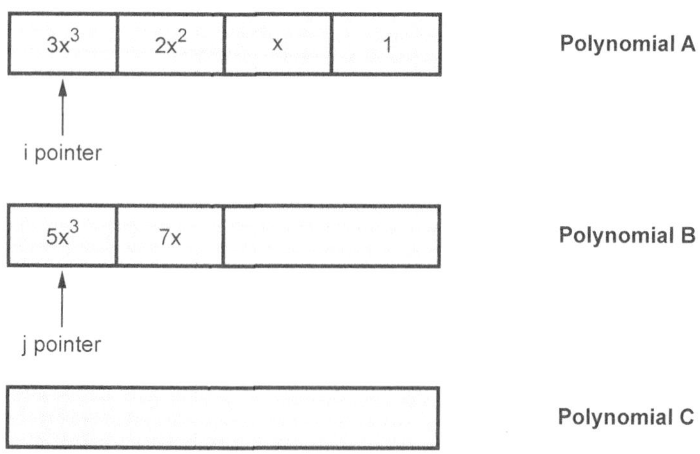

As the terms pointed by i and j shows that both the terms have equal exponent, we can perform addition of these terms and we will store the result in polynomial C.

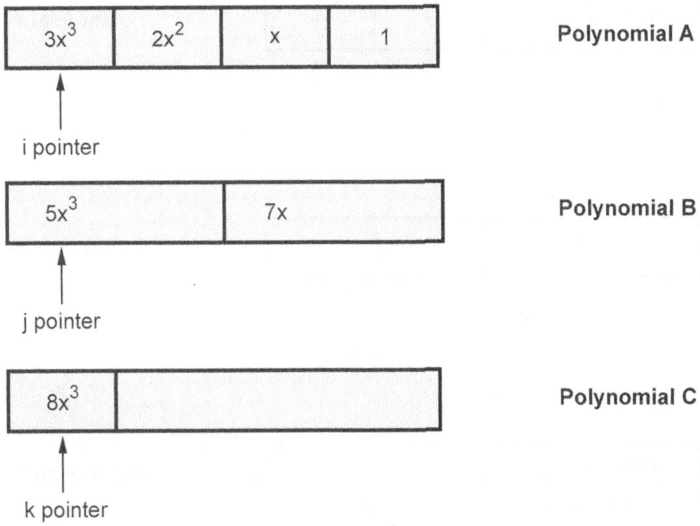

Now increment i, j, and k pointers.

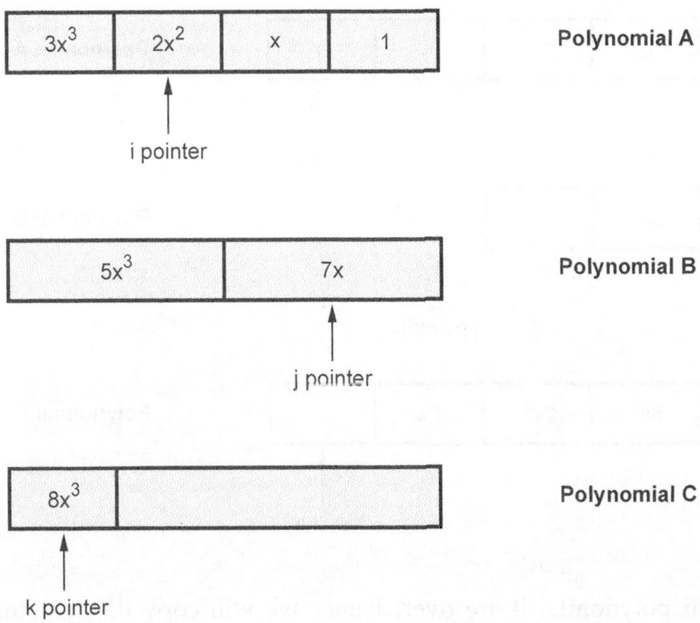

Now pointer i points to $2x^2$ and pointer j points to 7x. As $2x^2 > 7x$. We will copy $2x^2$ in the polynomial C. And we will simply increment i and k pointers

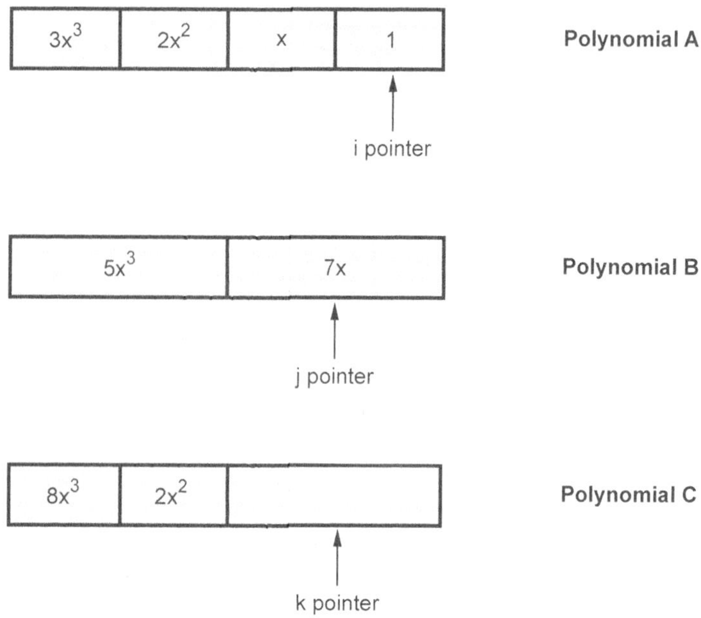

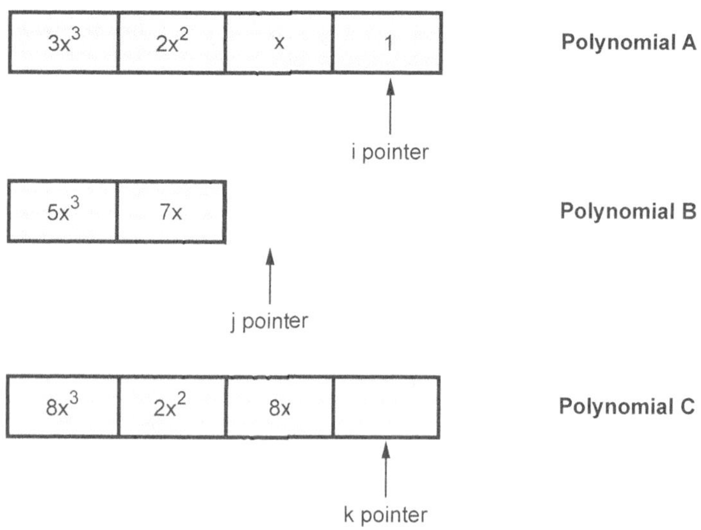

Now terms in polynomial B are over. Hence we will copy the remaining terms from polynomial A to polynomial C.

$3x^3$	$2x^2$	x	1

Polynomial A

$5x^3$	7x

Polynomial B

$8x^3$	$2x^2$	8x	1

Polynomial C

Thus the addition of polynomials A and B is in polynomial C.

Python Program

```
# A[] represents coefficients of first polynomial
# B[] represents coefficients of second polynomial
# m and n are sizes of A[] and B[] respectively
def add(A, B, m, n):
    size = max(m, n);
    C = [0 for i in range(size)]

    for i in range(0, m, 1):
    #Each term from first polynomial to C array
        C[i] = A[i]
    # Add each term of second poly and add it to C
    for i in range(n):
        C[i] += B[i]

    return C

# A function to print a polynomial
def display(poly, n):
    for i in range(n):
        print(poly[i], end = “”)
        if (i != 0):
            print(“x^”, i, end = “”)
        if (i != n - 1):
            print(“ + ”, end = “”)

# Driver Code
if __name__ == ‘__main__’:

    # The following array represents
    # polynomial 1 + 1x +2x^2+ 3x^3
    A = [1, 1, 2, 3]

    # The following array represents
    # polynomial 7x + 5x^3
```

```
B = [0, 7,0, 5]
m = len(A)
n = len(B)

print("\nFirst polynomial is")
display(A, m)
print("\nSecond polynomial is")
display(B, n)

C = add(A, B, m, n)
size = max(m, n)

print("\n Addition of polynomial is")
display(C, size)
```

Output

```
First polynomial is
1 + 1x^ 1 + 2x^ 2 + 3x^ 3
Second polynomial is
0 + 7x^ 1 + 0x^ 2 + 5x^ 3
Addition of polynomial is
1 + 8x^ 1 + 2x^ 2 + 8x^ 3
>>>
```

C++ Code

```
/*******************************************************************
 Program To Perform The Polynomial Addition And To Print
 The Resultant Polynomial.
*******************************************************************/
#include<iostream>
using namespace std;
class APADD
{
	private:
		struct p
		{
			int coeff;
			int expo;
		};
	public:
		p p1[10],p2[10],p3[10];
		int Read(p p1[10]);
		int add(p p1[10],p p2[10],int t1,int t2,p p3[10]);
		void Print(p p2[10],int t2);
};
```

```
/*
------------------------------------------------------------------------
The Read Function Is For Reading The Two Polynomials
------------------------------------------------------------------------
/*
int APADD::Read(p p[10])
{
        int t1,i;
        cout<<"\n Enter The Total number Of Terms in The Polynomial: ";
        cin>>t1;
        cout<<"\n Enter The Coef and Exponent In Descending Order";
        for(i=0;i<t1;i++)
        {
                cout<<"\n Enter Coefficient and exponent: ";
                cin>>p[i].coeff;
                cin>>p[i].expo;
        }
        return(t1);
}

/*
------------------------------------------------------
The add Function Is For adding The Two Polynomials
------------------------------------------------------*/
int APADD::add(p p1[10],p p2[10],int t1,int t2,p p3[10])
{
        int i,j,k;
        int t3;
        i=0;
        j=0;
        k=0;
        while(i<t1 &&j<t2)
        {
                if(p1[i].expo==p2[j].expo)
                {
                        p3[k].coeff=p1[i].coeff+p2[j].coeff;
                        p3[k].expo =p1[i].cxpo;
                        i++;j++;k++;
                }
                else if(p1[i].expo>p2[j].expo)
                {
                        p3[k].coeff=p1[i].coeff;
                        p3[k].expo =p1[i].expo;
                        i++;k++;
                }
                else
                {
```

```
                    p3[k].coeff=p2[j].coeff;
                    p3[k].expo =p2[j].expo;
                    j++;k++;
                }
        }
        while(i<t1)
        {
                p3[k].coeff=p1[i].coeff;
                p3[k].expo =p1[i].expo;
                i++;k++;
        }
        while(j<t2)
        {
                p3[k].coeff=p2[j].coeff;
                p3[k].expo =p2[j].expo;
                j++;k++;
        }
        t3=k;
        return(t3);
}
/*
-------------------------------------------------------------
The Print Function Is For Printing The Two Polynomials
-------------------------------------------------------------
*/
void APADD::Print(p pp[10],int term)
{
        int k;
        cout<<"\n Printing The Polynomial";
        for(k=0;k<term-1;k++)
                cout<<" "<<pp[k].coeff<<"X^"<<pp[k].expo<<"+ ";
        cout<<pp[k].coeff<<"X^"<<pp[k].expo;
}
/*
-------------------------------------------------------------
 The main function
-------------------------------------------------------------
*/
int main()
{
        APADD obj;
        int t1,t2,t3;
        cout<<"\n Enter The First Polynomial";
        t1=obj.Read(obj.p1);
        cout<<"\n The First Polynomial is: ";
        obj.Print(obj.p1,t1);
        cout<<"\n Enter The Second Polynomial";
```

```
    t2=obj.Read(obj.p2);
    cout<<"\n The Second Polynomial is: ";
    obj.Print(obj.p2,t2);
    cout<<"\n The Addition is: ";
    t3=obj.add(obj.p1,obj.p2,t1,t2,obj.p3);
    obj.Print(obj.p3,t3);
    return 0;
}
```

2.9.3 Polynomial Multiplication

We will now discuss another operation on polynomials and that is multiplication.

For example

If two polynomials are given as

$$
\begin{array}{rl} & 3x^3 + 2x^2 + x + 1 \\ \times & 5x^3 + 7x \end{array}
$$

Then we will perform multiplication by multiplying each term of polynomial A by each term of polynomial B.

$$
\begin{array}{rl} & 3x^3 + 2x^2 + x + 1 \\ \times & 5x^3 + 7x \\ \hline & \underbrace{15x^6 + 10x^5 + 5x^4 + 5x^3}_{\text{Multiplied poly A by } 5x^3} + \underbrace{21x^4 + 14x^3 + 7x^2 + 7x}_{\text{Multiplied poly A by } 7x} \end{array}
$$

Now rearranging the terms

$15x^6 + 10x^5 + 26x^4 + 19x^3 + 7x^2 + 7x$ is a resultant polynomial

Python Program

```
# A[] represents coefficients of first polynomial
# B[] represents coefficients of second polynomial
# m and n are sizes of A[] and B[] respectively
def mul(A, B, m, n):

    #allocating total size for resultant array
    C = [0]* (m+n-1)
    for i in range(0, m, 1):
    #multiplying by current term of first polynomial
    #to each term of second polynomial
      for j in range(n):
        C[i+j] += A[i]*B[j]

    return C
```

```
# A function to print a polynomial
def display(poly, n):
   for i in range(n):
      print(poly[i], end = "")
      if (i != 0):
         print("x^", i, end = "")
      if (i != n - 1):
         print(" + ", end = "")

# Driver Code
if __name__ == '__main__':

   # The following array represents
   # polynomial 1 + 1x +2x^2+ 3x^3
   A = [1, 1, 2, 3]

   # The following array represents
   # polynomial 7x + 5x^3
   B = [0, 7,0, 5]
   m = len(A)
   n = len(B)

   print("\nFirst polynomial is")
   display(A, m)
   print("\nSecond polynomial is")
   display(B, n)

   C = mul(A, B, m, n)

   print("\n Multiplication of polynomial is...")
   display(C, m+n-1)
```

Output

```
First polynomial is
1 + 1x^ 1 + 2x^ 2 + 3x^ 3
Second polynomial is
0 + 7x^ 1 + 0x^ 2 + 5x^ 3
 Multiplication of polynomial is...
0 + 7x^ 1 + 7x^ 2 + 19x^ 3 + 26x^ 4 + 10x^ 5 + 15x^ 6
>>>
```

2.9.4 Polynomial Evaluation

We will now discuss the algorithm for evaluating the polynomial.

Consider the polynomial for evaluation –

$$-10x^7 + 4x^5 + 3x^2$$

where x = 1,

$= -10 + 4 + 3 = -6 + 3$

$= 3$ is the result of polynomial evaluation.

Now, let us see the algorithm for polynomial.

Algorithm :

Step 1 : Read the polynomial array A

Step 2 : Read the value of x.

Step 3 : Initialize the variable sum to zero.

Step 4 : Then calculate coeff * pow (x, exp) of each term and add the result to sum.

Step 5 : Display " sum"

Step 6 : Stop

Python Program

```
def evalPoly(A,n,x):
    result = A[0]
    for i in range(1,n):
        result = result + A[i]*x**i
    return result

def display(poly, n):
    for i in range(n):
        print(poly[i], end = "")
        if (i != 0):
            print("x^", i, end = "")
        if (i != n - 1):
            print(" + ", end = "")

# Driver Code
if __name__ == '__main__':

    # The following array represents
    # polynomial 1 + 1x +2x^2+ 3x^3
    A = [1, 1, 2, 3]
    n = len(A)
    print("\n Polynomial is: ");
    display(A,n)

    x = int(input("\nEnter the value of x: "))
    print("\nThe result of evaluation of polynomial is: ",evalPoly(A,n,x))
```

Output

```
    Polynomial is:
1 + 1x^ 1 + 2x^ 2 + 3x^ 3
Enter the value of x: 2
The result of evaluation of polynomial is: 35
>>>
```

C++ Code

```
/************************************************************
    Program to evaluate a polynomial in single variable for a
    given value of x.
************************************************************/
#include <iostream>
#include <cmath>
using namespace std;
#define     size 20
class APEVAL
{
    private:
    struct p
    {
        int coef;
        int expo;
    };
    public:
    p p1[size];
    int get_poly(p p1[size]);
    void display(p p1[size],int n1);
    float eval(int n1, p p1[]);
};

/*-------------------------------------------------------
 Function get_poly
-------------------------------------------------------*/
int APEVAL::get_poly( p p1[] )
{
    int term,n;

    cout<<"\nHow Many Terms are there? ";
    cin>>n;
    if (n>size)
    {
        cout<<"Invalid number Of Terms\n";
        getch();
        return;
    }
    cout<<"\nEnter the terms of the Polynomial ";
    cout<<"in descending order of the exponent\n";
```

```
    for (term = 0; term < n ; term ++ )
    {
        cout<<"Enter  coefficient and exponenet: ";
        cin>>p1[term].coef;
        cin>>p1[term].expo;
    }
    return( n);
}

/*
----------------------------------------------------------
 This Function is to display the polynomial
 Parameter Passing: By reference and value
----------------------------------------------------------*/
void APEVAL::display(p p1[ ],int n)
{
    int term;
    for (term = 0; term < n-1 ; term ++ )
     cout<<p1[term].coef<<"x^"<<p1[term].expo<<"+ ";
     cout<<p1[term].coef<<"x^"<<p1[term].expo;
}

/*----------------------------------------------------------
Function eval
----------------------------------------------------------*/
float APEVAL::eval(int n1, p p1[])
{
    int i,sum, x;
    cout<<"\nEnter the value for x for evaluation : ";
    cin>>x;
    sum = 0;
    for(i=0; i < n1;i++ )
        sum= sum+p1[i].coef *pow( x, p1[i].expo);
    return( sum );
}

/*
----------------------------------------------------------
  Function main
----------------------------------------------------------
*/
int main()
{
    int n1;
    int value;
    APEVAL obj;
```

```
    cout<<"\n Enter the Polynomial";
    n1 =obj.get_poly(obj.p1);
    cout<<"The First polynomial is : \n";
    obj.display(obj.p1,n1);
    value = obj.eval(n1,obj.p1);
    cout<<"\n The Resultant Value of the polynomial is : "<<value<<"\n";
    return 0;
}
```

Review Question

1. *Explain polynomial representation using arrays with suitable example.*

SPPU : May-17, 18, Marks 3

2.10 Sparse Matrix

SPPU : May-17, 19, Dec.-19, Marks 6

- In a matrix, if there are m rows and n columns then the space required to store the numbers will be $m \times n \times s$ where s is the number of bytes required to store the value. Suppose, there are 10 rows and 10 columns and we have to store the integer values then the space complexity will be bytes.

  $10 \times 10 \times 2 \;=\; 200$ bytes

  (Here 2 bytes are required to store an integer value.)
- It is observed that, many times we deal with matrix of size m × n and values of m and n are reasonably higher and only a few elements are non zero. Such matrices are called **sparse matrices.**
- **Definition:** Sparse matrix is a matrix containing few non zero elements.
- For example - if the matrix is of size 100 × 100 and only 10 elements are non zero. Then for accessing these 10 elements one has to make 10000 times scan. Also only 10 spaces will be with non-zero elements remaining spaces of matrix will be filled with zeros only. i.e. we have to allocate the memory of 100 × 100 × 2 = 20000.
- Hence sparse matrix representation is a kind of representation in which only non zero elements along with their rows and columns is stored.

1	2	3
4	5	6
7	8	9

Dense Matrix

1	0	0
0	0	0
0	1	0

Sparse Matrix

2.10.1 Sparse Matrix Representation using Array

- The representation of sparse matrix will be a **triplet** only. That means it stores rows, columns and values.
- The 0th row will store total rows of the matrix, total columns of the matrix, and total non-zero values.
- For example – Suppose a matrix is 6×7 and number of non zero terms are say 8. In our sparse matrix representation the matrix will be stored as

Index	Row No.	Col. No.	Value
0	6	7	8
1	0	6	– 10
2	1	0	55
3	2	5	– 23
4	3	1	67
5	3	6	88
6	4	3	14
7	4	4	– 28
8	5	0	99

Python Program

```
# function display a matrix
def display(matrix):
    for row in matrix:
        for element in row:
            print(element, end =" ")
        print()

# function to convert the matrix
# into a sparse matrix
def convert(matrix):
    SP =[]
    # searching values greater
    # than zero
    for i in range(len(matrix)):
        for j in range(len(matrix[0])):
            if matrix[i][j] != 0 :

                # creating a temporary sublist
                temp = []

                # appending row value, column
                # value and element into the
```

```
                # sublist
                temp.append(i)
                temp.append(j)
                temp.append(matrix[i][j])

                # appending the sublist into
                # the sparse matrix list
                SP.append(temp)

    # displaying the sparse matrix
    print("\nSparse Matrix: ")
    print("Row Col Non_Zero_Value")
    display(SP)

# Driver code
#Original Matrix
A =[    [10, 0, 0, 0],
    [0, 20, 0, 0],
    [0, 0, 30, 0],
    [0, 0, 0, 40],
    [0, 50, 0, 0]]

# displaying the matrix
display(A)

# converting the matrix to sparse
convert(A)
```

Output

```
10   0    0    0
0    20   0    0
0    0    30   0
0    0    0    40
0    50   0    0

Sparse Matrix:
Row Col Non_Zero_Value
0   0   10
1   1   20
2   2   30
3   3   40
4   1   50
>>> |
```

2.10.2 Sparse Matrix Addition

Algorithm :

1. Start
2. Read the two sparse matrices say SP1 and SP2 respectively.
3. The index for SP1 and SP2 will be i and j respectively. Non zero elements are n1 and n2 for SP1 and SP2.
4. The k index will be for sparse matrix SP3 which will store the addition of two matrices.
5. If SP1 [0][0] > SP2 [0][0] i.e. total number of rows then

   SP3 [0][0] = SP1 [0][0]

   else

   SP3 [0][0] = SP2 [0][0]

   Similarly check in SP1 and SP2 the value of total number of columns which ever value is greater transfer it to SP3.

   Set i = 1, j = 1, k = 1.
6. When i < n1 and j < n2.
7. a) If row values of SP1 and SP2 are same then check also column values are same, if so add the non-zero values of SP1 and SP2 and store them in SP3, increment i, j, k by 1.

   b) Otherwise if colno of SP1 is less than colno of SP2 copy the row, col and nonzero value of SP1 to SP3. Increment i and k by 1.

   c) Otherwise copy the row, col and non-zero value of SP2 to SP3. Increment j and k by 1.
8. When rowno of SP1 is less than SP2 copy row, col and non-zero element of SP1 to SP3. Increment i and k by 1.
9. When rowno of SP2 is less than SP1 copy row, col and non-zero element of SP2 to SP3. Increment j, k by 1. Repeat step 6 to 9 till condition is true.
10. Finally whatever k value that will be total number of non-zero values in SP3 matrix.

    ∴ SP3 [0][2] = k
11. Print SP3 as a result.
12. Stop.

Python Program

```
def create(s,row_num,col_num,non_zero_values):
    s[0][0]= row_num
    s[0][1] = col_num
    s[0][2] = non_zero_values
    for k in range(1,non_zero_values+1):
        row = int(input("Enter row value: "))
        col = int(input("Enter col value: "))
        element = int(input("Enter the element: "))
        s[k][0]= row
        s[k][1] = col
        s[k][2] = element

def display(s):
    print("Row\tcol\t Non_Zero_values")
    for i in range(0,(s[0][2]+1)):
        for j in range(0,3):
            print(s[i][j], "\t", end='')
        print()

def add(s1,s2):
    i = 1
    j = 1
    k = 1
    s3 = []
    if ((s1[0][0] == s2[0][0]) and (s1[0][1] == s2[0][1])):
        #traversing thru all the terms
        while ((i <= s1[0][2]) and (j <= s2[0][2])):
            if (s1[i][0] == s2[j][0]):
                temp =[]
                if (s1[i][1] == s2[j][1]):
                    temp.append(s1[i][0])
                    temp.append(s1[i][1])
                    temp.append(s1[i][2]+s2[j][2])
                    s3.append(temp)
                    i += 1
                    j += 1
                    k += 1
                elif (s1[i][1]<s2[j][1]):
                    temp.append(s1[i][0])
                    temp.append(s1[i][1])
                    temp.append(s1[i][2])
                    s3.append(temp)
                    i += 1
                    k += 1
                else:
                    temp.append(s2[j][0])
```

```
                temp.append(s2[j][1])
                temp.append(s2[j][2])
                s3.append(temp)
                j += 1
                k += 1
            elif (s1[i][0]<s2[j][0]):
                temp =[]
                temp.append(s1[i][0])
                temp.append(s1[i][1])
                temp.append(s1[i][2])
                s3.append(temp)
                i +=1
                k +=1
            else:
                temp =[]
                temp.append(s1[j][0])
                temp.append(s1[j][1])
                temp.append(s1[j][2])
                s3.append(temp)
                j +=1
                k +=1
#copying remaining terms
        while (i <= s1[0][2]): #s1 is greater than s2
            temp = []
            temp.append(s1[i][0])
            temp.append(s1[i][1])
            temp.append(s1[i][2])
            s3.append(temp)
            i += 1
            k += 1
        while (j <= s2[0][2]): #s2 is greater than s1
            temp = []
            temp.append(s2[j][0])
            temp.append(s2[j][1])
            temp.append(s2[j][2])
            s3.append(temp)
            j += 1
            k += 1
        #assigning total rows, total columns
        #and total non zero values as a first row
        #in resultant matrix
        s3.insert(0,[s1[0][0],s1[0][1],k-1])
    else:
        print("\n Addition is not possible")

    print("Addition of Sparse Matrix ...")
    print("\nRow  Col  Non_Zero_values")
```

```
    for row in s3:
        for element in row:
            print(element, end ="    ")
        print()
#Driver Code
row_num1 = int(input("Input total number of rows for first matrix: "))
col_num1 = int(input("Input total number of columns for first matrix: "))
non_zero_values1 = int(input("Input total number of non-zero values: "))
cols =3
s1 = [[0 for col in range(cols)] for row in range(non_zero_values1+1)]
#creating first sparse matrix
create(s1,row_num1,col_num1,non_zero_values1)
print("First sparse matrix is")
display(s1)

row_num2 = int(input("Input total number of rows for second matrix: "))
col_num2 = int(input("Input total number of columns for second matrix: "))
non_zero_values2 = int(input("Input total number of non-zero values: "))
s2 = [[0 for col in range(cols)] for row in range(non_zero_values2+1)]
#creating second sparse matrix
create(s2,row_num2,col_num2,non_zero_values2)
print("Second sparse matrix is")
display(s2)
#Performing and displaying addition of two sparse matrices
add(s1,s2)
```

Output

```
Input total number of rows for first matrix: 2
Input total number of columns for first matrix: 2
Input total number of non-zero values: 3
Enter row value: 1
Enter col value: 1
Enter the element: 10
Enter row value: 1
Enter col value: 2
Enter the element: 20
Enter row value: 2
Enter col value: 1
Enter the element: 30
First sparse matrix is
Row  col    Non_Zero_values
2    2      3
1    1      10
1    2      20
2    1      30
Input total number of rows for second matrix: 2
Input total number of columns for second matrix: 2
```

```
Input total number of non-zero values: 2
Enter row value: 2
Enter col value: 1
Enter the element: 5
Enter row value: 2
Enter col value: 2
Enter the element: 40
Second sparse matrix is
Row  col    Non_Zero_values
2    2    2
2    1    5
2    2    40
Addition of Sparse Matrix ...

Row Col Non_Zero_values
2  2  4
1  1  10
1  2  20
2  1  35
2  2  40
>>>
```

C++ code

Following is a C++ function for addition of two sparse matrices

```
void add(int s1[10][3],int s2[10][3],int s3[10][3])
{
        int i, j, k;
        i = 1; j = 1; k = 1;
        if ((s1[0][0] == s2[0][0]) && (s1[0][1] == s2[0][1]))
        {
                s3[0][0] = s1[0][0];
                s3[0][1] = s1[0][1];
        //traversing thru all the terms
                while ((i <= s1[0][2]) && (j <= s2[0][2]))
                {
                        if (s1[i][0] == s2[j][0])
                        {
                                if (s1[i][1] == s2[j][1])
                                {
                                        s3[k][2] = s1[i][2] + s2[j][2];
                                        s3[k][1] = s1[i][1];
                                        s3[k][0] = s1[i][0];
                                        i++;
                                        j++;
                                        k++;
                                }
                                else if (s1[i][1]<s2[j][1])
```

```
                {
                        s3[k][2] = s1[i][2];
                        s3[k][1] = s1[i][1];
                        s3[k][0] = s1[i][0];
                        i++;
                        k++;
                }
                else
                {
                        s3[k][2] = s2[j][2];
                        s3[k][1] = s2[j][1];
                        s3[k][0] = s2[j][0];
                        j++;
                        k++;
                }
        }//end of 0 if
        else if (s1[i][0]<s2[j][0])
        {
                s3[k][2] = s1[i][2];
                s3[k][1] = s1[i][1];
                s3[k][0] = s1[i][0];
                i++;
                k++;
        }
        else
        {
                s3[k][2] = s2[j][2];
                s3[k][1] = s2[j][1];
                s3[k][0] = s2[j][0];
                j++;
                k++;
        }
}//end of while
 //copying remaining terms
while (i <= s1[0][2])
{
        s3[k][2] = s1[i][2];
        s3[k][1] = s1[i][1];
        s3[k][0] = s1[i][0];
        i++;
        k++;
}
while (j <= s2[0][2])
{
        s3[k][2] = s2[j][2];
        s3[k][1] = s2[j][1];
        s3[k][0] = s2[j][0];
```

```
            j++;
            k++;
        }
        s3[0][2] = k - 1;
    }
    else
        cout<<"\n Addition is not possible";
}
```

2.10.3 Transpose of Sparse Matrix

We will now discuss the algorithm for performing transpose of sparse matrix.

For eg :

Index	Row No.	Col. No.	Value
0	6	7	8
1	0	6	– 10
2	1	0	55
3	2	5	– 23
4	3	1	67
5	3	6	88
6	4	3	14
7	4	4	– 28
8	5	0	99

will become

Index	Row No.	Col. No.	Value
0	7	6	8
1	0	1	55
2	0	5	99
3	1	3	67
4	3	4	14
5	4	4	– 28
6	5	2	– 23
7	6	0	– 10
8	6	3	88

During the transpose of matrix (i) Interchange rows and columns (ii) Also maintain the rows in sorted order.

Python Program

```
row_num = int(input("Input number of rows: "))
col_num = int(input("Input number of columns: "))
non_zero_values = int(input("Input total number of non-zero values: "))
cols =3
s1 = [[0 for col in range(cols)] for row in range(non_zero_values+1)]
s2 = [[0 for col in range(cols)] for row in range(non_zero_values+1)]

def create(s1,row_num,col_num,cols,non_zero_values):
    s1[0][0]= row_num
    s1[0][1] = col_num
    s1[0][2] = non_zero_values
    for k in range(1,non_zero_values+1):
        row = int(input("Enter row value: "))
        col = int(input("Enter col value: "))
        element = int(input("Enter the element: "))
        s1[k][0]= row
        s1[k][1] = col
        s1[k][2] = element

def display(s,cols,non_zero_values):
    print("Row\tcol\t Non_Zero_values")
    for i in range(0,non_zero_values+1):
        for j in range(0,cols):
            print(s[i][j], "\t", end='')
        print()

def transpose(s1,row_num,col_num,s2,cols,non_zero_values):
    s2[0][0]= col_num
    s2[0][1] = row_num
    s2[0][2] = non_zero_values
    nxt=1
    for c in range(0,col_num):
    # for each column scan all the terms for a 'term' in that column
        for Term in range(1,non_zero_values+1):
            if (s1[Term][1] == c):
                # Interchange Row and Column
                s2[nxt][0] = s1[Term][1]
                s2[nxt][1] = s1[Term][0]
                s2[nxt][2] = s1[Term][2]
                nxt=nxt+1
#Driver Code
create(s1,row_num,col_num,cols,non_zero_values)
print("Original sparse matrix is")
display(s1,cols,non_zero_values)
transpose(s1,row_num,col_num,s2,cols,non_zero_values)
print("Transposed sparse matrix is")
display(s2,cols,non_zero_values)
```

Output

```
Input number of rows: 3
Input number of columns: 3
Input total number of non-zero values: 4
Enter row value: 0
Enter col value: 0
Enter the element: 10
Enter row value: 0
Enter col value: 2
Enter the element: 20
Enter row value: 1
Enter col value: 1
Enter the element: 30
Enter row value: 2
Enter col value: 1
Enter the element: 40
Original sparse matrix is
Row     col         Non_Zero_values
3       3       4
0       0       10
0       2       20
1       1       30
2       1       40
Transposed sparse matrix is
Row     col         Non_Zero_values
3       3       4
0       0       10
1       1       30
1       2       40
2       0       20
```

Logic Explanation :

In above program we look for column values of s1 array starting from 0 to total number of column value and interchange row and column one by one. For instance – Consider the output of above program s1[0][0] =10, the column value is 0 here, we swap the row and column and copy the column, row and non zero value to s2 array

Locate zero in **Col,** swap row, col and copy it to s2. At the same time copy corresponding non-zero-value to s2

s1

Row	Col	Non_Zero_values
0	(0)	10
0	2	20
1	1	30
2	1	40

s2

Row	Col	Non_Zero_values
0	0	10

Locate 1 in **Col,** swap row, col and copy it to s2. At the same time copy corresponding non-zero-value to s2

Row	Col	Non_Zero_values
0	0	10
0	(2)	20
1	1	30
2	1	40

Row	Col	Non_Zero_values
0	0	10
1	1	30

Row	Col	Non_Zero_values
0	0	10
0	2	20
1	(1)	30
2	1	40

Row	Col	Non_Zero_values
0	0	10
1	1	30
1	2	40

Locate 2 in **Col,** swap row, col and copy it to s2. At the same time copy corresponding non-zero-value to s2

Row	Col	Non_Zero_values
0	0	10
0	(2)	20
1	1	30
2	1	40

Row	Col	Non_Zero_values
0	0	10
1	1	30
1	2	40
2	1	20

Thus we get transposed matrix in the form of sparse matrix representation.

C++ Code

```
void transp(int s1[size + 1][3], int s2[size + 1][3])
{
	int  nxt, c, Term;
	int    n, m, terms;
/*Read Number of rows, columns and terms of given matrix */
	n = s1[0][0];
	m = s1[0][1];
	terms = s1[0][2];

	/* Interchange Number of rows with number of columns */
	s2[0][0] = m;
	s2[0][1] = n;
	s2[0][2] = terms;
	if (terms > 1) /* if nonzero matrix then */
	{
		nxt = 1; /* Gives next position in the transposed matrix */
				/* Do the transpose columnwise */
		for (c = 0; c <= m; c++)
		{
		/* for each column scan all the terms for a term in that column */
			for (Term = 1; Term <= terms; Term++)
			{
				if (s1[Term][1] == c)
```

```
                        {
                            /* Interchange Row and Column */
                            s2[nxt][0] = s1[Term][1];
                            s2[nxt][1] = s1[Term][0];
                            s2[nxt][2] = s1[Term][2];
                            nxt++;
                        }
                    }
                }
            }
}
```

Time complexity of simple transpose:

The simple transpose of sparse matrix can be performed using two nested for loops. Hence the time complexity is $O(n^2)$

2.10.4 Fast Transpose

The fast transpose is a transpose method in which matrix transpose operation is performed efficiently. In this method an auxiliary array are used to locate the position of the elements to be transposed sequentially.

Here is an implementation of fast transpose of sparse matrix in Python.

Python Program

```
row_num = int(input("Input number of rows: "))
col_num = int(input("Input number of columns: "))
non_zero_values = int(input("Input total number of non-zero values: "))
cols =3
s1 = [[0 for col in range(cols)] for row in range(non_zero_values+1)]
s2 = [[0 for col in range(cols)] for row in range(non_zero_values+1)]

def create(s1,row_num,col_num,cols,non_zero_values):
    s1[0][0]= row_num
    s1[0][1] = col_num
    s1[0][2] = non_zero_values
    for k in range(1,non_zero_values+1):
        row = int(input("Enter row value: "))
        col = int(input("Enter col value: "))
        element = int(input("Enter the element: "))
        s1[k][0]= row
        s1[k][1] = col
        s1[k][2] = element


def display(s,cols,non_zero_values):
    print("Row\tcol\t Non_Zero_values")
    for i in range(0,non_zero_values+1):
```

```
        for j in range(0,cols):
            print(s[i][j], "\t", end='')
        print()

def transpose(s1,row_num,col_num,s2,cols,non_zero_values):
    s2[0][0]= col_num
    s2[0][1] = row_num
    s2[0][2] = non_zero_values
    rterm = []
    rpos = []
    if non_zero_values > 0:
        for  i in range(col_num):
            rterm.insert(i,0)
        for  i in range(1,non_zero_values+1):
            #rterm[s1[i][1]]++
            index = s1[i][1]
            val = rterm.pop(index)
            rterm.insert(index,val+1)
        rpos.insert(0,1)
        for i in range(1,col_num+1):
            #rpos[i]=rpos[i-1]+ rterm[(i - 1)]
            rpos_val=rpos[i-1]
            rterm_val=rterm[i-1]
            rpos.insert(i,(rpos_val+rterm_val))
        for i in range(1,non_zero_values+1):
            j = rpos[s1[i][1]]
            s2[j][0] = s1[i][1]
            s2[j][1] = s1[i][0]
            s2[j][2] = s1[i][2]
            rpos[s1[i][1]] = j + 1
#Driver Code
create(s1,row_num,col_num,cols,non_zero_values)
print("Original sparse matrix is")
display(s1,cols,non_zero_values)
transpose(s1,row_num,col_num,s2,cols,non_zero_values)
print("Transposed sparse matrix is")
display(s2,cols,non_zero_values)
```

Output

```
Input number of columns: 3
Input total number of non-zero values: 4
Enter row value: 0
Enter col value: 1
Enter the element: 10
Enter row value: 1
Enter col value: 0
Enter the element: 20
Enter row value: 2
Enter col value: 0
Enter the element: 30
Enter row value: 2
Enter col value: 1
Enter the element: 40
Original sparse matrix is
Row       col       Non_Zero_values
3         3         4
0         1         10
1         0         20
2         0         30
2         1         40
Transposed sparse matrix is
Row       col       Non_Zero_values
3         3         4
0         1         20
0         2         30
1         0         10
1         2         40
>>> |
```

Logic for Fast Transpose

Consider the sparse matrix representative as

S1

Index	Row	Col	Non-Zero values
0	3	3	4
1	0	1	10
2	1	0	20
3	2	0	30
4	2	1	40

We will first consider one dimensional array, named **rterm[]**. In this array we will store non zero terms present in each column.

At 0th column there are two non zero terms. At 1st column also there are two non zero terms but there is non zero term in 2nd column.

rterm

	rterm
0	2
1	2
2	0

Similarly we will take another one dimensional array named **rpos[]**. We initialize 0th location of **rpos[]** by 1. so,

rpos

	rpos
0	1

Now we use following formula to fill up the **rpos** array.

$$rpos[i] = rpos[i-1] + rterm[i-1]$$

i = 1

rpos[1] = rpos[0] + rterm[0]

= 1+ 2

rpos = 3

i = 2

rpos[2] = rpos[1] + rterm[1]

= 3 + 2

rpos[2] = 5

i = 3

rpos[3] = rpos[2] + rterm[2]

= 5 + 0 = 5

rpos[3] = 5

	rpos
0	1
1	3
2	5
3	5

Now we will read values of S1 array from 1 to 4.

We must find the triplet from S1 array which is at index 1. it is (0, 1, 10)

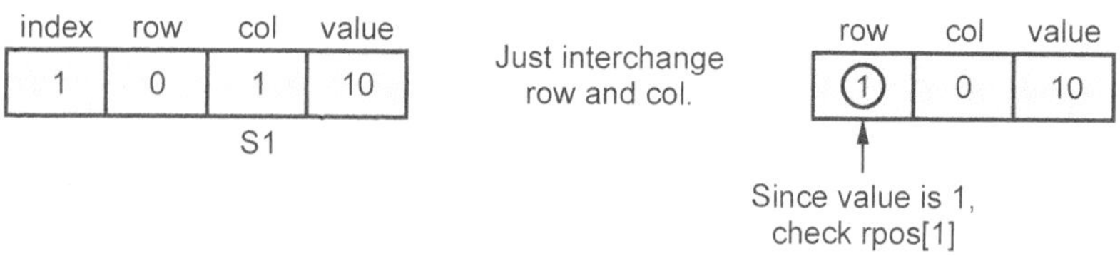

rpos[1] points to value 3. That means place the triplet (1, 0, 10) at index 3 in S2 array.

S2

	Row	Col	Non-Zero values
0			
1			
2			
3	1	0	10
4			

Now since rpos[1] is read just now, increment rpos[1] value by 1.

Hence

	rpos
0	1
1	~~3~~4
2	5
3	5

Read next element from S1 array

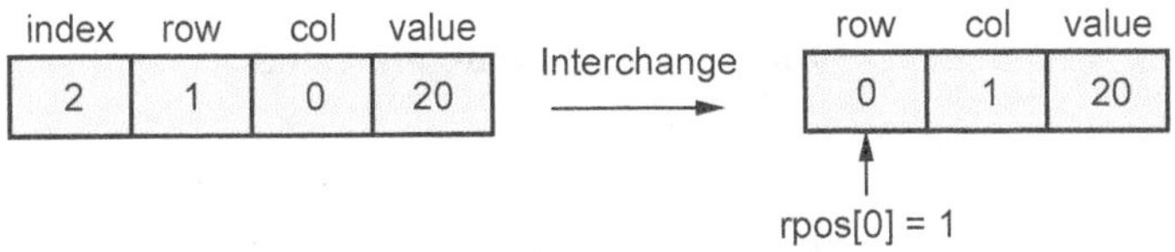

That mean place triplet (0, 1, 20) at index 1 in S2 array

S2

	Row	Col	Non-Zero values
0			
1	0	1	20
2			
3	1	0	10
4			

Since rpos[0] is read just now, increment rpos[0] by 1.

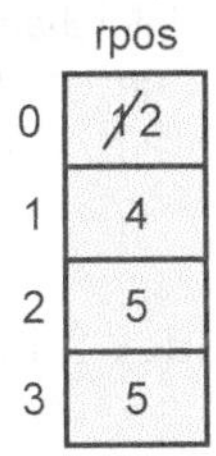

Read next element from S1 array

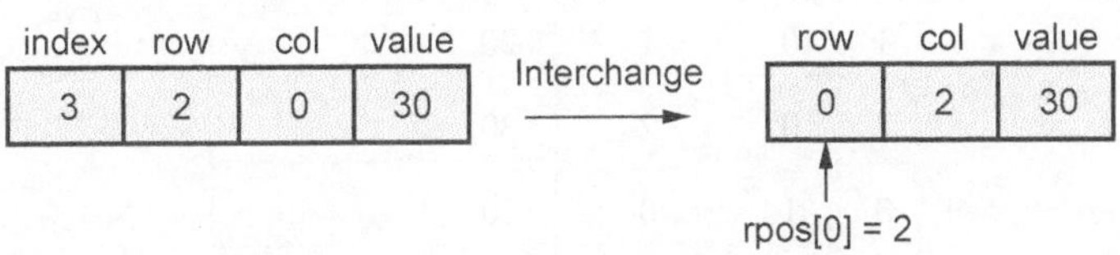

That means place triplet (0, 2, 30) at index 2 in S2 array.

S2

	Row	Col	Non-Zero values
0			
1	0	1	20
2	0	2	30
3	1	0	10
4			

Since rpos[0] is read just now increment rpos[0] by 1.

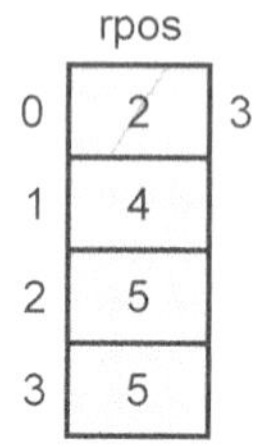

Read next element from S1 array

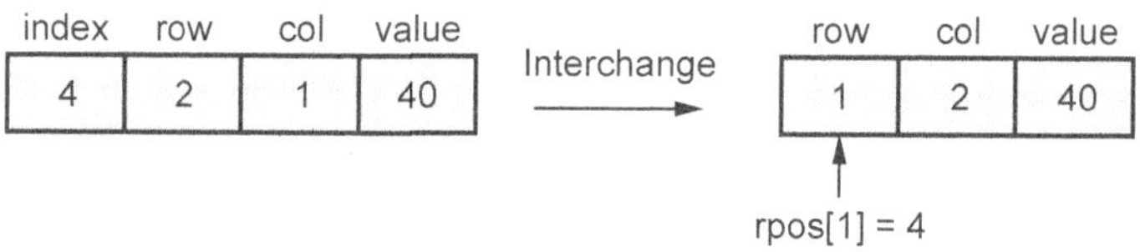

That means place triple (1, 2, 40) at index 2 in S2 array.

S2

	Row	Col	Non-Zero values
0			
1	0	1	20
2	0	2	30
3	1	0	10
4	1	2	40

Thus we get transposed sparse matrix.

Finally we fill up S2[0] by total number of rows, total number of colums and total number of non-zero values.

Thus we get

	Row	Col	Non-Zero values
0	3	3	4
1	0	1	20
2	0	2	30
3	1	0	10
4	1	2	40

C++ Code

```
void trans (int s1[max1][3],int s2[max1][3] )
{
    int rterm[max1],rpos[max1];
    int j,i ;
    int row,col,num ;

    row= s1[0][0];
    col= s1[0][1];
    num= s1[0][2];

    s2[0][0] = col;
    s2[0][1] = row;
    s2[0][2] = num;
    if ( num > 0 )
    {
        for ( i = 0; i <= col ; i ++ )
            rterm[i] = 0;
        for ( i = 1; i <= num ; i ++ )
            rterm[s1[i][1]] ++;
        rpos[0] = 1;  /*setting the rowwise position*/
        for ( i = 1; i <= col; i++ )
         rpos[i]=rpos[i-1]+ rterm[(i - 1)];
        for ( i = 1; i <= num ; i ++ )
        {
            j = rpos[s1[i][1]];
            s2[j][0] = s1[i][1];
            s2[j][1] = s1[i][0];
            s2[j][2] = s1[i][2];
            rpos[s1[i][1]] = j + 1;
        }
    }
}
```

Time Complexity of Fast Transpose

For transposing the elements using simple transpose method we need two nested for loops but in case of fast transpose we are determining the position of the elements that get transposed using only one for loop. Hence the time complexity of fast transpose is O(n)

Review Questions

1. *Explain fast transpose of sparse matrix with suitable example. Discuss time complexity of fast transpose.* **SPPU : May-17, Marks 6**
2. *Write pseudo code to perform simple transpose of sparse matrix.* **SPPU : May-19, Marks 4**
3. *What is sparse matrix ? Explain its representation with an example.* **SPPU : May-19, Marks 4**
4. *Write a pseudo code to perform the simple transpose of sparse matrix. Also discuss the time complexity.* **SPPU : Dec.-19, Marks 6**

2.11 Time and Space Tradeoff

Basic concept : Time space trade-off is basically a situation where either a space efficiency (memory utilization) can be achieved at the cost of time or a time efficiency (performance efficiency) can be achieved at the cost of memory.

Example 1 : Consider the programs like compilers in which symbol table is used to handle the variables and constants. Now if entire symbol table is stored in the program then the time required for searching or storing the variable in the symbol table will be reduced but memory requirement will be more. On the other hand, if we do not store the symbol table in the program and simply compute the table entries then memory will be reduced but the processing time will be more.

Example 2 : Suppose, in a file, if we store the uncompressed data then reading the data will be an efficient job but if the compressed data is stored then to read such data more time will be required.

Example 3 : This is an example of reversing the order of the elements. That is, the elements are stored in an ascending order and we want them in the descending order. This can be done in two ways -

- We will use another array **b[]** in which the elements in descending order can be arranged by reading the array **a[]** in reverse direction. This approach will actually increase the memory but time will be reduced.
- We will apply some extra logic for the same array **a[]** to arrange the elements in descending order. This approach will actually reduce the memory but time of execution will get increased.

The illustration of above mentioned example is given be following C program -

C Program

```
#include<stdio.h>
#include<conio.h>
void main()
{
 int a[10],b[10],n,mid,i,j,temp;
 clrscr();
 printf("\n How many elements do you want? ");
 scanf("%d",&n);
 printf("\n Enter the elements in the ascending order ");
 for(i=0;i<n;i++)
 {
  printf("\n Enter the element ");
  scanf("%d",&a[i]);
 }
 printf("\nThe elements in descending order(By Method 1) are ...\n");
 j=0;
 for(i=n-1;i>=0;i-)//    reading the array in    reverse direction
 {
  b[j]=a[i];//storing them in another array
  j++;
 }
 for(j=0;j<n;j++)
  printf(" %d",b[j]);


 printf("\nThe elements in descending
order(By Method 2) are ...\n");
 mid=n/2;
 for(i=0;i<mid;i++)
 {
  j=(n-1)-i;
  temp=a[i];
  a[i]=a[j];
  a[j]=temp;
 }
 for(i=0;i<n;i++)
  printf(" %d",a[i]);
 getch();
}
```

This method makes use of some **computations** for storing the elements in descending order. It makes use of the same array. Hence **less amount of space** is needed at the cost of **addition computational time**.

Output (Run 1)

```
How many elements do you want? 5

Enter the elements in the ascending order
Enter the element 11
```

```
Enter the element 22
Enter the element 33

Enter the element 44

Enter the element 55
The elements in descending order(By Method 1) are ...
55 44 33 22 11
The elements in descending order(By Method 2) are ...
55 44 33 22 11
```

Output (Run 2)

```
How many elements do you want? 6

Enter the elements in the ascending order
Enter the element 11

Enter the element 22

Enter the element 33

Enter the element 44

Enter the element 55

Enter the element 66

The elements in descending order(By Method 1) are ...
66 55 44 33 22 11
The elements in descending order(By Method 2) are ...
66 55 44 33 22 11
```

Thus time space trade-off is a situation of compensating one performance measure at the cost of another.

❑❑❑

Unit - III

3 Searching and Sorting

Syllabus

Searching : *Search Techniques-Sequential Search/Linear Search, Variant of Sequential Search-Sentinel Search, Binary Search, Fibonacci Search, and Indexed Sequential Search.*

Sorting : *Types of Sorting-Internal and External Sorting, General Sort Concepts-Sort Order, Stability, Efficiency, and Number of Passes, Comparison Based Sorting Methods-Bubble Sort, Insertion Sort, Selection Sort, Quick Sort, Shell Sort, Non-comparison Based Sorting Methods-Radix Sort, Counting Sort, and Bucket Sort, Comparison of All Sorting Methods and their complexities.*

Contents

Part I : Searching

3.1 Introduction to Searching and Sorting

Importance of Searching and Sorting

Searching technique is essential for locating the position of the required element from the heap of data.

Application of Sorting

Sorting is useful for arranging the data in desired order. After sorting the required element can be located easily.

1. The sorting is useful in database applications for arranging the data in desired order.
2. In the dictionary like applications the data is arranged in sorted order.
3. For searching the element from the list of elements, the sorting is required.
4. For checking the uniqueness of the element the sorting is required.
5. For finding the closest pair from the list of elements the sorting is required.

3.2 Search Techniques

- When we want to find out particular record efficiently from the given list of elements then there are various methods of searching that element. These methods are called **searching methods.** Various algorithms based on these searching methods are known as **searching algorithms**.
- The **basic characteristic** of any searching algorithm is -

  i. It should be **efficient**

  ii. **Less number of computations** must be involved in it.

  iii. The **space** occupied by searching algorithms must be **less.**
- The most commonly used searching algorithms are -

  i. Sequential or linear search

  ii. Indexed sequential search

  iii. Binary search
- The element to be searched from the given list is called the **key** element.

Let us discuss various searching algorithms.

3.2.1 Sequential Search/Linear Search

- Sequential search is technique in which the given list of elements is scanned from the beginning. The key element is compared with every element of the list. If the match is found the searching is stopped otherwise it will be continued to the end of the list.
- Although this is a **simple method,** there are some **unnecessary comparisons** involved in this method.
- The time complexity of this algorithm is **O(n).** The time complexity will increase linearly with the value of n.
- For **higher value of n** sequential search is **not satisfactory solution.**
- **Example**

Array

	Roll no	Name	Marks
0	15	Parth	96
1	2	Anand	40
2	13	Lalita	81
3	1	Madhav	50
4	12	Arun	78
5	3	Jaya	94

Fig. 3.2.1 Represents students Database for sequential search

From the above Fig. 3.2.1 the array is maintained to store the students record. The record is not sorted at all. If we want to search the student's record whose roll number is 12 then with the key-roll number we will see the every record whether it is of roll number = 12. We can obtain such a record at Array [4] location.

C++ Function

```
int search(int a[size],int key)
{
 for(i=0;i<n;i++)
     {
           if(a[i]==key)
                 return 1;
     }
return 0;
}
```

Python Program

```
def search(arr,x):

    for i in range(len(arr)):
        if arr[i] == x:
            return i
    return -1

print("\nHow many elements are there in Array?")
n = int(input())
array = []
i=0
for i in range(n):
    print("\n Enter element in Array")
    item = int(input())
    array.append(item)

print("Resultant array is\n")
print(array)

print("\n Enter the key element to be searched: ")
key = int(input())

location = search(array,key)
print("The element is present at index:",location)
```

Output

```
How many elements are there in Array?
5
 Enter element in Array
30
 Enter element in Array
10
 Enter element in Array
40
 Enter element in Array
50
 Enter element in Array
20
Resultant array is
[30, 10, 40, 50, 20]
 Enter the key element to be searched:
40
The element is present at index: 2
>>>
```

Advantages of sequential searching

1. It is simple to implement.
2. It does not require specific ordering before applying the method.

Disadvantages of sequential searching

1. It is less efficient.

3.2.2 Variant of Sequential Search-Sentinel Search

- The sentinel value is a specialized value that acts as a flag or dummy data. This specialized value is used in context of an algorithm which uses its presence as a condition of termination.

Typical examples of sentinel values are -

1. Null character used at the end of the string.
2. Null pointer at the end of the linked list.
3. End of file character.

- In sentinel search, when searching for a particular value in an unsorted list, every element will be compared against this value.
- In this search, the last element of the array is replaced with the element to be searched and then the linear search is performed on the array without checking whether the current index is inside the index range of the array or not because the element to be searched will definitely be found inside the array even if it was not present in the original array since the last element got replaced with it. So, the index to be checked will never be out of bounds of the array.

For example

```
Input: [10,20,30,40,50,60]
Key: 40
Result: The element is present

Input: [10,20,30,40,50,60]
Key: 99
Result: The element is not present in the list.
```

Python Program

```
def Sentsearch(arr,x):
    l = len(arr)
    arr.append(x)
    i = 0
    while(arr[i]!=x):
        i = i+1
    if(i!=l):
```

```
        return i
    else:
        return -1

print("\nHow many elements are there in Array?")
n = int(input())
array = []
i=0
for i in range(n):
    print("\n Enter element in Array")
    item = int(input())
    array.append(item)

print("Resultant array is\n")
print(array)

print("\n Enter the key element to be searched: ")
key = int(input())

location = Sentsearch(array,key)
if(location != -1):
    print("The element is present at index:",location)
else:
    print("\n The element is not present in the list")
```

Output

```
How many elements are there in Array?
5
 Enter element in Array
30
 Enter element in Array
10
 Enter element in Array
50
 Enter element in Array
20
 Enter element in Array
40
Resultant array is
[30, 10, 50, 20, 40]
 Enter the key element to be searched:
50
The element is present at index: 2
```

3.2.3 Binary Search

- **Concept :** Binary search is a searching algorithm in which the list of elements is divided into two sublists and the key element is compared with the middle element. If the match is found then, the location of middle element is returned otherwise, we search into either of the halves(sublists) depending upon the result produced through the match.

This algorithm is considered as an efficient searching algorithm.

Algorithm for Binary Search

1. if(low>high)
2. return;
3. mid =(low+high)/2;
4. if(x==a[mid])
5. return (mid);
6. if(x<a[mid])
7. search for x in a[low] to a[mid-1];
8. else
9. search for x in a[mid+1] to a[high];

Example :

As mentioned earlier the necessity of this method is that all the elements should be sorted. So let us take an array of sorted elements.

array

0	1	2	3	4	5	6	7
– 40	11	33	37	42	45	99	100

Step 1 : Now the key element which is to be searched is = 99 ∴ key = 99.

Step 2 : Find the middle element of the array. Compare it with the key

if middle $\overset{?}{=}$ key

i.e. if 42 $\overset{?}{=}$ 99

if 42 < 99 search the sublist 2

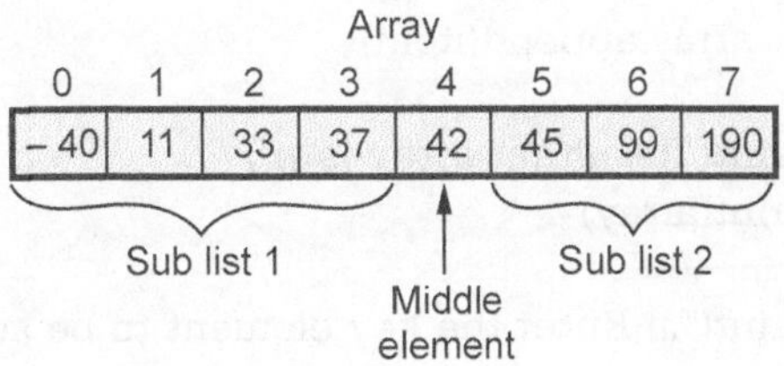

Now handle only sublist 2. Again divide it, find mid of sublist 2

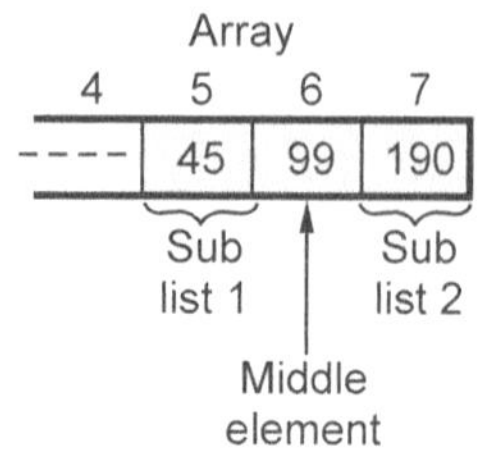

if middle $\stackrel{?}{=}$ key

i.e. if 99 $\stackrel{?}{=}$ 99

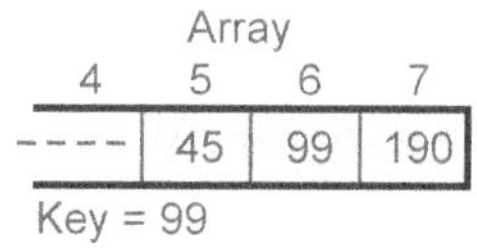

So match is found at 7th position of array i.e. at array [6]

Thus by binary search method we can find the element 99 present in the given list at array $[6]^{th}$ location.

Non Recursive Python Program

```
def Binsearch(arr,KEY):
    low = 0
    high = len(arr)-1
    m = 0
    while(low<=high):
        m =(low+high) //2          #mid of the array is obtained
        if(KEY<arr[m]):
            high = m-1             #search the left sub list
        elif(KEY>arr[m]):
            low = m+1              #search the right sub list
        else:
            return m

    return -1                      #if element is not present in the list
print("\nHow many elements are there in Array?")
n = int(input())
array = []
i=0
for i in range(n):
    print("\n Enter element in Array")
    item = int(input())
    array.append(item)

print("Resultant array is\n")
print(array)

print("\n Enter the key element to be searched: ")
key = int(input())

location = Binsearch(array,key)
```

```
if(location != -1):
    print("The element is present at index:",location)
else:
    print("\n The element is not present in the list")
```

Output

```
How many elements are there in Array?
5
 Enter element in Array
10
 Enter element in Array
20
 Enter element in Array
30
 Enter element in Array
40
 Enter element in Array
50
Resultant array is
[10, 20, 30, 40, 50]

Enter the key element to be searched:
40
The element is present at index: 3
>>>
```

Recursive Python Program

```
def BinRsearch(arr,KEY,low,high):
    if(high >= low):
        m =(low+high)//2                          #mid of the array is obtained
        if(arr[m] == KEY):
            return m
        elif(arr[m]>KEY):
            return BinRsearch(arr,KEY,low,m-1)    #search the left sub list
        else:
            return BinRsearch(arr,KEY,m+1,high)   #search the right sub list
    else:
        return -1                                 #if element is not present in the list

print("\nHow many elements are there in Array?")
n = int(input())
array = []
i=0
for i in range(n):
    print("\n Enter element in Array")
    item = int(input())
    array.append(item)
```

```
print("Resultant array is\n")
print(array)

print("\n Enter the key element to be searched: ")
key = int(input())
location = BinRsearch(array,key,0,len(array)-1)
if(location != -1):
   print("The element is present at index:",location)
else:
   print("\n The element is not present in the list")
```

Output

```
How many elements are there in Array?
5
 Enter element in Array
10
 Enter element in Array
20
 Enter element in Array
30
 Enter element in Array
40
 Enter element in Array
50
Resultant array is
[10, 20, 30, 40, 50]
 Enter the key element to be searched:
20
The element is present at index: 1
>>>
```

Example 3.2.1 *How many comparisons are required to find 73 in the following array using binary search 12, 25, 32, 37, 41, 48, 58, 60, 66, 73, 74, 79, 83, 91, 95 ?*

Solution :

Step 1 :

0	1	2	3	4	5	6	7	8	9	10	11
12	25	32	37	41	48	58	60	66	73	74	79

↑ (at 58)

Compare 73 with 58

Number of comparison = 1.

Step 2 : As 73 > 58. Search 73 between A[7] to A[11]

7	8	9	10	11
60	66	73	74	79

↑ Compare 73 with 73

Number 73 is found.

∴**Number of comparison = 2.**

Thus with two comparisons number 73 is found.

Example 3.2.2 *Apply binary search method to search 60 from the list 10, 20, 30, 40, 50, 60, 70.*

Solution : Consider a list of elements stored in array A as

0	1	2	3	4	5	6
10	20	30	40	50	60	70
↑ Low						↑ High

The KEY element (i.e. the element to be searched) is 60.

Now to obtain middle element we will apply a formula :

$$m = (low + high)/2$$

$$m = (0 + 6)/2$$

$$m = 3$$

Then Check $A[m] \stackrel{?}{=} KEY$

i.e. $A[3] \stackrel{?}{=} 60$ NO A[3] = 40 and 40 < 60

∴ Search the right sublist.

0	1	2	3	4	5	6
10	20	30	40	50	60	70
Left sublist			↑ m	Right sublist		

The right sublist is

...	50	60	70

Now we will again divide this list and check the mid element.

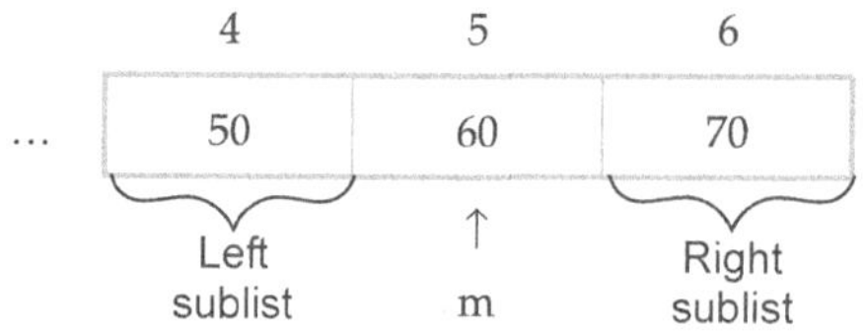

$m = (low + high)/2$

$m = (4 + 6)/2$

$\therefore\ m = 5$

is $A[m] \stackrel{?}{=} KEY$

i.e. $A[5] \stackrel{?}{=} 60$ Yes, i.e. the number is present in the list.

Thus we can search the desired number from the list of elements.

Advantages and Disadvantages of Binary Search

Advantage

(1) It is efficient technique.

Disadvantages

(1) It requires specific ordering before applying the method.

(2) It is complex to implement.

Comparison between Linear Search and Binary Search

Sr. No.	Linear search method	Binary search method
1.	The linear search is a searching method in which the element is searched by scanning the entire list from first element to the last.	The binary search is a searching method in which the list is sub divided into two sub-lists. The middle element is then compared with the key element and then accordingly either left or right sub-list is searched.
2.	Many times entire list is searched.	Only sub-list is searched for searching the key element.
3.	It is simple to implement.	It involves computation for finding the middle element.
4.	It is less efficient searching method.	It is an efficient searching method.

3.2.4 Fibonacci Search

In binary search method we divide the number at mid and based on mid element i.e. by comparing mid element with key element we search either the left sublist or right sublist. Thus we go on dividing the corresponding sublist each time and comparing mid element with key element. If the key element is really present in the list, we can reach to the location of key in the list and thus we get the message that the "element is present in the list" otherwise get the message. "element is not present in the list."

In Fibonacci search rather than considering the mid element, we consider the indices as the numbers from fibonacci series. As we know, the Fibonacci series is -

0 1 1 2 3 5 8 13 21 ...

To understand how Fibonacci search works, we will consider one example, suppose, following is the list of elements.

arr [ ]

10	20	30	40	50	60	70
1	2	3	4	5	6	7

Here n = total number of elements = 7

We will always compute 3 variables i.e. a, b and f.

Initially f = n = 7.

For setting a and b variables we will consider elements from Fibonacci series.

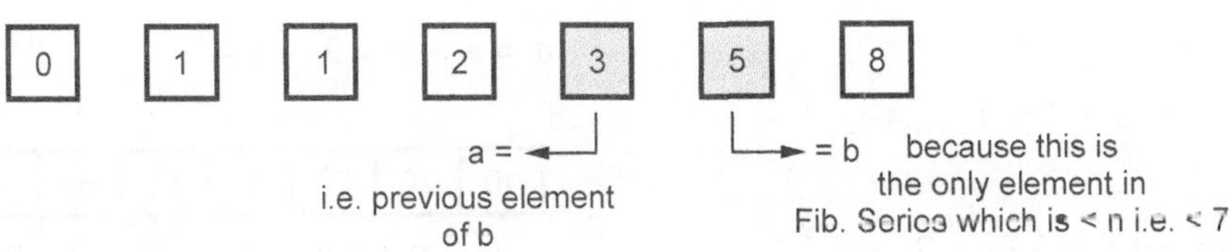

Now we have

f = 7

b = 5

a = 3

With these initial values we will start searching the key element from the list. Each time we will compare key element with arr [f]. That means

If (Key < arr [f])

f = f − a

b = a

a = b − a

If (Key > arr [f])

f = f + a

b = b − a

a = a − b

Suppose we have **f = 7, b = 5, a = 3**

		a		b		f
10	20	30	40	50	60	70
1	2	3 ↑	4	5 ↑	6	7 ↑

If **Key = 20**

i.e. Key < arr[f]

i.e. 20 < 70

∴f = f − a = 7 − 3 = 4

b = a = 3

a = b − a = 2

Again we compare if (Key < arr [f])

i.e. 20 < arr [4]

i.e. if (20 < 40) → Yes

At Present f = 4, b = 3, a = 2

∴f = f − a = 4 − 2 = 2

b = a = 2

a = b − a = 3 − 2 = 1

Now we get f = 2, b = 2, a = 1

a	f/b					
10	20	30	40	50	60	70
1	2	3	4	5	6	7

If **Key = 60**

i.e. Key < arr [f]

60 < 70

∴f = f − a = 7 − 3 = 4

b = a = 3

a = b − a = 2

Again we compare if (Key > arr [f])

∴i.e. 60 > arr [f] i.e. 40

∴f = f + a = 4 + 2 = 6

b = b − a = 3 − 2 = 1

a = a − b = 2 − 3 = − 1

a	b				f	
10	20	30	40	50	60	70
1	2	3	4	5	6	7

If (Key < arr [f])

i.e. if (60 < 60) → No

If (Key < arr [f]) i.e. if (20 < 20) → No

If Key > arr [f]) i.e. if (20 > 20) → No

That means "**Element is present at f = 2 location**"

If (key > arr [f])

i.e. if (60 > 60) → No

That means "**Element is present at f = 6 location.**"

Analysis : The time complexity of fibonacci search is **O(logn).**

Algorithm

Let the length of given array be **n [0...n-1]** and the element to be searched be **key**

Then we use the following steps to find the element with minimum steps :

1. Find the **smallest Fibonacci number greater than or equal to n.** Let this number be f(m^{th} element).
2. Let the two Fibonacci numbers preceding it be **a**($m\text{-}1^{th}$ element) and **b**($m\text{-}2^{th}$ element)

   While the array has elements to be checked :

   Compare key with the last element of the range covered by **b**

   (a) If **key** matches, return index value

   (b) Else if **key is less** than the element, move the third Fibonacci variable two Fibonacci down, indicating removal of approximately two-third of the unsearched array.

   (c) Else key is greater than the element, move the third Fibonacci variable one Fibonacci down. Reset offset to index. Together this results into removal of approximately front one-third of the unsearched array.
3. Since there might be a single element remaining for comparison, check if **a** is '1'. If Yes, compare key with that remaining element. If match, return index value.

For example -

According to the algorithm we have to sort the elements of the array prior to applying Fibonacci search. Consider sorted array of elements as -

0	1	2	3	4	5	6
10	20	30	40	50	60	70

∴ n = 7, we want to find key = 60

Now check Fibbonacci series.

As n < 8

set f = 8

a = 5

b = 3

			b		a			f
0	1	2	3	4	5	6		8
10	20	30	40	50	60	70	...	

Set offset = – 1

∴ i = 2 ∵ 1 = min (offset + b, n – 1)

A[i] = A[2] < (key = 60)

Here key is greater than the element

We move f one fibbonacci down (step 2C of algorithm)

∴ f = 5

a = 3

b = 2

		b	a		f	
0	1	2	3	4	5	6
10	20	30	40	50	60	70

Set offset = i i.e. = **2**

Now i = 4 ∵ i = min (offset + b, n – 1)

Here key is again greater than the element. So we move f, one fibbonacci down

∴ f = 3

a = 2

b = 1

	b	a	f			
0	1	2	3	4	5	6
10	20	30	40	50	60	70

Set offset = i i.e. **4**

Now new i = 5 ∵ i = min (offset + b, n – 1)

Here a[i] = key. Hence return value of i as the position of key element.

Note that due to fibonacci numbering the search portion is restricted and we need to compare very less number of elements.

Python Program

```
def FibSearch(arr, key, n):
    # Initialize Fibonacci numbers
    b = 0
    a = 1
    f = b + a

    # f is going to store the smallest
    # Fibonacci Number greater than or equal to n
    while (f < n):
        b = a
        a = f
        f = b + a
    # Marks the eliminated range from front
    offset = -1;

    # while there are elements to be inspected.
    # we compare arr[i] with key.
    while (f > 1):

        # Check if b is a valid location
        i = min(offset+b, n-1)

        # If key is greater than the value at
        # index b, cut the subarray array
        # from offset to i
        if (arr[i] < key):
            f = a
            a = b
            b = f - a
            offset = i

        # If key is lesser than the value at
        # index b, cut the subarray
        # after i+1
        elif (arr[i] > key):
            f = b
            a = a - b
            b = f - a

        # element found. return index
        else :
            return i

    # comparing the last element with key
    if(a and arr[offset+1] == key):
        return offset+1;
```

```
    # element not found. return -1
    return -1

print("\n Program For Fibonacci Search")
print("\nHow many elements are there in Array?")
n = int(input())
array = []
i=0
for i in range(n):
    print("\n Enter element in Array")
    item = int(input())
    array.append(item)

print("Resultant array is\n")
print(array)

print("\n Enter the key element to be searched: ")
key = int(input())
print("\n The element is present at index: ",FibSearch(array,key,n))
```

Output

```
Program For Fibonacci Search
How many elements are there in Array?
7
 Enter element in Array
10
 Enter element in Array
20
 Enter element in Array
30
 Enter element in Array
40
 Enter element in Array
50
 Enter element in Array
60
 Enter element in Array
70
Resultant array is
[10, 20, 30, 40, 50, 60, 70]
 Enter the key element to be searched:
60
 The element is present at index:  5
>>>
```

Analysis : From the above algorithm it is clear if we have to search the larger section of the array then the time taken will be more and will result into worst case and it's complexity wil be O(log n). If on the very first search, we get our element then it will be considered as the best case and complexcity will be O(1).

3.2.5 Indexed Sequential Search

- Index sequential search is a searching technique in which a separate table containing the indices of the actual elements is maintained.
- The actual search of the element is done with the help of this index table.

For example -

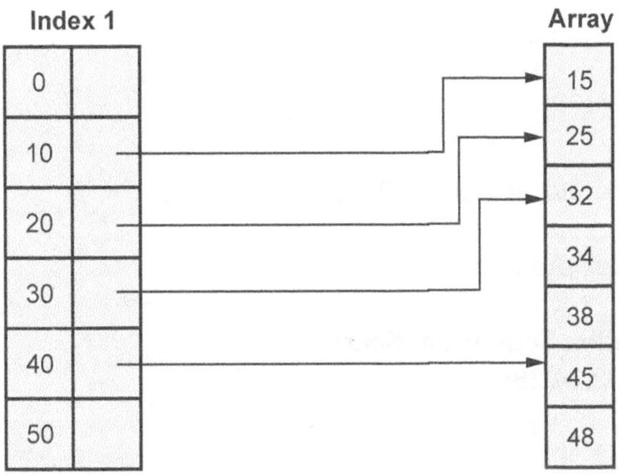

- Note that the sorted index table is maintained. First we search the index table and then with the help of an index, actual array is searched for the element.
- For instance - If we want to search an element 34, then we first locate to index 30 which is present in the index table and then, we compare element 32 and then 34 in the actual array.

Python Program

```
def IndexSeq(arr,key,n):
    Elements = [0]*10
    Index = [0]*10
    flag = 0
    ind = 0
    start=end=0
    for i in range(0,n,2) :
        # Storing element
        Elements[ind] = arr[i]
        # Storing the index
        Index[ind] = i
        ind += 1
```

```
    if (key < Elements[0]):
        print("Element is not present")
        exit(0)

    else:
        for i in range(1, ind + 1) :
            if(key < Elements[i]) :
                start = Index[i - 1]
                end = Index[i]
                break

    for i in range(start, end + 1) :
        if (key == arr[i] ):
            flag = 1
            break

    if flag == 1 :
        print("Element is Found at index", i)
    else :
        print("Element is not present")

print("\n Program For Index Sequential Search")
array = [11,15,22,24,26,32,34,38]
n = len(array)
key=32
IndexSeq(array,key,n)
```

Output

```
Program For Index Sequential Search
Element is Found at index 5
```

Part II : Sorting

3.3 Types of Sorting-Internal and External Sorting

Definition : Sorting is systematic arrangement of data.

3.3.1 Internal and External Sorting

Sorting can be of two types **internal sorting and external sorting.**

Internal Sorting :

- The internal sorting is a sorting in which the data resides in the main memory of the computer.

- Various methods that make use of internal sorting are -
- 1. Bubble Sort 2. Insertion Sort 3. Selection Sort 4. Quick Sort 5. Radix Sort and so on.

- **External Sorting :**
    - For many applications it is not possible to store the entire data on the main memory for two reasons, i) amount of **main memory available is smaller** than amount of data. ii)Secondly the **main memory is a volatile device** and thus will lost the data when the power is shut down. To overcome these problems the data is stored on the secondary storage devices. The technique which is used to sort the data which resides on the secondary storage devices are called **external sorting.**
    - The data stored on secondary memory is part by part loaded into main memory, sorting can be done over there. The sorted data can be then stored in the intermediate files. Finally these intermediate files can be merged repeatedly to get sorted data. Thus **huge amount of data** can be sorted using this technique.

For example : Consider that there are 10,000 records that has to be sorted. Clearly we need to apply external sorting method. Suppose main memory has a capacity to store 500 records in blocks, with each block_size of 100 records.

The sorted 5 blocks (i.e. 500 records) are stored in intermediate file. This process will be repeated 20 times to get all the records sorted in chunks.

In the second step, we start merging a pair of intermediate files in the main memory to get output file.

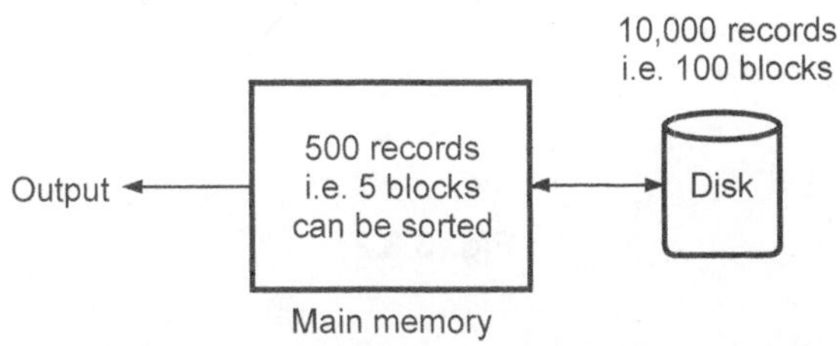

Fig. 3.3.1

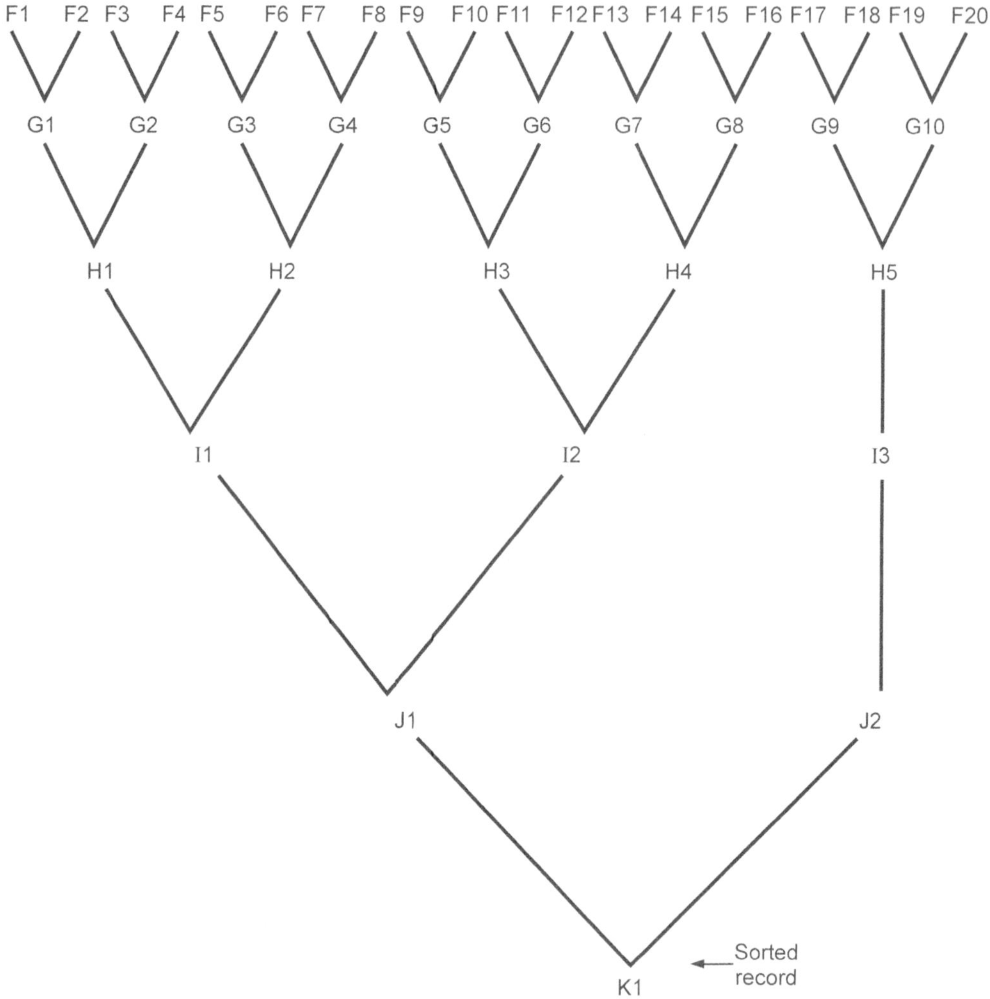

Fig. 3.3.2

3.4 General Sort Concepts

Before learning the actual sorting techniques let us understand some basic concepts of sorting.

3.4.1 Sort Order

The sorting is a technique by which we expect the list of elements to be arranged as we expect. Sorting order is nothing but the arrangement of the elements in some specific manner. Usually the sorting order is of two types -

Ascending order : It is the sorting order in which the elements are arranged from low value to high value. In other words elements are in increasing order.

For example : 10, 50, 40, 20, 30

can be arranged in ascending order after applying some sorting technique as

10, 20, 30, 40, 50

Descending Order : It is the sorting order in which the elements are arranged from high value to low value. In other words elements are in decreasing order. It is reverse of the ascending order.

For example : 10, 50, 40, 20, 30

can be arranged in descending order after applying some sorting technique as

50, 40, 30, 20, 10

While sorting the elements, we always consider a specific order and expect our data to be arranged in that order.

3.4.2 Sort Stability

The sorting stability means comparing the records of same value and expecting them in the same order even after sorting them.

For example :

(Pune, BalGandharva)

(Pune, Shaniwarwada)

(Nasik, Panchavati)

(Mumbai, Gateway-of-India)

Now in the above list, we will sort the list according to the first alphabet of the city. The ascending order for the alphabets P(for Pune), N(for Nasik), M(for Mumbai) will be M, N, P. The sorting stability can be achieved by arranging the records as follows.

(Mumbai, Gateway-Of-India)

(Nasik, Panchavati)

(Pune, BalGandharva)

(Pune, Shaniwarwada)

Note that in the above list same record as Pune is twice. But we have preserved the original sequence as it is after comparing them. Thus the stability is achieved in sorting the records.

3.4.3 Efficiency and Passes

One of the major issue in the sorting algorithms is its efficiency. If we can efficiently sort the records then that adds value to the sorting algorithm. We usually denote the efficiency of sorting algorithms in terms of time complexity. The time complexities are given in terms of big-on notations.

Commonly there are $O(n^2)$ and O(nlogn) time complexities for various algorithms. The sorting techniques such as bubble sort, insertion sort, selection sort, shell sort has the time complexity $O(n^2)$ and the techniques such as merge sort, quick sort has the time complexity as O(nlogn). The quick sort is the fastest algorithm and bubble sort is the slowest one! Efficiency also depends on number of records to be sorted. After all sorting efficiency is nothing but how much time that algorithm have taken to sort the elements. That is why it is convenient to give the efficiency of sorting algorithms in terms of time complexity.

While sorting the elements in some specific order there is lot of arrangement of elements. The phases in which the elements are moving to acquire their proper position is called **passes**.

For example : 10, 30, 20, 50, 40

Pass 1 : 10, 20, 30, 50, 40

Pass 2 : 10, 20, 30, 40, 50

In the above method we can see that data is getting sorted in two passes distinctly. By applying a logic as comparison of each element with its adjacent element gives us the result in two passes.

Sorting Techniques

As mentioned above sorting is an important activity and every time we insert or delete the data we need to sort the remaining data. Therefore it should be carried out efficiently. Various algorithms are developed for sorting such as

1. Bubble Sort 2. Selection Sort 3. Insertion Sort
4. Radix Sort 5. Shell Sort 6. Merge Sort 7. Quick Sort

3.5 Comparison based Sorting Methods

3.5.1 Bubble Sort

This is the simplest kind of sorting method in this method. We do this bubble sort procedure in several iterations, which are called passes.

Example bubble sort :

Consider 5 unsorted elements are

45 – 40 190 99 11

First store those elements in the array a

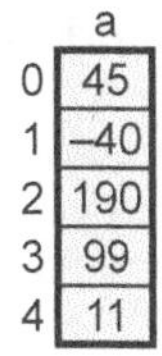

Pass 1

In this pass each element will be compared with its neighbouring element.

Compare 45 and – 40

Is 45 > – 40 ∴ Interchange

i.e. compare a[0] and a[1], after interchange

∴ a[0] = – 40

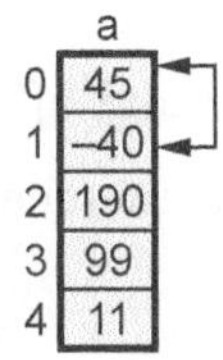

Compare a[1] and a[2]

Is 45 > 190 ∴ No interchange

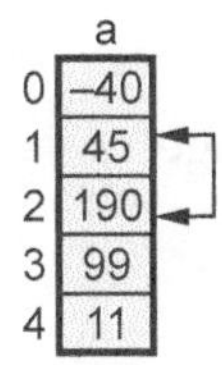

Compare a[2] and a[3]

Is 190 > 99 ∴ Interchange

a[2] = 99

a[3] = 190

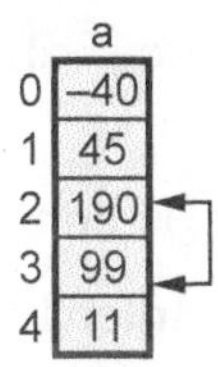

Compare a[3] and a[4]

Is 190 > 11 ∴ Interchange

a[3] = 11

a[4] = 190

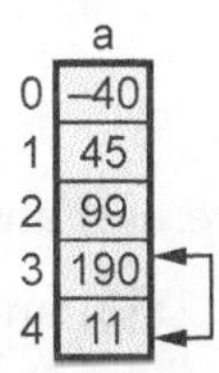

After first pass the array will hold the elements which are sorted to some extent.

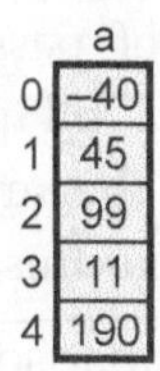

Pass 2

Compare a[0] and a[1]

No interchange

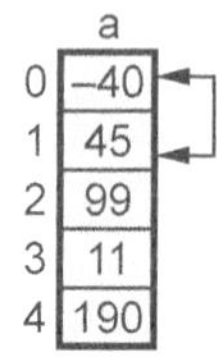

Compare a[0] and a[1]

No interchange.

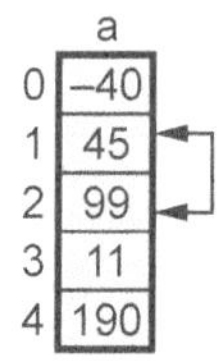

Compare a[2] and a[3]

Since 99 > 11 interchange

∴ a[2] = 11

a[3] = 99

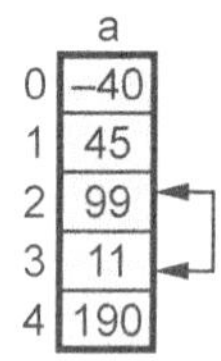

No interchange

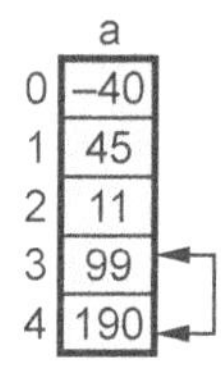

Pass 3

First compare a[0] and a[1], no interchange

∴ Compare a[1] and a[2]

45 > 11 ∴ Interchange

a[1] = 11

a[2] = 45

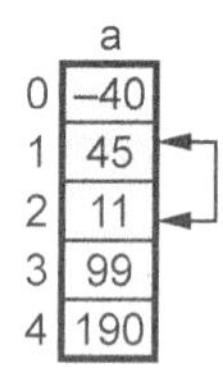

Next compare a[2] and a[3] similarly

a[3] and a[4]

No interchange.

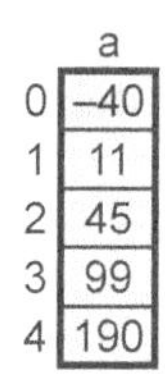

This is end of pass 3. This process will be thus continued till pass 4. Finally at the end of last pass the array will hold all the sorted elements like this,

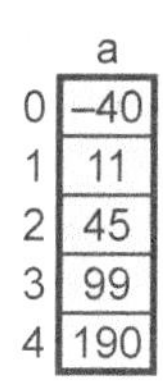

Since the comparison positions look like bubbles, therefore it is called **bubble sort**.

Algorithm :

1. Read the total number of elements say n
2. Store the elements in the array
3. Set the i = 0 .
4. Compare the adjacent elements.
5. Repeat step 4 for all n elements.
6. Increment the value of i by 1 and repeat step 4, 5 for i< n
7. Print the sorted list of elements.
8. Stop.

Python Program

```
def Bubble(arr,n):
  i = 0

  for i in range(n-1):
    for j in range(0,n-i-1):
      if(arr[j] > arr[j+1]):
        temp = arr[j]
        arr[j] = arr[j+1]
        arr[j+1] = temp
    print("\nPass#",(i+1))
    print(arr)

print("\n Program For Bubble Sort")
print("\nHow many elements are there in Array?")
n = int(input())
array = []
i=0
for i in range(n):
  print("\n Enter element in Array")
  item = int(input())
  array.append(item)

print("Original array is\n")
print(array)

print("\n Sorted Array is")
Bubble(array,n)
```

Output

```
Program For Bubble Sort
How many elements are there in Array?
5
 Enter element in Array
```

```
30
 Enter element in Array
10
 Enter element in Array
20
 Enter element in Array
50
 Enter element in Array
40
Original array is
[30, 10, 20, 50, 40]
 Sorted Array is
Pass# 1
[10, 20, 30, 40, 50]
Pass# 2
[10, 20, 30, 40, 50]
Pass# 3
[10, 20, 30, 40, 50]
Pass# 4
[10, 20, 30, 40, 50]
>>>
```

Analysis : In above algorithm basic operation if (a[j] > a[j +1]) which is executed within nested for loops. Hence time complexity of bubble sort is $\Theta(\mathbf{n})^2$.

Example 3.5.1 *Show the output of each pass for the following list*
10, 5, 4, 18, 17, 1, 2

Solution : Let, 10, 5, 4, 18, 17, 1, 2 be the given list of elements. We will compare adjacent elements say A[i] and A[j]. If A[i] > A[j] then swap the elements.

Pass I

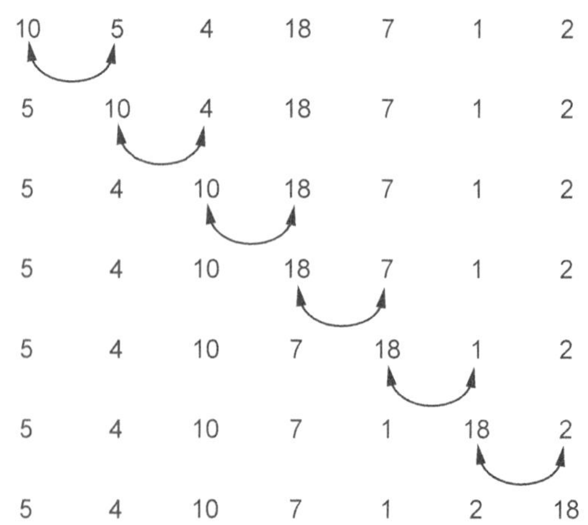

Pass II

5 4 10 7 1 2 18

4 5 10 7 1 2 18

4 5 10 7 1 2 18

4 5 7 10 1 2 18

4 5 7 1 10 2 18

4 5 7 1 2 10 18

4 5 7 1 2 10 18

Pass III

4 5 7 1 2 10 18

4 5 1 7 2 10 18

4 5 1 2 7 10 18

Pass IV

4 5 1 2 7 10 18

4 1 5 2 7 10 18

4 1 2 5 7 10 18

4 1 2 5 7 10 18

Pass V

4 1 2 5 7 10 18

1 4 2 5 7 10 18

1 2 4 5 7 10 18

1 2 4 5 7 10 18

Pass VI

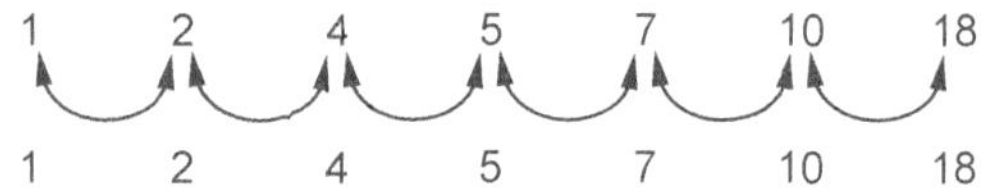

This is the sorted list of elements.

3.5.2 Insertion Sort

In this method the elements are inserted at their appropriate place. Hence is the name **insertion sort**. Let us understand this method with the help of some example -

For Example

Consider a list of elements as,

0	1	2	3	4	5	6
30	70	20	50	40	10	60

The process starts with first element

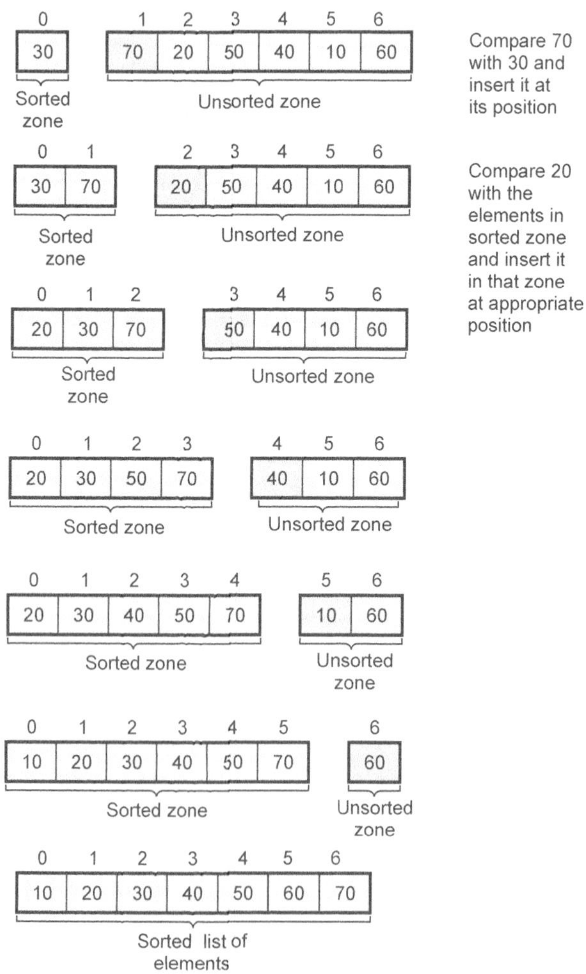

Algorithm

Although it is very natural to implement insertion using recursive(top down) algorithm but it is very efficient to implement it using bottom up(iterative) approach.

```
Algorithm Insert_sort(A[0...n-1])
//Problem Description: This algorithm is for sorting the
//elements using insertion sort
//Input: An array of n elements
//Output: Sorted array A[0...n-1] in ascending order
 for i ← 1 to n-1 do
{
        temp ← A[i]//mark A[i]th element
        j ← i-1//set j at previous element of A[i]
        while(j>=0)AND(A[j]>temp)do
        {
    //comparing all the previous elements of A[i] with
    //A[i].If any greater element is found then insert
    //it at proper position
        A[j+1] ← A[j]
        j ← j-1
        }
        A[j+1] ← temp //copy A[i] element at A[j+1]
}
```

Analysis

When an array of elements is almost sorted then it is **best case** complexity. The best case time complexity of insertion sort is **O(n).**

If an array is randomly distributed then it results in **average case** time complexity which is $O(n^2)$.

If the list of elements is arranged in descending order and if we want to sort the elements in ascending order then it results in **worst case** time complexity which is $O(n^2)$.

Advantages of insertion sort

1. *Simple* to implement.
2. This method is *efficient* when we want to sort small number of elements. And this method has excellent performance on almost sorted list of elements.
3. More efficient than most other simple $O(n^2)$ algorithms such as selection sort or bubble sort.
4. This is a *stable* (does not change the relative order of equal elements).

5. It is called *in-place* sorting algorithm (only requires a constant amount O(1) of extra memory space). The in-place sorting algorithm is an algorithm in which the input is overwritten by output and to execute the sorting method it does not require any more additional space.

Python Program

```
def InsertSort(arr,n):
  i = 1
  for i in range(n):
    temp = arr[i]
    j = i-1
    while((j>=0) & (arr[j]>temp)):
      arr[j+1] = arr[j]
      j = j-1
    arr[j+1] = temp

  print(arr)
print("\n Program For Insertion Sort")
print("\nHow many elements are there in Array?")
n = int(input())
array = []
i=0
for i in range(n):
  print("\n Enter element in Array")
  item = int(input())
  array.append(item)

print("Original array is\n")
print(array)

print("\n Sorted Array is")
InsertSort(array,n)
```

Output

```
Program For Insertion Sort

How many elements are there in Array?
5
 Enter element in Array
30
 Enter element in Array
10
 Enter element in Array
50
 Enter element in Array
40
 Enter element in Array
```

```
20
Original array is

[30, 10, 50, 40, 20]

 Sorted Array is
[10, 20, 30, 40, 50]
>>>
```

Logic Explanation :

For understanding the logic of above python program consider a list of unsorted elements as,

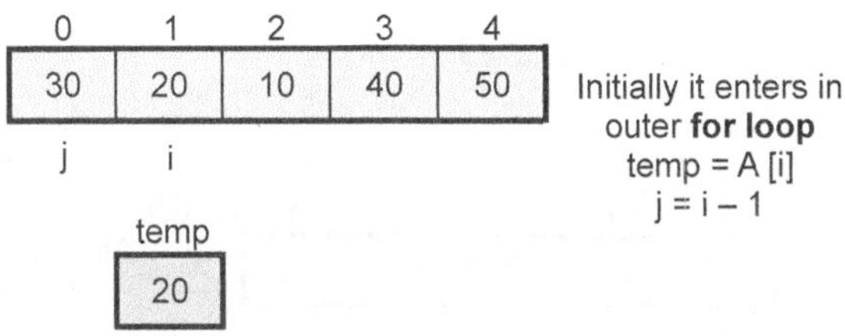

Then the control moves to **while loop**. As j >= 0 and A[j] > temp is **True**, the while loop will be executed.

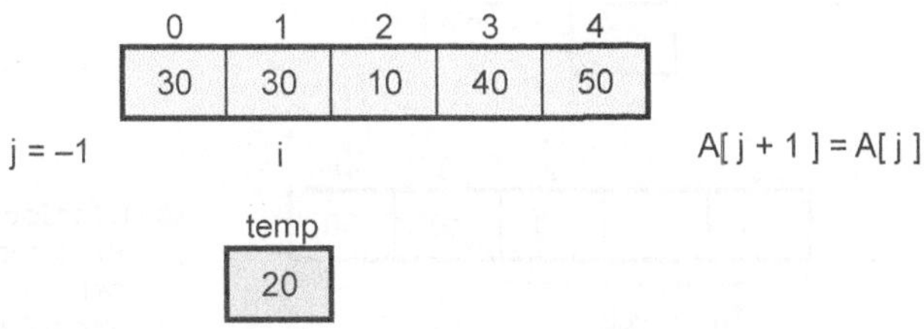

Now since j >= 0 is false, control comes out of while loop.

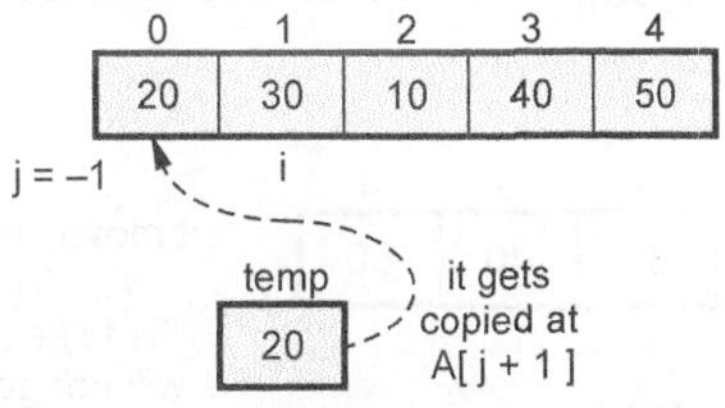

Then list becomes,

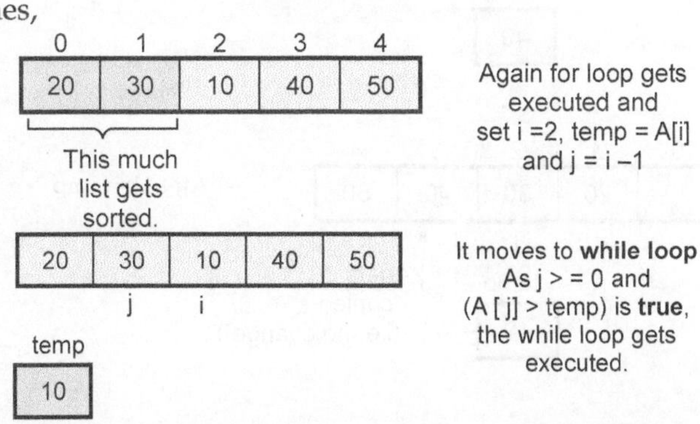

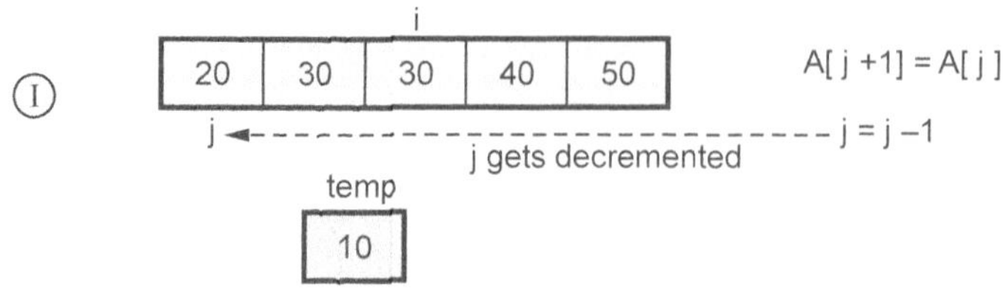
I
i
20 30 30 40 50
A[j +1] = A[j]
j
j = j –1
j gets decremented
temp
10

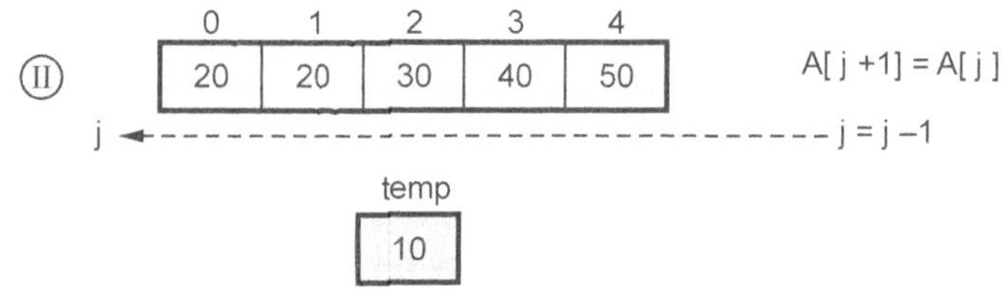
II
0 1 2 3 4
20 20 30 40 50
A[j +1] = A[j]
j
j = j –1
temp
10

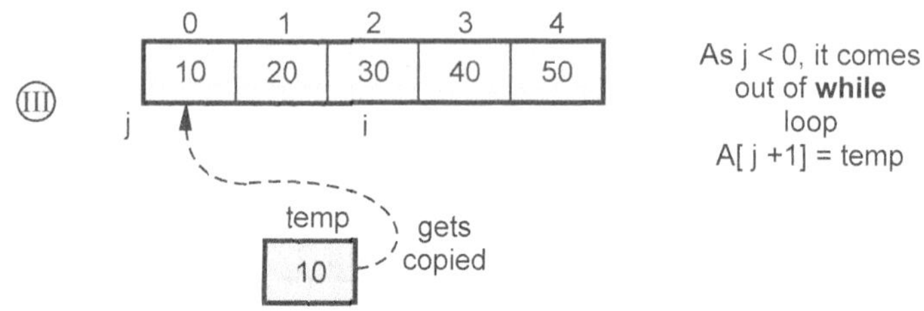
III
0 1 2 3 4
10 20 30 40 50
j
i
As j < 0, it comes out of while loop
A[j +1] = temp
temp
10
gets copied

Thus,

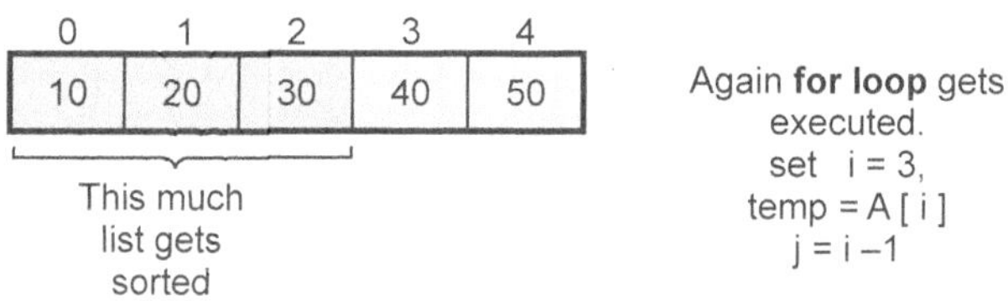
0 1 2 3 4
10 20 30 40 50
This much list gets sorted
Again for loop gets executed.
set i = 3,
temp = A [i]
j = i –1

Then,

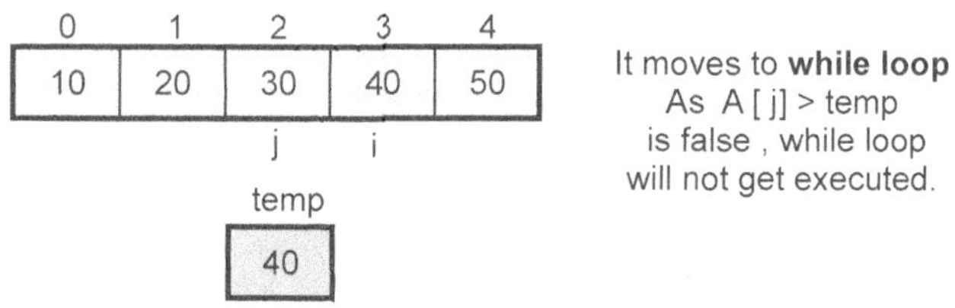
0 1 2 3 4
10 20 30 40 50
j i
It moves to while loop
As A [j] > temp
is false , while loop
will not get executed.
temp
40

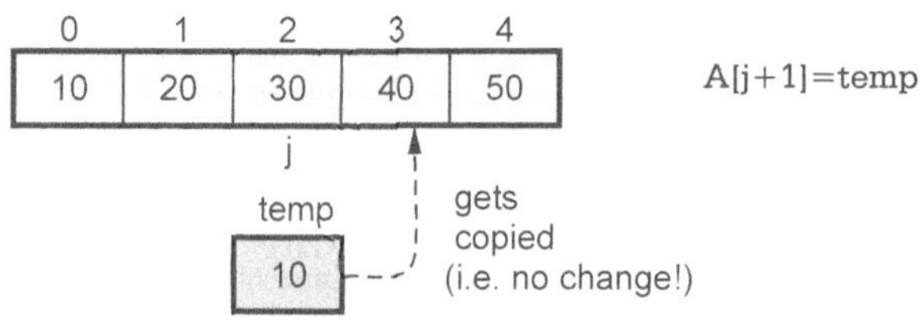
0 1 2 3 4
10 20 30 40 50
A[j+1]=temp
j
temp
10
gets copied
(i.e. no change!)

Then,

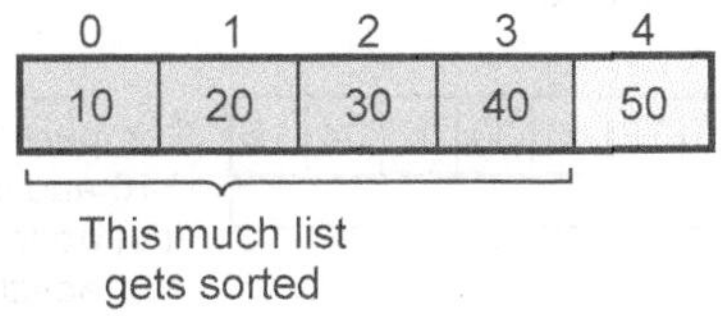

Again for loop gets executed
set i = 4
temp = A [i]
j = i –1

Then,

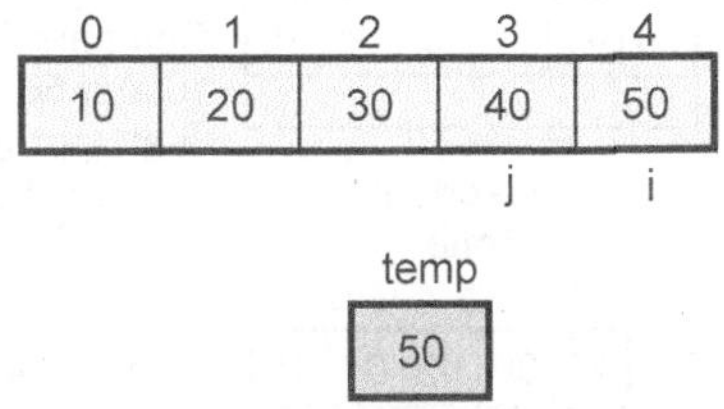

It moves to **while loop**
As A[j] > temp is false, while loop will not get executed.

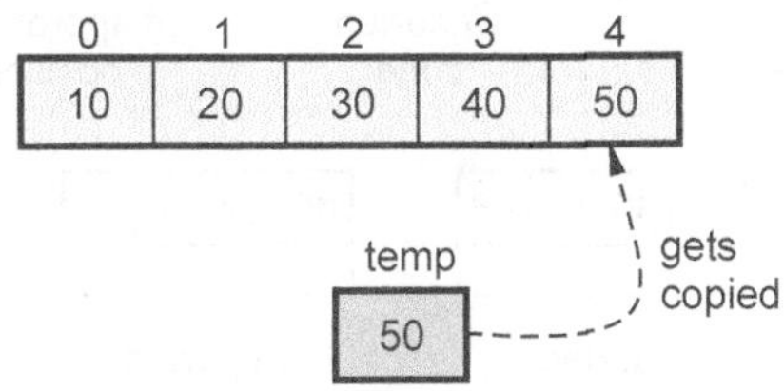

A[j+1]=temp

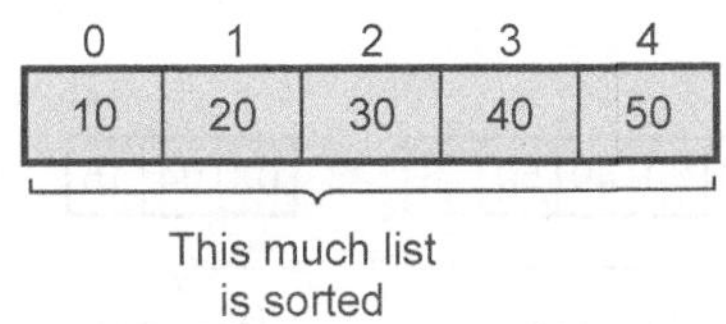

Thus we have scanned the entire list and inserted the elements at corresponding locations. Thus we get the sorted list by insertion sort.

Example 3.5.2 *Sort the following numbers using insertion sort. Show all passes*
50, 10, 78, 40, 30, 02, 04, 15

Solution : Consider the list of elements as -

0	1	2	3	4	5	6	7
50	10	78	40	30	02	04	15

The process starts with first element.

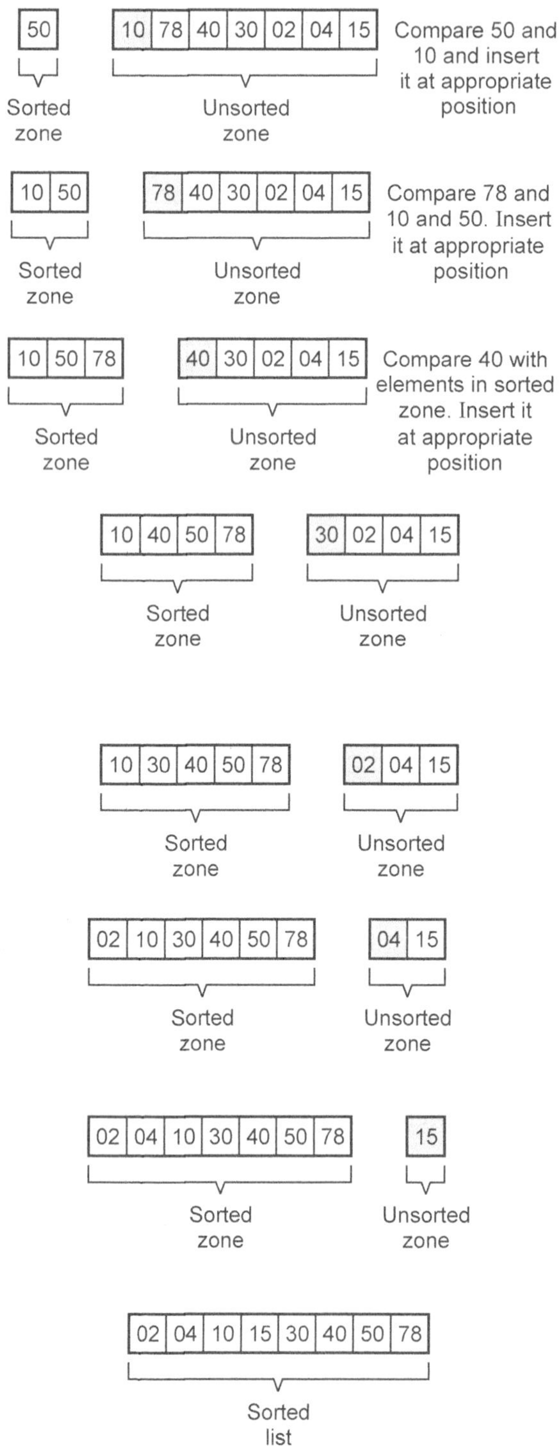

Example 3.5.3 *Compare the insertion sort and selection sort with*
i) Efficiency ii) Sort stability iii) Passes

Solution : i) Efficiency : The code for selection sort is as follows

```
for(i=0;i<n-1;i++)
        for(j=i+1;j<n;j++)
        {
                if(ai>aj)
                        swap ai and aj
        }
```

In the ith pass, n-i comparisons will be needed to select the smallest element. n-1 passes are required to sort the array. Thus, the number of comparisons needed to sort an array having n elements

$$= (n-1)+(n-2)+...+ 2+1 = \frac{n(n-1)}{2} = \frac{1}{2}(n^2 - n)$$

$$\approx O(n^2)$$

Insertion sort :

```
for(i=1;i<n;i++)
{
        k=a[i];
        for(j=i-1;j>=0&&y<a[i])
                a[j+1]=a[j];
                a[j+1]=1;
}
```

Inner loop is data sensitive. If the input list is presented for sorting is presorted then the test a[i] > y in the inner loop will fail immediately. Thus, only one comparison will be made in each pass.

Thus the total number of comparisons (Best case)

$= n - 1 \approx n$ for large n.

If the numbers to be sorted are initially in descending order then the inner loop will make i iterations in i^{th} pass.

∴ Total number of comparisons.

$$= 1+2+3+...+(n-1) = \frac{n(n-1)}{2} = \frac{1}{2}(n^2 - n) \approx n^2 \text{ for large n.}$$

ii) Sort stability : Both the techniques are stable. Both of them have same time complexity.

iii) Passes : Both selection and insertion sort requires n-1 passes.

Insertion sort is more stable than selection sort.

Insertion sort requires less overhead while sorting data. Selection sort requires more number of comparisons. In both the algorithms, elements are read in linear fashion and adjacent elements are compared. Hence identical numbers will maintain their relative sequence even in the sort list.

3.5.3 Selection Sort

Scan the array to find its smallest element and swap it with the first element. Then, starting with the second element scan the entire list to find the smallest element and swap it with the second element. Then starting from the third element the entire list is scanned in order to find the next smallest element. Continuing in this fashion we can sort the entire list.

Generally, on pass i $(0 \le i \le n-2)$, the smallest element is searched among last $n-i$ elements and is swapped with A[i]

$$A[0] \le A[1] \le \ldots \le A[i-1] \mid \overbrace{A[i], \ldots, A[k], \ldots, A[n-1]}^{\text{Last } n-i \text{ elements}}$$

A[k] is smallest element

so swap A[i] and A[k]

The list gets sorted after n–1 passes.

Example 1 :

Consider the elements

70, 30, 20, 50, 60, 10, 40

We can store these elements in array A as :

70	30	20	50	60	10	40
A[0]	A[1]	A[2]	A[3]	A[4]	A[5]	A[6]

↑ ↑

Initially set Min j

1st pass :

A[0]	A[1]	A[2]	A[3]	A[4]	A[5]	A[6]
70	30	20	50	60	10	40

↑ Min — Scan the array for finding smallest element

70	30	20	50	60	10	40

↑ i — ↑ Smallest element found

Now swap A[i] with smallest element. Then we get,

10	30	20	50	60	70	40

2nd pass :

A[0]	A[1]	A[2]	A[3]	A[4]	A[5]	A[6]
10	30	20	50	60	70	40

↑ i, Min — Scan the array for finding smallest element

10	30	20	50	60	70	40

↑ i ↑ Smallest element

Swap A[i] with smallest element. The array becomes,

10	20	30	50	60	70	40

3rd pass :

A[0]	A[1]	A[2]	A[3]	A[4]	A[5]	A[6]
10	20	30	50	60	70	40

↑ i, Min — Smallest element is searched in this list

As there is no smallest element than 30 we will increment i pointer.

4th pass :

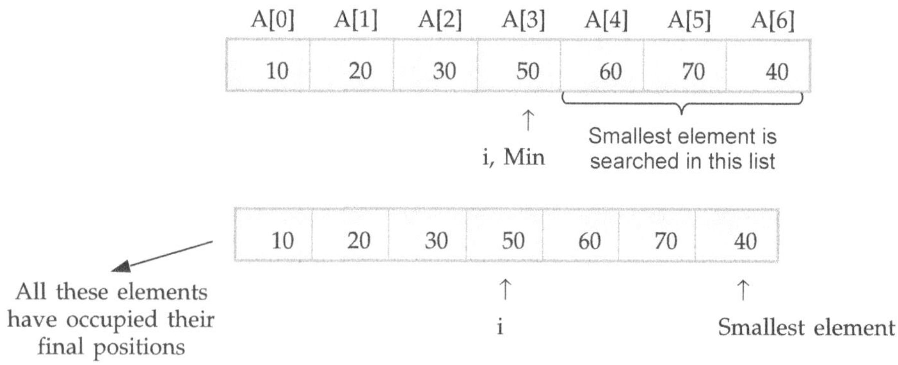

Swap A[i] with smallest element. The array then becomes,

5th pass :

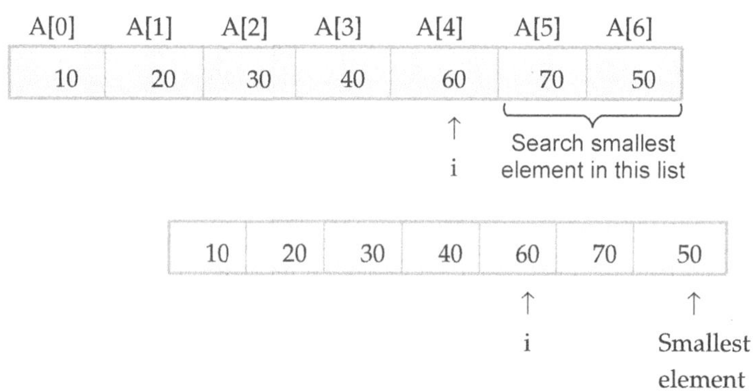

Swap A[i] with smallest element. The array then becomes,

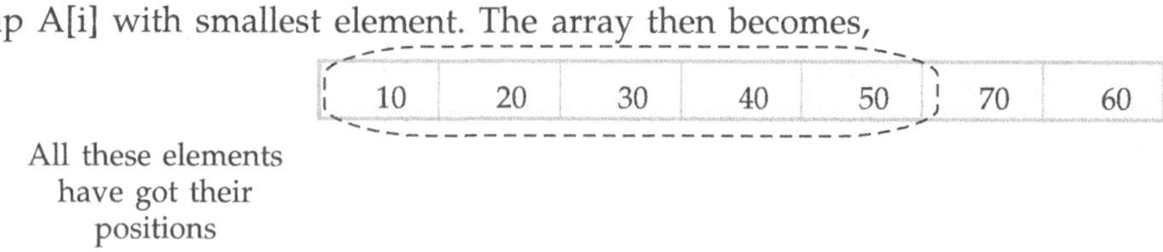

6th pass :

10	20	30	40	50	70	60
					↑ i	↑ Smallest element

Swap A[i] with smallest element. The array then becomes,

A[0]	A[1]	A[2]	A[3]	A[4]	A[5]	A[6]
10	20	30	40	50	60	70

This is a sorted array.

Python Program

```
def SelectionSort(arr,n):
    for i in range(n):
        Min = i
        for j in range(i+1,n):
            if(arr[j]<arr[Min]):
                Min = j
        temp=arr[i]
        arr[i]=arr[Min]
        arr[Min]=temp

    print(arr)

print("\n Program For Selection Sort")
print("\nHow many elements are there in Array?")
n = int(input())
array = []
i=0
for i in range(n):
    print("\n Enter element in Array")
    item = int(input())
    array.append(item)

print("Original array is\n")
print(array)

print("\n Sorted Array is")
SelectionSort(array,n)
```

Output

```
Program For Selection Sort
How many elements are there in Array?
5
 Enter element in Array
30
```

```
 Enter element in Array
50
 Enter element in Array
10
 Enter element in Array
20
 Enter element in Array
40
Original array is
[30, 50, 10, 20, 40]
 Sorted Array is
[10, 20, 30, 40, 50]
>>>
```

Example 3.5.4 *Sort the following and show the status after every pass using selection sort : 34, 9, 78, 65, 12, -8*

Solution : Let

34	9	78	65	12	–8

be the given elements.

Pass 1 : Consider the elements A[0] as the first element. Assume this as the minimum element.

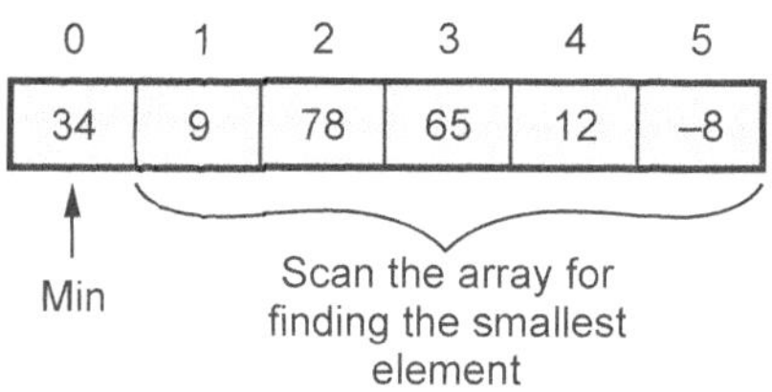

If smallest element is found, swap it with A[0]

0	1	2	3	4	5
–8	9	78	65	12	34

Pass 2 :

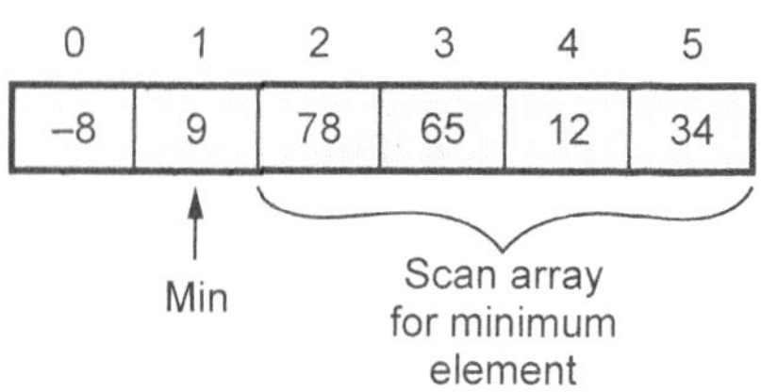

Pass 3 :

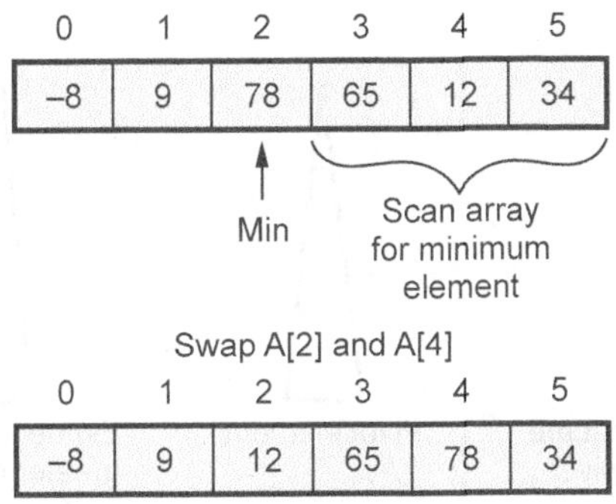

Pass 4 :

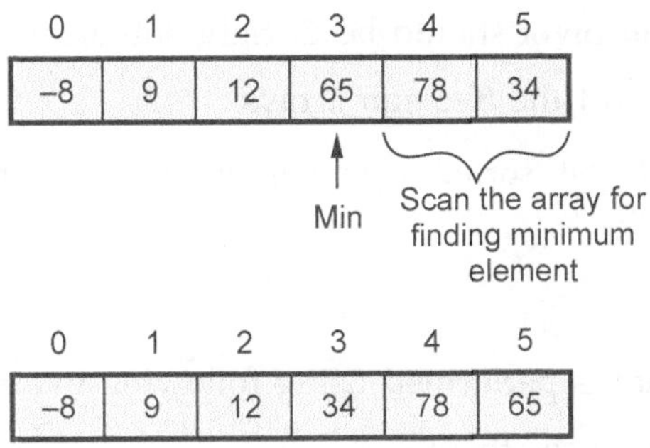

Pass 5 :

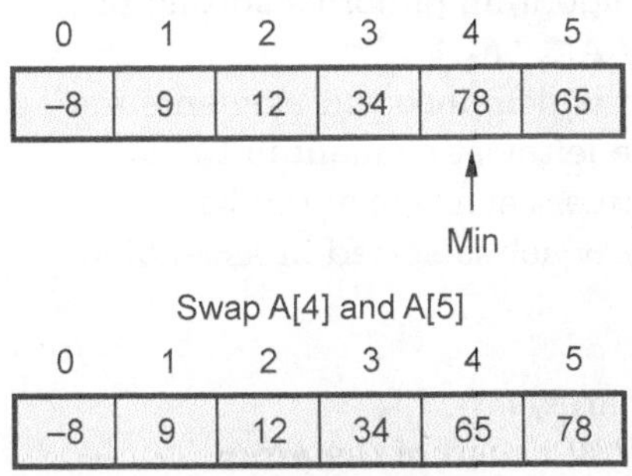

This is a sorted list

3.5.4 Quick Sort

Quick sort is a sorting algorithm that uses the divide and conquer strategy. In this method division is dynamically carried out. The three steps of quick sort are as follows :

Divide : Split the array into two sub arrays that each element in the left sub array is less than or equal the middle element and each element in the right sub array is greater than the middle element. The splitting of the array into two sub arrays is based on pivot

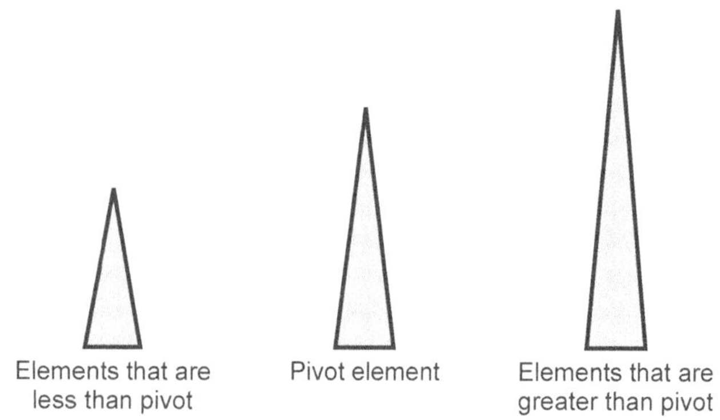

Fig. 3.5.1

element. All the elements that are less than pivot should be in left sub array and all the elements that are more than pivot should be in right sub array.

Conquer : Recursively sort the two sub arrays.

Combine : Combine all the sorted elements in a group to form a list of sorted elements.

Algorithm

The quick sort algorithm is performed using following two important functions - *Quick* and *partition*. Let us see them -

```
Algorithm Quick(A[0...n-1],low,high)
//Problem Description : This algorithm performs sorting of
//the elements given in Array A[0...n-1]
//Input: An array A[0...n-1] in which unsorted elements are
//given. The low indicates the leftmost element in the list
//and high indicates the rightmost element in the list
//Output: Creates a sub array which is sorted in ascending
//order
if(low<high)then
//split the array into two sub arrays
m ← partition(A[low...high])// m is mid of the array
Quick(A[low...m-1])
Quick(A[mid+1...high] )
```

In above algorithm call to partition algorithm is given. The *partition* performs arrangement of the elements in ascending order. The recursive *quick* routine is for dividing the list in two sub lists. The pseudo code for *Partition* is as given below -

```
Algorithm Partition (A[low...high])
//Problem Description: This algorithm partitions the
//subarray using the first element as pivot element
//Input: A subarray A with low as left most index of the
```

```
//array and high as the rightmost index of the array.
//Output: The partitioning of array A is done and pivot
//occupies its proper position. And the rightmost index of
//the list is returned
pivot ← A[low]
i ← low
j ← high+1
while(i<=j) do
{
 while(A[i]<=pivot) do
  i ← i+1
 while(A[j]>=pivot) do
  j ← j-1;
 if(i<=j) then
            swap(A[i],A[j])//swaps A[i] and A[j]
}
swap(A[low],A[j])//when i crosses j swap A[low] and A[j]
return j//rightmost index of the list
```

The partition function is called to arrange the elements such that all the elements that are less than pivot are at the left side of pivot and all the elements that are greater than pivot are all at the right of pivot. In other words pivot is occupying its proper position and the partitioned list is obtained in an ordered manner.

Analysis

When pivot is chosen such that the array gets divided at the mid then it gives the best case time complexity. The best case time complexity of quick sort is **$O(n\log_2 n)$**.

The worst case for quick sort occurs when the pivot is minimum or maximum of all the elements in the list. This can be graphically represented as -

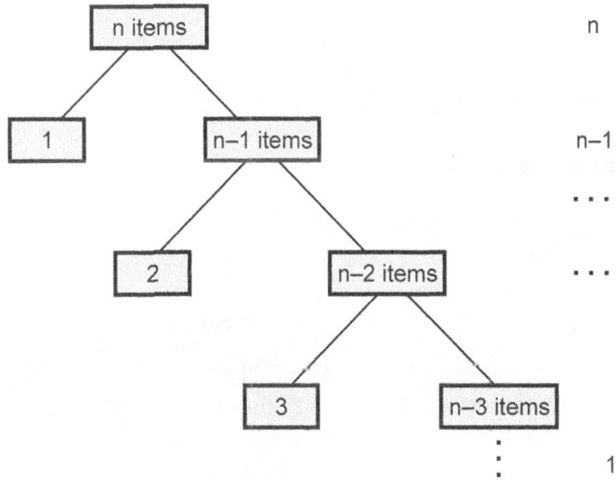

Fig. 3.5.2

This ultimately results in $O(n^2)$ time complexity. When array elements are randomly distributed then it results in average case time complexity, and it is **$O(n\log_2 n)$**.

Example 3.5.5 *Consider following numbers, sort them using quick sort. Show all passes to sort the values in ascending order*

25, 57, 48, 37, 12, 92, 86, 33

Solution : Consider the first element as a pivot element.

25	57	48	37	12	92	86	33
↑	↑						↑
Pivot	i						j

Now, if A[i] < Pivot element then increment i. And if A[j] > Pivot element then decrement j. When we get these above conditions to be false, Swap A[i] and A[j]

25	33	48	37	12	92	86	57
↑	i						j
Pivot							

25	33	48	37	12	92	86	57
↑	i			j			
Pivot							

Swap A[i] and A[j]

Low							High
25	12	48	37	33	92	86	57
	j	i					

As j > i Swap A[Low] and A[j]

After pass 1 :

[12]	25	[48	37	33	92	86	57]
		↑	↑				↑
		Pivot	i				j
12	25	[48	37	33	92	86	57]
					i		j
		Low					
12	25	[48	37	33	92	86	57]
				j	i		

As j > i, we will swap A[j] and A[Low]

After pass 2 :

12 25 [33 37] 48 [92 86 57]

After pass 3 :

12 25 33 37 48 [92 86 57]

Assume 92 to be pivot element

```
12   25   33   37   48   [92   86   57]
                          ↑    i    j
                        Pivot
12   25   33   37   48   92    86   57
                                    j    i
```

As j > i swap 92 with 57.

After pass 4 :

12 25 33 37 48 57 [86 92]

After pass 5 :

12 25 33 37 48 57 86 92

is a sorted list.

Python Program

```
def Quick(arr,low,high):
   if(low<high):
      m=Partition(arr,low,high)
      Quick(arr,low,m-1)
      Quick(arr,m+1,high)

def Partition(arr,low,high):
   pivot = arr[low]
   i=low+1
   j=high
   flag = False
   while(not flag):
      while(i<=j and arr[i]<=pivot):
         i = i + 1
      while(i<=j and arr[j]>=pivot):
```

```
        j = j - 1

    if(j<i):
        flag = True
    else:
        temp = arr[i]
        arr[i] = arr[j]
        arr[j] = temp

  temp = arr[low]
  arr[low] = arr[j]
  arr[j] = temp
  return j

print("\n Program For Quick Sort")
print("\nHow many elements are there in Array?")
n = int(input())
array = []
i=0
for i in range(n):
  print("\n Enter element in Array")
  item = int(input())
  array.append(item)

print("Original array is\n")
print(array)

Quick(array,0,n-1)
print("\n Sorted Array is")
print(array)
```

Output

```
Program For Quick Sort
How many elements are there in Array?
8
 Enter element in Array
50
 Enter element in Array
30
 Enter element in Array
10
 Enter element in Array
90
 Enter element in Array
80
 Enter element in Array
20
 Enter element in Array
```

```
40
 Enter element in Array
70
Original array is
[50, 30, 10, 90, 80, 20, 40, 70]
 Sorted Array is
[10, 20, 30, 40, 50, 70, 80, 90]
>>>
```

3.5.5 Shell Sort

This method is a improvement over the simple insertion sort. In this method the elements at fixed distance are compared. The distance will then be decremented by some fixed amount and again the comparison will be made. Finally, individual elements will be compared. Let us take some example.

Example : If the original file is

	0	1	2	3	4	5	6	7
X array	25	57	48	37	12	92	86	33

Step 1 : Let us take the distance k = 5

So in the first iteration compare

(x [0], x[5])

(x [1], x [(6])

(x [2], x[7])

(x[3])

(x[4])

i.e. first iteration

After first iteration,

x[0]	x[1]	x[2]	x[3]	x[4]	x[5]	x[6]	x[7]
25	57	33	37	12	92	86	48

Step 2 : Initially k was 5. Take some d and decrement k by d. Let us take d = 2

∴ k = k – d i.e. k = 5 – 2 = 3

So now compare

(x[0], x[3], x[6]), (x[1], x[4], x[7])

(x[2], x[5])

Second iteration

x[0]	x[1]	x[2]	x[3]	x[4]	x[5]	x[6]	x[7]
25	57	33	37	12	92	86	48

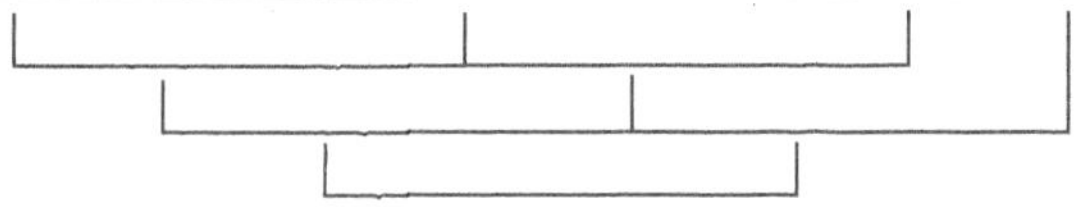

After second iteration

x[0]	x[1]	x[2]	x[3]	x[4]	x[5]	x[6]	x[7]
25	12	33	37	48	92	86	57

Step 3 : Now k = k – d ∴ k = 3 – 2 = 1

So now compare

(x[0], x[1], x[2], x[3], x[4], x[5], x[6], x[7])

This sorting is then done by simple insertion sort. Because simple insertion sort is highly efficient on sorted file. So we get

x[0]	x[1]	x[2]	x[3]	x[4]	x[5]	x[6]	x[7]
12	25	33	37	48	57	86	92

Python Program

```
def ShellSort(arr,n):
    d = n//2
    while d > 0:
        for i in range(d,n):
            temp = arr[i]
            j = i
            while(j >= d and arr[j-d] >temp):
                arr[j] = arr[j-d]
                j -= d

            arr[j] = temp
        d = d//2

print("\n Program For Shell Sort")
print("\nHow many elements are there in Array?")
n = int(input())
array = []
i=0
for i in range(n):
    print("\n Enter element in Array")
```

```
    item = int(input())
    array.append(item)

print("Original array is\n")
print(array)

ShellSort(array,n)
print("\n Sorted Array is")
print(array)
```

Output

```
Program For Shell Sort
How many elements are there in Array?
5
 Enter element in Array
30
 Enter element in Array
20
 Enter element in Array
10
 Enter element in Array
40
 Enter element in Array
50
Original array is
[30, 20, 10, 40, 50]
 Sorted Array is
[10, 20, 30, 40, 50]
>>>
```

Analysis :

Best Case : The best case in the shell sort is when the array is already sorted in the right order. The number of comparisons is less. In that case the inner loop does not need to any work and a simple comparison will be sufficient to skip the inner sort loop. the other loops gives O(nlogn). The best case of O(n) is reached by using a constant number of increments. Hence the best case time complexity of shell sort is **O(nlogn)**

Worst Case and Average Case : The running time of Shellsort depends on the choice of increment sequence. The problem with Shell's increments is that pairs of increments are not necessarily relatively prime and smaller increments can have little effect. The wort case and average case time complexity is **O(n)**.

3.6 Non-comparison based Sorting Methods

3.6.1 Radix Sort

In this mehod sorting can be done digit by digit and thus all the elements can be sorted.

Example for Radix sort

Consider the unsorted array of 8 elements.

45 37 05 09 06 11 18 27

Step 1 : Now sort the element according to the last digit.

Last digit	0	1	2	3	4	5	6	7	8	9
Elements		11				45, 05	06	37,27	18	09

Now sort this number

Last digit	Element
0	
1	11
2	
3	
4	
5	05,45
6	06
7	27,37
8	18
9	09

Step 2 : Now sort the above array with the help of second last digit.

Second last digit	Element
0	05,06,09
1	11,18
2	27
3	37
4	45
5	
6	
7	
8	
9	

Since the list of element is of two digit that is why, we will stop comparing. Now whatever list we have got (shown in above array) is of sorted elements. Thus finally the sorted list by radix sort method will be

05 06 09 11 18 27 37 45

Example 3.6.1 *Sort the following data in ascending order using Radix Sort :*
25, 06, 45, 60, 140, 50,

Solution :

Step 1 :

Sort the elements according to last digit and sort them.

Last digit	Element
0	50, 60, 140
1	
2	
3	
4	

5	25, 45
6	06
7	
8	
9	

Step 2 :

Sort the elements according to second last digit and sort them.

Second last digit	Element
0	06
1	
2	25
3	
4	45, 140
5	50
6	60
7	
8	

Step 3 :

Sort the elements according to 100th position of the element and sort them.

100th position	Element
0	06, 25, 45, 50, 60
1	140
2	
3	
4	
5	

6	
7	
8	
9	

Thus the sorted list of elements is

06, 25, 45, 50, 60, 140

Algorithm :

1. Read the total number of elements in the array.
2. Store the unsorted elements in the array.
3. Now the simple procedure is to sort the elements by digit by digit.
4. Sort the elements according to the last digit then second last digit and so on.
5. Thus the elements should be sorted for up to the most significant bit.
6. Store the sorted element in the array and print them.
7. Stop.

Python Program

```
def RadixSort(arr):
   MaxElement = max(arr)
   place = 1
   while MaxElement          //place > 0:
      countingSort(arr,place)
      place = place * 10

def countingSort(arr,place):
   n = len(arr)
   result – [0]*n
   count = [0] *10
   #calculating the count of elements based on digits place
   i = 0
   for i in range(n):
      index = arr[i]          // place
      count[index % 10] += 1

   for i in range(1, 10):
      count[i] = count[i]+count[i - 1]
   #placing the elements in sorted order
   i = n - 1
   while i >= 0:
```

```
        index = arr[i]              // place
        result[count[index % 10] - 1] = arr[i]
        count[index % 10] -= 1
        i = i-1
    #placing back the sorted elements in original
    for i in range(0, n):
        array[i] = result[i]

print("\n Program For Radix Sort")
print("\nHow many elements are there in Array?")
n = int(input())
array = []
i=0
for i in range(n):
    print("\n Enter element in Array")
    item = int(input())
    array.append(item)

print("Original array is\n")
print(array)

RadixSort(array)
print("\n Sorted Array is")
print(array)
```

Output

```
Program For Radix Sort
How many elements are there in Array?
6
 Enter element in Array
121
 Enter element in Array
235
 Enter element in Array
55
 Enter element in Array
973
 Enter element in Array
327
 Enter element in Array
179
Original array is
[121, 235, 55, 973, 327, 179]
 Sorted Array is
[55, 121, 179, 235, 327, 973]
>>>
```

3.6.2 Counting Sort

Concept : Counting sort is a sorting algorithm that sorts the elements of an array by counting the number of occurrences of each unique element in the array. The count is stored in an auxiliary array and the sorting is done by mapping the count as an index of the auxiliary array.

Let us understand this technique with the help of an example

Example 3.6.2 *Apply counting sort for the following numbers to sort in ascending order.*
4, 1, 3, 1, 3

Solution : Step 1 : We will find the min and max values from given array. The min = 1 and max = 4. Hence create an array A from 1 to 4.

A	1	2	3	4

Now create another array named **count.** Just count the number of occurrences of each element and store that count in count array at corresponding location of element i.e. element 1 appeared twice, element 2 is not present, element 3 appeared twice and element 4 appeared once.

A	1	2	3	4
Count	2	0	2	1

Step 2 : Now we will create another array B in which we will store sum of counts for given index.

A	1	2	3	4
Count	2	0	2	1
	↓			
B	2			

Simply copy first index value of count array to B.

For filling up rest of the elements to B array copy the sum of previous index value of B with current index value of count array.

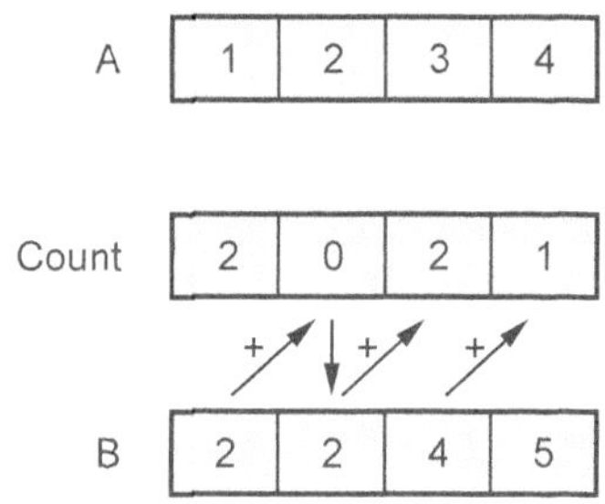

Step 3 : Now consider array A and B for creating two more arrays namely **Position** and **Element.**

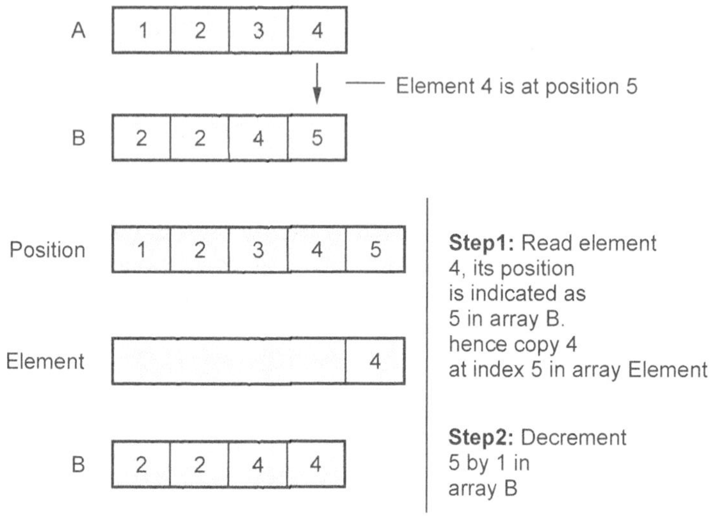

Step 4 : Next element is 1. The position of it is 2.

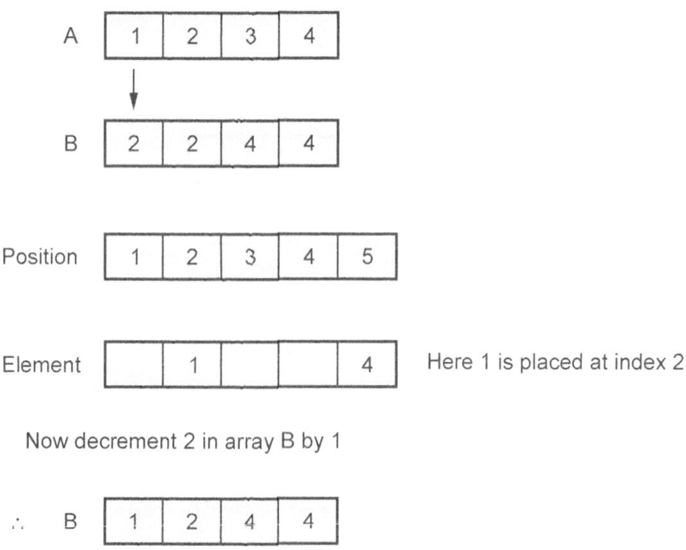

Step 5 : Next element is 3. The position of it is 4 in array B.

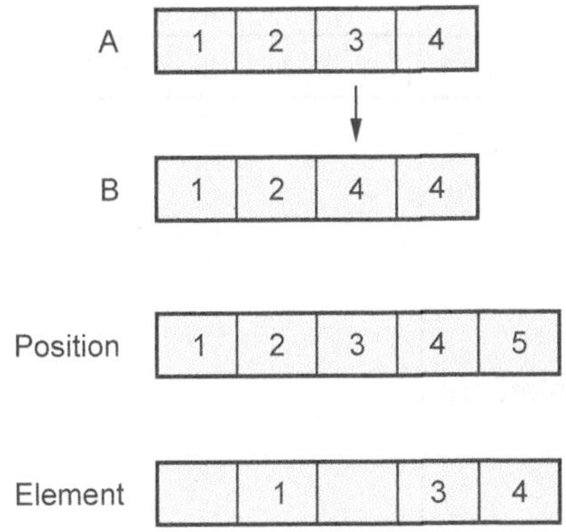

Now decrement 4 in array B by 1

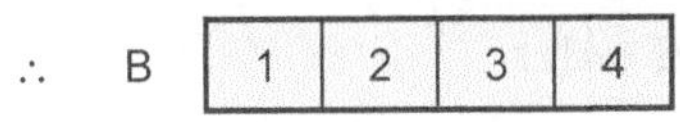

Step 6 : Next element is 1. The position of it in array B is 1.

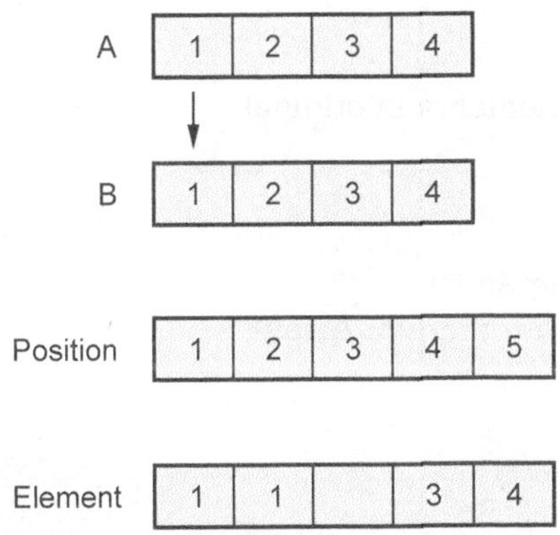

Step 7 : Next element is 3. In array B its position is 3.

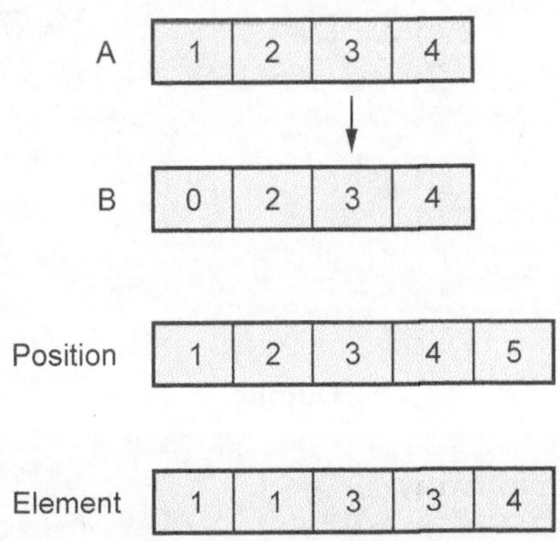

Step 8 : Thus we get sorted list in array **Element** as

1	1	3	3	4

Python Program

```
def countingSort(arr):
    n = len(arr)
    result = [0]*n
    count = [0] *10
    #calculating the count of elements
    i = 0
    for i in range(n):
        count[arr[i]] += 1

    for i in range(1, 10):
        count[i] = count[i]+count[i - 1]
    #placing the elements in sorted order
    i = n - 1
    while i >= 0:
        result[count[arr[i]] - 1] = arr[i]
        count[arr[i]] -= 1
        i = i-1
    #placing back the sorted elements in original
    for i in range(0, n):
        array[i] = result[i]

print("\n Program For Counting Sort")
print("\nHow many elements are there in Array?")
n = int(input())
array = []
i=0
for i in range(n):
    print("\n Enter element in Array")
    item = int(input())
    array.append(item)

print("Original array is\n")
print(array)

countingSort(array)
print("\n Sorted Array is")
print(array)
```

Output

```
Program For Counting Sort
How many elements are there in Array?
7
```

```
 Enter element in Array
5
 Enter element in Array
3
 Enter element in Array
5
 Enter element in Array
1
 Enter element in Array
3
 Enter element in Array
5
 Enter element in Array
4
Original array is
[5, 3, 5, 1, 3, 5, 4]

 Sorted Array is
[1, 3, 3, 4, 5, 5, 5]
>>>
```

3.6.3 Bucket Sort

Bucket sort is a sorting technique in which array is partitioned into buckets. Each bucket is then sorted individually, using some other sorting algorithm such as insertion sort.

Algorithm

1. Set up an array of initially empty buckets.
2. Put each element in corresponding bucket.
3. Sort each non empty bucket.
4. Visit the buckets in order and put all the elements into a sequence and print them.

Example 3.6.3 *Sort the elements using bucket sort. 56, 12, 84, 56, 28, 0, -13, 47, 94, 31, 12, -2.*

Solution : We will set up an array as follows

	0	1	2	3	4	5	6	7	8	9	10
Range	–20 to –1	0 to 10	10 to 20	20 to 30	30 to 40	40 to 50	50 to 60	60 to 70	70 to 80	80 to 90	90 to 100

Now we will fill up each bucket by corresponding elements

0	1	2	3	4	5	6	7	8	9	10
–13 –2	0	12 12	28	31	47	56 56			84	94

Now sort each bucket

0	1	2	3	4	5	6	7	8	9	10
–13 –2	0	12 12	28	31	47	56 56			84	94

Print the array by visiting each bucket sequentially.

-13, -2, 0, 12, 12, 28, 31, 47, 56, 56, 84, 94.

This is the sorted list.

Example 3.6.4 *Sort the following elements in ascending order using bucket sort. Show all passes 121, 235, 55, 973, 327, 179*

Solution : We will set up an array as follows -

0 to 100	100 to 200	200 to 300	300 to 400	400 to 500	500 to 600	600 to 700	700 to 800	800 to 900	900 to 1000

Now we will fill up each bucket by corresponding element in the list

55	121, 179	235	237						973
0 to 100	100 to 200	200 to 300	300 to 400	400 to 500	500 to 600	600 to 700	700 to 800	800 to 900	900 to 1000

Now visit each bucket and sort it individually.

Finally read each element of the bucket and place in some array say b[]. The elements from array b are printed to display the sorted list

55	121	179	235	327	973

Python Program

```
def BucketSort(arr):
    bucket = []
    slot = 10
    for i in range(slot):
        bucket.append([])
    #fill the bucket with elements
    for j in arr:
        k = int(slot*j)
        bucket[k].append(j)
    #sort individual bucket
    for i in range(len(array)):
        bucket[i] = sorted(bucket[i])
    #Retrieve sorted elements from bucket to original array
        m = 0
        for i in range(len(arr)):
            for j in range(len(bucket[i])):
                arr[m] = bucket[i][j]
                m = m + 1
        return arr

print("\n Program For Bucket Sort")
print("\nHow many elements are there in Array?")
n = int(input())
array = []
i=0
for i in range(n):
    print("\n Enter element in Array")
    item = int(input())
    array.append(item)

print("Original array is\n")
print(array)

BucketSort(array)
print("\n Sorted Array is")
print(array)
```

Drawbacks

1. For bucket sort the maximum value of the element must be known.
2. We must have to create enough buckets in the memory for every element to place in the array.

Analysis

The best case, worst case and average case time complexity of this algorithm is O(n)

3.7 Comparison of all Sorting Methods and their Complexities

Sorting technique	Best case	Average case	Worst case
Insertion sort	O(n)	$O(n^2)$	$O(n^2)$
Selection sort	$O(n^2)$	$O(n^2)$	$O(n^2)$
Radix sort	O(nlogn)	O(nlogn)	O(nlogn)
Quick sort	O(nlogn)	O(nlogn)	$O(n^2)$
Heap sort	O(nlogn)	O(nlogn)	O(nlogn)
Shell sort	O(nlogn)	O(n)	O(n)

❑❑❑

Unit - IV

4 Linked List

Syllabus

Introduction to Static and Dynamic Memory Allocation, Linked List: Introduction, of Linked Lists, Realization of linked list using dynamic memory management, operations, Linked List as ADT, Types of Linked List: singly linked, linear and Circular Linked Lists, Doubly Linked List, Doubly Circular Linked List, Primitive Operations on Linked List-Create, Traverse, Search, Insert, Delete, Sort, Concatenate. Polynomial Manipulations-Polynomial addition. Generalized Linked List (GLL) concept, Representation of Polynomial using GLL.

Contents

4.1 Introduction to Static and Dynamic Memory Allocation

- The **static memory management** means allocating or deallocating of memory at compilation time while the word **dynamic** refers to allocation or deallocation of memory while program is running (after compilation).
- The **advantage of dynamic memory management** in handling the linked list is that we can create as many nodes as we desire and if some nodes are not required we can deallocate them. Such a deallocated memory can be reallocated for some other nodes.
- Thus the total memory utilization is possible using dynamic memory allocation.

Sr. no.	Static memory	Dynamic memory
1.	The memory allocation is done at compile time.	Memory allocation is done at dynamic time.
2.	Prior to allocation of memory some fixed amount of it must be decided.	No need to know amount of memory prior to allocation.
3.	Wastage of memory or shortage of memory.	Memory can be allocated as per requirement.
4.	e.g. Array.	e.g. Linked list.

- As shown in Fig. 4.1.1, the program uses the memory which is divided into three parts **static area, local data** and **heap.**
- The static area stores the global data. The stack is for local data area i.e for local variables and heap area is used to allocate and deallocate memory under program's control.
- The **stack** and **heap** area are the part of dynamic memory management. Note that the stack and heap grow towards each other. Their areas are flexible.

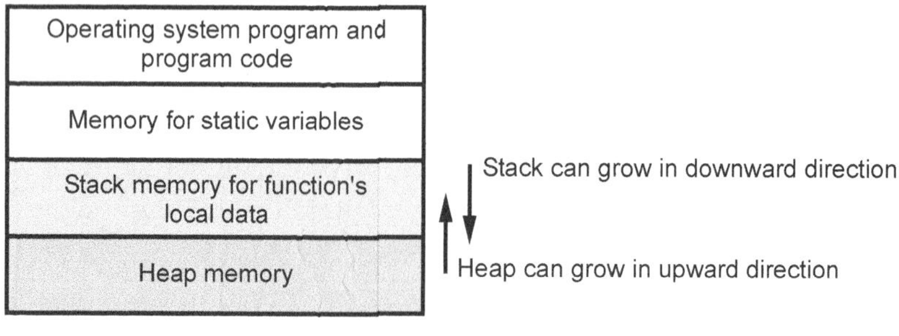

Fig. 4.1.1 Memory model

4.2 Introduction of Linked Lists

A linked list is a set of nodes where each node has two fields ' **data'** and **'link'**. The 'data' field stores actual piece of information and 'link' field is used to point to next node. Basically 'link' field is nothing but **address only**.

Fig. 4.2.1 Structure of node

Hence link list of integers 10, 20, 30, 40 is

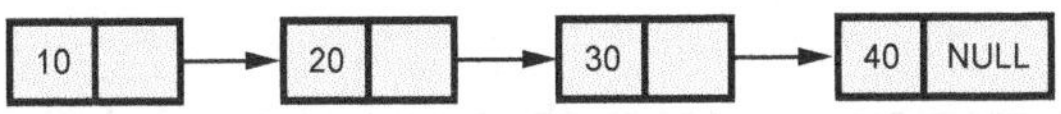

Fig. 4.2.2

Note that the **'link'** field of **last node consists of NULL** which indicates **end of list**.

4.2.1 Linked List Vs. Array

The comparison between linked list and arrays is as shown below -

Sr. No.	Linked List	Array
1.	The linked list is a collection of nodes and each node is having one data field and next link field. For example 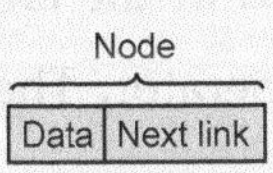	The array is a collection of similar types of data elements. In arrays the data is always stored at some index of the array. For example 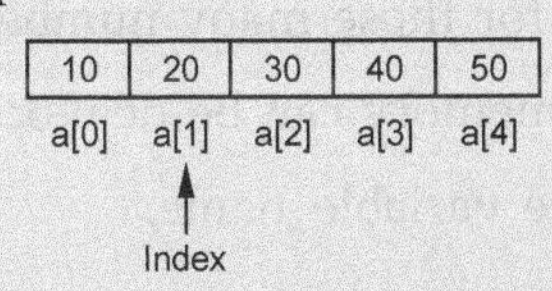
2.	Any element can be accessed by sequential access only.	Any element can be accessed randomly i.e. with the help of index of the array.
3.	Physically the data can be deleted.	Only logical deletion of the data is possible.
4.	Insertions and deletion of data is easy.	Insertions and deletion of data is difficult.
5.	Memory allocation is dynamic. Hence developer can allocate as well as deallocate the memory. And so no wastage of memory is there.	The memory allocation is static. Hence once the fixed amount of size is declared then that much memory is allocated. Therefore there is a chance of either memory wastage or memory shortage.

4.3 Realization of Linked List using Dynamic Memory Management

For performing the linked list operations we need to allocate or deallocate the memory dynamically. The dynamic memory allocation and deallocation can be done using new and delete operators in C++.

The dynamic memory allocation is done using an operator **new**. The syntax of dynamic memory allocation using **new** is

new data type;

For example :

```
int *p;
p=new int;
```

We can allocate the memory for more than one element. For instance if we want to allocate memory of size in for 5 elements we can declare.

```
int *p;
p=new int[5];
```

In this case, the system dynamically assigns space for five elements of type *int* and returns a pointer to the first element of the sequence, which is assigned to p. Therefore, now, *p* points to a valid block of memory with space for five elements of type *int*.

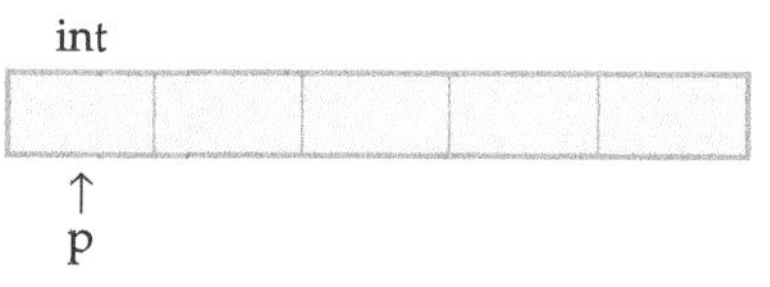

The program given below allocates the memory for any number of elements and the memory for those many number of elements get deleted at the end of the program.

The memory can be deallocated using the **delete** operator. The syntax is

delete variable_name;

For example

```
delete p;
```

4.4 Linked List as ADT

In ADT the implementation details are hidden. Hence the ADT will be -

Abstract DataType List

{

Instances : List is a collection of elements which are arranged in a linear manner.

Operations : Various operations that can be carried out on list are -

1. Insertion : This operation is for insertion of element in the list.
2. Deletion : This operation removed the element from the list.

3. Searching : Based on the value of the key element the desired element can be searched.
4. Modification : The value of the specific element can be changed without changing its location.
5. Display : The list can be displayed in forward or in backward manner.

}

4.5 Representation of Linked List

Representation of Linked List using C++

```
class node
{
 public:
        int data;
        node *next;
};
class sll
{
 private:
        node *head;       ← Data members of list
public:
        void create();
        void print();     ← Operations on list
        .
        .
        .
};
```

4.6 Primitive Operations on Linked List

Various operations that can be performed on list are -

1. Creation
2. Insertion
3. Deletion
4. Reverse
5. Search
6. Display

1. Creation of linked list

```
void sll :: create()
{
        node *temp, *New;
        int val,flag;
        char ans ='y';
        flag=TRUE;
        do
```

```
    {
        cout<<"\nEnter the data :";
        cin>>val;
        // allocate memory to new node
         New = new node;
        if ( New == NULL )

            cout<<"Unable to allocate memory\n";
        New-> data  = val ;
        New-> next = NULL;
        if( flag==TRUE ) // Executed only for the first time
        {
         head=New;
         temp = head;
         flag=FALSE;
        }
        else
        {
            /*temp last keeps track of the most recently
              created node*/
          temp->next = New;
          temp = New;
        }
        cout<<"\n Do you want to enter more elements?(y/n)";
        ans = getche();
    }while(ans=='y'||ans=='Y');
    cout<<"\nThe Singly Linked List is created\n";
    getch();
    clrscr();
}
```

Creation of linked list (logic explanation part) :

Initially one variable flag is taken whose value is initialized to TRUE (i.e. 1). The purpose of flag is for making a check on creation of first node. That means if flag is TRUE then we have to create head node or first node of linked list. Naturally after creation of first node we will reset the flag (i.e. assign FALSE to flag) Consider that we have entered the element value 10 initially then,

Step 1 :

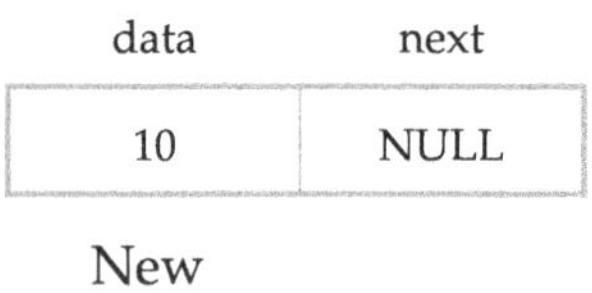


```
New = new node ;
/* memory gets allocated for
New node */
New → data = Val;
/* value 10 will be put in data field of New */
```

Step 2 :

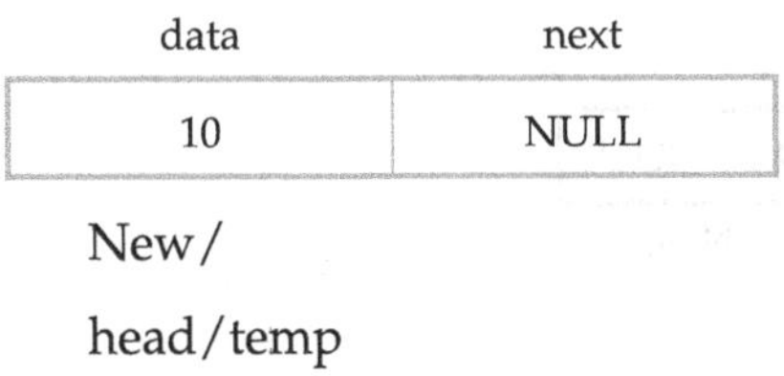


```
if (flag = = TRUE)
{
head = New
temp = head;
/* We have also called this node as temp because
head's address will be preserved in 'head' and we can
change 'temp' node as per requirement */
flag = FALSE;
/* After creation of first node flag is reset */
```

Step 3 :

If **head** node of linked list is created we can further create a linked list by attaching the subsequent nodes. Suppose we want to insert a node with value 20 then,

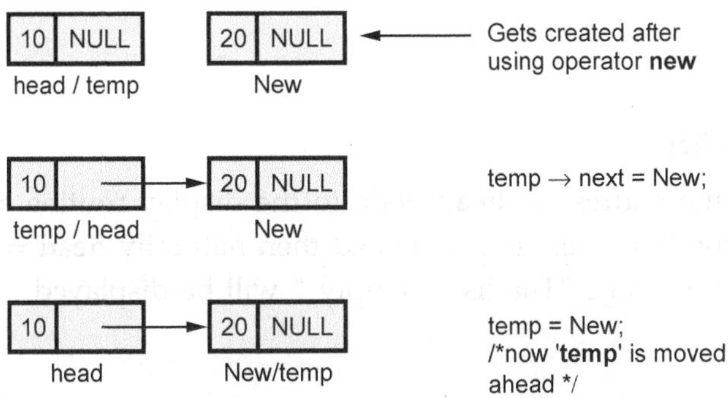

Step 4 :

If user wants to enter more elements then let say for value 30 the scenario will be,

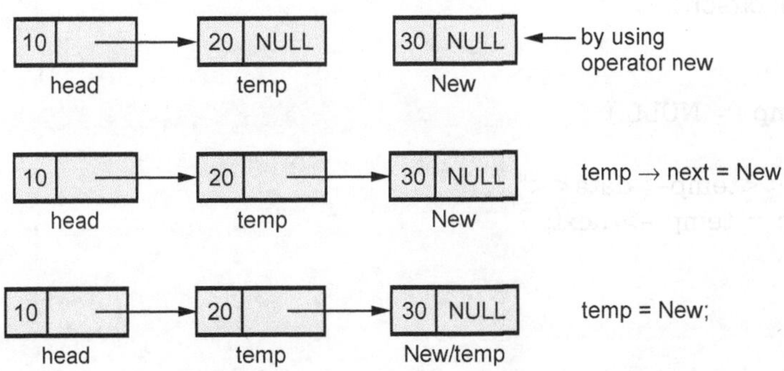

Then for value 40 -

Step 5 :

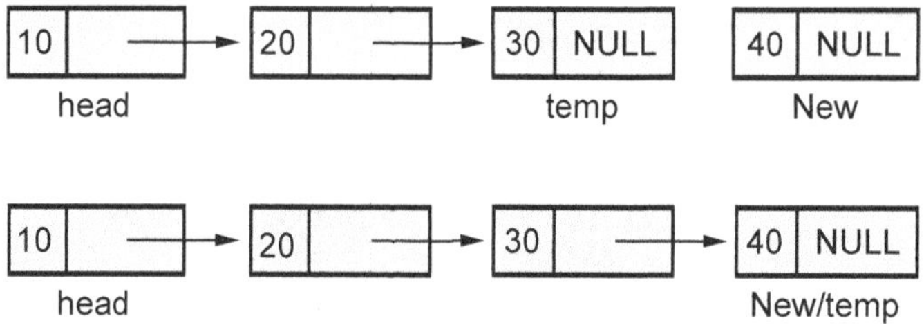

Next if we enter 50 then

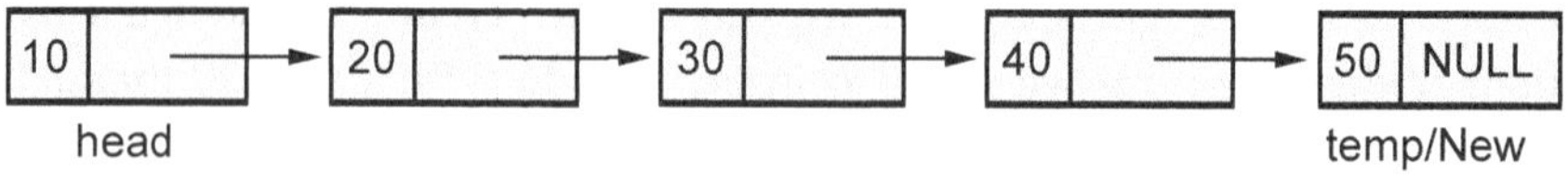

is the final linked list.

2. Display of linked list

We are passing the address of **head** node to the display routine and calling head as the **'temp'** node. If the linked list is not created then naturally **head = temp** node will be **NULL.** Therefore the message "The list is empty " will be displayed.

```
void sll ::display()
{
    node *temp ;
    temp = head;
    if ( temp == NULL )
    {
        cout<<"\nThe list is empty\n";
        getch(); clrscr();
        return;
    }
    while ( temp != NULL )
    {
        cout<<temp->data<<" ";
        temp = temp -> next;
    }
    getch();

}
```

If we have created some linked list like this then -

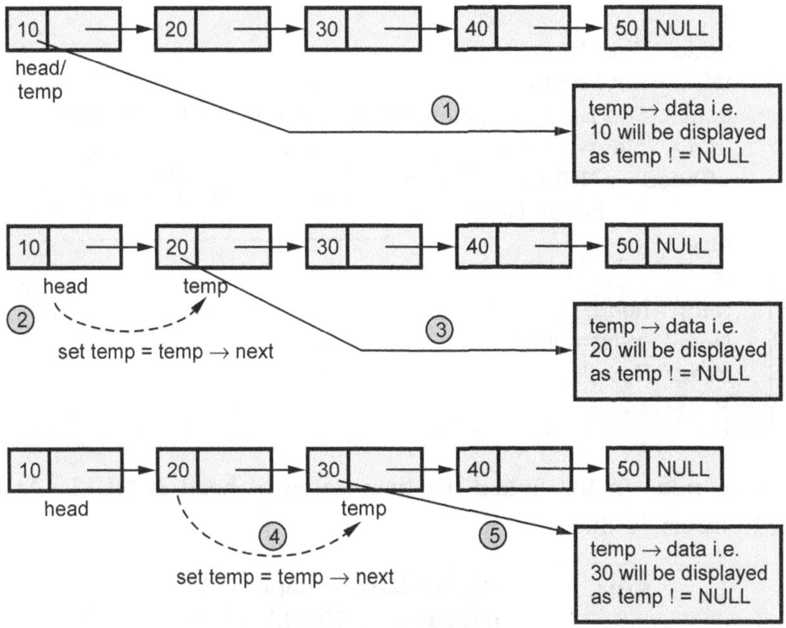

Continuing in this fashion we can display remaining nodes 40, 50. When

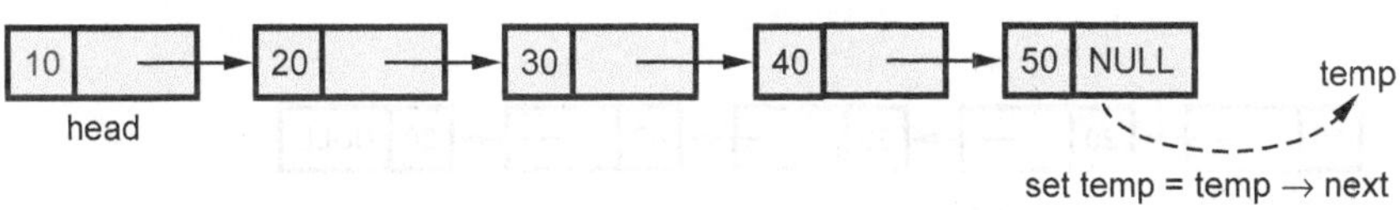

As now value of temp becomes NULL we will come out of **while** loop. As a result of such display routine we will get,

10 → 20 → 30 → 40 → 50 → NULL

will be printed on console.

3. Insertion of any element at anywhere in the linked list

There are three possible cases when we want to insert an element in the linked list -

a) Insertion of a node as a head node

b) Insertion of a node as a last node

c) Insertion of a node after some node.

We will see the case a) first -

```
void sll:: insert_head()
{
node *New,*temp;
 New=new node;
cout<<"\n Enter The element which you want to insert";
 cin>>New->data;
 if(head==NULL)
            head=New;
else
 {
temp=head;
New->next=temp;
head=New;
}
}
```

There is no node in the linked list. That means the linked list is empty

If there is no node in the linked list then value of head is NULL. At that time if we want to insert 10 then

10	NULL

head / New

Cin >>New → data
if (head = = NULL)
head = New;

Otherwise suppose linked list is already created like this

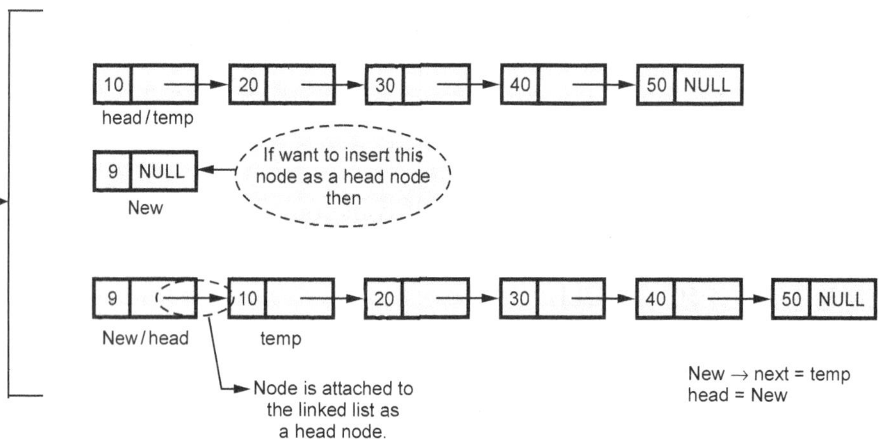

Now we will insert a node at the end -

```
void sll::insert_last()
{
 node *New,*temp;
 cout<<"\nEnter The element which you want to insert";
 cin>>New->data;
 if(head==NULL)
      head=New;
 else
 {
      temp=head;
      while(temp->next!=NULL)
           temp=temp->next;
      temp->next=New;
      New->next=NULL;
 }
}
```

Finding the end of the linked list. Then **temp** will be a last node.

To attach a node at the end of linked list assume that we have already created a linked list like this -

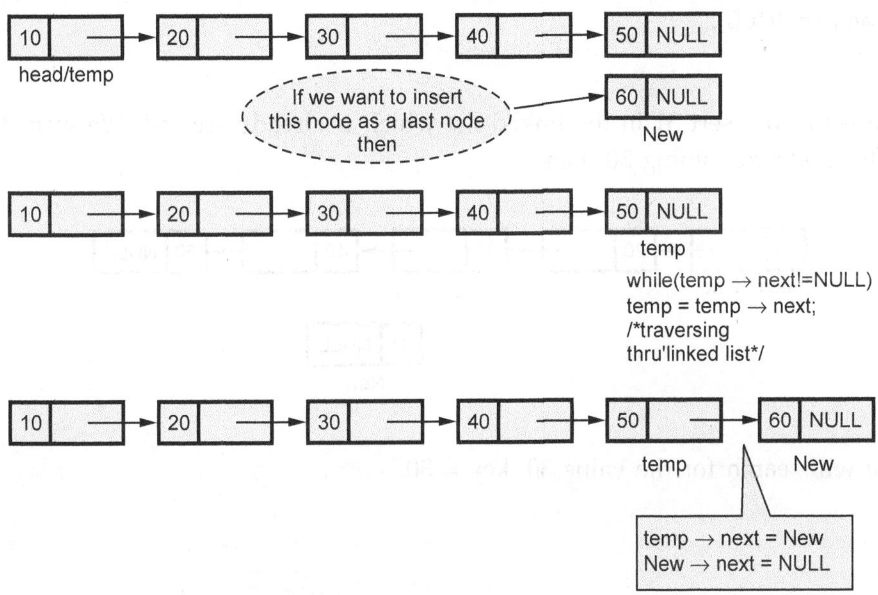

Now we will insert a new node after some node at intermediate position

```
void sll:: insert_after()
{
 int key;
 node  *temp,*New;
 New= new node;
```

```
cout<<"\n Enter The element which you want to insert";
cin>>New->data;
if(head==NULL)
{
 head=New;
}
else
{
 cout<<"\n Enter The element after which you want to insert the node";
 cin>>key;
 temp=head;
 do
 {
      if(temp->data==key)
      {
           New->next=temp->next;
           temp->next=New;
           break;
      }
    else
         temp=temp->next;
 }while(temp!=NULL);
}
}
```

If we want to insert 31 in the linked list which is already created. We want to insert this 31 after node containing 30 then

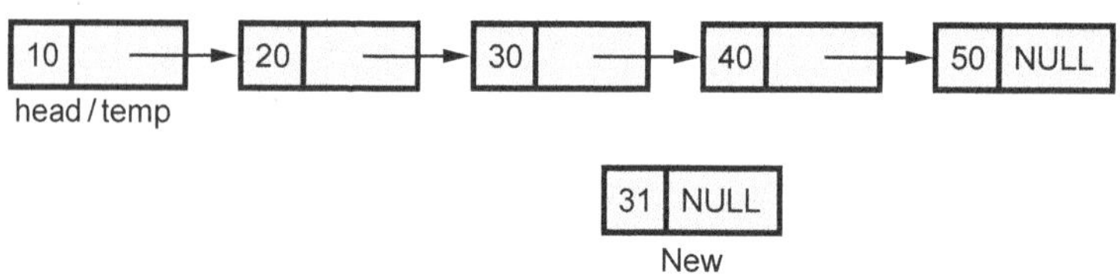

As we will search for the value 30, key = 30.

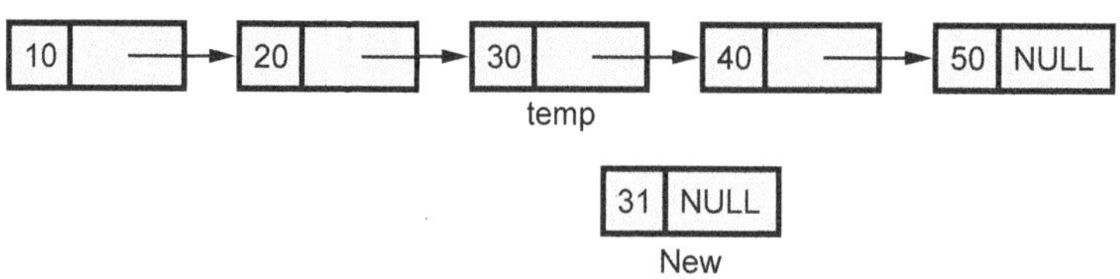

Then,

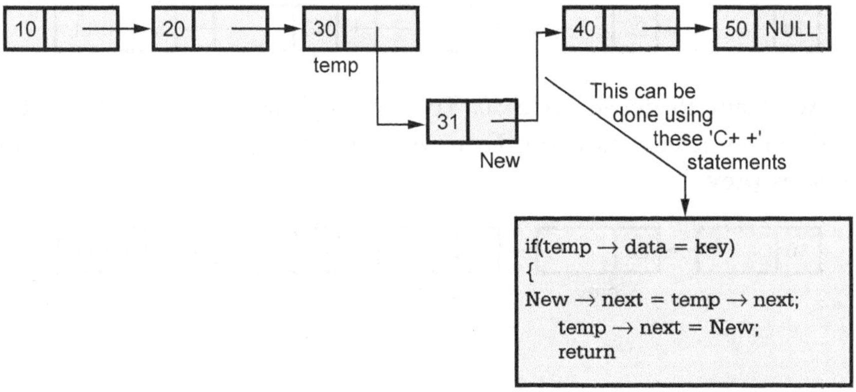

Thus desired node gets inserted at desired position.

4. Deletion of any element from the linked list

```
void sll:: dele()
{
	node *temp, *prev ;
	int  key;
	temp=head;
	clrscr();
	cout<<"\nEnter the data of the node you want to delete: ";
	cin>>key;
	while(temp!=NULL)
	{
	 if(temp->data==key)
		break;
	 prev=temp;
	 temp=temp->next;
  }
  if(temp==NULL)
  cout<<"\nNode not found";
  else
  {
	 if(temp==head) //first node
		head=temp->next;
	 else
		prev->next=temp->next;  //intermediate or end node
	delete temp;
	cout<<"\nThe Element is deleted\n";
  }
	getch();

}
```

Firstly Node to be deleted is searched in the linked list

Once the node to be deleted is found then get the previous node of that node in variable **prev**

If we want to delete the head node then set its adjacent node as a new head node and then release the memory

Suppose we have,

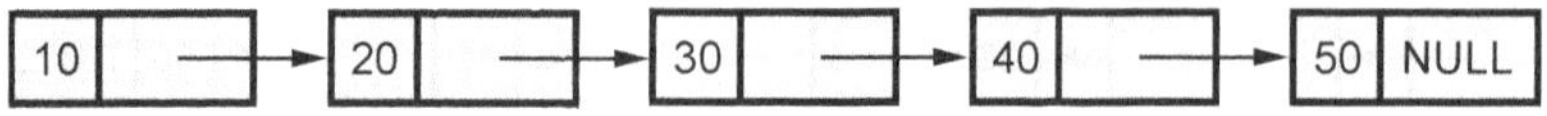

Suppose we want to delete node 30. Then we will search the node containing 30. Mark the node to be deleted as **temp**. Then we will obtain previous node of **temp** Mark previous node as **prev**

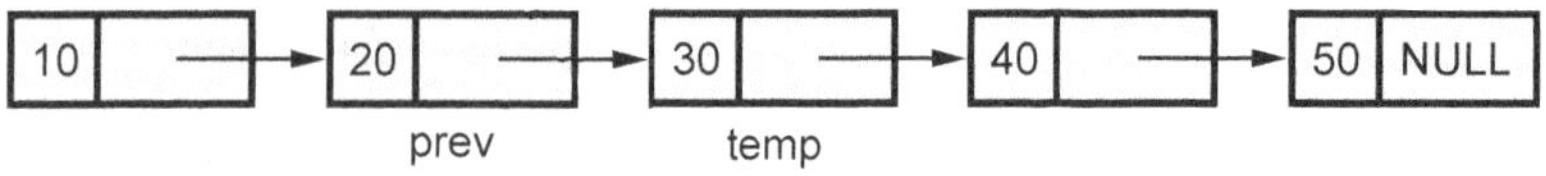

Then,

prev → next = temp → next

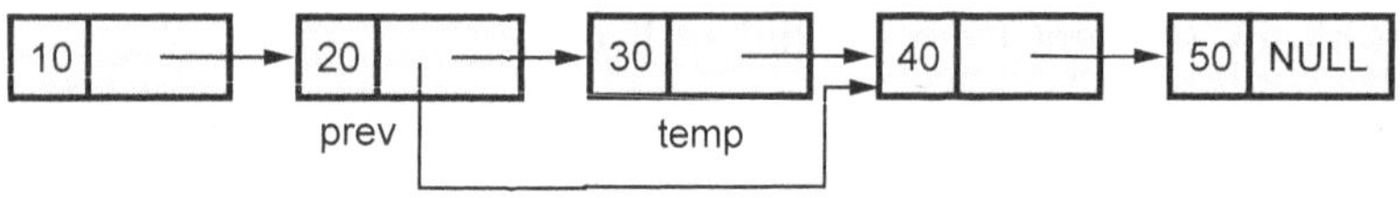

Now we will **delete** the **temp** node. Then the linked list will be

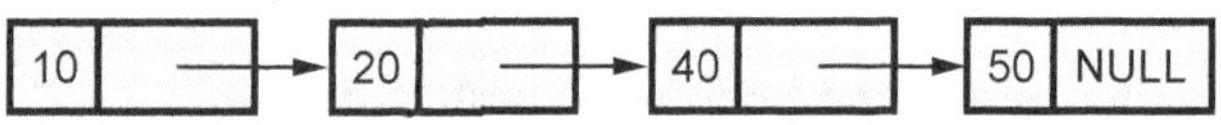

Another case is, if we want to delete a head node then -

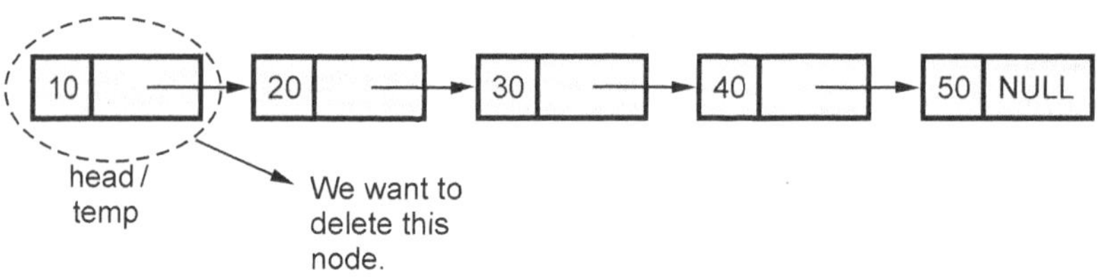

This can be done using following statements

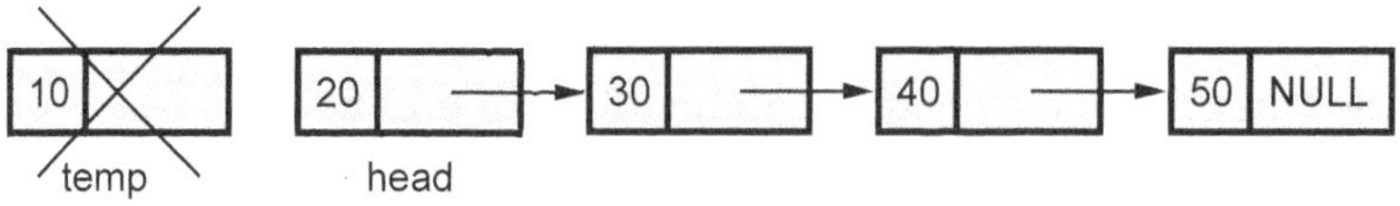


```
head = temp → next;
delete temp;
```

5. Searching of desired element in the linked list

The search function is for searching the node containing desired value. We pass the head of the linked list to this routine so that the complete linked list can be searched from the beginning.

```
void sll::search(int key)
{
 node *temp;
 int found;
 temp = head;
 if ( temp == NULL )
 {
  cout<<"The Linked List is empty\n";
  getch();
  clrscr();
 }
 found = FALSE;
 while ( temp != NULL && found==FALSE)
 {
  if ( temp->data != key)
    temp = temp -> next;
  else
    found = TRUE;
 }
 if ( found==TRUE )
 {
  cout<<"\nThe Element is present in the list\n";
  getch();
 }
 else
 {
  cout<<"The Element is not present in the list\n";
  getch();
 }
}
```

If node containing desired data is obtained in the linked list then set **found** variable to **TURE**

Consider that we have created a linked list as

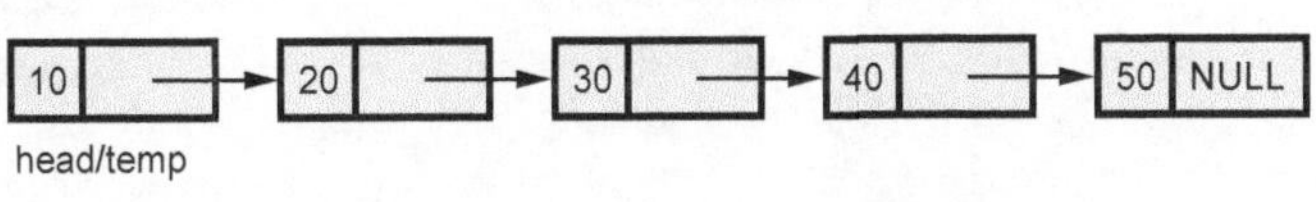

Suppose key = 30 i.e. we want a node conaining value 30 then compare **temp → data** and **key** value. If there is no match then we will mark next node as **temp**.

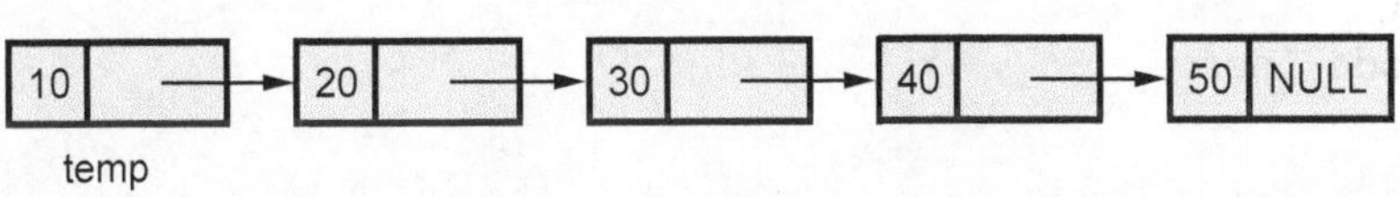

Is temp $\rightarrow$ data $\stackrel{?}{=}$ key No

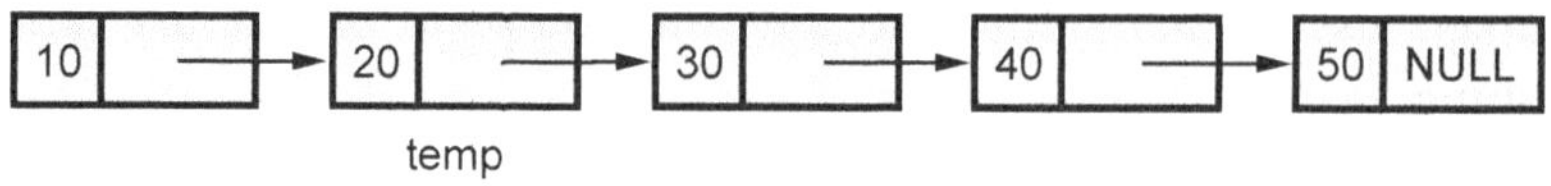

Is temp $\rightarrow$ data $\stackrel{?}{=}$ key No

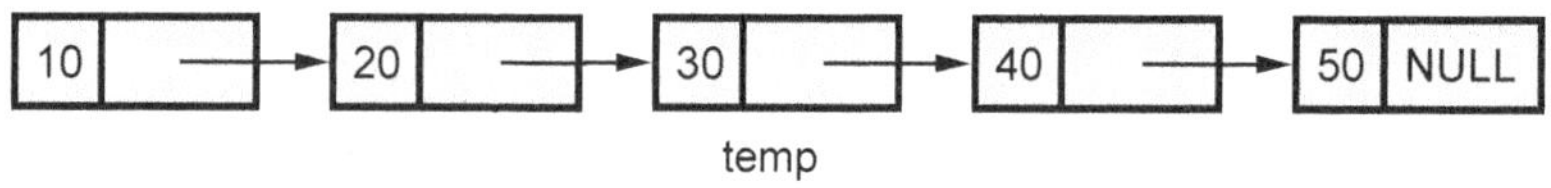

Is temp $\rightarrow$ data $\stackrel{?}{=}$ key Yes

Hence print the message **"The Element is present in the list"**

Thus in search operation the entire list can be scanned in search of desired node. And still, if required node is not obtained then we have to print the message.

"The Element is not present in the list"

Let us see the complete program for it -

'C++' Program

```
/*********************************************************************
 Demonstration Program to perform various operations on
 singly link lists.
*********************************************************************/

// List of include files

#include<iostream.h>
#include <conio.h>
#define TRUE 1
#define FALSE 0
// class

class sll
{
private:
 struct node
 {
        int data;
        structnode  *next;
 }*head;
public:
sll();
```

```
void create();
void display();
void search(int key);
void insert_head();
void insert_after();
void insert_last();
void dele();
~sll();
};

/*
----------------------------------------------------------------------
The  Constructor defined
----------------------------------------------------------------------
*/
sll::sll()
 {
  head=NULL;//initialize head to NULL
 }
/*
----------------------------------------------------------------------
       The Destructor defined
----------------------------------------------------------------------
*/
sll::~sll()
{
  node *temp,*temp1;
  temp=head->next;
  delete head;
  while(temp!=NULL) //free the memory allocated
   {
    temp1=temp->next;
    delete temp;
    temp=temp1;
   }
}
/*
----------------------------------------------------------------------
       The Create function
----------------------------------------------------------------------
*/
void sll :: create()
{

       node *temp, *New;
       int val,flag;
       char ans ='y';
```

```
    flag=TRUE;
    do
    {
        cout<<"\nEnter the data :";
        cin>>val;
        // allocate memory to new node
         New = new node;
        if ( New == NULL )
            cout<<"Unable to allocate memory\n";
        New-> data  = val ;
        New-> next = NULL;
        if( flag==TRUE ) // Executed only for the first time
        {
         head=New;
         temp = head;
         flag=FALSE;
        }
        else
        {
            /*temp last keeps track of the most recently
              created node*/
          temp->next = New;
          temp = New;
        }
        cout<<"\n Do you want to enter more elements?(y/n)";
        ans = getche();
    }while(ans=='y'||ans=='Y');
    cout<<"\nThe Singly Linked List is created\n";
    getch();
    clrscr();
}

/*
-----------------------------------------------------------------------
    The display function
-----------------------------------------------------------------------
*/
void sll ::display()
{
    node *temp ;
    temp = head;
    if ( temp == NULL )
    {
       cout<<"\nThe list is empty\n";


       getch(); clrscr();
```

```
            return;
        }
        while ( temp != NULL )
        {
            cout<<temp->data<<" ";
            temp = temp -> next;
        }
        getch();

}

void sll::search(int key)
{
 node *temp;
 int found;
 temp = head;
 if ( temp == NULL )
 {
  cout<<"The Linked List is empty\n";
  getch();
  clrscr();
 }
 found = FALSE;
 while ( temp != NULL && found==FALSE)
 {
  if ( temp->data != key)
    temp = temp -> next;
  else
    found = TRUE;
 }
 if ( found==TRUE )
 {
  cout<<"\nThe Element is present in the list\n";
  getch();
 }
 else
 {
  cout<<"The Element is not present in the list\n";
  getch();
 }
}

/*
----------------------------------------------------------------
        The dele function
----------------------------------------------------------------
*/
```

```
void sll:: dele()
{
      node *temp, *prev ;
      int  key;
      temp=head;
      clrscr();
      cout<<"\nEnter the data of the node you want to delete: ";
      cin>>key;
      while(temp!=NULL)
      {
        if(temp->data==key)//traverse till required node to delete
        break;          //is found
        prev=temp;
        temp=temp->next;
 }
 if(temp==NULL)
 cout<<"\nNode not found";
 else
 {
        if(temp==head) //first node
             head=temp->next;
        else
             prev->next=temp->next; //intermediate or end node
      delete temp;
      cout<<"\nThe Element is deleted\n";
      }

      getch();

}

/*
-------------------------------------------------------------------
        Function to insert at end
-------------------------------------------------------------------
*/
void sll::insert_last()
{
 node *New,*temp;
 cout<<"\nEnter The element which you want to insert";
 cin>>New->data;
 if(head==NULL)
      head=New;
 else
 {
      temp=head;
```

```
      while(temp->next!=NULL)
            temp=temp->next;
      temp->next=New;
      New->next=NULL;
 }
}

/*
---------------------------------------------------------------------
       Function to insert after a node
---------------------------------------------------------------------
*/
void sll:: insert_after()
{
 int key;
 node  *temp,*New;
 New= new node;
 cout<<"\n Enter The element which you want to insert";
 cin>>New->data;
 if(head==NULL)
 {
  head=New;
 }
 else
 {
  cout<<"\n Enter The element after which you want to insert the node";
  cin>>key;
  temp=head;
  do
  {
      if(temp->data==key)
      {
          New->next=temp->next;
          temp->next=New;
          break;
      }
    else
        temp=temp->next;
  }while(temp!=NULL);
 }
}
/*
---------------------------------------------------------------------
Function to insert at the beginning
---------------------------------------------------------------------
*/
```

```
void sll:: insert_head()
{
 node *New,*temp;
 New=new node;
 cout<<"\n Enter The element which you want to insert";
 cin>>New->data;
 if(head==NULL)
        head=New;
 else
 {
  temp=head;
  New->next=temp;
  head=New;
 }
}
/*
-----------------------------------------------------------------------
      The main function
      Input : None
      Output: None
      Parameter Passing Method : None
-----------------------------------------------------------------------
*/
void main()
{
      sll s;
      int choice,val,ch1;
      char ans = 'y';
      do
      {
      clrscr();
      cout<<"\nProgram to Perform Various operations on Linked List";
      cout<<"\n1.Create";
      cout<<"\n2.Display";
      cout<<"\n3.Search";
      cout<<"\n4.Insert an element in a list";
      cout<<"\n5.Delete an element from list";
      cout<<"\n6.Quit";
      cout<<"\nEnter Your Choice ( 1-6) ";
      cin>>choice;
      switch( choice)
       {
            case 1:  s.create();
                     break;

            case 2:  s.display();
                     break;
```

```
        case 3:  cout<<"Enter the element you want to search";
                 cin>>val;
                 s.search(val);
                 break;
        case 4:  clrscr();
                 cout<<"\nThe list is:\n";
                 s.display();
                 cout<<"\nMenu";
                 cout<<"\n1.Insert at beginning\n2.Insert after";
                         cout<<"\n3.Insert at end";
                         cout<<"\nEnter your choice";
                         cin>>ch1;
                         switch(ch1)
                         {
                         case 1:s.insert_head();
                                             break;
                         case 2:s.insert_after();
                                             break;
                         case 3:s.insert_last();
                                             break;
                         default:cout<<"\nInvalid choice";
                         }
                     break;
    case 5: s.dele();
                     break;
    default: cout<<"\nInvalid choice";
    }
    cout<<"\nContinue?";
    cin>>ans;
    }while(ans=='y'||ans=='Y');
    getch();
    return;
}
```

Output

```
Program to Perform Various operations on Linked List
1.Create
2.Display
3.Search
4.Insert an element in a list
5.Delete an element from list
6.Quit
Enter Your Choice ( 1-6) 1

Enter the data :10

 Do you want to enter more elements?(y/n)y
Enter the data :20
```

```
Do you want to enter more elements?(y/n)y
Enter the data :30

Do you want to enter more elements?(y/n)y
Enter the data :40

Do you want to enter more elements?(y/n)y
Enter the data :50

Do you want to enter more elements?(y/n)n
The Singly Linked List is created
Continue?
Program to Perform Various operations on Linked List
1.Create
2.Display
3.Search
4.Insert an element in a list
5.Delete an element from list
6.Quit
Enter Your Choice ( 1-6) 2
10 20 30 40 50
Continue?

Program to Perform Various operations on Linked List
1.Create
2.Display
3.Search
4.Insert an element in a list
5.Delete an element from list
6.Quit
Enter Your Choice ( 1-6) 3
Enter the element you want to search 30

The Element is present in the list
```

4.6.1 Programming Examples based on Linked List Operations

Example 4.6.1 *Given a singly linked list, write a function swap to swap every two nodes e.g. 1->2->3->4->5->6 should become 2->1->4->3->6->5.*

Solution : Assumption

1. The linked is created using create routine.
2. The display routine is written to display the nodes of the linked list.

3. The swap routine for swapping two nodes is as follows -

```
void swap(node **head)
{

  // If linked list is empty or there is only one node in list
  if (*head == NULL || (*head)->next == NULL)
     return;

  node *prev = *head;//maintaining the previous node
  node *current = (*head)->next;//and current node.
     //Thus two nodes are focused at a time

  *head = current;  // Change head before proceeeding

  // Traverse the list
  while (true)
  {
     node *temp = current->next;
     current->next = prev; // Change next of current as previous node


     if (temp == NULL || temp->next == NULL)
     {
        prev->next = temp;
        break;
     }

     // Change next of previous to next of temp
     prev->next = temp->next;

     // Update previous and current nodes
     prev = temp;
     current = prev->next;
  }
}
```

Example 4.6.2 *Write a C program to implement insertion to the immediate left of kth node in singly linked list.*

Solution :

```
#include<iostream.h>
//using namespace std;
#define TRUE 1
#define FALSE 0
// class definition

class sll
```

```
{
private:
        struct node
        {
                int data;
                structnode  *next;
        }*head;
public:
        sll();
        void create();
        void display();
        void insert(int k);
        ~sll();
};

/*
--------------------------------------------------------------------------------
The  Constructor defined
--------------------------------------------------------------------------------
*/
sll::sll()
{
        head = NULL;//initialize head to NULL
}
/*
--------------------------------------------------------------------------------
The Destructor defined
--------------------------------------------------------------------------------
*/
sll::~sll()
{
        node *temp, *temp1;
        temp = head->next;
        delete head;
        while (temp != NULL) //free the memory allocated
        {
                temp1 = temp->next;
                delete temp;
                temp = temp1;
        }
}
/*
--------------------------------------------------------------------------------
The Create function
--------------------------------------------------------------------------------
*/
void sll::create()
```

```
{
    node *temp, *New;
    temp = NULL;
    int val, flag;
    char ans = 'y';
    flag = TRUE;
    do
    {
        cout << "\nEnter the data :";
        cin >> val;
        // allocate memory to new node
        New = new node;
        if (New == NULL)
            cout << "Unable to allocate memory\n";
        New-> data = val;
        New-> next = NULL;
        if (flag == TRUE) // Executed only for the first time
        {
            head = New;
            temp = head;
            flag = FALSE;
        }
        else
        {
            /*temp last keeps track of the most recently
            created node*/
            temp->next = New;
            temp = New;
        }
        cout << "\n Do you want to enter more elements?(y/n)";
        cin >> ans;
    } while (ans == 'y' || ans == 'Y');
    cout << "\nThe Singly Linked List is created\n";

}

/*
------------------------------------------------------------------
The display function
------------------------------------------------------------------
*/
void sll::display()
{
    node *temp;
    temp = head;
    if (temp == NULL)
```

```
	{
		cout << "\nThe list is empty\n";
		return;
	}
	while (temp != NULL)
	{
		cout << temp->data << " ";
		temp = temp -> next;
	}
}

void sll::insert(int k)
{
	node *temp,*prev_node,*New;
	int count;
	temp = head;
	prev_node = head;
	count = 1;
	if (temp == NULL)
	{
		cout << "The Linked List is empty\n";
	}
	while (temp != NULL)
	{
		if(count==k)
			break;
		else
		{
		//keeping track of previous node
			prev_node = temp;
			temp = temp->next;
			count++;
		}
	}
	if (count==k)
	{
		New = new node;
		cout << "\n Enter the new node: ";
		cin >> New->data;
		prev_node->next = New;
		New->next = temp;
		cout << "\n The element is inserted in the linked list!!!";
	}
	else
	{
		cout << "The Element is not present in the list\n";
```

```
	}
}

void main()
{
	sll s;
	int choice, val;
	char ans = 'y';
	do
	{
		cout << "\nProgram to Perform Various operations on Linked List";
		cout << "\n1.Create";
		cout << "\n2.Display";
		cout << "\n3.Insert left to Kth node ";
		cout << "\n4.Quit";
		cout << "\nEnter Your Choice ( 1-4) ";
		cin >> choice;
		switch (choice)
		{
		case 1:		s.create();
			break;
		case 2:		s.display();
			break;
		case 3:		cout << "Enter the number of a node";
			cin >> val;
			s.insert(val);
			break;
		default: cout << "\nInvalid choice";
		}
		cout << "\nContinue?";
		cin >> ans;
	} while (ans == 'y' || ans == 'Y');
	return;
}
```

Example 4.6.3 *Given an ordered linked list whose node represented by 'key' as information and next as 'link' field. Write C program to implement deleting number of nodes(consecutive) whose 'key' values are greater than or equal to 'Kmin' and less than 'Kmax'*

Solution :

i) The Pseudo code for deleting elements less than or equal to Kmax is as follows -

```
void sll::delet()
{
	node *temp,*NextNode;
	int Kmax;
	temp = head;
```

```
    cout << "\n Enter the node value as Kmin";
    cin >> Kmax;
    if (temp == NULL)
    {
        cout << "The Linked List is empty\n";
    }
    while (temp != NULL)
    {
        if (Kmax == temp->data)
            break;
        else
        {
            NextNode = temp->next;
            temp->next = NULL;
            delete(temp);
            temp = NextNode;
        }
    }
    NextNode = temp->next;
    temp->next = NULL;
    delete(temp);
    temp = NextNode;
    head = temp;
}
```

ii) The Pseudo code for deleting elements greater than or equal to Kmin is as follows -

```
void sll::delet()
{
    node *temp,*NextNode;
    int Kmin;
    temp = head;
    cout << "\n Enter the node value as Kmin";
    cin >> Kmin;
    if (temp == NULL)
    {
        cout << "The Linked List is empty\n";
    }
    while(Kmin != temp->data)
    {
        if(Kmin==temp->data)
            break;
        else
        {
            temp = temp->next;
        }
    }
    while (temp != NULL)
```

```
    {
        NextNode = temp->next;
        temp->next = NULL;
        delete(temp);
        temp = NextNode;
    }
}
```

Example 4.6.4 *Write an algorithm to count the number of nodes between given two nodes in a linked list.*

Solution :

```
void count_between_nodes(node *temp1, node *temp2)
{
 int count=0;
 //temp1 represents the starting node
 //temp2 represents the end node
 //we have to count number of nodes between temp1 and temp2
 while(temp1->next!=temp2)
  count++;
 printf("\n Total number of nodes between % and %d is %d ", temp1->data, temp2->data,
count);
}
```

Example 4.6.5 *Write an algorithm to find the location of an element in the given linked list. Is the binary search will be suitable for this search ? Explain the reason.*

Solution :

```
void search_element(node *head,int key)
 {
  node *Temp;
  int count=1;
  //head is a starting node of the linked list
  //key is the element that is to be searched in the linked list.
  Temp=head;
   while(Temp->next!=NULL)
   {
    if(temp->data==key)
    {
      printf("\n The element is present at location %d",count);
      break;
    }
    count++;
    Temp=Temp->next;
   }
}
```

The binary search can be suitable for this algorithm only if the elements in the linked list are arranged in sorted order. Otherwise this method will not be suitable because sorting the linked list is not efficient as it requires the swapping of the pointers.

Example 4.6.6 *Write a C++ function to perform the merging of two linked lists.*

Solution :

```
node *merge(node *temp1,node *temp2)
{
    node *prev_node1,*next_node2,*head;
    if(temp1==NULL)
    {
        temp1=temp2;
        head=temp2;
    }
if(temp1->data<temp2->data)
        head=temp1;
else
        head=temp2;
while(temp1!=NULL && temp2!=NULL)
{
/*while data of 1st list is smaller then traverse*/
        while((temp1->data<temp2->data) && (temp1!=NULL))
        {
            prev_node1=temp1; /*store prev node of Sll1 */
            temp1=temp1->next;
        }
        if(temp1==NULL)
            break;
    /*when temp1's data>temp1 it will come out
    Of while loop so adjust links with temp1's prev node*/
        prev_node1->next=temp2;
        next_node2=temp2->next; /*store next node of Sll2*/
        temp2->next=temp1;
        temp1=temp2;
        temp2=next_node2;
}
if(temp1==NULL&&temp2!=NULL) /*attach rem nodes of Sll2*/
{
        while(temp2!=NULL)
        {
            prev_node1->next=temp2;
            prev_node1=temp2;
            temp2=temp2->next;
        }
}
return head;
}
```

Example 4.6.7 *Write a C function to concatenate two singly linked list.*

Solution :

```
void concat(node *head1,node *head2)
{
      node *temp1,*temp2;
      temp1=head1;
      temp2=head2;
      while(temp1->next!=NULL)
            temp1=temp1->next;/*searching end of first list*/
      temp1->next=temp2;/*attaching head of the second list*/
      printf("\n The concatenated list is ...\n");
      temp1=head1;
      while(temp1!=NULL)
      { /*printing the concatenated list*/
            printf(" %d",temp1->Data);
            temp1=temp1->next;
      }
}
```

Example 4.6.8 *Write a C++ code to recursive routine to erase a linked list (delete all node from the linked list).*

Solution :

```
node sll::*list_free(struct node *temp)
{
 if(temp->next!=NULL)
 {
      temp1=temp->next;/*temp1 is declared globally*/
      temp->next=NULL;
      delete temp;
      list_free(temp1);/*recursive call*/
 }
 temp=NULL;
 return temp;
}
```

Example 4.6.9 *Write a program in C++ to return the position of an element X in a list L.*

Solution : The routine is as given below -

```
Return_position(node *head,int key)
{
  /* head represents the starting node of the List*/
 /* key represents the element X in the list*/
 int count=0;
 node *temp;
 temp=head;
 while(temp->data!=key)&&(temp!=NULL)
 {
```

```
   temp=temp->next;
   count=count+1;
 }
 if(temp->data==key)
   return count;
else if(temp==NULL)
   return -1; /* -1 indicates that the element X is not present in the list*/
}
```

4.7 Types of Linked List

There are four types of linked list.

1. Singly linked list : It is called singly linked list because it contains only **one link** which points to the next node. The very first node is called **head** or **first.**

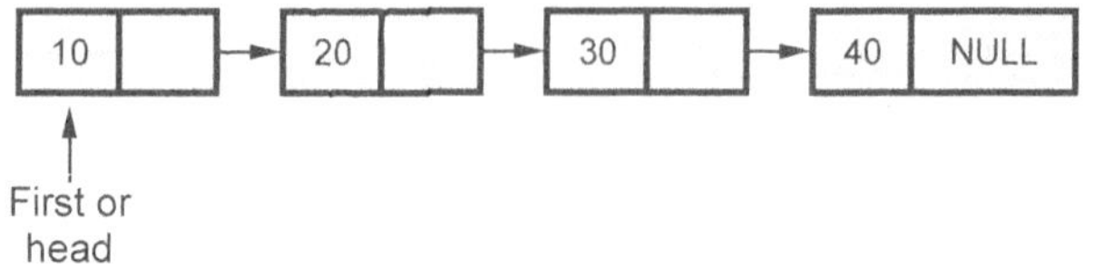

2. Singly circular linked list : In this type of linked list the next link of the last node points to the first node. Thus the overall structure looks circular. Following figure represents this type of linked list.

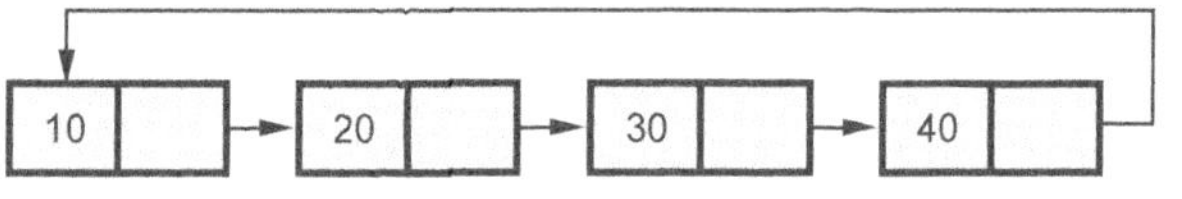

3. Doubly linear list : In this type of linked list there are two pointers associated with each node. The two pointer are - **next** and **previous.** As the name suggests the next pointer points to the next node and the previous pointer points to the previous node.

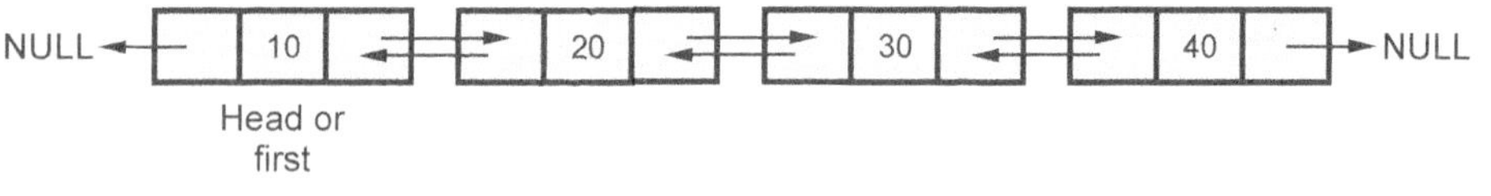

4. Doubly circular linked list : In this type of linked list there are two pointers **next** and **previous** to each node and the next pointer of last node points to the first node and previous pointer of the first node points to the last node making the structure circular.

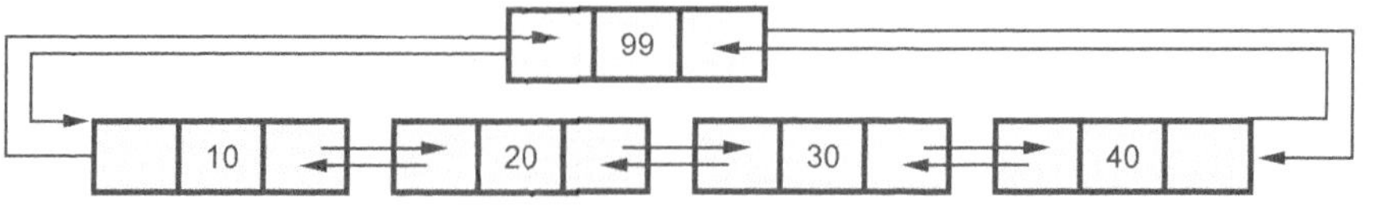

4.8 Doubly Linked List

The typical structure of each node in doubly linked list is like this.

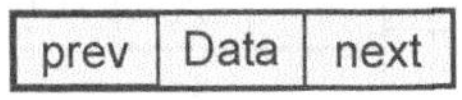

Fig. 4.8.1

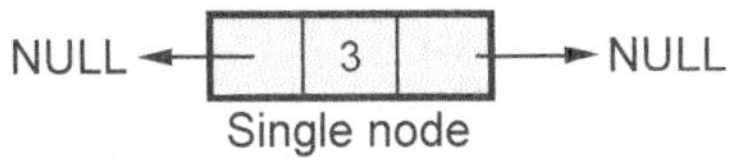

'C++' structure of doubly linked list :

```
typedef struct node
{
    int Data;
    struct node *prev;
    struct node *next;
}
```

The linked representation of a doubly linked list is

Thus the doubly linked list can traverse in both the directions, forward as well as backwards.

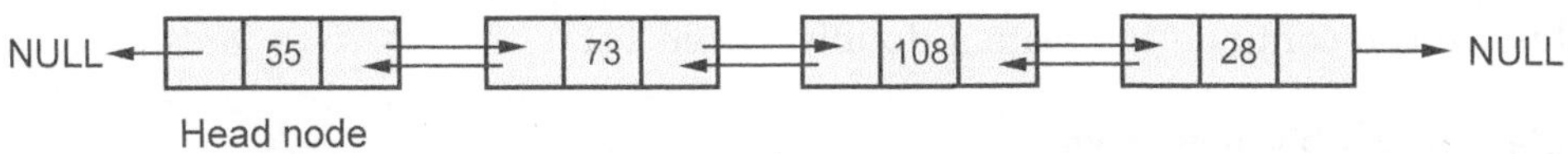

Logic for doubly linked list

In doubly linked list there are following operations

1. Create 2. Display 3. Insert 4. Delete

The node in doubly linked list (DLL) will look like this

4.8.1 Operations on Doubly Linked List

1. Creation of node

Initially set new node as

For the first time flag = 0

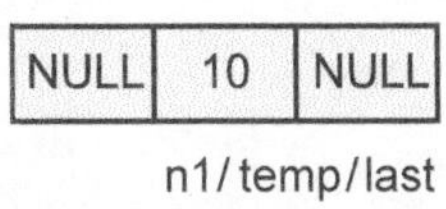


```
temp = n1;
last = temp;
```

Now set flag = 1, if we want to create more node then -

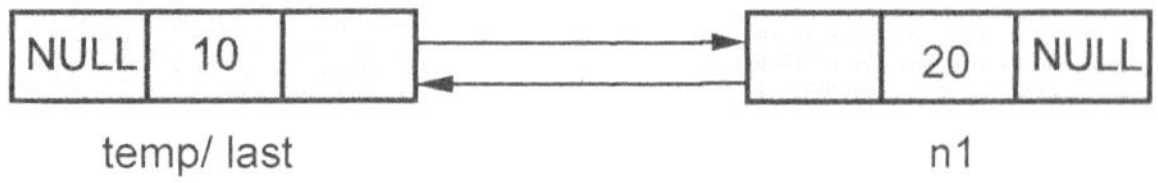

last → next = n1
n1 → prev = last

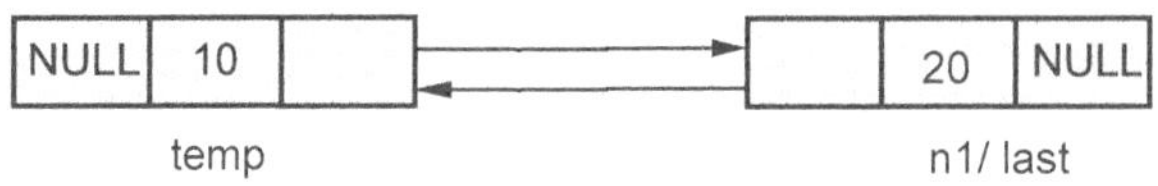

last = n1

If we want to attach node 30 then

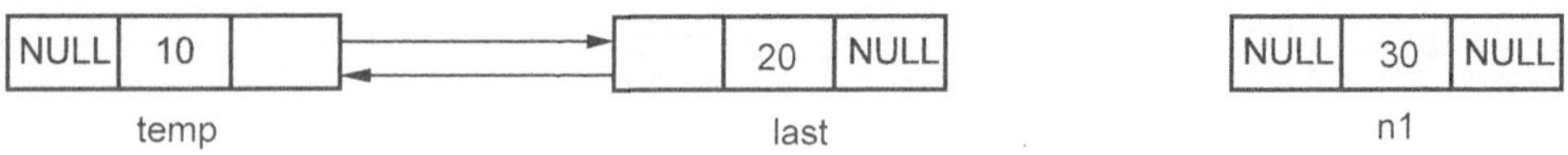

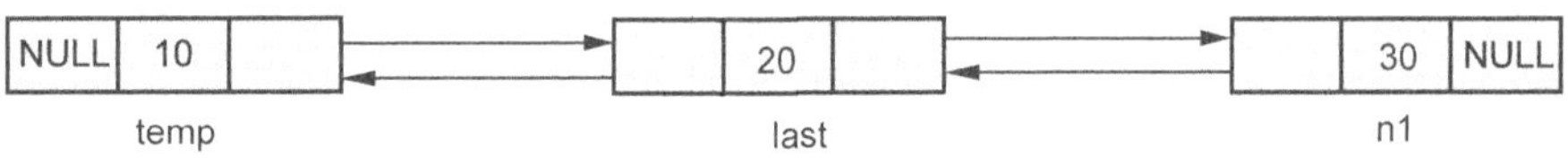

last → next = n1
n1 → prev = last

This we can continue to create a doubly linked list.

2. Display of Doubly linked list

We assign **head** node address to **temp** node.

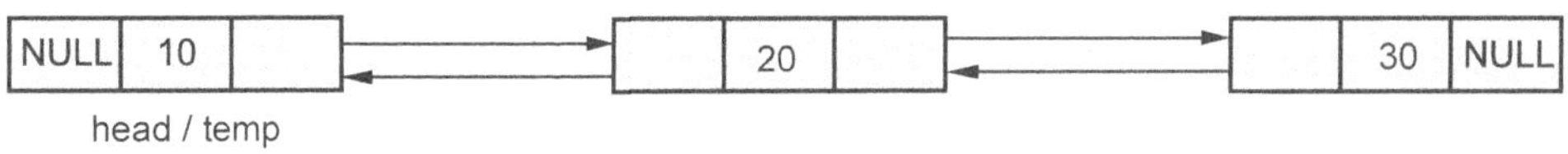


```
while (temp → next ! = NULL)
{
    " display data at temp node.
    temp = temp → next
}
```

This will display **10 20 30** as a doubly linked.

3. Deletion of a node in doubly linked list

Consider,

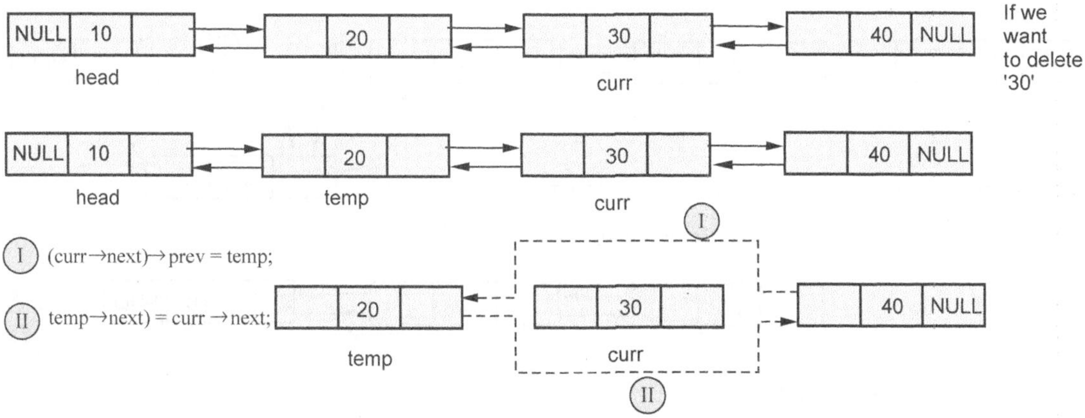

Then **delete curr.**

4. Insertion of a node

Consider a list

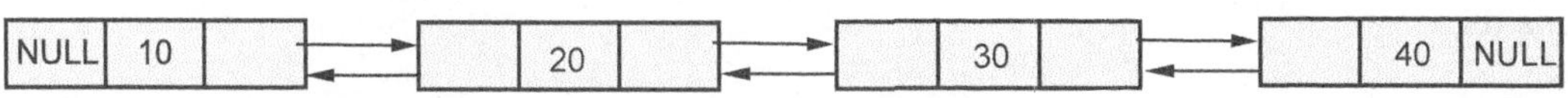

Suppose we want to insert 31 after 30 then first search for node 30 call it as **temp** node. Then create a node containing value 31.

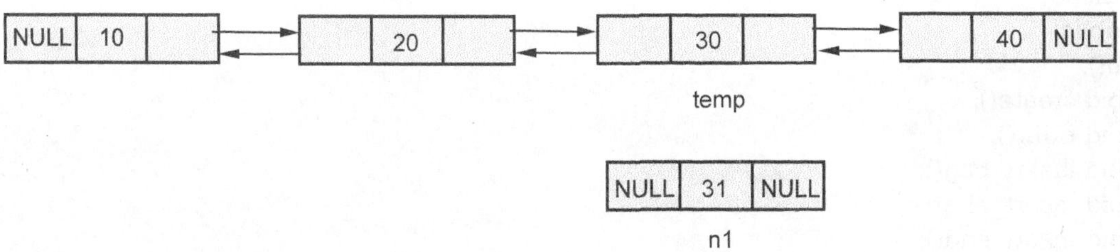

Then

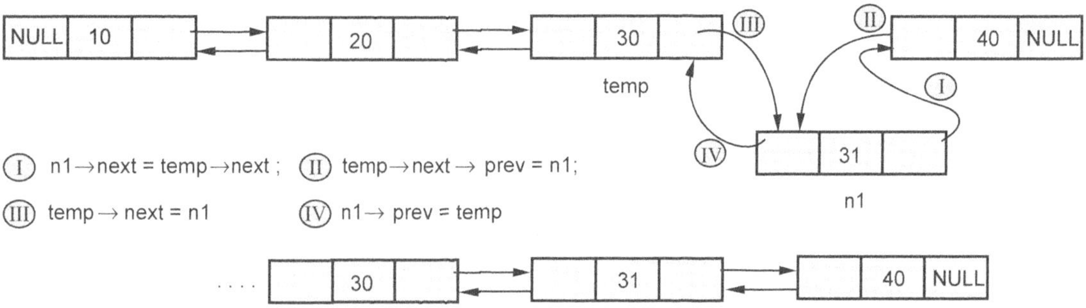

Thus **"Node inserted"**.

```
/**********************************************************************
 Demonstration Program to perform various operations such as insertion,
 deletion,finding the lenghth of the doublly linked list.
**********************************************************************/

// List of include files
#include<iostream.h>
#include <conio.h>
// class
class dll
{
 private:
 struct node
 {
     int Data;
     struct  node *next;
     struct  node *prev;
 }*head;
 public:
 dll();
 void create();
 void print();
 void insert_beg();
 void insert_after();
 void insert_end();
 void del();
 int length();
 ~dll();
};
```

```
/*
-------------------------------------------------------------------
The Constructor defined
-------------------------------------------------------------------
*/
 dll::dll()
 {
  head=NULL;
 }

/*
-------------------------------------------------------------------
The destructor defined
-------------------------------------------------------------------
*/
dll::~dll()
{
 node *temp,*temp1; //free the memory
 temp=head;
 while(temp!=NULL)
 {
    temp1=temp->next;
    delete temp;
    temp=temp1;
 }
}
/*
-------------------------------------------------------------------
      The Create function
-------------------------------------------------------------------
*/
void dll :: create()
{
      // Local declarations here
      node  *n1,*last,*temp;
      char ans ='y';
      int flag=0;
      int val;
      do
      {
            cout<<"\nEnter the data :";
            cin>>val;

            // allocate new node
            n1 = new node;
            if ( n1 == NULL )
```

```
            cout<<"Unable to allocate memory\n";
        n1 -> Data  = val ;
        n1 -> next = NULL;
        n1 -> prev = NULL;
        if (flag==0) // Executed only for the first time
        {
            temp=n1;
            last=temp;
            flag=1;
        }
        else
        {
            // last keeps track of the most recently
            // created node

            last->next=n1;
            n1->prev=last;
            last=n1;
        }
        cout<<"\n\nEnter more?";
        ans = getche();
    }while(ans=='y's||ans=='Y');
    cout<<"\nThe List is created\n";
    head=temp;
    getch();
}

/*
----------------------------------------------------------------------
    The length function
    Output:Returns number of items in list
    Calls : None
----------------------------------------------------------------------
*/

int dll ::length()
{
    node *curr ;
    int  count;

    count = 0;
    curr = head;
    if ( curr == NULL )
    {
        cout<<"The list is empty\n";
        getch();
        return 0;
```

```
    }
    while ( curr != NULL )
    {
        count++;
        curr = curr -> next; // traverse till end
    }
    getch();
    return count;
}

/*
-------------------------------------------------------------------
    The print function
    Output:None, Displays data
    Calls : None
-------------------------------------------------------------------
*/
void dll ::print()
{
    node *temp ;

    temp = head;
    if ( temp == NULL )
    {
        cout<<"\nThe list is empty\n";
        getch(); clrscr();
        return;
    }
    else
    {
    cout<<"\nThe list is:";
    while(temp != NULL)
    {
        cout<<temp->Data<<" ";
        temp = temp -> next;
    }
    }
    getch();

}

/*
-------------------------------------------------------------------
    The del function
    Output:deletes an item from the list
-------------------------------------------------------------------
*/
```

```
void dll:: del()
{
	node *curr, *temp;
	int  data;
	curr=head;
	cout<<"\nEnter the data of the node you want to delete: ";
	cin>>data;
	while(curr!=NULL)
	{
	 if(curr->Data==data) //traverse till the required node to delete
	 break;              //is found
	 curr=curr->next;
  }
  if(curr==NULL)
  cout<<"\nNode not found";
  else
  {
	 if(curr==head)
	 {
		if(head->next==NULL&&head->prev==NULL)//only one node
				head=NULL;
		else
		{
		head=curr->next;// first node
		head->prev=NULL;
		}
	 }
	 else
	 {
		temp=curr->prev; //intermediate or end node
		if(curr->next!=NULL)
		(curr->next)->prev=temp;
		temp->next=curr->next;
	 }
		delete curr; //free memory
		cout<<"\nThe item is deleted\n";
	}

	getch();

}

/*-------------------------------------------------------------------
	Function to insert at end
-------------------------------------------------------------------*/
void dll::insert_end()
```

```
{
 node *temp,*n1;
 int val,flag=0;
 cout<<"\nEnter the data of the new node to insert";
 cin>>val;
 temp=head;
 if(temp==NULL)
  flag=1;
 else
 {
  while(temp->next!=NULL)  // traverse till end
       temp=temp->next;
 }

 // allocate new node
 n1 = new node;
 if ( n1 == NULL )
        cout<<"\nUnable to allocate memory\n";
  n1-> Data  = val ;
  n1 -> next = NULL;
  n1 -> prev = NULL;
  if(flag==0)
  {
  temp->next=n1;  // attach at end
  n1->prev=temp;
  }
  else
  head=n1;       //if list empty make this node as head node
  cout<<"\nNode inserted";
}


/*--------------------------------------------------------------------
        Function to insert after a node
--------------------------------------------------------------------*/
void dll:: insert_after()
{
 node *temp,*n1;
 int val,val1;
 cout<<"\nEnter the data of the new node to insert";
 cin>>val;
 cout<<"\nEnter the data of the node after which to insert";
 cin>>val1;
 temp=head;
 while(temp!=NULL)
 {
  if(temp->Data==val1) //traverse till the required node after which to insert
```

```
        break;
    temp=temp->next;
  }
  if(temp!=NULL)
  {
  /* allocate new node */
  n1 = new node;
  if ( n1 == NULL )
        cout<<"Unable to allocate memory\n";
    n1 -> Data  = val ;
    n1 -> next = NULL;
    n1 -> prev = NULL;
    /* after temp attach*/
    n1->next=temp->next;
    temp->next->prev=n1;
    temp->next=n1;
    n1->prev=temp;
    cout<<"\nNode inserted";
  }
  else
  cout<<"\nNode after which to insert not found";
}
/* -----------------------------------------------------------------
Function to insert at the beginning
-------------------------------------------------------------------*/

void dll:: insert_beg()
{
  node *temp,*n1;
  int data;

  cout<<"\nEnter the data of the new node to insert";
  cin>>data;

  /* allocate new node */
  n1 = new node;
  if ( n1 == NULL )
  cout<<"Unable to allocate memory\n";
   n1 -> Data  = data ;
   n1 -> next = NULL;
   n1 -> prev = NULL;
  if(head)
  {
   n1->next=head; //attach before head
   head->prev=n1;
  }
  head=n1; //make this node as head
```

```
 cout<<"\nNode inserted";
}


/*
-------------------------------------------------------------------
      The main function
      Input : None
      Output: None
      Parameter Passing Method : None
-------------------------------------------------------------------
*/
void main()
{
      dll d;
      int ch,ch1,cnt;
      char ans = 'y';
      do
      {
      clrscr();
      cout<<"\n"<<"MENU";
      cout<<"\n1.Create\n2.Display\n3.Insert\n4.Delete\n5.Length";
      cout<<"\nEnter ur choice:";
      cin>>ch;
      switch(ch)
      {
      case 1: d.create();
              break;
      case 2: d.print();
               break;
      case 3: clrscr();
           d.print();
           cout<<"\nMenu";
           cout<<"\n1.Insert at beginning\n2.Insert after";
           cout<<"\n3.Insert at end";
           cout<<"\nEnter your choice";
           cin>>ch1;
           switch(ch1)
           {
           case 1: d.insert_beg();
                 d.print();
                 break;
           case 2: d.insert_after();
                  d.print();
                  break;
           case 3: d.insert_end();
```

```
                d.print();
                break;
        default:cout<<"\nInvalid choice";
            }
          break;
    case 4: d.print();
                d.del();
                d.print();
                break;
    case 5: cnt=d.length();
                cout<<"The length is: "<<cnt;
                break;
    default: cout<<"\nInvalid choice";
    }
    cout<<"\n Do You Want To Continue?";
    cin>>ans;
    }while(ans=='y'||ans=='Y');
    getch();
    return;
}
```

Output

```
MENU
1.Create
2.Display
3.Insert
4.Delete
5.Length
Enter ur choice:1
Enter the data :1

Enter more?y
Enter the data :2

Enter more?y
Enter the data :3

Enter more?y
Enter the data :4

Enter more?y
Enter the data :5

Enter more?n
The List is created
```

```
 Do You Want To Continue?

MENU
1.Create
2.Display
3.Insert
4.Delete
5.Length
Enter ur choice:2

The list is:1  2  3  4  5
 Do You Want To Continue?y
```

4.8.2 Comparison between Singly and Doubly Linked List

Sr. No.	Singly Linked List	Doubly Linked List
1.	Singly linked list is a collection of nodes and each node is having one data field and next link field. For example : 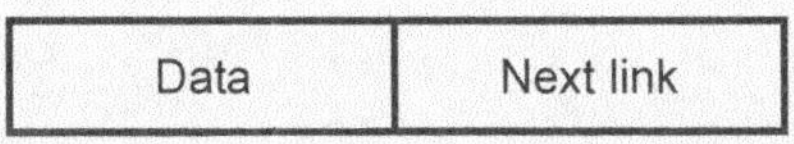	Doubly linked list is a collection of nodes and each node is having one data field, one previous link field and one next link field. For example : 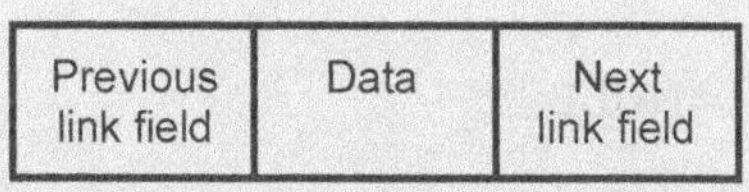
2.	The elements can be accessed using next link.	The elements can be accessed using both previous link as well as next link.
3.	No extra field is required; hence node takes less memory in SLL.	One field is required to store previous link hence node takes more memory in DLL.
4.	Less efficient access to elements.	More efficient access to elements.

Example 4.8.1 *Write a method in C++ to join two doubly linked lists into a single doubly linked list. In a join elements of second list are appended to the end of first list.*

Solution :

```
/*******************************************************************
Program to join two doubly linked list
*******************************************************************/

// List of include files

#include<iostream.h>
```

```
#include <conio.h>
// class defination
class dll
{
 private:
 struct node
 {
      int Data;
      structnode  *next;
      structnode  *prev;
 }*head;
 public:
 dll();
 void create();
 void print();
 void join(dll,dll);
};

/*
-------------------------------------------------------------------
 Constructor
-------------------------------------------------------------------
*/
dll::dll()
{
 head=NULL;
}
/*
------------------------------------------------------------------------
      The Create function
------------------------------------------------------------------------
*/
void dll :: create()
{
      node *New,last,*temp;
      int num,flag=0;
      char ans;
      // flag to indicate whether a new node
       //is created for the first time or not
      do
      {
            cout<<"\n Enter the Element :";
            cin>>num;
            /* allocate new node */
            New =new node;
            New -> Data  = num;
            New -> next = NULL;
```

```
            New->prev=NULL;
            if ( flag == 0 )
            {
             head = New; // First node is created
             temp=New;
             flag=1;
            }
            else
            {
               temp->next=New;//remaining nodes are created
               New->prev=temp;
               temp=New;
            }
            cout<<"\n Do You Want to insert More Elements?";
            ans=getch();
        }while(ans=='y');
        cout<<"\n The List Is Created";
}

/*
-------------------------------------------------------------------
        The print function
-------------------------------------------------------------------
*/
void dll ::print()
{
        node *temp ;
        temp = head;
        if ( temp == NULL )
        {
           cout<<"\nThe list is empty\n";
           getch(); clrscr();
           return;
        }
        else
        {
        cout<<"\nThe list is:";
        while(temp != NULL)
        {
           cout<<temp->Data<<" ";
           temp = temp -> next;
        }
        }
        getch();
}
```

```
/*
-------------------------------------------------------------------
The join Function
-------------------------------------------------------------------
*/
void dll::join(dll d1,dll d2)
{
 node *temp1,*temp2,*prev_node1,*next_node2;
 temp1=d1.head;
 temp2=d2.head;
 if(temp1==NULL)
 temp1=temp2;
 while(temp1->next!=NULL)
 {
  temp1=temp1->next;//reaching at the end of first DLL
 }
 temp1->next=temp2;

}
/*
----------------------------------------------------------------------
      The main function
----------------------------------------------------------------------
*/
void main()
{
     dll d1,d2;
     int ch,ch1,cnt;
     char ans = 'y';
     do
     {
       clrscr();
       cout<<"\nEnter the data for 1 st Doubly Linked List ";
       d1.create();
       d1.print();
       cout<<"\nEnter the data for 2nd Doubly Linked List ";
       d2.create();
       d2.print();
       d1.join(d1,d2);
       d1.print();
       cout<<"\nDo you want to Continue?";
       cin>>ans;
       }while(ans=='y'||ans=='Y');
       return;
}
```

Output

```
Enter the data for 1 st Doubly Linked List
Enter the Element :10

Do You Want to insert More Elements?
Enter the Element :20

Do You Want to insert More Elements?
Enter the Element :30

Do You Want to insert More Elements?
The List Is Created
The list is:10  20  30
Enter the data for 2nd Doubly Linked List
Enter the Element :40

Do You Want to insert More Elements?
Enter the Element :50

Do You Want to insert More Elements?
The List Is Created
The list is:40  50
The list is:10  20  30  40  50
```

Review Questions

1. *Explain the representation of doubly linked list.*
2. *Write about operations performed on doubly linked list.*
3. *List and Explain doubly linked list operations.*

Advantages of Doubly Linked List over Singly Linked List

- The doubly linked list has two pointer fields. One field is previous link field and another is next link field.
- Because of these two pointer fields we can access any node efficiently whereas in singly linked list only one pointer field is there which stores forward pointer, which makes accessing of any node difficult one.

4.9 Circular Linked List

The circular linked list is as shown below -

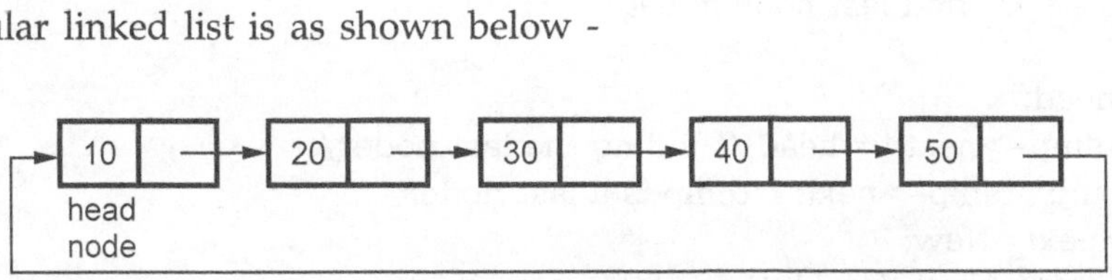

or

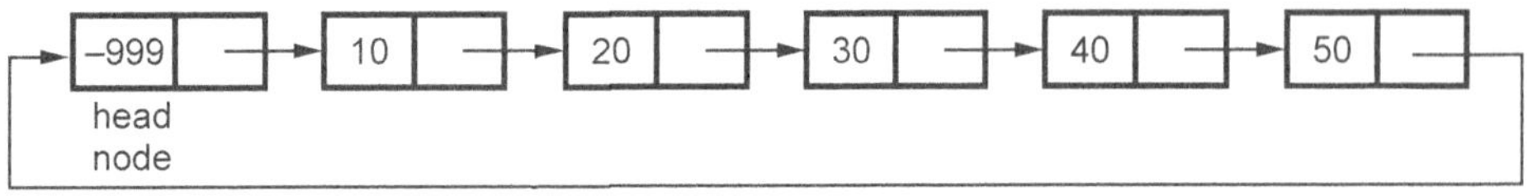

The Circular Linked List (CLL) is similar to singly linked list except that the last node's next pointer points to first node.

Various operations that can be performed on circular linked list are,

1. Creation of circular linked list.
2. Insertion of a node in circular linked list.
3. Deletion of any node from linked list.
4. Display of circular linked list.

We will see each operation along with some example.

1. Creation of circular linked list

```
void sll ::Create()
{
 char ans;
 int flag=1;
 node *New,*temp;
 clrscr();
 do
 {
      New = new node;
      New->next=NULL;
      cout<<"\n\n\n\tEnter The Element\n";
      cin>>New->data;
      if(flag==1)    /*flag for setting the starting node*/
      {
           head = New;
           New->next=head;      Single node in the Circular list
           flag=0;/*reset flag*/
      }
      else             /* find last node in list */
      {
       temp=head;
       while (temp->next != head)/*finding the last node*/
            temp=temp->next; /*temp is a last node*/
       temp->next=New;
       New->next=head; /*each time making the list
```

```
            circular*/
    }
    cout<<"\n Do you want to enter more nodes?(y/n)";
    ans=getch();
    }while(ans=='y'||ans=='Y');
}
```

Initially we will allocate memory for **New** node using a function **get_node()** . There is one variable **flag** whose purpose is to check whether first node is created or not. That means flag is 1 (set) then first node is not created. Therefore after creation of first node we have to reset the flag (making flag = 0).

Initially,

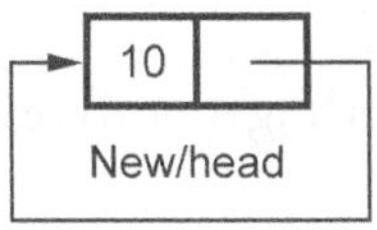

Suppose we have taken element '10' the flag = 1,

```
head = New;
New ← next = head;
flag = 0;
```

Here variable **head** indicates starting node.

Now as flag = 0, we can further create the nodes and attach them as follows.

When we have taken element '20'

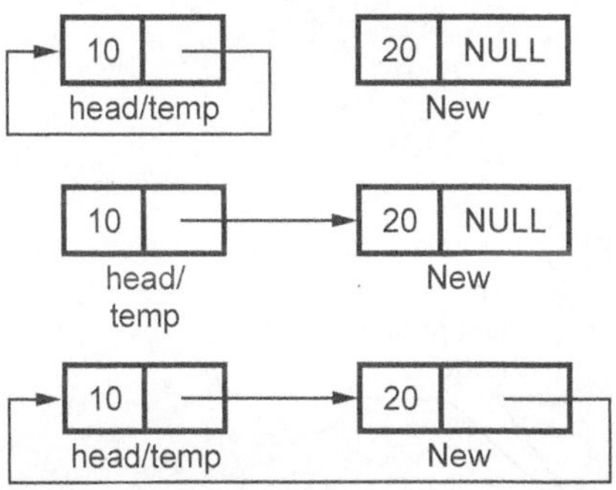

temp = head;
when temp → next = head;

temp → next = New;

New → next = head;

If we want to insert 30 then

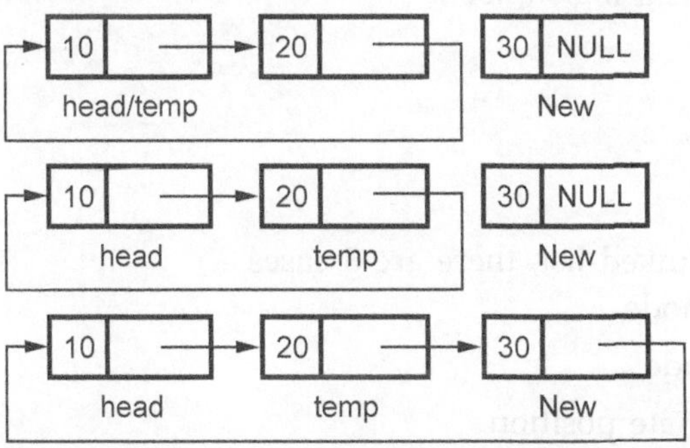

As temp → next ! = head;
temp = temp → next;

As temp → next = head;

temp → next = New;
New → next = head;

If we want to insert 40 then

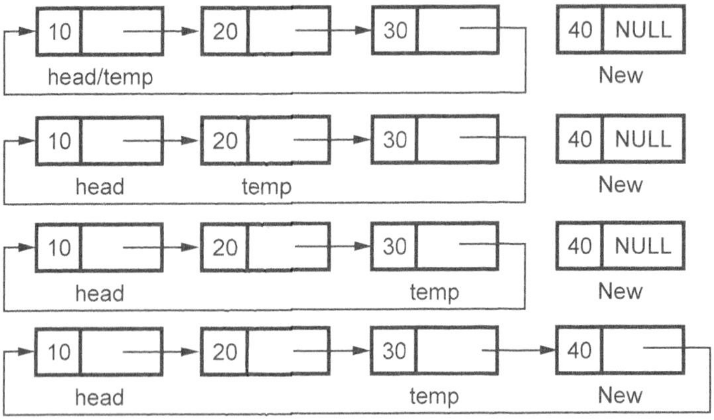

Thus we can create a circular linked list by inserting one more element 50. It is as shown below -

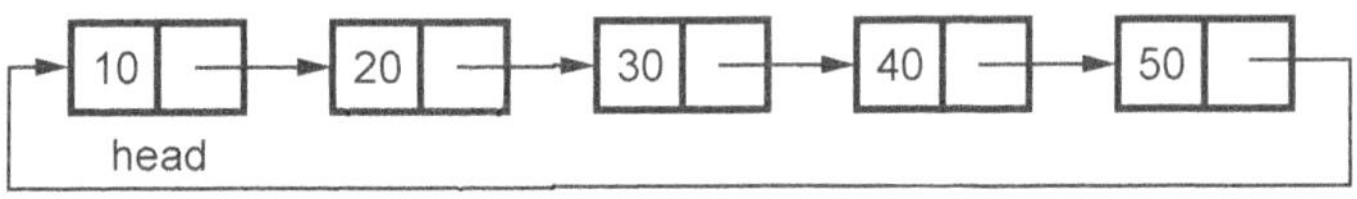

2. Display of Circular linked list

```
void sll::Display()
{
    node *temp;
    temp = head;
    if(temp == NULL)
     cout<<"\n Sorry ,The List Is Empty\n";
    else
    {
     do
     {
          cout<<"\t"<<temp->data;
          temp = temp->next;
     }while(temp != head);/*Circular linked list*/
    }
    getch();
}
```

The next node of last node is head node

3. Insertion of circular linked list

While inserting a node in the linked list, there are 3 cases –

a) inserting a node as a head node

b) inserting a node as a last node

c) inserting a node at intermediate position

The functions for these cases is as given below –

```
void sll::insert_head()
{
 node *New,*temp;
 New=new node;
 New->next=NULL;
 cout<<"\n Enter The element which you want to insert ";
 cin>>New->data;
 if(head==NULL)
       head=New;
 else
 {
            temp=head;
            while(temp->next!=head)
                   temp=temp->next;
            temp->next=New;
            New->next=head;
            head=New;
            cout<<"\n The node is inserted!";
 }
}
/*Insertion of node at last position*/
void sll::insert_last()
{
      node *New,*temp;
      New=new node;
      New->next=NULL;
      cout<<"\n Enter The element which you want to insert ";
      cin>>New->data;
      if(head==NULL)
             head=New;
      else
      {
       temp=head;
       while(temp->next!=head)
                    temp=temp->next;
       temp->next=New;
       New->next=head;
       cout<<"\n The node is inserted!";
      }
}
void sll::insert_after()
{
 int key;
 node *New,*temp;
 New= new node;
 New->next=NULL;
```

```
    cout<<"\n Enter The element which you want to insert ";
    cin>>New->data;
    if(head==NULL)
    {
      head=New;
    }
    else
    {
        cout<<"\n Enter The element after which you want to insert the node ";
        cin>>key;
        temp=head;
        do
        {
            if(temp->data==key)
            {
                New->next=temp->next;
                temp->next=New;
                cout<<"\n The node is inserted";
                return;
            }
            else
                temp=temp->next;
        }while(temp!=head);
    }
}
```

Suppose linked list is already created as -

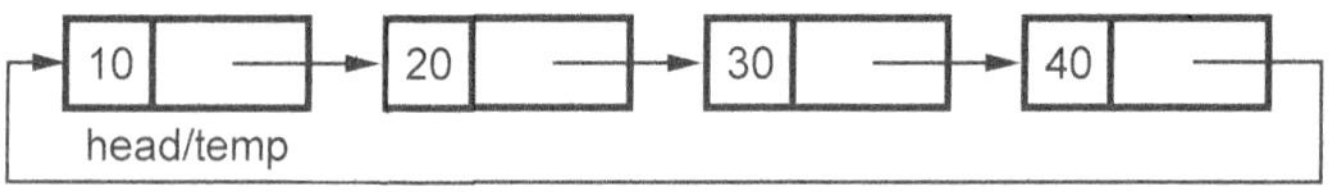

If we want to insert a **New** node as a head node then,

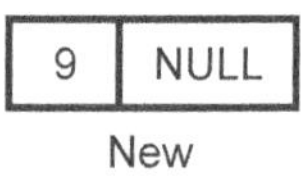

Then

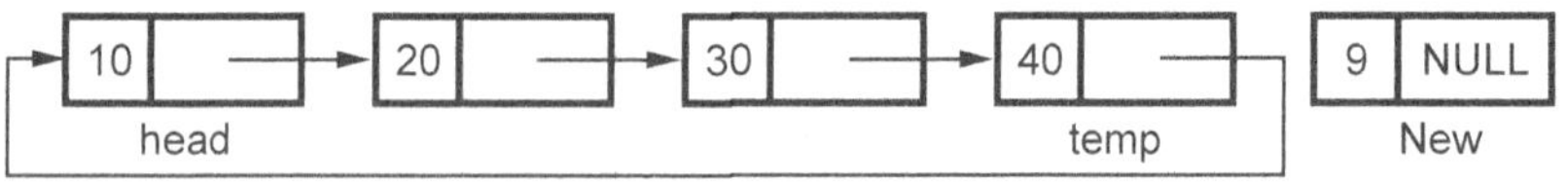

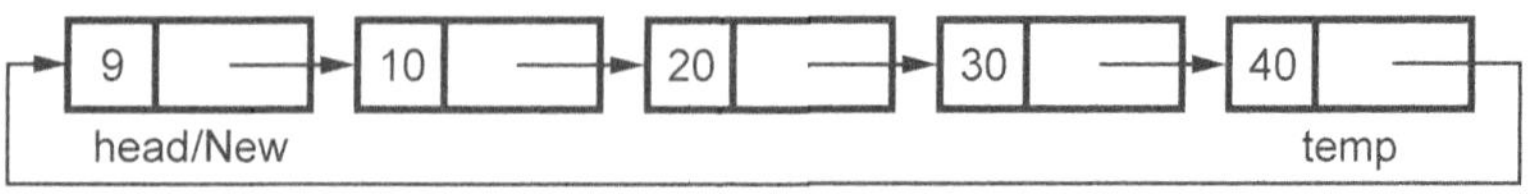

temp → next = New;
New → next = head;
head = New;

If we want to insert a New node as a last node consider a linked list

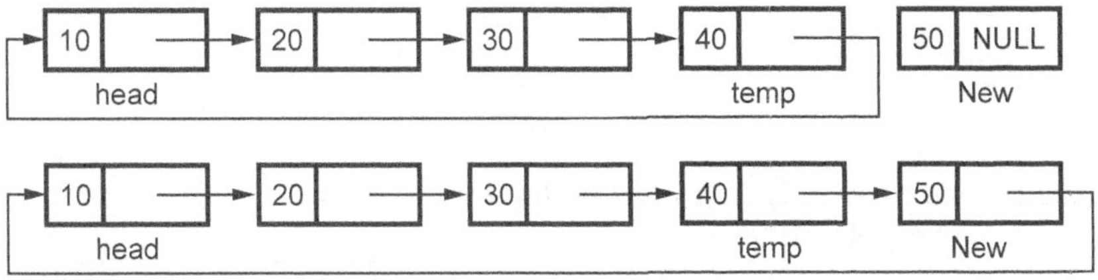

If we want to insert an element 35 after node 30 then,

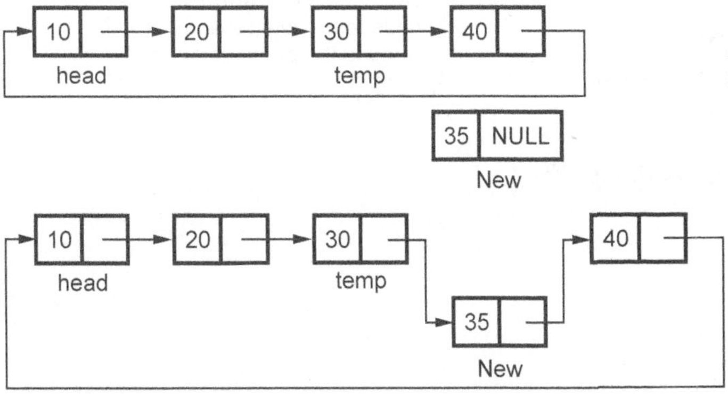

As key = 30
and temp → data = 30

New → next = temp → next;
temp → next = New;

4. Deletion of any node

```
void sll::Delete()
{
 int key;
 struct node *temp,*temp1;
 cout<<"\n Enter the element which is to be deleted";
 cin>>key;
 temp=head;
 if(temp->data==key)/*If header node is to be deleted*/

{
        temp1=temp->next;
        if(temp1==temp)
  /*if single node is present in circular linked list
  and we want to delete it*/
        {
               temp=NULL;
               head=temp;
               cout<<"\n The node is deleted";
        }
        else /*otherwise*/
        {
          while(temp->next!=head)
            temp=temp->next;/*searching for the last node*/
               temp->next=temp1;
```

If a single node is present in the list and we want to delete it

```
            head=temp1;/*new head*/
            cout<<"\n The node is deleted";
        }
}
else
{
    while(temp->next!=head) /* if intermediate node is to
                              be deleted*/
    {
    if((temp->next)->data==key)
    {
            temp1=temp->next;
            temp->next=temp1->next;
            temp1->next=NULL;
            delete temp1;
            cout<<"\n The node is deleted";
    }
    else
            temp=temp->next;
    }
}
}
```

The previous node of the node to be deleted is searched. Here **temp 1** is the node to be deleted and **temp** is the previous node of **temp 1**

Suppose we have created a linked list as,

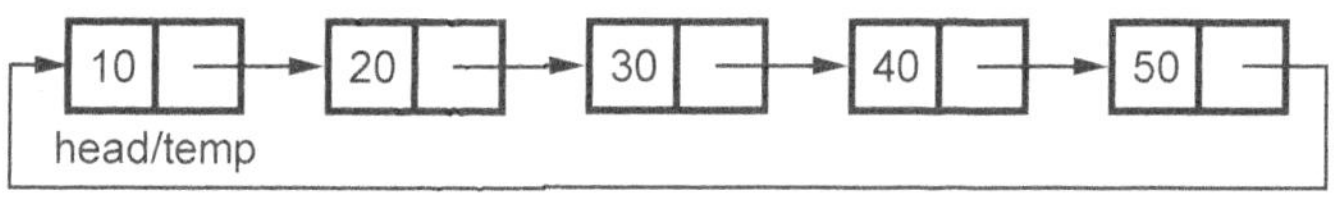

If we want to delete temp → data i.e. node 10 then,

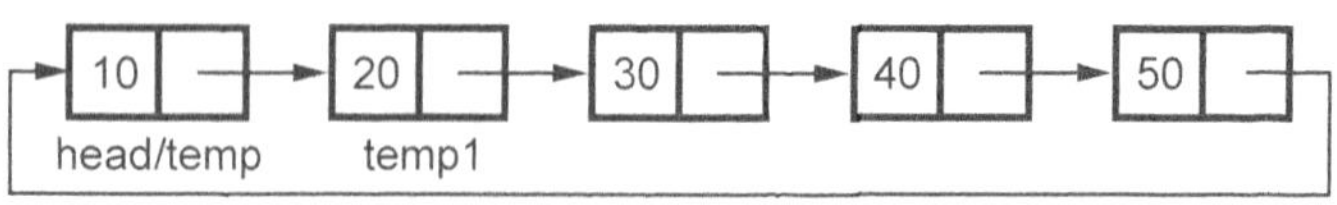

temp1 = temp → next;

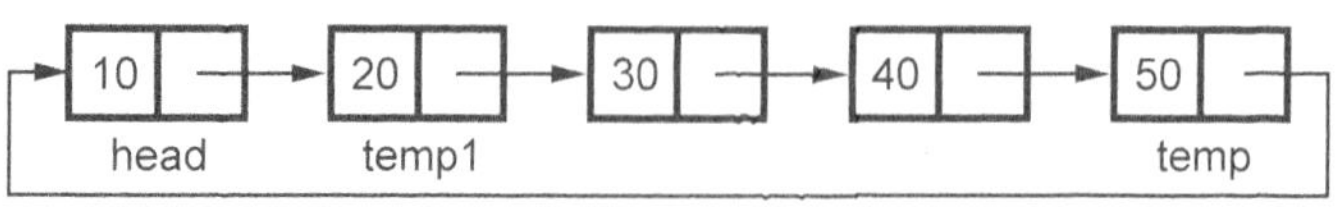

while (temp → next ! head)
temp = temp → next;

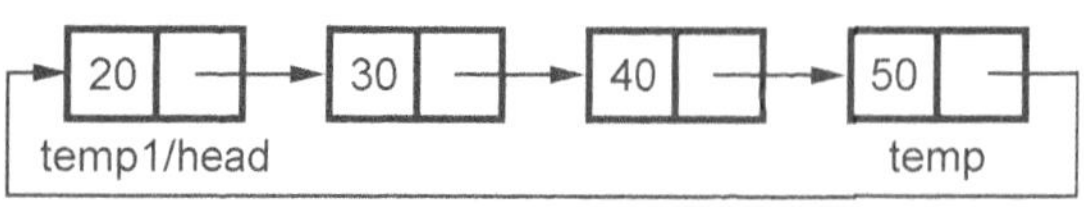

temp → next = temp1;
head = temp1;

If we want to delete an intermediate node from a linked list which is given below

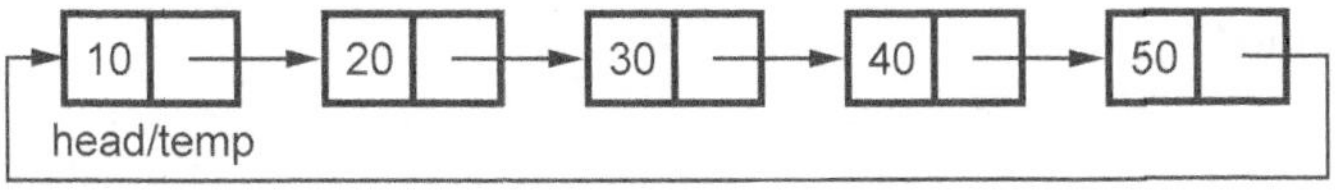

We want to delete node with '30' then

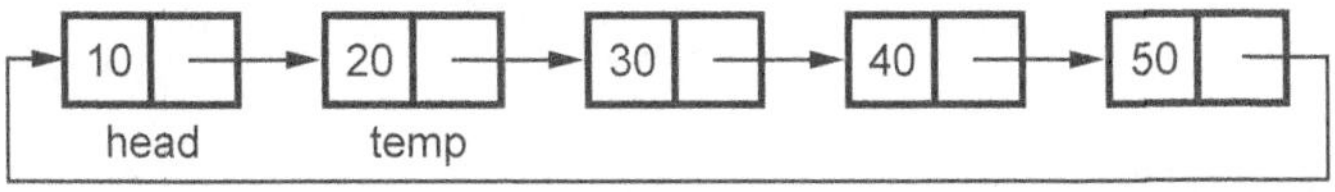

Key = 30 and temp → next → data = key, hence

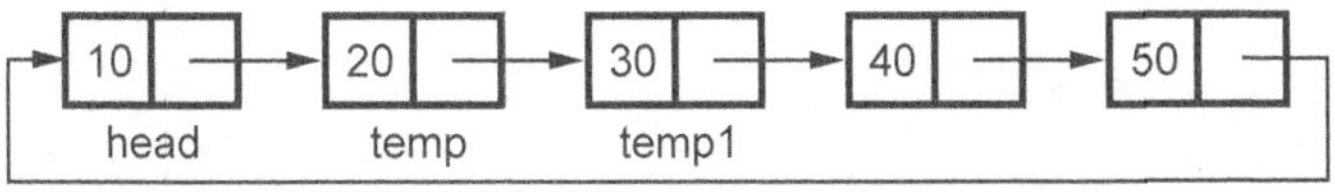

temp1 = temp → next;

Now

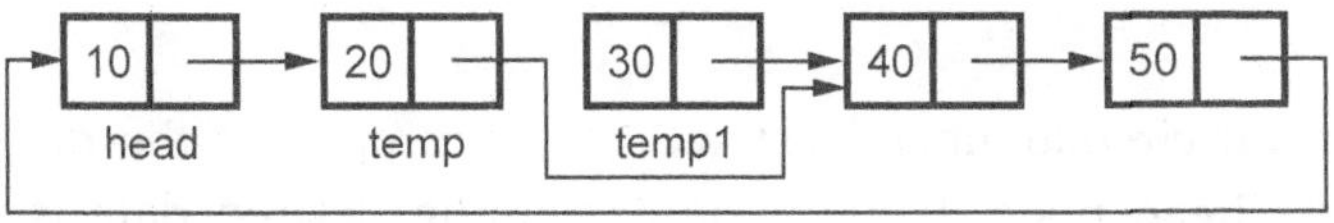

temp → next = temp1 → next;

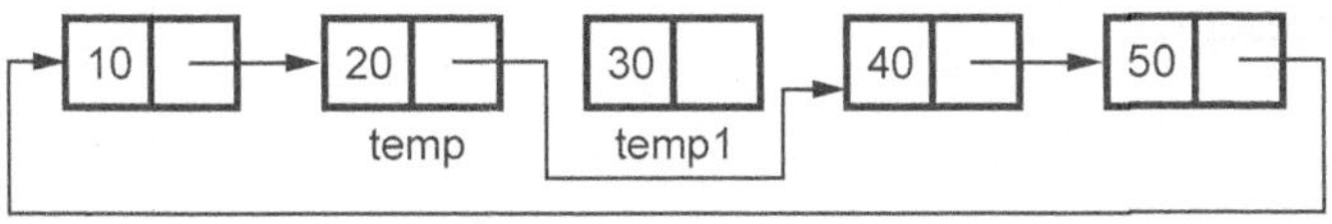

temp1 → next = NULL

Then delete temp1 ; / * to deallocate memory */

The linked list can be -

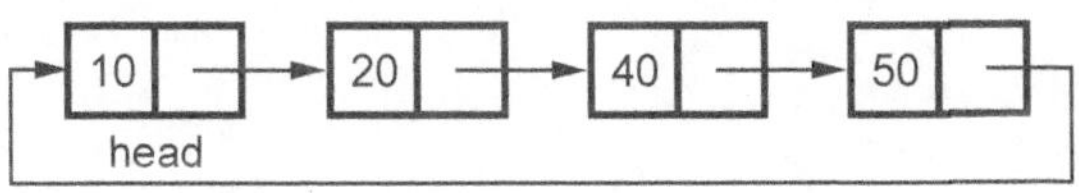

Thus node with value 30 is deleted from CLL.

5. Searching a node from circular linked list

```
void sll::Search(int num)
{
        node *temp;
        int found;
        temp=head;
        if ( temp == NULL )
         {
          cout<<"The Linked List is empty\n";
          getch();
          clrscr();
         }
        found=0;
        while(temp->next!=head && found==0)
```

```
    {
     if(temp->data == num)
      found=1;/*if node is found*/
     else
       temp=temp->next;
    }
    if(found==1)
     {
     cout<<"\n The node is present";
     getch();
    }
    else
    {
     cout<<"\n The node is not present";
     getch();
    }
}
```

while searching a node from circular linked list we go on comparing the data field of each node starting from the **head** node. If the node containing desired data is found we declare that the node is present.

'C++' Program

```
/*
*****************************************************************
 Program To Perform The Various Operations On The Circular Linked List
*****************************************************************
*/

#include<iostream.h>
#include <conio.h>
#include<stdlib.h>
// class


class sll
{
private:
struct node
{
 int data;
 struct node *next;
}*head;
public:
sll();
void Create();
void Display();
```

```
void Search(int key);
void insert_head();
void insert_after();
void insert_last();
void Delete();
~sll();
};

/*
----------------------------------------------------------------------
The  Constructor defined
----------------------------------------------------------------------
*/
sll::sll()
 {
  head=NULL;//initialize head to NULL
 }
/*
----------------------------------------------------------------------
The Destructor defined
----------------------------------------------------------------------
*/
sll::~sll()
{
  node *temp,*temp1;
  temp=head->next;
  delete head;
  while(temp!=NULL) //free the memory allocated
  {
   temp1=temp->next;
   delete temp;
   temp=temp1;
  }
}
/*
----------------------------------------------------------------------
       The Create function
----------------------------------------------------------------------
*/
void sll ::Create()
{
 char ans;
 int flag=1;
 node *New,*temp;
 clrscr();
 do
 {
```

```
        New = new node;
        New->next=NULL;
        cout<<"\n\n\n\tEnter The Element\n";
        cin>>New->data;
        if(flag==1)     /*flag for setting the starting node*/
        {
                head = New;
                New->next=head; /*the circular list of a single
                        node*/
                flag=0;/*reset flag*/
        }
        else            /* find last node in list */
        {
         temp=head;
         while (temp->next != head)/*finding the last node*/
                temp=temp->next; /*temp is a last node*/
         temp->next=New;
         New->next=head; /*each time making the list
                circular*/
        }
        cout<<"\n Do you want to enter more nodes?(y/n)";
        ans=getch();
        }while(ans=='y'||ans=='Y');
}
void sll::Display()
{
        node *temp;
        temp = head;
        if(temp == NULL)
         cout<<"\n Sorry ,The List Is Empty\n";
        else
        {
         do
         {
                cout<<"\t"<<temp->data;
                temp = temp->next;
         }while(temp != head);/*Circular linked list*/
        }
        getch();
}

void sll::insert_head()
{
 node *New,*temp;
 New=new node;
 New->next=NULL;
 cout<<"\n Enter The element which you want to insert ";
```

```
cin>>New->data;
if(head==NULL)
      head=New;
else
{
            temp=head;
            while(temp->next!=head)
                     temp=temp->next;
            temp->next=New;
            New->next=head;
            head=New;
            cout<<"\n The node is inserted!";
}
}
/*Insertion of node at last position*/
void sll::insert_last()
{
      node *New,*temp;
      New=new node;
      New->next=NULL;
      cout<<"\n Enter The element which you want to insert ";
      cin>>New->data;
      if(head==NULL)
            head=New;
      else
      {
       temp=head;
       while(temp->next!=head)
               temp=temp->next;
       temp->next=New;
       New->next=head;
       cout<<"\n The node is inserted!";
      }
}
void sll::insert_after()
{
 int key;
 node *New,*temp;
 New= new node;
 New->next=NULL;
 cout<<"\n Enter The element which you want to insert ";
 cin>>New->data;
 if(head==NULL)
 {
   head=New;
 }
 else
```

```
  {
      cout<<"\n Enter The element after which you want to insert the node ";
      cin>>key;
      temp=head;
      do
      {
          if(temp->data==key)
          {
              New->next=temp->next;
              temp->next=New;
              cout<<"\n The node is inserted";
              return;
          }
          else
              temp=temp->next;
      }while(temp!=head);
  }
}

void sll::Search(int num)
{
    node *temp;
    int found;
    temp=head;
    if ( temp == NULL )
     {
      cout<<"The Linked List is empty\n";
      getch();
      clrscr();
     }
    found=0;
    while(temp->next!=head && found==0)
    {
     if(temp->data == num)
      found=1;/*if node is found*/
     else
       temp=temp->next;
    }
    if(found==1)
     {
     cout<<"\n The node is present";
     getch();
    }
    else
    {
     cout<<"\n The node is not present";
     getch();
```

```
        }
}
void sll::Delete()
{
 int key;
 struct node *temp,*temp1;
 cout<<"\n Enter the element which is to be deleted";
 cin>>key;
 temp=head;
 if(temp->data==key)/*If header node is to be deleted*/
 {
        temp1=temp->next;
        if(temp1==temp)
  /*if single node is present in circular linked list
  and we want to delete it*/
        {
              temp=NULL;
              head=temp;
              cout<<"\n The node is deleted";
        }
        else  /*otherwise*/
        {
          while(temp->next!=head)
            temp=temp->next;/*searching for the last node*/
              temp->next=temp1;
              head=temp1;/*new head*/
              cout<<"\n The node is deleted";
        }
 }
 else
 {
        while(temp->next!=head) /* if intermediate node is to
                          be deleted*/
        {
         if((temp->next)->data==key)
         {
              temp1=temp->next;
              temp->next=temp1->next;
              temp1->next=NULL;
              delete temp1;
              cout<<"\n The node is deleted";
         }
         else
              temp=temp->next;
        }
 }
}
```

```
void main()
{
	sll s;
	char ch='y';
	int num,choice,choice1;
	do
	{
	 clrscr();
	 cout<<"\n Program For Circular Linked List\n";
	 cout<<" 1.Insertion of any node\n\n";
	 cout<<" 2. Display of Circular List\n\n";
	 cout<<" 3. Insertion of a node in Circular List\n\n";
	 cout<<" 4. Deletion of any node \n\n";
	 cout<<" 5. Searching a Particular Element in The List\n\n";
	 cout<<" 6.Exit ";
	 cout<<"\n Enter Your Choice ";
	 cin>>choice;
	 switch(choice)
	 {
		case 1 :s.Create();
			break;
		case 2 :s.Display();
			break;
		case 3: cout<<"\n 1. Insert a node as a head node";
			cout<<"\n 2. Insert a node as a last node";
			cout<<"\n 3. Insert a node at intermediate position in the linked list";
			cout<<"\n Enter your choice for insertion of node";
			cin>>choice1;
			switch(choice1)
			{
			 case 1:s.insert_head();
				break;
			 case 2:s.insert_last();
				break;
			 case 3:s.insert_after();
				break;
			}
			 break;
		case 4:s.Delete();
		       break;
		case 5:cout<<"\n Enter The Element Which Is To Be Searched ";
		       cin>>num;
		       s.Search(num);
		       break;
		case 6:exit(0);
	}
```

```
        cout<<"\nDo you want to go to Main Menu?\n";
        ch = getch();
 }while(ch == 'y' || ch == 'Y');
}
```

Output

```
Program For Circular Linked List
1. Insertion of any node

2. Display of Circular List

3. Insertion of a node in Circular List

4. Deletion of any node

5. Searching a Particular Element in The List

6.Exit
Enter Your Choice 1



Enter The Element
10
Do you want to enter more nodes?(y/n)

Enter The Element
20
Do you want to enter more nodes?(y/n)

Enter The Element
30
Do you want to enter more nodes?(y/n)

Enter The Element
40

Do you want to enter more nodes?(y/n)
Do you want to go to Main Menu?

Program For Circular Linked List
1.Insertion of any node

2. Display of Circular List

3. Insertion of a node in Circular List
```

```
 4. Deletion of any node

 5. Searching a Particular Element in The List

 6. Exit
 Enter Your Choice 2
      10    20    30    40
Do you want to go to Main Menu?

Program For Circular Linked List
1.Insertion of any node

2. Display of Circular List

3. Insertion of a node in Circular List

4. Deletion of any node

5. Searching a Particular Element in The List

6. Exit
Enter Your Choice 3

1. Insert a node as a head node
2. Insert a node as a last node
3. Insert a node at intermediate position in the linked list
Enter your choice for insertion of node 1

Enter The element which you want to insert 9

 The node is inserted!
Do you want to go to Main Menu?

 Program For Circular Linked List
 1.Insertion of any node

 2. Display of Circular List

 3. Insertion of a node in Circular List

 4. Deletion of any node

 5. Searching a Particular Element in The List

 6.Exit
 Enter Your Choice 2
    9    10    20    30    40
```

```
Do you want to go to Main Menu?

 Program For Circular Linked List
 1.Insertion of any node

 2. Display of Circular List

 3. Insertion of a node in Circular List

 4. Deletion of any node

 5. Searching a Particular Element in The List

 6.Exit
 Enter Your Choice 3

 1. Insert a node as a head node
 2. Insert a node as a last node
 3. Insert a node at intermediate position in the linked list
 Enter your choice for insertion of node2

 Enter The element which you want to insert 50

 The node is inserted!
Do you want to go to Main Menu?

 Program For Circular Linked List
 1.Insertion of any node

 2. Display of Circular List

 3. Insertion of a node in Circular List

 4. Deletion of any node

 5. Searching a Particular Element in The List

 6.Exit
 Enter Your Choice 2
     9    10    20    30    40    50
Do you want to go to Main Menu?

 Program For Circular Linked List
 1.Insertion of any node

 2. Display of Circular List
```

```
3. Insertion of a node in Circular List

4. Deletion of any node

5. Searching a Particular Element in The List

6.Exit
Enter Your Choice 3

1. Insert a node as a head node
2. Insert a node as a last node
3. Insert a node at intermediate position in the linked list
Enter your choice for insertion of node 3

Enter The element which you want to insert 35

Enter The element after which you want to insert the node 30

The node is inserted
Do you want to go to Main Menu?

Program For Circular Linked List
1.Insertion of any node

2. Display of Circular List

3. Insertion of a node in Circular List

4. Deletion of any node

5. Searching a Particular Element in The List

6.Exit
Enter Your Choice 2
      9     10     20     30     35     40     50
Do you want to go to Main Menu?

Program For Circular Linked List
1.Insertion of any node

2. Display of Circular List

3. Insertion of a node in Circular List

4. Deletion of any node

5. Searching a Particular Element in The List
```

```
6.Exit
Enter Your Choice 4

Enter the element which is to be deleted 30

The node is deleted
Do you want to go to Main Menu?

Program For Circular Linked List
1.Insertion of any node

2. Display of Circular List

3. Insertion of a node in Circular List

4. Deletion of any node

5. Searching a Particular Element in The List

6.Exit
Enter Your Choice 2
    9     10     20     35     40     50

Program For Circular Linked List
1.Insertion of any node

2. Display of Circular List

3. Insertion of a node in Circular List

4. Deletion of any node

5. Searching a Particular Element in The List

6.Exit
Enter Your Choice 5

Enter The Element Which Is To Be Searched 40

The node is present
Do you want to go to Main Menu?

Program For Circular Linked List
1.Insertion of any node

2. Display of Circular List
```

```
3. Insertion of a node in Circular List

4. Deletion of any node
5. Searching a Particular Element in The List

6.Exit
Enter Your Choice 5

Enter The Element Which Is To Be Searched 75

The node is not present
Do you want to go to Main Menu?

Program For Circular Linked List
1.Insertion of any node

2. Display of Circular List

3. Insertion of a node in Circular List

4. Deletion of any node

5. Searching a Particular Element in The List

6.Exit
Enter Your Choice 6
```

Advantages of Doubly Linked List over Singly Linked List

- In circular list the next pointer of last node points to head node, whereas in doubly linked list each node has **two pointers** : One previous pointer and another is next pointer.
- The **main advantage** of circular list over doubly linked list is that with the help of single pointer field we can **access head** node quickly.
- Hence some amount of memory get saved because in circular list only one pointer field is reserved.

4.10 Doubly Circular Linked List

The doubly circular linked list can be represented as follows

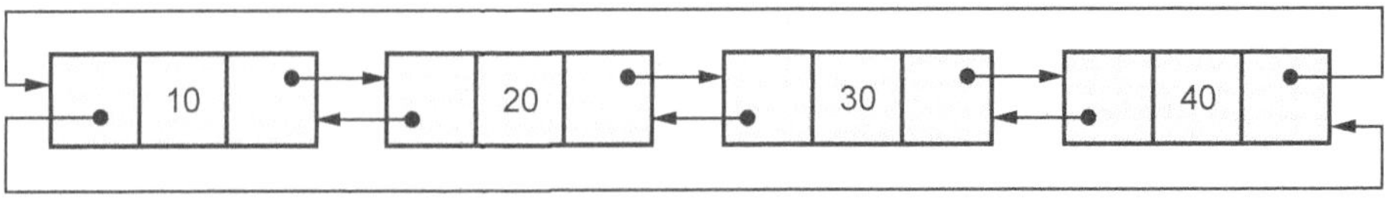

Fig. 4.10.1 Doubly circular list

```
The node structure will be
struct node
{
      int data;
      struct node *next;
      struct node *prev;
};
```

C++ Function for creation of doubly Circular List

```
struct node *Create()
{
      char ans;
      int flag = 1;
      struct node *head, *New, *temp;
      struct node *get_node();
      head = NULL;
      do
      {
            New = new node;
            cout<<"\n\n\n\tEnter The Element\n";
            cin>>New->data;

            if (flag == 1)   /*flag for setting the starting node*/
            {
                  head = New;
                  New->next = head;  /*the circular list of a single node*/
                  head->prev = New;
                  flag = 0;/*reset flag*/
            }
            else             /* find last node in list */
            {
                  temp = head;
                  while (temp->next != head)/*finding the last node*/
                        temp = temp->next; /*temp is a last node*/
                  temp->next = New;
                  New->prev = temp;
                  head->prev = New;
                  New->next = head; /*each time making the list circular*/
            }
            cout<<"\n Do you want to enter more nodes ? ";
            cin>>ans;
      } while (ans == 'y' || ans == 'Y');
      return head;
}
```

4.11 Applications of Linked List

Various applications of linked list are -

1. Linked list can be used to implement linear data structures such as stacks, and qeues.
2. Linked list is useful for implementing the non-linear data structures, such as tree and graph.
3. Polynomial representation, and operations such as addition, multiplication and evaluation can be performed using linked list.

4.12 Polynomial Manipulations

4.12.1 Representation of a Polynomial using Linked List

As we know a polynomial has the main fields as coefficient, exponent in linked list, it will have one more field called **'link'** field to point to next term in the polynomial. If there are n terms in the polynomial then n such nodes has to be created.

The typical node will look like this,

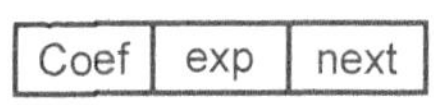

Fig. 4.12.1 Node of polynomial

For example : To represent $3x^2 + 5x + 7$ the link list will be,

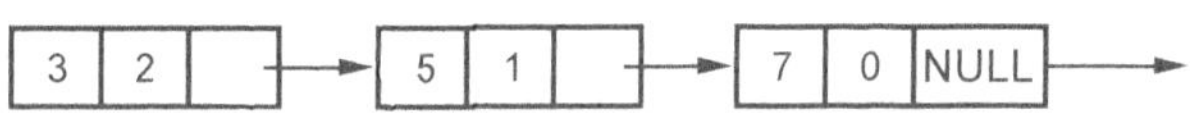

In each node, the exponent field will store exponent corresponding to that term, the coefficient field will store coefficient corresponding to that term and the link field will point to next term in the polynomial. Again for simplifying the algorithms such as addition of two polynomials we will assume that the polynomial terms are stored in descending order of exponents.

The node structure for a singly linked list for representing a term of polynomial can be defined as follows :

```
typedef struct Pnode
{
    float coef;
    int exp;
    struct node *next;
} p;
```

Advantages of linked representation over arrays :

1. Only one pointer will be needed to point to first term of the polynomial.
2. No prior estimation on number of terms in the polynomial is required. This results in flexible and more space efficient representation.
3. The insertion and deletion operations can be carried out very easily without movement of data.

Disadvantage of linked representation over arrays :

1. We can not access any term randomly or directly we have to go from start node always.

4.12.2 Addition of Two Polynomials Represented using Singly Linear Link List

Logic for polynomial addition by linked list :

Step 1 : First of all we create two linked polynomials.

For example

$$P_1 = 3x^3 + 2x^2 + 1x$$

$$P_2 = 5x^5 + 3x^2 + 7$$

Each node in the polynomial will look like this,

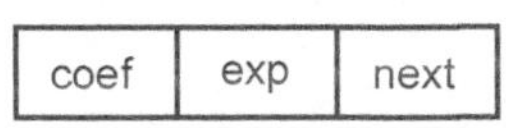

p node

The linked list for p_1 will be,

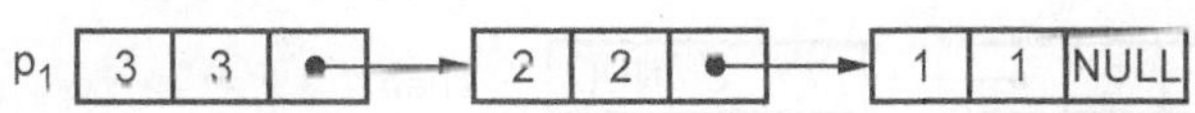

Similarly the p_2 will be,

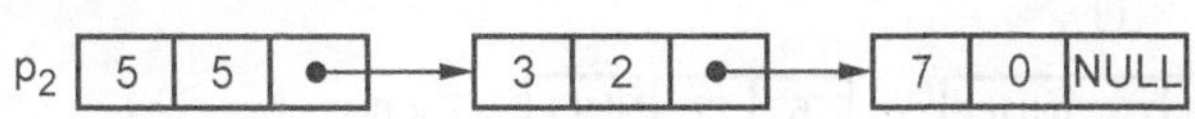

Step 2 :

For addition of two polynomials if exponents of both the polynomials are same then we add the coefs. For storing the result we will create the third linked list say p_3. The processing will be as follows :

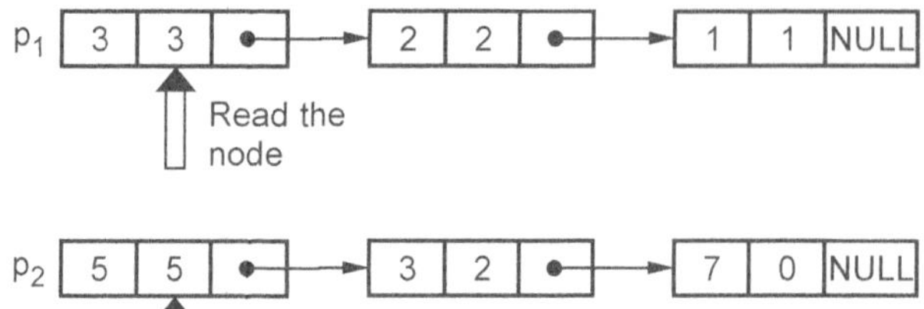

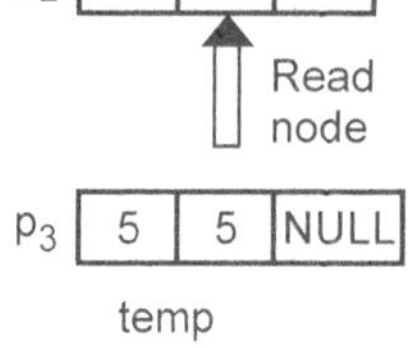

If $p_2 \rightarrow exp > p_1 \rightarrow exp$

$p_3 \rightarrow coef = p_2 \rightarrow coef$

$p_3 \rightarrow exp = p_2 \rightarrow exp$

$p_2 = p_2 \rightarrow next$

Step 3 :

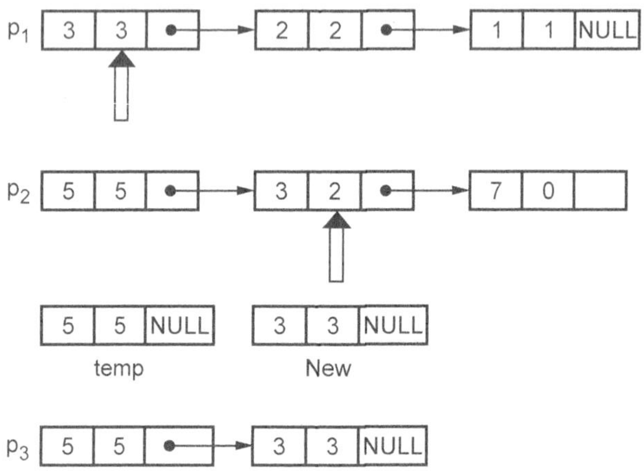

If $p_1 \rightarrow exp = p_2 \rightarrow exp$

$p_3 \rightarrow coef = p_1 \rightarrow coef$

$p_3 \rightarrow exp = p_1 \rightarrow exp$

create (temp, New)

$p_1 = p_1 \rightarrow next$

Step 4 :

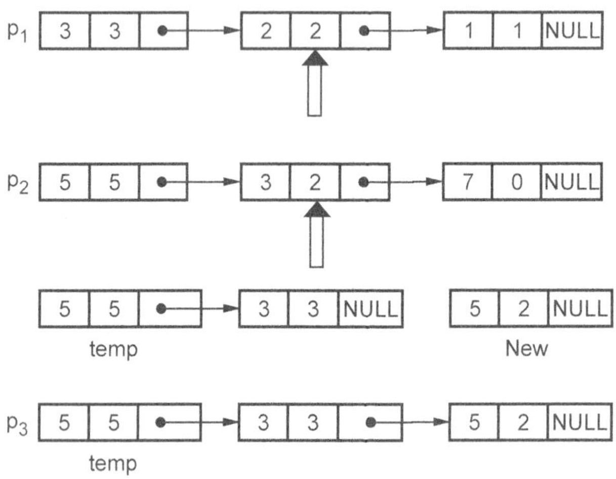

If $p_1 \rightarrow exp = p_2 \rightarrow exp$

$p_3 \rightarrow coef = p_1 \rightarrow coef + p_2 \rightarrow coef$

$p_3 \rightarrow exp = p_1 \rightarrow exp$

Then

Increment both the pointers

Then

Attach temp list

with New node.

Step 5 :

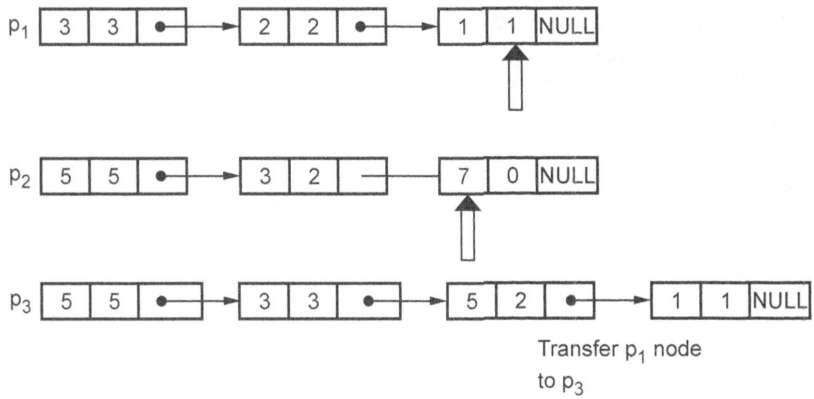

Step 6 :

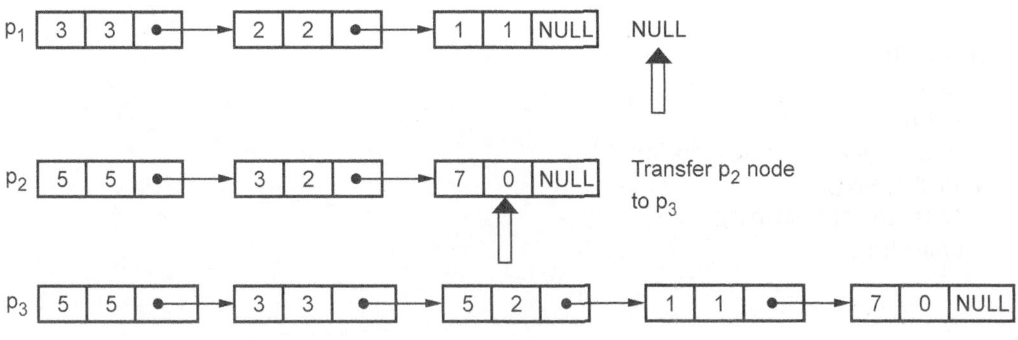

Finally

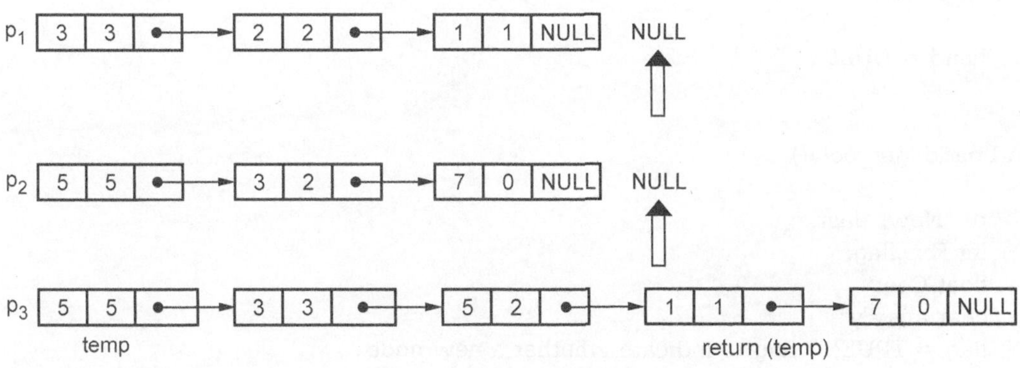

p_3 list is the addition of two polynomials.

'C++' Program

```
/************************************************************************
      Program To Perform Addition Of Two Polynomials Using
      Singly Linear Linked List
************************************************************************/
#include <iostream.h>
#include <conio.h>
#include <stdlib.h>

#define TRUE  1
#define FALSE   0
class Lpadd
{
      private:
      typedef struct  pnode
      {
            float coef;
            int exp;
            structpnode  *next;
      }p;
      p *head;
      public:
      Lpadd();
      void get_poly(),add(Lpadd,Lpadd);
      void display();
      p *Attach(int,float,p *);
      ~Lpadd();
};
/*
------------------------------------------------------------------------
The constructor defined
------------------------------------------------------------------------
*/
Lpadd::Lpadd()
{
      head = NULL ;
}

void Lpadd::get_poly()
{
      p  *New, *last;
      int Exp,flag;
      float Coef;
      char ans='y';
      flag = TRUE; // flag to indicate whether a new node
            // is created for the first time or not
      cout<<"\nEnter the polynomial in desending order of exponent\n";
```

```
    do
    {
        cout<<"\nEnter the Coefficient and Exponent of a term :";
        cin>>Coef>>Exp;
        // allocate new node
        New=new p;
        New->next=NULL;
        if ( New == NULL )
         cout<<"\nMemory can not be allocated";
         New -> coef = Coef;
      //putting coef,exp values in the node
         New -> exp  = Exp ;
         if ( flag==TRUE ) // Executed only for the first time
         {                   //for creating the first node
             head = New;
             last = head;
             flag = FALSE;
         }
         else
          {
             // last keeps track of the most recently
               // created node
             last ->next = New;
             last = New;
         }
        cout<<"\n Do you Want To Add more Terms?(y/n)";
        ans=getch();
    }while(ans=='y');
    return;
}
void Lpadd::display()
{
    p *temp ;
    temp=head;
    if ( temp == NULL )
    {
        cout<<"The polynomial is empty\n";
        getch();
        return;
    }
    cout<<endl;
    while ( temp->next != NULL )
    {
        cout<<temp->coef<<" x^  "<<temp->exp<<"+ ";
        temp = temp -> next;
    }
    cout<<temp ->coef<<" x^  "<<temp ->exp;
```

```
    getch();
}

void Lpadd::add(Lpadd p1,Lpadd p2)
{
    p *temp1, *temp2,*dummy;
    float Coef;
    temp1 =p1.head;
    temp2 =p2.head;
    head = new p;
    if ( head == NULL )
        cout<<"\nMemory can not be allocated";
    dummy = head;//dummy is a start node
    while ( temp1 != NULL && temp2 != NULL )
    {
        if(temp1->exp==temp2->exp)
        {
            Coef = temp1->coef + temp2->coef;
            head = Attach(temp1->exp,Coef,head);
            temp1 = temp1->next;
            temp2 = temp2->next;
        }
        else if(temp1->exp<temp2->exp)
        {
            Coef = temp2 -> coef;
            head =Attach(temp2->exp, Coef,head);
            temp2 = temp2 -> next ;
        }
        else if(temp1->exp>temp2->exp)
        {
            Coef = temp1 -> coef;
            head =Attach(temp1->exp, Coef,head);
            temp1 = temp1 -> next ;
        }
    }
    //copying the contents from first polynomial to the resultant
    //poly
    while ( temp1 != NULL )
    {
        head = Attach(temp1->exp,temp1->coef,head);
        temp1 = temp1 -> next;
    }
    //copying the contents from second polynomial to the resultant poly.
    while ( temp2 != NULL )
    {
        head = Attach(temp2->exp,temp2->coef,head);
        temp2 = temp2 -> next;
```

```
        }
        head ->next = NULL;
        head = dummy -> next;//Now set temp as starting node
        delete dummy;
        return;
}
p *Lpadd::Attach( int Exp, float Coef, p *temp)
{
        p *New, *dummy;

        New = new p;
        if (New == NULL )
          cout<<"\n Memory can not be allocated \n";
        New->exp  = Exp;
        New->coef = Coef;
        New->next = NULL;
        dummy = temp;
        dummy -> next = New;
        dummy = New;
        return(dummy);
}
Lpadd::~Lpadd()
{
        p *temp;
        temp=head;
        while(head!=NULL)
        {
              temp=temp->next;
              delete head;
              head=temp;
        }
}
void main()
{
        Lpadd p1,p2,p3;
        cout<<"\n Enter the first polynomial\n\n";
        p1.get_poly();
        cout<<"\nEnter the Second polynomial\n\n";
        p2.get_poly();
        cout<<"\nThe first polynomial is \n";
        p1.display();
        cout<<"\nThe second polynomial is\n";
        p2.display();
        p3.add(p1,p2);
        cout<<"\nThe Addition of the Two polynomials is...\n";
        p3.display();
        exit(0);
}
```

Output

```
Enter the first polynomial

Enter the polynomial in desending order of exponent

Enter the Coefficient and Exponent of a term : 3 3

Do you Want To Add more Terms?(y/n)
Enter the Coefficient and Exponent of a term : 2 2

Do you Want To Add more Terms?(y/n)
Enter the Coefficient and Exponent of a term : 1 1

Do you Want To Add more Terms?(y/n)
Enter the Coefficient and Exponent of a term : 5 0

Do you Want To Add more Terms?(y/n)n

Enter the Second polynomial

Enter the polynomial in desending order of exponent

Enter the Coefficient and Exponent of a term : 5 1

Do you Want To Add more Terms?(y/n)
Enter the Coefficient and Exponent of a term : 7 0
Do you Want To Add more Terms?(y/n)
The first polynomial is
3 x^ 3+ 2 x^ 2+ 1 x^ 1+ 5 x^ 0
The second polynomial is
5 x^ 1+ 7 x^ 0
The Addition of the Two polynomials is...
3 x^ 3+ 2 x^ 2+ 6 x^ 1+ 12 x^ 0
```

4.13 Generalized Linked List (GLL)

4.13.1 Concept of Generalized Linked List

A generalized linked list A, is defined as a finite sequence of n>=0 elements,

$a_1, a_2 a_3, \ldots, a_n$, such that ai are either atoms or the list of atoms. Thus

$A = (a_1, a_2 a_3, \ldots, a_n)$

Where n is total number of nodes in the list.

Now to represent such a list of atoms we will have certain assumptions about the node structure

Flag	Data	Down pointer	Next pointer

Flag = 1 means down pointer exists.

= 0 means next pointer exists.

Data means the atom

Down pointer is address of node which is down of the current node.

Next pointer is the address of the node which is attached as the next node.

With this typical node structure let us represent the generalized linked list for the above. Let us take few example to learn how actually the generalized linked list can be shown,

Typical 'C' structure of GLL -

```
typedef struct node
 {
   char c;              /*Data*/
   int ind;             /*Flag*/
   struct node *next,*down; /*next & down  pointer */
 }gll;
```

Example of GLL [List representation]

1. (a , (b , c), d)

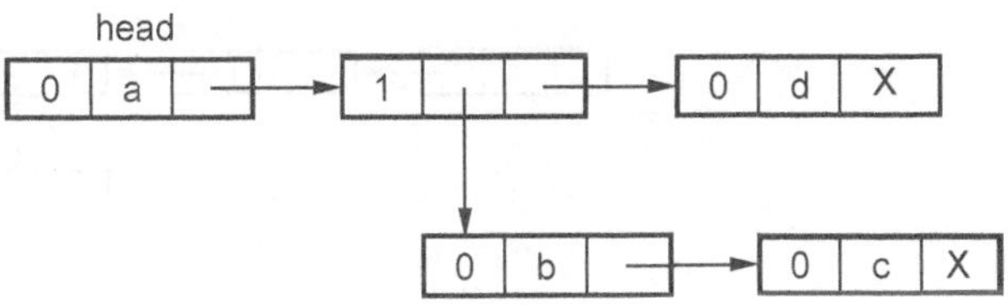

In above example the head node is 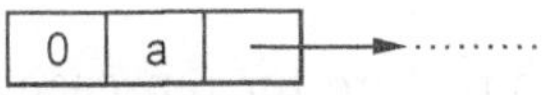

In this case the first field is 0, it indicates that the second field is variable. If first field is 1 means the second field is a down pointer, means some list is starting.

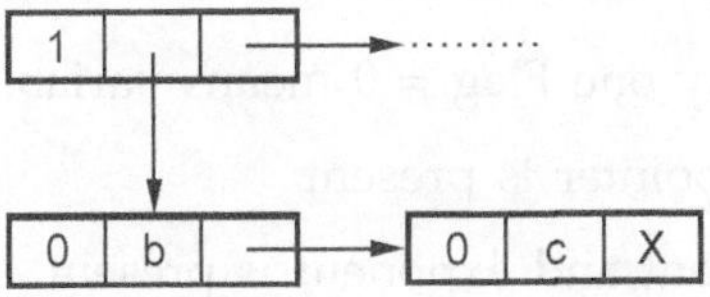

The above figure indicates (b , c). In this way the generalised linked list can be built. The X in the next pointer field indicates NULL value.

2. G = (p , q, (r, s, (t, u, v), w), x, y)

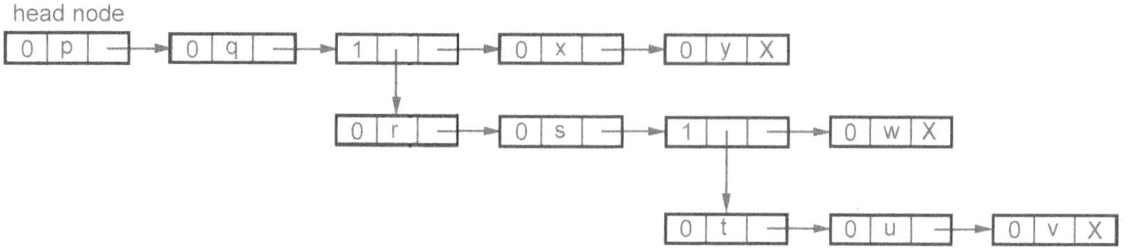

3. ((a, b, (c, d, (e))), (a, b))

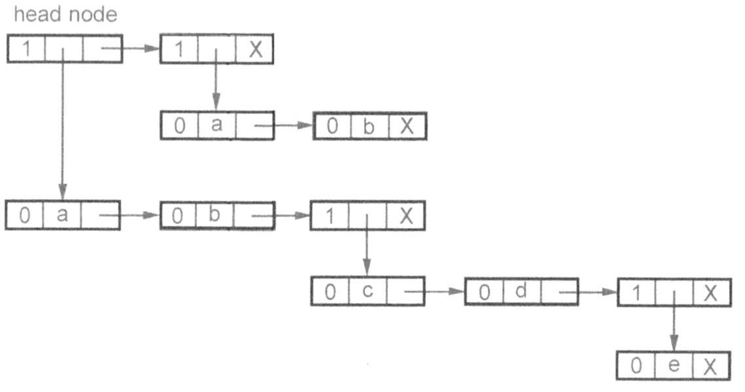

4.13.2 Polynomial Representation using Generalized Linked List

The typical node structure for representation of polynomial is

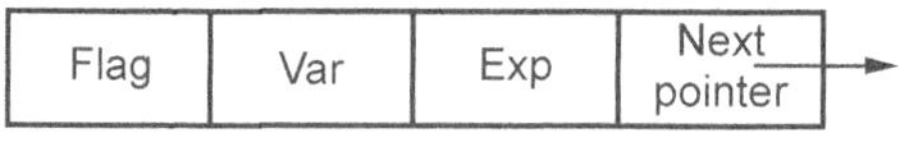

Let us see each field one by one Flag = 0 means variable is present

Flag = 1. Means down pointer is present

Flag = 2. Means coefficient and exponent is present

Example 1 : $9x^5 + 7xy^4 + 10xz$

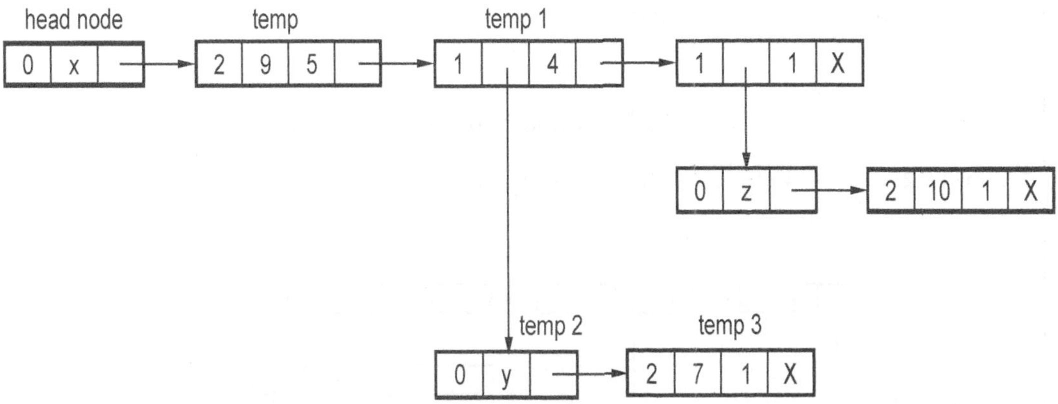

In the above example the head node is of variable x. The temp node shows the first field as 2 means coefficient and exponent are present.

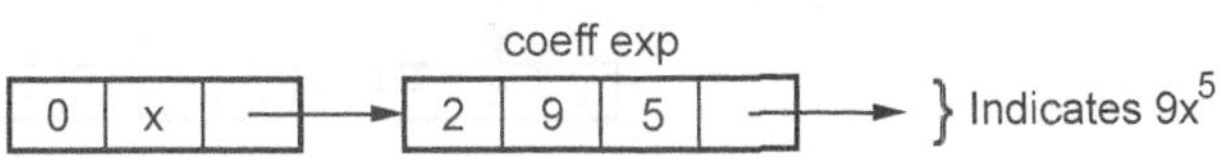

Since temp node is attached to head node and head node is having variable x, temp node having coefficient = 9 and exponent = 5. The above two nodes can be read as $9x^5$. Similarly in the figure.

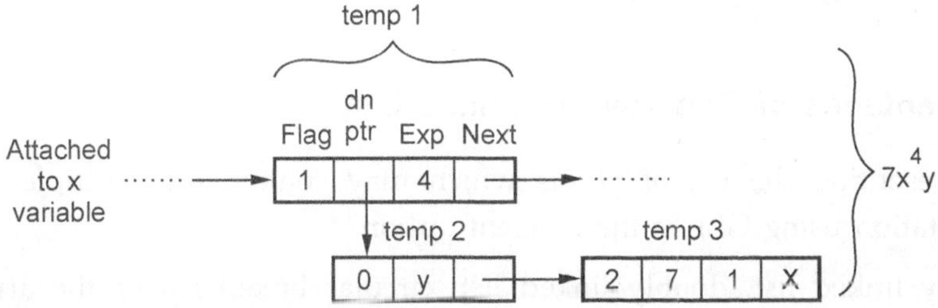

The node temp1 can be read as x^4. The flag field is 1 means down pointer is there

The temp2 = y

temp3 = coefficient = 7

exponent = 1

Flag = 2 means the node contains coefficient and exponent values temp2 is attached to temp3 this means $7y^1$ and temp2 is also attached to temp1 means

$$\begin{array}{ccc} \text{temp1} & \times & \text{temp2} \\ x^4 & \times & 7y^1 \\ & = & 7x^4y^1 \end{array}$$

value is represented by above figure.

Example 2 : $-4x^4y^2z^3 + 10x^2yz^2 + 7xyz + 45$

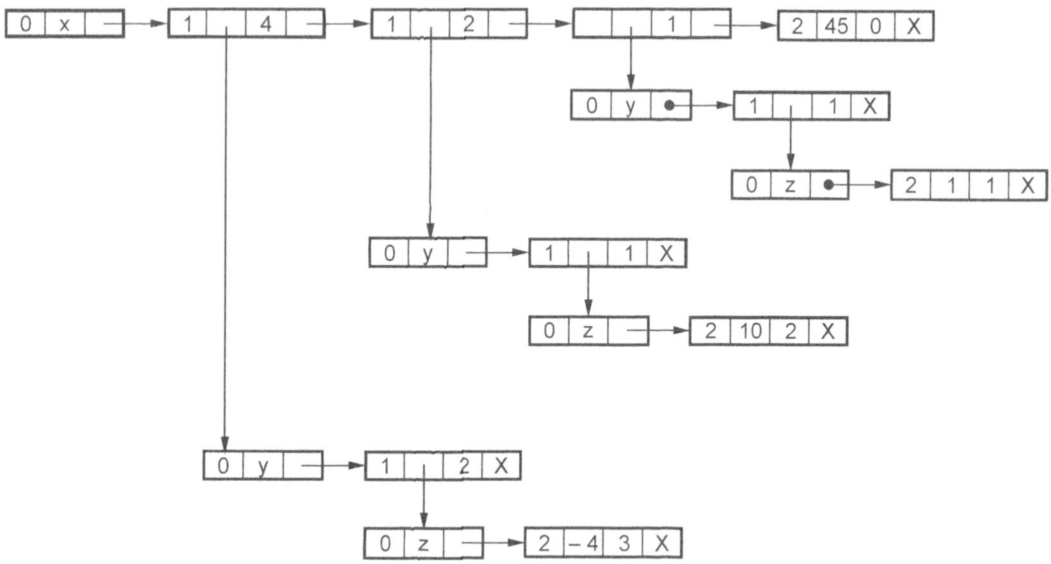

4.13.3 Advantages of Generalized Linked List

1. For representing the list of atoms which may contain the multiple sub-lists the representation using GLL is the efficient option.
2. As singly linked list, doubly linked list, circular linked list or the arrays are not efficient ways for multi-variable polynomials. The use of GLL in performing various operations on multi-variable polynomial increases the efficiency of the algorithm.

❑❑❑

Unit - V

5 Stack

Syllabus

Basic concept, stack Abstract Data Type, Representation of Stacks Using Sequential Organization, stack operations, Multiple Stacks, Applications of Stack- Expression Evaluation and Conversion, Polish notation and expression conversion, Need for prefix and postfix expressions, Postfix expression evaluation, Linked Stack and Operations. Recursion- concept, variants of recursion- direct, indirect, tail and tree, Backtracking algorithmic strategy, use of stack in backtracking.

Contents

5.1 Basic Concept

Let us have the formal definition of the stack.

Definition :

A stack is an **ordered list** in which all insertions and deletions are made at **one end**, called the **top**. If we have to make stack of elements 10, 20, 30, 40, 50, 60 then 10 will be the bottommost element and 60 will be the topmost element in the stack. A stack is shown in Fig. 5.1.1.

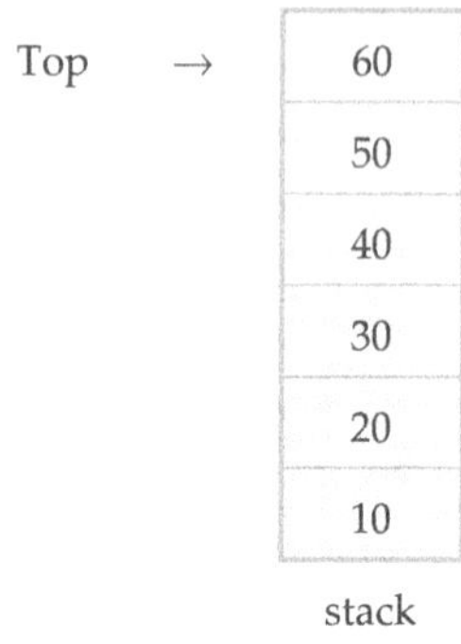

Fig. 5.1.1 Stack

Example

The typical example can be a stack of coins. The coins can be arranged one on another, when we add a new coin it is always placed on the previous coin and while removing the coin the recently placed coin can be removed. The example resembles the concept of stack exactly.

5.2 Stack Abstract Data Type

Stack is a data structure which posses LIFO i.e. Last In First Out property. The abstract data type for stack can be as given below.

Abstract DataType stack

{

Instances : Stack is a collection of elements in which insertion and deletion of elements is done by one end called top.

Preconditions :

1. Stfull () : This condition indicates whether the stack is full or not. If the stack is full then we cannot insert the elements in the stack.
2. Stempty () : This condition indicates whether the stack is empty or not. If the stack is empty then we cannot pop or remove any element from the stack.

Operations :

1. Push : By this operation one can push elements onto the stack. Before performing push we must check stfull () condition.
2. Pop : By this operation one can remove the elements from stack. Before popping the elements from stack We should check stempty () condition.

}

Review Question

1. *What is ADT ? Write ADT for stack operations.*

5.3 Representation of Stacks using Sequential Organization

Declaration 1 :

```
#define size 100
int stack[size], top = -1;
```

In the above declaration stack is nothing but an array of integers. And most recent index of that array will act as a top.

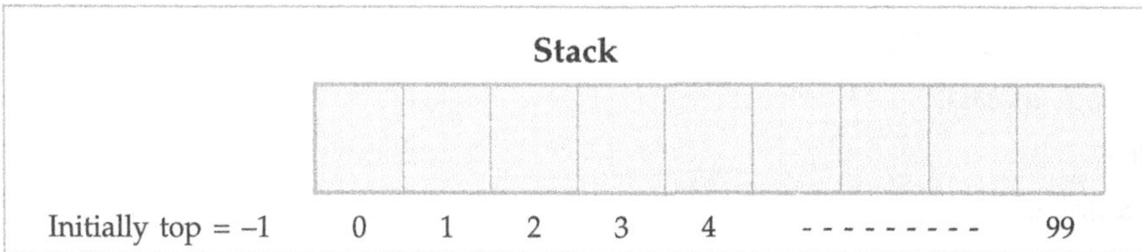

Fig. 5.3.1 Stack using one dimensional array

The stack is of the size 100. As we insert the numbers, the top will get incremented. The elements will be placed from 0th position in the stack. At the most we can store 100 elements in the stack, so at the most last element can be at (size-1) position, i.e., at index 99.

Declaration 2 :

```
#define size 10
struct stack {
        int s[size];
            int top;
                }st;
```

In the above declaration stack is declared as a structure.

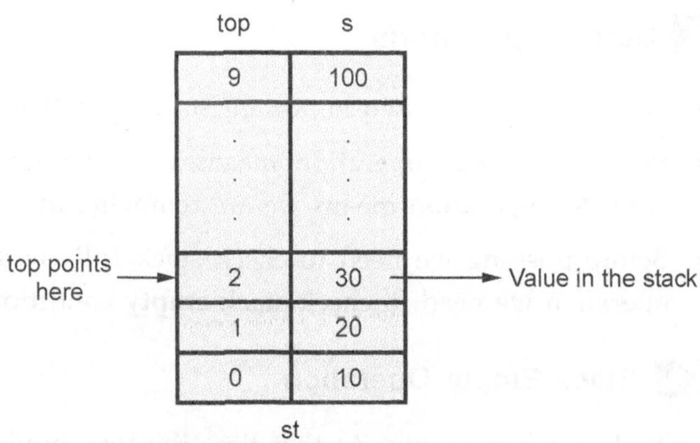

Fig. 5.3.2 Stack using structure

Now compare declaration 1 and 2. Both are for stack declaration only. But the second declaration will always preferred. Why ? Because in the second declaration we have used a structure for stack elements and top. By this we are binding or co-relating top variable with stack elements. Thus top and stack are associated with each other by putting them together in a structure. The stack can be passed to the function by simply passing the structure variable.

We will make use of the second method of representing the stack in our program.

The stack can also be used in the databases. For example if we want to store marks of all the students of forth semester we can declare a structure of stack as follows

```
# define size 60
typedef struct student
    {
        int roll.no;
        char name[30];
        float marks;
    }stud;
    stud S1[size];
    int top = -1;
```

The above structure will look like this

Thus we can store the data about whole class in our stack. The above declaration means creation of stack. Hence we will write only push and pop function to implement the stack. And before pushing or popping we should check whether stack is empty or full.

	roll_no	name	marks
59			
⋮			
top = 3 →	40	Mita	66
2	30	Rita	91
1	20	Geeta	88.3
0	10	Seeta	76.5

5.4 Stack Operations

- Basically there are two important stack operations - **(1) Push** and **(2) Pop.**
- Performing **Push operation** means we are inserting the elements onto the stack. And **Pop operation** means we are removing the element from the stack.
- Before pushing we need to check **stack full condition** and before performing pop operation we need to check **stack empty condition.**

5.4.1 Stack Empty Operation

Initially stack is empty. At that time the top should be initialized to – 1 or 0. If we set top to – 1 initially then the stack will contain the elements from 0th position and if we set top to 0 initially, the elements will be stored from 1st position, in the stack. Elements may be pushed onto the stack and there may be a case that all the elements are removed from the stack. Then the stack becomes empty. Thus whenever top reaches to – 1 we can say the stack is empty.

```
int stempty()
{
 if(st.top==-1)
  return 1;
 else
  return 0;
}
```

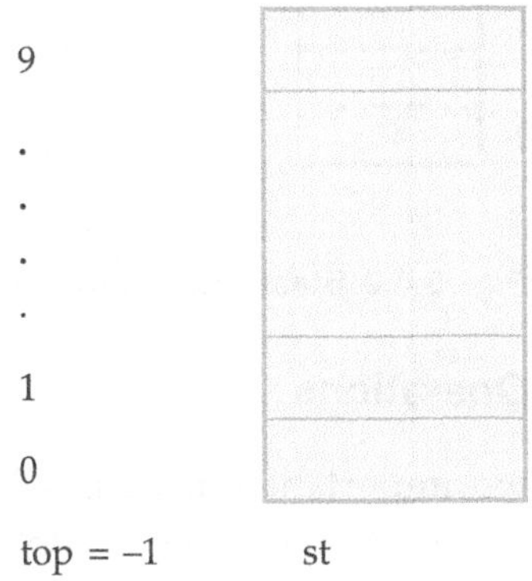

Fig. 5.4.1 Stack empty condition

Key Point *If top = – 1 means stack empty.*

5.4.2 Stack Full Operation

In the representation of stack using arrays, size of array means size of stack. As we go on inserting the elements the stack gets filled with the elements. So it is necessary before inserting the elements to check whether the stack is full or not. Stack full condition is achieved when stack reaches to maximum size of array.

```
int stfull()
{
 if(st.top>=size-1)
  return 1;
 else
  return 0;
}
```

Thus stfull is a Boolean function if stack is full it returns 1 otherwise it returns 0.

Key Point *If top >= size means stack is full.*

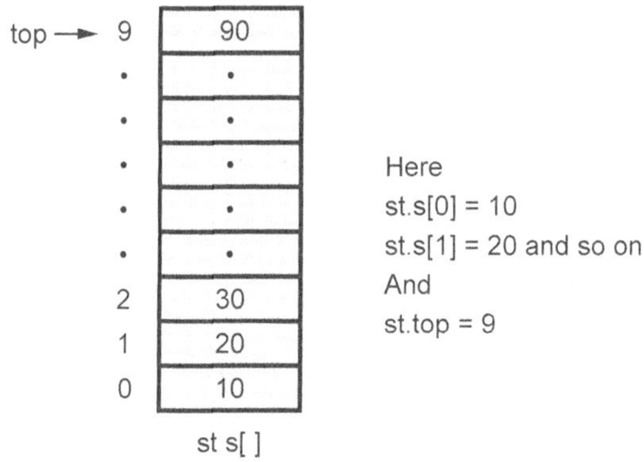

Fig. 5.4.2 Stack full condition

5.4.3 The Push and Pop Operations

We will now discuss the two important functions which are carried out on a stack. push is a function which inserts new element at the top of the stack. The function is as follows.

```
void push(int item)
{
 st.top++; / * top pointer is set to next location */
 st.s[st.top] =item; /* placing the element at that location */
}
```

Note that the push function takes the parameter **item** which is actually the element which we want to insert into the stack - means we are pushing the element onto the stack. In the function we have checked whether the stack is full or not, if the stack is not full then only the insertion of the element can be achieved by means of push operation.

Now let us discuss the operation pop, which deletes the element at the top of the stack. The function pop is as given below -

Note that always top element can be deleted.

```
int pop()
{
 int item;
 item = st.s[st.top];
 st.top – –;
 return(item);
}
```

In the choice of pop- it invokes the function 'stempty' to determine whether the stack is empty or not. If it is empty, then the function generates an error as stack underflow ! If not, then pop function returns the element which is at the top of the stack. The value at the top is stored in some variable as item and it then decrements the value of the top, which now points to the element which is just under the element being retrieved from the stack. Finally it returns the value of the element stored in the variable item. Note that this is what called as logical deletion and not a physical deletion, i.e. even when we decrement the top, the element just retrieved from the stack remains there itself, but it no longer belongs to the stack. Any subsequent push will overwrite this element.

Push operation can be shown by following Fig. 5.4.3.

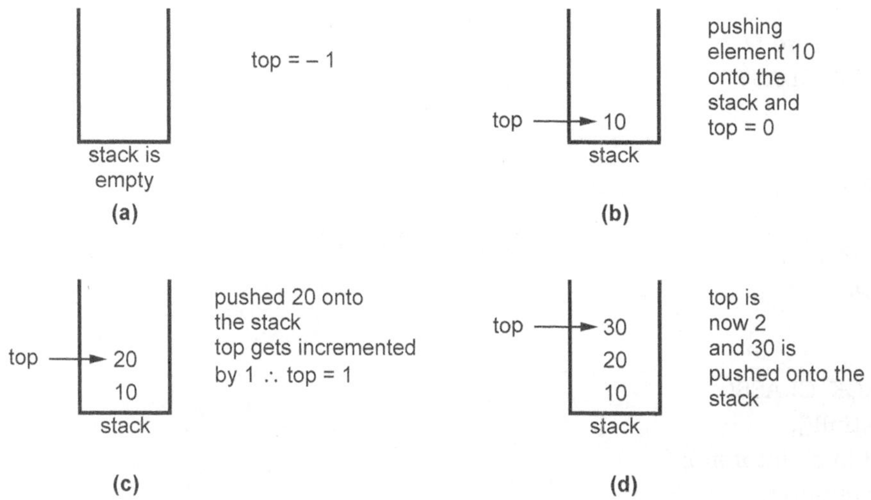

Fig. 5.4.3 Performing push operation

The pop operation can be shown by following Fig. 5.4.4.

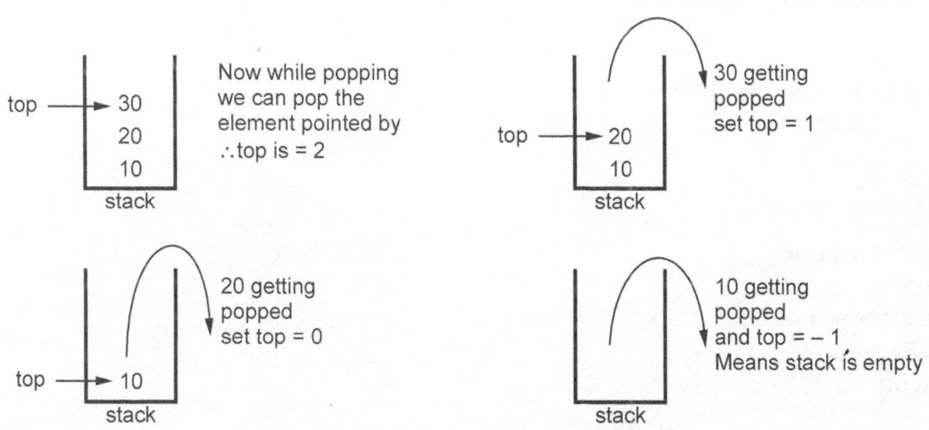

Fig. 5.4.4 Performing pop operation

Key Point *If stack is empty we cannot pop and if stack is full we cannot push any element.*

'C++' Program

```
/****************************************************************
Program for implementing a stack using arrays.It involves various operations such as
push, pop, stack empty, stack full and display.
****************************************************************/
#include<iostream.h>
#include<conio.h>
#include<stdlib.h>
#define size 5
/* stack structure */
class STACK_CLASS
{
 private:
 struct stack
 {
     int s[size];
     int top;
  } st;
 public:
       STACK_CLASS();
       int stfull();
       void push(int item);
       int stempty();
       int pop();
       void display();
};
//constructor is used to initialise stack
STACK_CLASS::STACK_CLASS()
{
       st.top=-1;
       for(int i=0;i<size;i++)
              st.s[i]=0;
}

/*
 The stfull Function
 Input:none
 Output:returns 1 or 0 for stack full or not
 Called By:main
 Calls:none
*/
int STACK_CLASS::stfull()
{
 if(st.top>=size-1)
      return 1;
 else
```

```
        return 0;
}
/*
 The push Function
 Input:item which is to be pushed
 Output:none-simply pushes the item onto the stack
 Called By:main
 Calls:none
*/
void STACK_CLASS::push(int item)
{
 st.top++;
 st.s[st.top] =item;
}
/*
 The stempty Function
 Input:none
 Output:returns 1 or 0 for stack empty or not
 Called By:main
 Calls:none
*/
int STACK_CLASS::stempty()
{
 if(st.top==-1)
  return 1;
 else
  return 0;
}
/*
 The pop Function
 Input:none
 Output:returns the item which is popped from the stack
 Called By:main
 Calls:none
*/
int STACK_CLASS::pop()
{
 int item;
 item=st.s[st.top];
 st.top --;
 return(item);
}
/*
 The display Function
 Input:none
 Output:none-displays the contents of the stack
 Called By:main
```

```
 Calls:none
*/
void STACK_CLASS::display()
{
 int i;
 if(stempty())
   cout<<"\n Stack Is Empty!";
 else
 {
  for(i=st.top;i>=0;i--)
  cout<<"\n"<<st.s[i];
 }
}
/*
 The main Function
 Input:none
 Output:none
 Called By:O.S.
 Calls:push,pop,stempty,stfull,display
*/
void main(void)
{
       int item,choice;
       char ans;
       STACK_CLASS obj;
       clrscr();
       cout<<"\n\t\t Implementation Of Stack";
       do
       {
              cout<<"\n Main Menu";
              cout<<"\n1.Push\n2.Pop\n3.Display\n4.exit";
              cout<<"\n Enter Your Choice: ";
              cin>>choice;
              switch(choice)
              {
                case 1:   cout<<"\n Enter The item to be pushed ";
                          cin>>item;
                          if(obj.stfull())
                          cout<<"\n Stack is Full!";
                      else
                           obj.push(item);
                           break;
                case 2:if(obj.stempty())
                         cout<<"\n Empty stack!Underflow !!";
                      else
                      {
                        item=obj.pop();
```

```
                    cout<<"\n The popped element is "<<item;
                   }
                   break;
           case 3:obj.display();
                        break;
           case 4:exit(0);
          }
          cout<<"\n Do You want To Continue?";
          ans=getche();
      }while(ans ==Y ||ans ==y);
      getch();
}
/******************** End Of Program ************************/
```

Output

```
         Implementation Of Stack
 Main Menu
1.Push
2.Pop
3.Display
4.exit
 Enter Your Choice: 1

 Enter The item to be pushed 10

 Do You want To Continue?y
 Main Menu
1.Push
2.Pop
3.Display
4.exit
 Enter Your Choice: 1

 Enter The item to be pushed 20

 Do You want To Continue?y
 Main Menu
1.Push
2.Pop
3.Display
4.exit
 Enter Your Choice: 1

 Enter The item to be pushed 30

 Do You want To Continue?y
 Main Menu
```

```
1.Push
2.Pop
3.Display
4.exit
 Enter Your Choice: 2
 The popped element is 30
 Do You want To Continue?y
 Main Menu
1.Push
2.Pop
3.Display
4.exit
 Enter Your Choice: 3
20
10
 Do You want To Continue?y
```

5.5 Multiple Stacks

- In a single array any number of stacks can be adjusted. And push and pop operations on each individual stack can be performed.
- The following Fig. 5.5.1 shows how multiple stacks can be stored in a single dimensional array

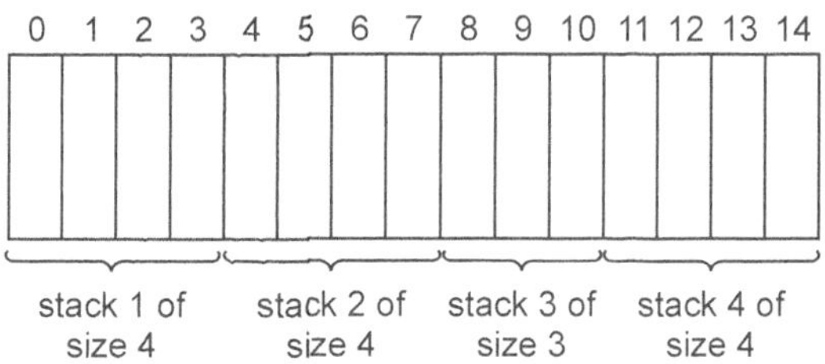

Fig. 5.5.1 Multiple stacks in one dimensional array

- Each stack in one dimensional array can be of any size.
- The only one thing which has to be maintained that total size of all the stacks < = size of single dimensional array.

Example

Let us perform following operations on the stacks -

1. push 10 in stack 4
2. push 20 in stack 3
3. push 30 in stack 1
4. push 40 in stack 2

5. push 50 in stack 3

6. push 60 in stack 3

The multiple stack will then be as follows -

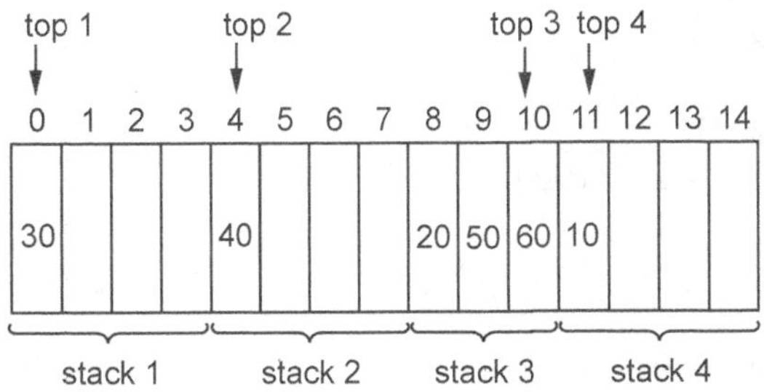

- Here stack 3 is now full and we can not insert the elements in stack 3.
- The top 1, top 2, top 3, top 4 indicates the various top pointers for stack 1, stack 2, stack 3 and stack 4 respectively.
    - **stack 1**-array [0] will be lower bound and array [3] will be upper bound. That is we can perform stack 1 operation for array [0] to array [3] only.
    - **stack 2**-The area for stack 2 will be from array [4] to array [7]
    - **stack 3**-From array [8] to array [10]
    - **stack 4**-From array [11] to array [14]

Thus you can declare any number of stacks having different sizes of them.

Let us see the implementation of multiple stacks

C++ Program

```
/*****************************************************************
Program to implement multiple stacks using single array
*****************************************************************/
#include<iostream>
using namespace std;
#define MAX 20
class MultipleStack {
	private:
		int stack[MAX];
		int lb,ub;
	public:
		int size[MAX];
	/*Constructor defined*/
		MultipleStack()
		{
			for(int i=1;i<=MAX;i++)
				stack[i]=-1;/*for initialization of the entire array of stacks*/
```

```
    }
/* set_stack Function */
    void set_stack(int index)
    {
        int sum,i;
        if(index==1)
        {
            lb=1;
            ub=size[index];
        }
        else
        {
            sum=0;
            for(i=1;i<index;i++)
                sum=sum+size[i];
            lb=sum+1;
            ub=sum+size[index];
        }
    }
/* stfull Function */
    int stfull(int index)
    {
        int top,i,sum;
        set_stack(index);
        for(top=lb;top<=ub;top++)
        {
            if(stack[top]==-1)
                break;
        }
        if(top-1==ub)
            return 1;
        else
            return 0;
    }
/*  stempty Function */
    int stempty(int index)
    {
        int top;
        set_stack(index);
        for(top=lb;top<=ub;top++)
        {
            if(stack[top]!=-1)
                return 0;
            return 1;
        }
    }
/*  push Function */
```

```
        void push(int item)
        {
                int top;
                for(top=lb;top<=ub;top++)
                        if(stack[top]==-1)
                                break;
                stack[top]=item;
                return;
        }

    /* pop Function */
        int pop()
        {
                int top,item;;
                for(top=lb;top<=ub;top++)
                        if(stack[top]==-1)
                                break;
                top--;
                item=stack[top];
                stack[top]=-1;
                return item;
        }
    /*  display Function */
        void display(int index)
        {
                int top;
                set_stack(index);
                for(top=lb;top<=ub;top++)
                {
                        if(stack[top]!=-1)
                                cout<<"  "<<stack[top];
                }
        }

/*  display_all Function */
        void display_all(int n)
        {
                int top,index;
                for(index=1;index<=n;index++)
                {
                        cout<<"\nstack number "<<index<<" is";
                        set_stack(index);
                        for(top=lb;top<=ub;top++)
                        {
                                if(stack[top]!=-1)
                                        cout<<"  "<<stack[top];
                        }
```

```
            }
        }
};
/*  main Function */
int main(void)
{
    int n,index,i,item,choice;
    char ans;
    ans='y';
    MultipleStack ms;
    cout<<"\n\t Program For multiple stacks using single array";
    cout<<"\n Enter how many stacks are there";
    cin>>n;
    cout<<"\n Enter the size for each stack";
    for(i=1;i<=n;i++)
    {
        cout<<"\n size for stack"<<i<<" is: ";
        cin>>ms.size[i];
    }
    do
    {
        cout<<"\n\t\t Main Menu";
        cout<<"\n 1.Push \n2.Pop \n3.Display \n4.Dispaly all";
        cout<<"\n Enter Your choice";
        cin>>choice;
        switch(choice)
        {
            case 1:cout<<"\n Enter the item to be pushed";
                cin>>item;
                cout<<"\n In Which stack?";
             cin>>index;
             if(ms.stfull(index))
                cout<<"\n Stack is Full,can not Push";
            else
                ms.push(item);
            break;
            case 2:cout<<"\n From Which stack?";
                cin>>index;
                if(ms.stempty(index))
                    cout<<"\n Stack number: "<<index<<" is empty!";
                else
                {
                    item=ms.pop();
                    cout<<"\n"<<item<<" is popped from stack "<<index;
                }
            break;
            case 3:cout<<"\n Which stack has to be displayed?";
```

```
                    cin>>index;
                    ms.display(index);
                break;
                case 4:ms.display_all(n);
                break;
                default:cout<"\n Exitting";
            }
            cout<<"\n Do you wish to continue?";
            cin>>ans;
    }while(ans=='y'||ans=='Y');
    return 0;
}
```

Output

```
      Program For multiple stacks using single array
Enter how many stacks are there 4
Enter the size for each stack
size for stack1 is: 2
size for stack2 is: 3
size for stack3 is: 4
size for stack4 is: 5
            Main Menu
1.Push
2.Pop
3.Display
4.Dispaly all
Enter Your choice 1
Enter the item to be pushed 10
In Which stack?1
Do you wish to continue?y

            Main Menu
1.Push
2.Pop
3.Display
4.Dispaly all
Enter Your choice1

Enter the item to be pushed 20

In Which stack?3

Do you wish to continue?y

            Main Menu
1.Push
2.Pop
3.Display
```

```
4.Dispaly all
 Enter Your choice1

 Enter the item to be pushed 30

 In Which stack?3

 Do you wish to continue?y

              Main Menu
 1.Push
 2.Pop
 3.Display
 4.Dispaly all
 Enter Your choice1
 Enter the item to be pushed 40
 In Which stack?4
 Do you wish to continue?y
              Main Menu
 1.Push
 2.Pop
 3.Display
 4.Dispaly all
 Enter Your choice1
 Enter the item to be pushed 50
 In Which stack?2
 Do you wish to continue?y
              Main Menu
 1.Push
 2.Pop
 3.Display
 4.Dispaly all
 Enter Your choice 1
 Enter the item to be pushed 60
 In Which stack?2
 Do you wish to continue?y
              Main Menu
 1.Push
 2.Pop
 3.Display
 4.Dispaly all
 Enter Your choice4

stack number 1 is  10
stack number 2 is  50  60
stack number 3 is  20  30
stack number 4 is  40
```

```
Do you wish to continue?y

          Main Menu
1.Push
2.Pop
3.Display
4.Dispaly all
Enter Your choice2

From Which stack?3

30 is popped from stack 3
Do you wish to continue?y

          Main Menu
1.Push
2.Pop
3.Display
4.Dispaly all
Enter Your choice4

stack number 1 is  10
stack number 2 is  50  60
stack number 3 is  20
stack number 4 is s 40
Do you wish to continue?n
```

5.5.1 Two Stacks in Single Array

Two stacks can be adjusted in a single array with n numbers, which is as shown below

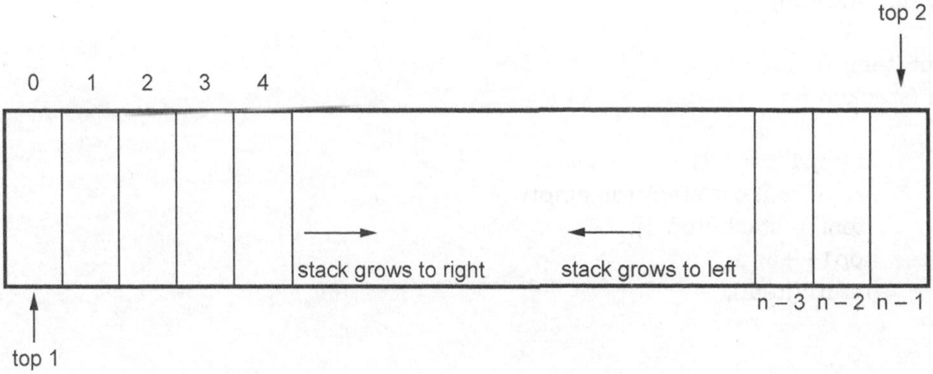

Fig. 5.5.2 Two stacks in single array

- One stack starts at the leftmost end of array and other at the rightmost end of array.
- The insertion in stack1 moves top1 to right while insertion in stack2 moves **top2** to left.
- When stack is full both the **top1** and **top2** positions are adjacent to each other.
- The **advantage** of this arrangement is that every location of the array can be utilized.
- The implementation routines are -

```
# define MAX 80
int stack[MAX];
int top1=-1, top2=n;
void push (int item, int stackno)
{
	if(stackno == 1)
	{
	/* pushing in stack1 */
		if(top1+1 == top2)

			cout<<"stack1 is full";
		top1++;
		stack [top1]=item;
	}
	else
	{
		if (top2-1 == top1)
		cout<<"stack2 is full";
		top2--
		stack[top2]=item;
	}
int pop (int stackno)
{
	int item;
	if (stackno == 1)
	{
		if (top1 == - 1)
			cout<<"stack1 is empty";
		item = stack [top 1];
		top1++
		return(item);
	}
	else
	{
		if (top2 == MAX)
			cout<<"stack2 is empty";
```

```
        item = stack [top2];
        top2--
        return(item);
    }
}
```

5.6 Applications of Stack

Various applications of stack are -

1. Stack is used for converting one form of expression to another.
2. Stack is also useful for evaluating the expression.
3. Stack is used for parsing the well formed parenthesis.
4. Decimal to binary conversion can be done by using stack.
5. The stack is used for reversing the string.
6. In recursive routines for storing the function calls the stack is used.

5.7 Polish Notation and Expression Conversion

- Expression is a string of operands and operators.
- Operands are some numeric values and operands are of two types - unary operators and binary operators.
- Unary operators are + **and** –.
- Binary operators are **+, –, /, *, % and exponential.**

There are three types of expressions :

1. Infix Expression :

In this type of expressions the arrangement of operands and operator is as follows :

Infix expression = operand1 operator operand2

For example 1. (a + b) 2. (a + b) ∗ (c – d) 3. (a + b/e) ∗ (d + f)

Parenthesis can be used in these expressions. Infix expression are the most natural way of representing the expressions.

2. Postfix Expression :

In this type of expressions the arrangement of operands and operator is as follows :

Postfix expression = operand1 operand2 operator

For example 1. *a*b+ 2. *a*b + cd – ∗ 3. *a*b + e / df + ∗

In postfix expression there is no parenthesis used. All the corresponding operands come first and then operator can be placed.

3. Prefix Expression :

In prefix expression the arrangement of operands and operators is as follows

Prefix expression = operator operand1 operand2

For example 1. + *a*b 2. * + *a*b – cd 3. * / + *a*be + df

This notation is also called as **Polish Notation**.

In prefix expression, there is no parenthesis used. All the corresponding operators come first and then operands are arranged.

Conversion of Infix to Postfix

Algorithm

1. Read the infix expression for left to right one character at a time.
2. Initially push $ onto the stack. For $ in stack set priority as – 1.

If input symbol read is '(' then push it on to the stack.

3. If the input symbol read is an operand then place it in postfix expression.
4. If the input symbol read is operator then
   a) Check if priority of operator in stack is greater than the priority of incoming (or input read) operator then pop that operator from stack and place it in the postfix expression. Repeat step 4(a) till we get the operator in the stack which has greater priority than the incoming operator.

   b) Otherwise push the operator being read, onto the stack.

   c) If we read input operator as ')' then pop all the operators until we get "(" and append popped operators to postfix expression. Finally just pop "(".
5. Final pop the remaining contents, from the stack until stack becomes empty append them to postfix expression.
6. Print the postfix expression as a result.

The priorities of different operators when they are in stack will be called as **instack** priorities. And the priorities of different operator when then are from input will be called as **incoming priorities**.

These priorities are as given below

Operator	Instack priority	Incoming priority
+ or –	2	1
* or /	4	3

∧ for any exponential operator	5	6
(	0	9
Operand	8	7
)	NA	0

Example 5.7.1 *Convert A*B+C $ postfix form.*

Solution :

Input	Stack	Output
none	empty	none
A	empty	A
*	*	A
B	*	AB
+	pop * and Push	AB*
C	+	AB*C
$	Empty	AB*C +

Example 5.7.2 *Convert (A+B)* (C–D) to postfix.*

Solution :

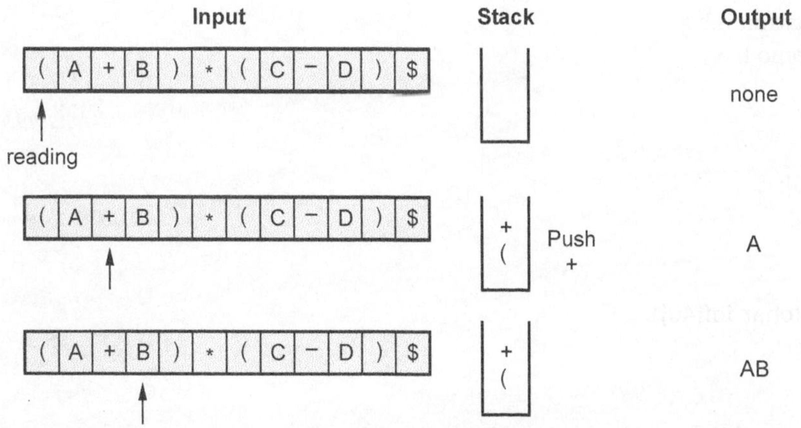

When closing parenthesis comes pop everything and print except '('

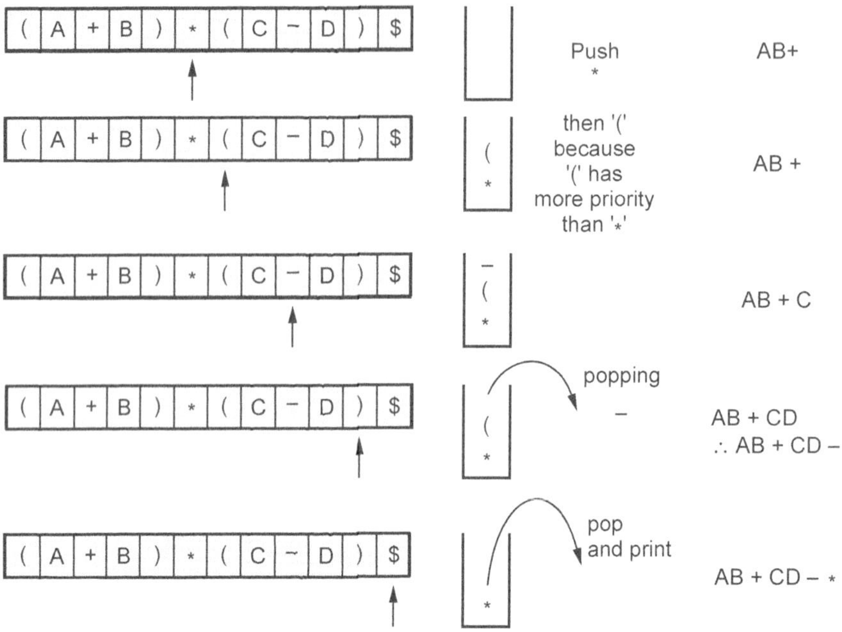

So finally the converted expression is

AB+CD–*

C++ Program

```
/******************************************************************
 Program for conversion of Infix expression to Postfix form.
******************************************************************/
#include<iostream.h>
#include<conio.h>
class EXP
{
 private:
 char post[40];
 int top,st[20];
 public:
 EXP();
 void postfix(char inf[40]);
 void push(int);
 char pop();
};
EXP::EXP()
```

```
{
 top=0;
}
/*
----------------------------------------------------------------
Postfix function
----------------------------------------------------------------
*/
void EXP::postfix(char inf[40])
 {
        int i,j=0;
        for(i=0;inf[i]!='\0';i++)
        {
        switch(inf[i])
        {
                case '+' :  while(st[top] >= 1)
                            post[j++] = pop();
                            push(1);
                            break;

                case '-' :  while(st[top] >= 1)
                            post[j++] = pop();
                            push(2);
                            break;

                case '*' :  while(st[top] >= 3)
                            post[j++] = pop();
                            push(3);
                            break;

                case '/' :  while(st[top] >= 3)
                            post[j++] = pop();
                            push(4);
                            break;

                case '^' :  while(st[top] >= 4)
                            post[j++] = pop();
                            push(5);
                            break;

                case '(' :  push(0);
                            break;

                case ')' :  while(st[top] != 0)
                            post[j++] = pop();
                            top--;
                            break;
```

```
            default  : post[j++] = inf[i];
        }
        }
        while(top>0)
        post[j++] = pop();
        cout<<"\n\tPostfix expression is =>\n\n\t\t "<<post;
 }
/*
-----------------------------------------------------------------
Push function
-----------------------------------------------------------------
*/
void EXP::push(int ele)
 {
        top++;
        st[top] = ele;
 }
/*
-----------------------------------------------------------------
pop Function
-----------------------------------------------------------------
*/
char EXP::pop()
 {
        int el;
        char e;
        el = st[top];
        top--;
        switch(el)
        {
            case 1 : e = '+';
                                    break;
            case 2 : e = '-';
                                    break;
            case 3 : e = '*';
                                    break;
            case 4 : e = '/';
                                    break;
            case 5 : e = '^';
                                    break;
        }
        return(e);
 }

/*
  The main Function
```

```
  Input:none
  Output:none
  Called By:O.S.
  Calls:postfix

*/
void main(void)
{
        EXP obj;
        char inf[40];
        clrscr();
        cout<<"\n\tEnter the infix expression :: \n";
        cin>>inf;
        cout<<"The infix expression entered by you is..."<<inf;
        obj.postfix(inf);
        getch();
 }
```

Output

```
Enter the infix expression ::
(a+b)*(c–d)
The infox expression entered by you is...(a+b)*(c–d)
        Postfix expression is =>

                    ab+cd–*
```

Example 5.7.3 *Convert the following expression into postfix. Show all steps : (a + (b * c/d) – e).*

Solution :

Step	Input	**Action**	Stack	Postfix expression
1.	(	Push (	(	
2.	a	Print a	(	a
3.	+	Push +	(+	a
4.	(	Push (	(+ (	a
5.	b	Print b	(+ (	ab
6.	*	Push *	(+ (*	ab
7.	c	Print c	(+ (*	abc
8.	/	Pop * print it then push / onto the stack	(+ (/	abc*
9.	d	Print d	(+ (/	abc*d

10.	)	Pop all the contents of the stack until (. Print all the popped contents. Then pop (.	(+	abc*d /
11.	–	pop + , print Then push –	(–	abc*d /+
12.	e	Print e		abc*d /+e
13.	)	pop all the contents until (, print the popped contents. Then pop)		abc*d /+e –

The postfix expression is **abc*d/+ e –**

Example 5.7.4 *Identify the expressions and convert them into remaining two forms :*

i) AB + C∗DE−FG+$, where $-exponent

ii) −A/B∗C$DE

Solution : i) AB + C * DE – FG + $ → postfix expression

i) Infix :

AB + C * DE – FG + $

(A + B) C * DE – FG + $

((A + B)* C) DE – RG + $

((A + B)* C) D – E FG + $

((A + B)* C) (D – E) (F + G) $ ⇒ ((A + B) * C) (D – E) $ (F + G)

ii) Prefix :

= AB + C * DE – FG + $

= (+ AB) C * DE – FG + $

= (* + ABC) DE – FG + $

= (* + ABC) (– DE) (+ FG) $

= *** + ABC $ – DE + FG**

ii) – A/B * C $ DE prefix

a) To postfix

Reverse the prefix expression

ED$C* B/A –

DE $ * C /B – A

reverse it

A – B/C *DE $ → postfix

b) To infix

= (A – B) / (C * D) $ E

Example 5.7.5 *Give the postfix and prefix expression - (a+b*c)/(x+y/z)*

Solution : Infix to postfix conversion

Input read	Action	Stack	Output
(	Push (	(	
a	Print a	(	a
+	Push +	(+	a
b	Print b	(+	ab
*	Push	(+ *	ab
c	Print c	(+ *	abc
)	Pop *, Print. Pop +, Print Pop (		abc * +
/	Push /	/	abc * +
(	Push (	/ (	abc * +
x	Print x	/ (	abc * + x
+	Push +	/ (+	abc * + x
y	Print y	/ (+	abc * + xy
/	Push /	/ (+ /	abc * + xy
z	Print z	/ (+ /	abc * + xyz
)	Pop /, Print. Pop +, Print Pop (	/	abc * + xyz / +
end of input	Pop /, Print		**abc * + xyz / + /** is required postfix expression.

Infix to Prefix Conversion

Reverse the input as) z/y + x (/) c * b + a (and then read each character one at a time.

Input read	Action	Stack	Output
)	Push)	)	
z	Print z	)	z
/	Push	) /	z
y	Print y	) /	zy
+	Pop /, Print push +	) +	zy /
x	Print x	) +	zy / x
(	Pop +, Print + Pop)		zy / x +
/	Push /	/	zy / x +
)	Push	/)	zy / x +
c	Print c	/)	zy / x + c
*	Push *	/) *	zy / x + c
b	Print b	/) *	zy / x + c
+	Pop *, Print it push +	/)	zy / x + cb *
a	Print	/) +	zy / x + cb * a
(	Pop +, Print + Pop)	/	zy/ x + cb * a +
end of input	Pop/, Print it	empty	zy / x + cb * a + /
	Reverse the output and print it.		**/ + a * bc + x / yz** is prefix expression.

Example 5.7.6 *Convert the following expression into postfix form. Show all the steps and stack content :*

$4\$2*3-3+8/4(1+1)$

Solution :

Input symbol	Action	Stack	Postfix expression
4	Print 4	empty	4
$	Push $	$	4
2	Print 2	$	42

*	POP $, Print it. Push *	*	42 $
3	Print 3	*	42 $ 3
–	POP *, Print it Push –	-	42 $ 3*
3	Print it	-	42 $ 3*3
+	POP –, Print it. Then push +	+	42 $ 3*3 –
8	Print 8	+	42 $ 3*3 – 8
/	Push /	+ /	42 $ 3*3 – 8
4	Print 4	+ /	42 $ 3*3 – 84
/	POP/, Print it Then Push/	+ /	42 $ 3*3 – 84 /
(	Push (	+ / (	42 $ 3*3 – 84 /
1	Print 1	+ / (	42 $ 3*3 – 84 / 1
+	Push +	+ / (+	42 $ 3*3 – 84 / 1
1	Print 1	+ / (+	42 $ 3*3 – 84 / 11
)	POP +, Print it POP (	+ /	42 $ 3*3 – 84 / 11 +
end of input	POP/, Print POP +, Print	empty	42 $ 3*3 – 84 / 11 + / +

The postfix expression is **42$3*3 – 84/11+/+**

5.7.1 Need for Prefix and Postfix Expressions

- Prefix expression is a kind of expression in which the operator is placed before the two operands. The postfix expression is kind of expression in which the operator is placed after the two operands. The advantage of this arrangement is that the operators are **no longer ambiguous** with respect to the operands that they work on.
- The **order of operations** within prefix and postfix expressions is completely determined by the position of the operator and nothing else.
- Hence during compilation of an expression, the infix expression is converted to postfix form first and then it is evaluated.

5.8 Postfix Expression Evaluation

Algorithm for evaluation of postfix

1. Read the postfix expression from left to right.
2. If the input symbol read is an operand then push it on to the stack.
3. If the operator is read POP two operands and perform arithmetic operations if operator is

   + then result = operand 1 + operand 2

   – then result = operand 1 – operand 2

   * then result = operand 1 * operand 2

   / then result = operand 1 / operand 2
4. Push the result onto the stack.
5. Repeat steps 1-4 till the postfix expression is not over.

For example - Consider postfix expression -

AB + C – BA + C $ – for A = 1, B = 2 and C = 3

Now as per the algorithm of postfix expression evaluation, we scan the input from left to right. If operand comes we push them onto the stack and if we read any operator, we must pop two operands and perform the operation using that operator. Here $ is taken as exponential operator.

As A = 1, push 1

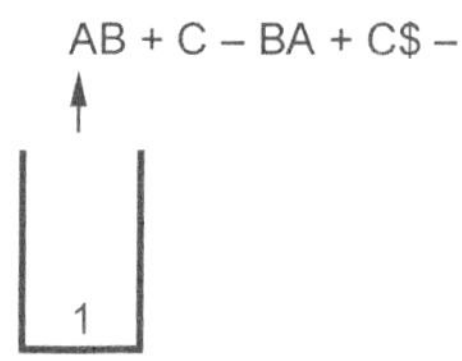

As B = 2, push 2

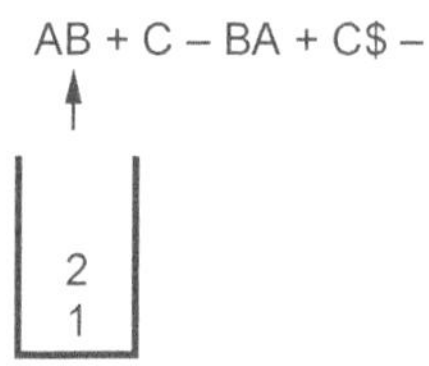

POP two operands and perform addition of 1 and 2. Then push the result onto the stack.

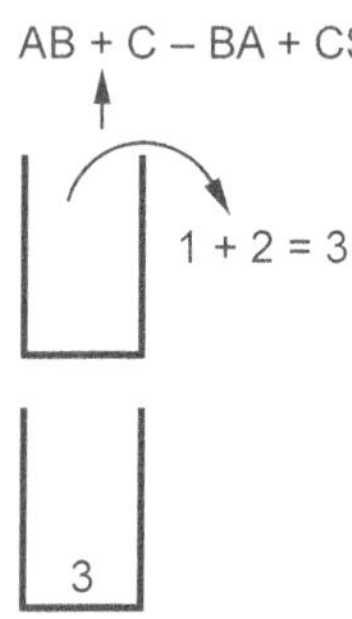

As C = 3, push 3 onto the stack.

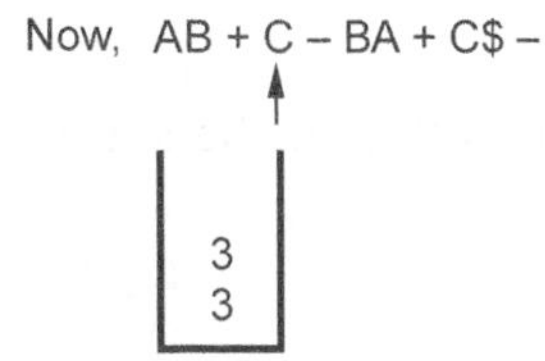

Perform subtraction

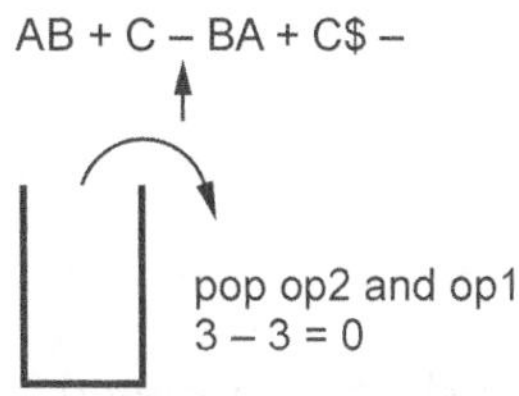

Then push the result onto the stack

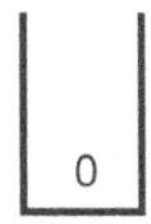

Push B = 2

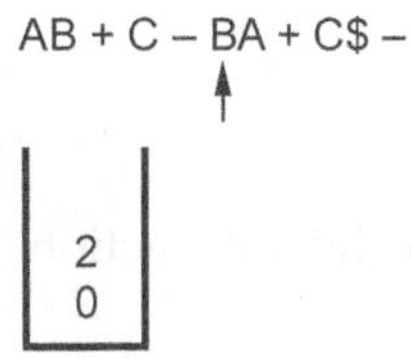

Push A = 1

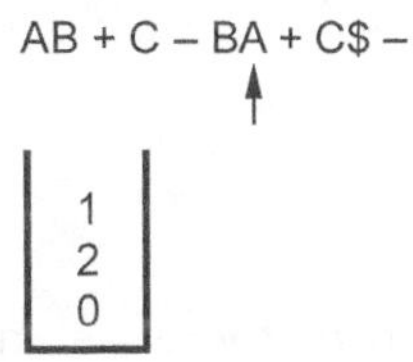

As operator comes perform operation by popping two operands.

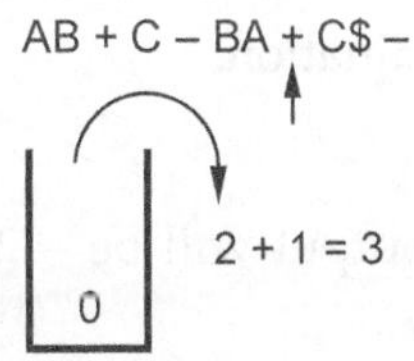

Then push the result onto the stack.

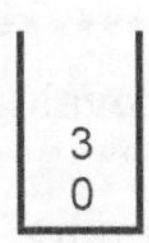

Push C = 3 onto the stack.

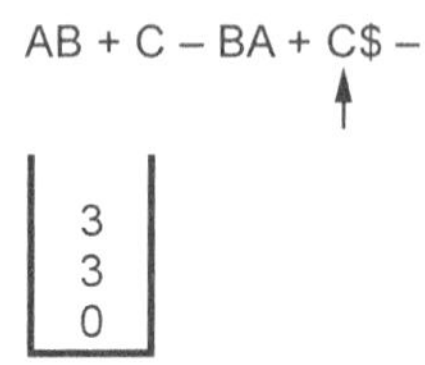

Then push the computed result

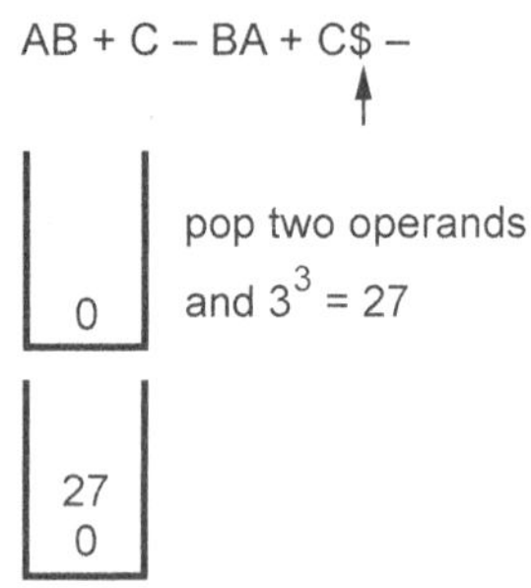

Perform the subtraction

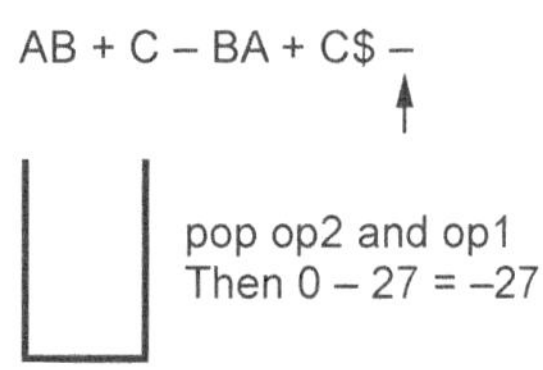

Now since there is no further input we should pop the contents of stack and print it as a result of evaluation.

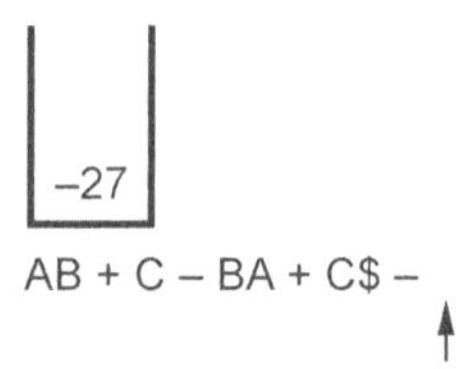

Hence output will be – 27.

C++ Program

```
/*****************************************************************
    Program to evaluate a given postfix expression.
*****************************************************************/
#include<iostream.h>
#include<conio.h>
#include<stdlib.h>
#include<string.h>
#include<math.h>
#define size 80
```

```
class EVAL
{
/*declaration of stack data structure*/
        private:
        struct stack
        {
                double s[size];
                int  top;
        }st;
        public:
                double post(char post[]);
                void push(double);
                double pop();
};
/*-----------------------------------------------------------------------------------
 The post function which is for evaluating postfix expression
 Input : A post Expression of single digit operand
 Output: Resultant value after evaluating the expression
 Parameter Passing Method : By reference
 Called By : main()
 Calls : push(), pop()
-------------------------------------------------------------------------------------
*/
double EVAL::post(char exp[])
{
    char   ch,*type;
    double  result, val, op1, op2;
    int i;
    st.top = 0;
    i=0;
    ch = exp[i];
    while ( ch !='$' )
    {
        if ( ch >= '0' && ch <= '9')
        type ="operand";

        else if ( ch == '+' || ch == '-'||
         ch == '*'|| ch == '/' ||
         ch == '^' )
        type="operator";
        if( strcmp(type,"operand")==0)/*if the character is operand*/
        {
        val = ch - 48;
        push(val);
        }
        else
```

The characters '0', '1', ... '9' will be converted to their values, so that they will perform arithmetic operation.

```
        if (strcmp(type,"operator")==0)/*if it is operator*/
        {
         op2 = pop();
         op1 = pop(); //popping two operands to perform arithmetic operation
         switch(ch)
        {
        case '+' : result = op1 + op2;
                    break;
        case '-' : result = op1 - op2;
                   break;
        case '*' : result = op1 * op2;
                  break;
        case '/' : result = op1 / op2;
                  break;
        case '^' : result = pow(op1,op2);
                  break;
    }/* switch */
    push(result);
    }
        i++;
        ch=exp[i];
    } /* while */
    result = pop(); /*pop the result*/
    return(result);
}
/*
-------------------------------------------------------------------------
    The push function
    Input : A value to be pushed on global stack
    Output: None, modifies global stack and its top
    Parameter Passing Method : By Value
    Called By : post()
    Calls : none
-------------------------------------------------------------------------
*/
void EVAL::push(double val)
{
    if ( st.top+1 >= size )
                cout<<"\nStack is Full\n";
    st.top++;
    st.s[st.top] = val;
}
/*-----------------------------------------------------------------------
    The pop function
    Input : None, uses global stack and top
    Output: Returns the value on top of stack
```

Finally result will be pushed onto the stack.

```
    Parameter Passing Method : None
    Called By : post()
    Calls : None
---------------------------------------------------------------
*/
double EVAL::pop()
{
    double val;
    if ( st.top == -1 )
        cout<<"\nStack is Empty\n";
    val = st.s[st.top];
    st.top --;
    return(val);
}
/*---------------------------------------------------------------
    The main function
    Input : None
    Output: None
    Parameter Passing Method :None
    Called By : OS
    Calls : post()
---------------------------------------------------------------
*/
void main ( )
{
    char exp[size];
    int len;
    double  Result;
    EVAL obj;
    clrscr();
    cout<<"Enter the postfix Expression\n";
    cin>>exp;
    len = strlen(exp);
    exp[len] = '$'; /* Append $ at the end as a endmarker*/
    Result =obj.post(exp);
    cout<<"The Value of the expression is  " <<Result;
    getch();
    exit(0);
}
```

Output

```
Enter the postfix Expression
12+34*+
The Value of the expression is  15
```

Logic of evaluation of postfix expression [Refer the above program]

Let us take some example of postfix expression and try to evaluate it

123+*

Step 1 : Assume the array exp [ ] contains the input

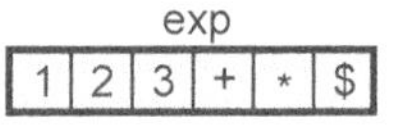

The $ symbol is used as an end marker. Read from first element of the array if it is **operand** push it onto the stack.

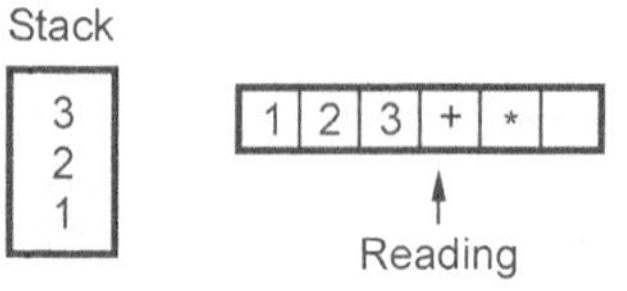

Step 2 : If the operator is read pop two operands

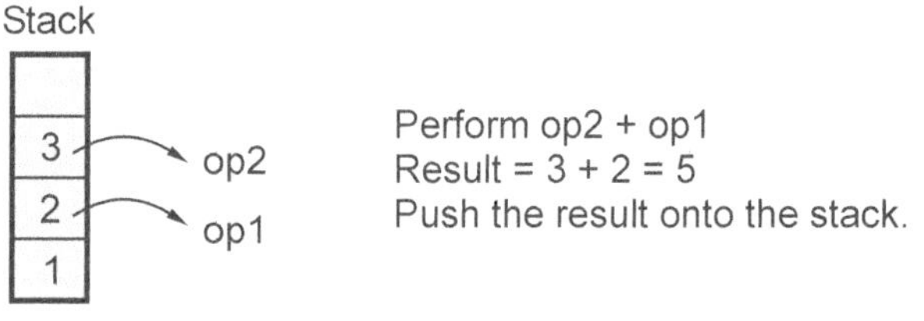

Step 3 : Again pop two operands and perform the operation.

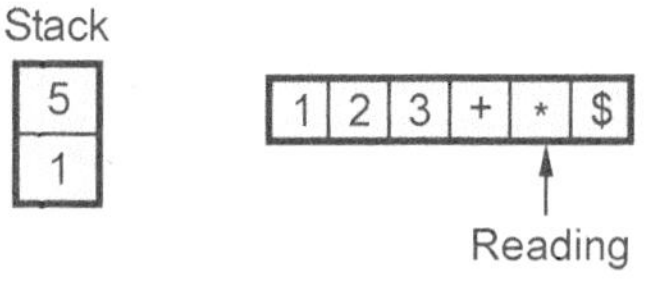

Step 4 : At this point the stack is empty and the input is read as $. So here stop the evaluation procedure and return the result = 5.

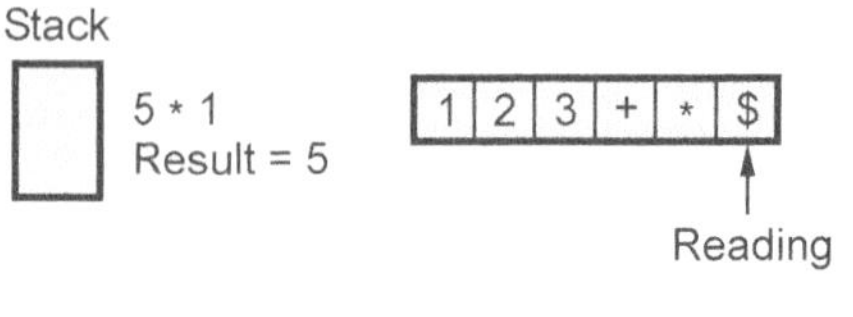

5.9 Linked Stack and Operations

- The advantage of implementing stack using linked list is that we need not have to worry about the size of the stack.
- Since we are using linked list as many elements we want to insert those many nodes can be created. And the nodes are dynamically getting created so there won't be any stack full condition.
- The typical structure for linked stack can be

```
struct stack
{
	int data;
	struct stack *next;
}node;
```

- Each node consists of data and the next field. Such a node will be inserted in the stack. Following figure represents stack using linked list.

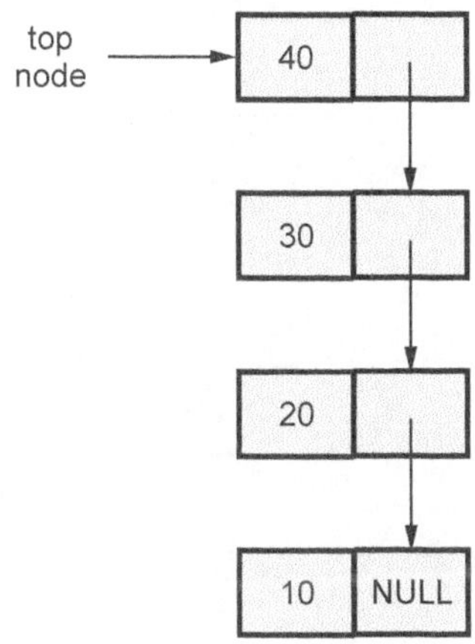

Fig. 5.9.1 Representing the linked stack

Let us now see the 'C++' implementation of it.

C++ Program

```
/***********************************************************
Program for creating the stack using the linked list. Program performs all the operations
such as push,pop and display. It takes care of stack underflow condition. There can not
be stack full condition in stack using linked list.
	************************************************************/
	#include <iostream.h>
	#include <conio.h>
	#include<stdlib.h>
	//Declaration for data structure of linked stack
	class Lstack
```

```
{
 private:
 typedef struct stack
 {
       int data;
       struct stack *next;
 }node;
 node *top;
 public:
 Lstack();
 ~Lstack();
 void create(),remove(),show();
 void Push(int , node **);
 void Display(node **);
 int Pop(node **);
 int Sempty(node *);
};
/*
--------------------------------------------------------------
The constructor defined
--------------------------------------------------------------
*/
Lstack::Lstack()
{
 top = NULL;
}
/*
--------------------------------------------------------------
The destructor defined
--------------------------------------------------------------
*/
Lstack::~Lstack()
{
 node *temp;
 temp=top;
 if(temp==NULL)
 delete temp;
 else
 {
  while(temp!=NULL)
  {
       temp=temp->next;
       top=NULL;
       top=temp;
  }
  delete temp;//de allocating memory
 }
```

```
}
/*
------------------------------------------------------------
The create function
------------------------------------------------------------
*/
void Lstack::create()
{
 int data;
 cout<<"\n Enter the data";
 cin>>data;
 Push(data,&top);
}
/*
------------------------------------------------------------
The remove function
------------------------------------------------------------
*/
void Lstack::remove()
{
 int item;
 if(Sempty(top))
        cout<<"\n stack underflow!";
 else
  {
        item = Pop(&top);
        cout<<"\n The popped node is  "<<item;
  }
}
/*
------------------------------------------------------------
The show function
------------------------------------------------------------
*/
void Lstack::show()
{
        Display(&top);
}

/*
------------------------------------------------------------
The Push function
------------------------------------------------------------
*/
void Lstack::Push(int Item, node **top)
{
        node *New;
```

```
        New = new node;
        New->data=Item;
        New -> next = *top;
      *top = New;
}
/*
------------------------------------------------------------
The Sempty Function
------------------------------------------------------------
*/
int Lstack::Sempty(node *temp)
{
 if(temp==NULL)
  return 1;
 else
  return 0;
}
/*
------------------------------------------------------------
        The Pop function
------------------------------------------------------------
*/
int Lstack::Pop(node **top)
{
        int    item;
        node *temp;
        item = (*top) ->data;
        temp = *top;
        *top = (*top) -> next;
        delete temp;
        return(item);
}
/*
----------------------------------------------------
        The Display function
-------------------------------------------------
*/
void Lstack::Display(node **head )
{
        node *temp ;
        temp = *head;
        if(Sempty(temp))
         cout<<"\n The stack is empty!";
        else
        {
         while ( temp != NULL )
         {
```

```
            cout<<" "<<temp-> data;
            temp = temp -> next;
           }
          }
         getch();
}
/*
------------------------------------------------
         The main function
------------------------------------------------
*/
void main ( )
{
         int choice;
         char ans,ch;
         Lstack st;
         clrscr();
         cout<<"\n\t\t Stack Using Linked List";
         do
         {
           cout<<"\n\n The main menu";
           cout<<"\n1.Push\n2.Pop\n3.Display\n4.Exit";
           cout<<"\n Enter Your Choice";
           cin>>choice;
           switch(choice)
           {
            case 1:st.create();
                        break;
            case 2:st.remove();
                        break;
            case 3:st.show();
                        break;
            case 4:exit(0);
           }
          cout<<"\n Do you want to continue?";
          ans =getche();
         getch();
         clrscr();
   }while(ans =='Y' ||ans =='y');
 getch();
 }
```

Output

```
The main menu
1.Push
2.Pop
3.Display
4.Exit
Enter Your Choice1

Enter the data10

Do you want to continue?
The main menu
1.Push
2.Pop
3.Display

4.Exit
Enter Your Choice1

Enter the data20

Do you want to continue?
The main menu
1.Push
2.Pop
3.Display
4.Exit
Enter Your Choice1

Enter the data30

Do you want to continue?
The main menu
1.Push
2.Pop
3.Display
4.Exit
Enter Your Choice1
Enter the data40

Do you want to continue?
The main menu
1.Push
2.Pop
3.Display
4.Exit
Enter Your Choice1
Enter the data50

Do you want to continue?
```

```
The main menu
1.Push
2.Pop
3.Display
4.Exit
Enter Your Choice3
 50  40  30  20  10
Do you want to continue?

The main menu
1.Push
2.Pop
3.Display
4.Exit
Enter Your Choice2

The popped node is  50
Do you want to continue?

The main menu
1.Push
2.Pop
3.Display
4.Exit
Enter Your Choice4
```

Program Explanation

We have defined constructor for stack in which simply top is intialized by NULL value.

```
LStack :: LStack()
{
top = NULL ;
}
```

And in the destructor we are deallocating the memory which was reserved for each node of stack.

For example : If the linked stack is created as follows -

Continuing in while loop.

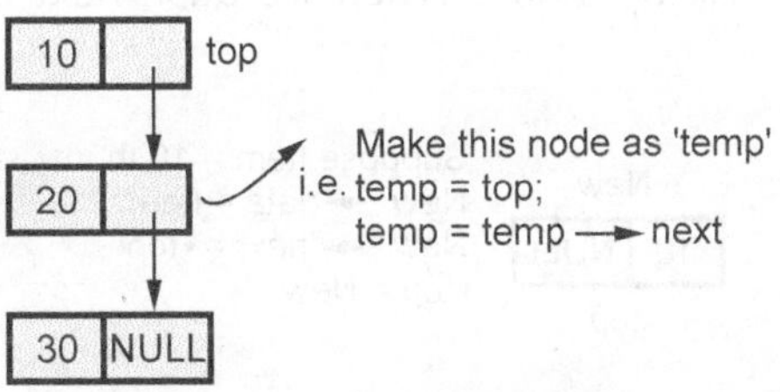

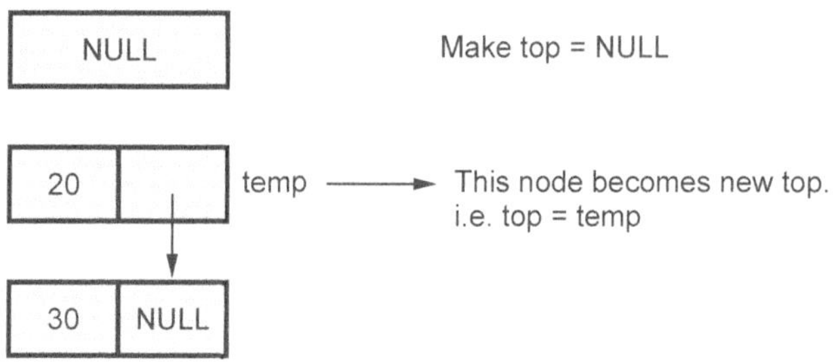

Hence,

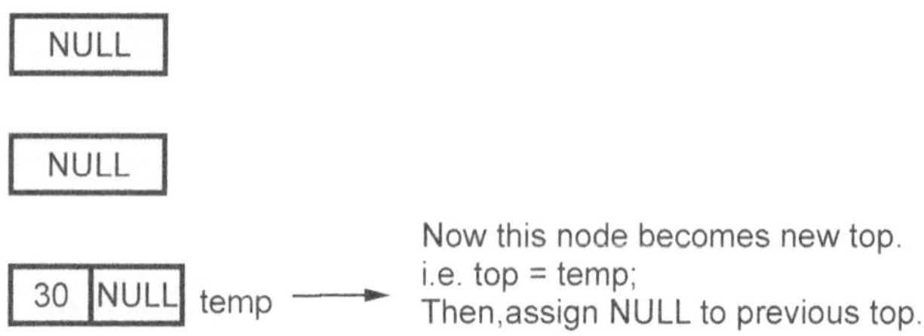

This shows that all the nodes are assigned NULL. Then the memory for these nodes

is deallocated by 'delete'.

In push function :

The memory for 'New ' node is allocated using new operator. In 'New' node we will put the data.

Initially top = NULL, hence

Now make 'New' node as 'top' node. When we push next item as 20 then,

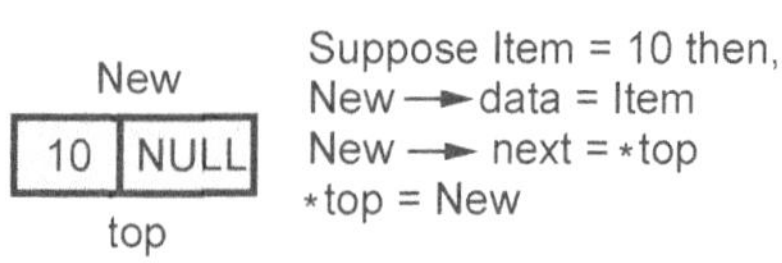

Now make 'New' node as 'top' node.

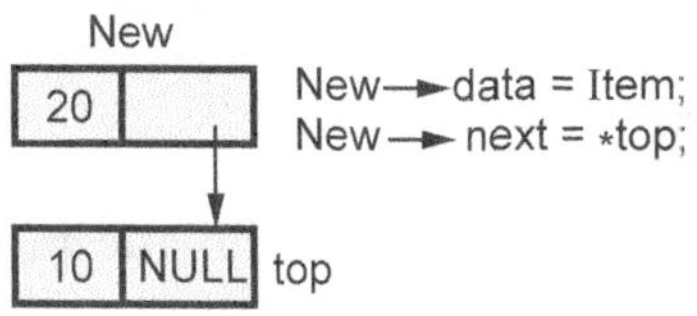

In POP function

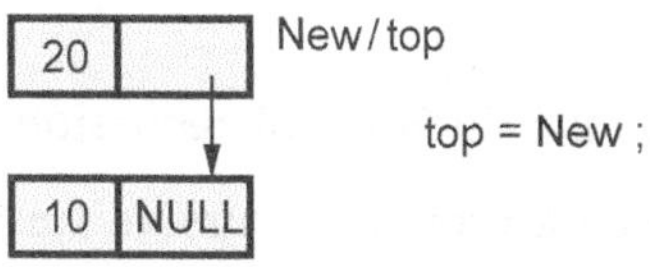

We will POP the element which is at the top. Consider a scenario that we have a stack of

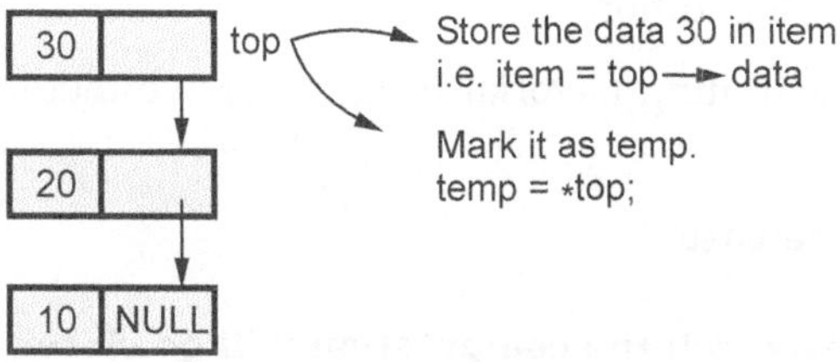

Then

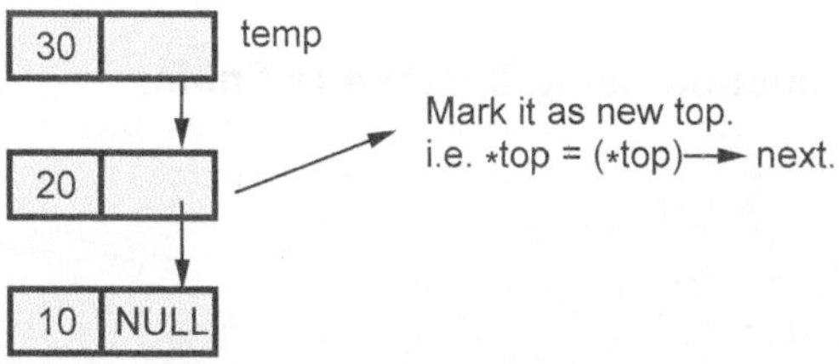

Then delete 'temp' node.

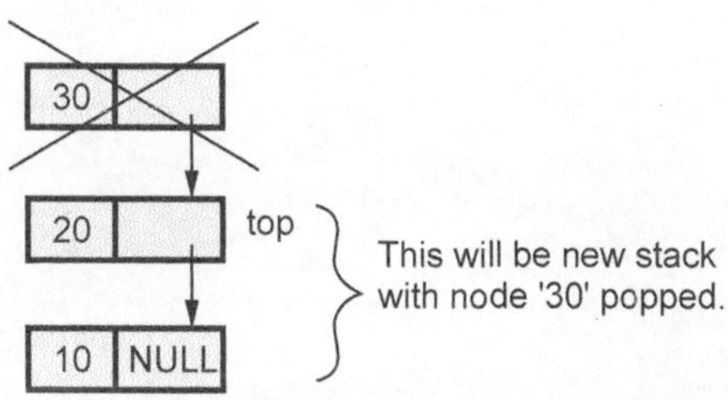

Review Question

1. *Explain the concept of linked stack with suitable example.*

5.10 Recursion- Concept

Definition : Recursion is a programming technique in which the function calls itself repeatedly for some input.

By recursion the same task can be performed repeatedly.

Properties of Recursion

Following are two fundamental principles of recursion

1. There must be at least one condition in recursive function which do not involve the call to recursive routine. This condition is called a "way out" of the sequence of recursive calls. The is called **base case property.**
2. The invoking of **each recursive call must reduce** to some manipulation and must go closer to base case condition.

For example - While computing factorial using recursive method -

```
if(n==0)
  return 1;  //This is a base case
else
  return n*fact(n-1);//on each call the computation will go closer to base case
```

Example

Algorithm for Factorial Function using Iterative Definition

1. prod = 1;
2. x=n;
3. while(x>0)
4. {
5. prod = prod*x;
6. x – –;
7. }
8. return(prod);

Algorithm for Factorial Function using Recursive Definition

```
1. if(n==0)
2. fact =1;
3. else
   {
4. x=n–1;
5. y= value of x!;
6. fact = n* y ;
7. } /*else ends here */
```

This definition is called the **recursive definition** of the factorial function. This definition is called recursive because again and again the same procedure of multiplication is followed but with the different input and result is again multiplied with the next input. Let us see how the recursive definition of the factorial function is used to evaluate the 5!

Step 1. 5! = 5 * 4!

Step 2. 4! = 4 * 3!

Step 3. 3! = 3 * 2!

Step 4. 1! = 1 * 0!

Step 5. 2! = 2 * 1!

Step 6. 0! = 1.

Actually the step 6 is the only step which is giving the direct result. So to solve 5! we have to backtrack from step 6 to step 1,collecting the result from each step. Let us see how to do this.

Step 6′. 0! =1

Step 5′. 1! = 1*0! = 1 from step 6′

Step 4′. 2! = 2*1! = 2 from step 5′

Step 3′. 3! = 3*2! = 6 from step 4′

Step 2′. 4! = 4*3! = 24 from step 3′

Step 1′. 5! = 5*4! = 120 from step 2′

Example 5.10.1 *Generate n^{th} term Fibonacci sequence with recursion.*

Solution :

```
#include<iostream>
using namespace std;
```

```
int fib(int n)
{
    int x,y;
    if(n<=1)
        return n;
    x=fib(n-1);
    y=fib(n-2);
    return (x+y);
}
int main(void)
{
    int n,num;
    cout<<"\n Enter location in fibonacci series: ";
    cin>>n;
    num=fib(n);
    cout<<"\n The number at "<<n<<" position is "<<num<<" in fibonacci series";
    return 0;
}
```

Output

```
Enter location in fibonacci series: 3
The number at 3 position is 2 in fibonacci series
```

5.10.1 Use of Stack in Recursive Functions

For illustrating the use of stack in recursive functions, we will consider an example of finding factorial. The recursive routine for obtaining factorial is as given below -

```
int fact (int num)
{
    int a, b;
    if (num = = 0)
        return 1 ;
    else
    {
        a = num – 1 ;
        b = fact (a) ;
        f = a * b;
        return f ;
    }
}
/* Call to the function */
ans = fact (4) ;
```

For the above recursive routine we will see the use of stack. For the stack the only principle idea is that – when there is a call to a function the values are pushed onto the stack and at the end of the function or at the return the stack is popped

Suppose we have num = 4. Then in function **fact** as num ! = 0 else part will be executed. We get

a = num – 1

a = 3

And a recursive call to fact (3) will be given. Thus internal stack stores

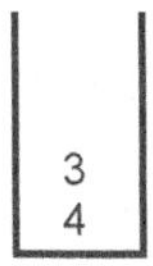

Next fact (2) will be invoked. Then

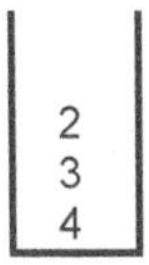

∵ a = num – 1

a = 3 – 1

b = fact (2)

Then,

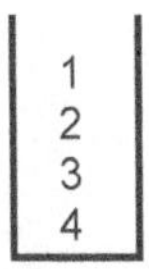

∵ a = num – 1

a = 2 – 1

b = fact (1)

Now next as num = 0, we return the value 1.

∴ a = 1, b = 1, we return f = a ∗ b = 1 from function **fact**. Then 1 will be popped off.

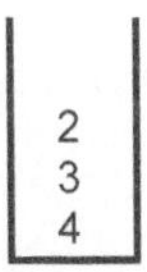

Now the top of the stack is the value of a

Then we get b = fact (2) = 1

∴ f = a ∗ b = 2 ∗ 1 = 2 will be returned.

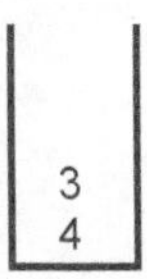

Here a = 3

Then b = fact (3)

b = 2

∴ f = a ∗ b = 6 will be returned.

The stack will be

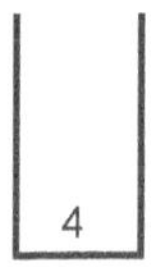

Here a = 4

Then b = fact (4)

= 6

$\therefore$ f = a $*$ b = 24 will be returned.

As now stack is empty. We return f = 24 from the function **fact**.

5.10.2 Variants of Recursion

Variants of recursion tells us different ways by which the recursive calls can be made depending upon the problem.

Let us understand them with the help of suitable examples -

5.10.2.1 Direct Recursion

Definition : A C function is directly recursive if it contains an explicit call to itself.

For example

```
int fun1(int n)
{
    if(n<=0)
        return n;
    else
        return fun1(n-1);        Call to itself
}
```

5.10.2.2 Indirect Recursion

Definition : A C function is indirectly recursive if function1 calls function2 and function2 ultimately calls function1.

For example

```
int fun1(int n)
{
    if(n<=0)
        return n;
    else
        return fun2(n);
}
int fun2(int m)
{
    return fun1(n-1);
}
```

5.10.2.3 Tail Recursion

Tail recursion is a kind of recursion in which there is no pending operation after returning from the recursive function.This concept was introduced by David H. D. Warren. This is a special kind of recursive approach which helps in improving the space and time efficiency of recursive function.

For example : Consider a simple example of computing factorial of number n. Following is a simple recursive function.

C program

```
/*********************************************************************
Implementing the FACTORIAL function without using tail recursion
*********************************************************************/
#include<stdio.h>
#include<conio.h>
void main()
{
      int fact(int n);
      int n;
      printf("\n Enter some number n ");
      scanf("%d",&n);
      printf("\n The factorial = %d",fact(n));
      getch();
}
int fact(int n)
{
        if(n==1)
              return 1;
        return n*fact(n-1);
}
```

Output

```
Enter some number n 4
```

The above given program does not have tail recursion, because it contains a recursive function fact and on return of this recursive call multiplication is performed. The multiplication operation is always a pending operation even after return of recursive call. We can convert the above code into a tail recursive form as follows -

```
/*********************************************************************
Implementation of tail recursion for computing FACTORIAL function
*********************************************************************/
#include<stdio.h>
#include<conio.h>
void main()
```

```
{
    int fact(int n);
    int n;
    printf("\n\t Program for finding factorial(n) using Tail Recursion ");
    printf("\n Enter some number n ");
    scanf("%d",&n);
    printf("\n The factorial = %d",fact(n));
    getch();
}
int fact(int n)
{
    int my_new_fact(int n,int f);
    return my_new_fact(n,1);
}
int my_new_fact(int n,int f)
{
    if(n==1)
        return f;
    my_new_fact(n-1,n*f);
}
```

> This is tail recursive function as after returning from this function there is no pending operation.

Output

```
    Program for finding factorial(n) using Tail Recursion
 Enter some number n 4

 The factorial = 24
```

Note that once the control returns from the function my_new_fact, there is no pending operation. The control always returns from this function with the final result in variable f.

Advantages of tail recursion

1. **Optimizes** the task of compiler for executing the recursive function.
2. Improves the **space and time efficiency** of the recursive code.

5.10.2.4 Tree

A tree recursion is a kind of recursion in which the recursive function contains the pending operation that involves another recursive call to the function.

The implementation of **fibonnaci** series is a classic example of tree recursion.

C Function

```
int fib(int n)
{
        if(n==0)
                return 0;
        if(n==1)
                return 1;
        return fib(n-1)+fib(n-2);
}
```

```
        fib(4)
     =  fib(3) + fib(2)
     =  [fib(2) + fib(1)] + [fib(1) + fib(0)]
     =  [(fib(1) + fib(0)] + [1] + [1 + 0]
     =  [1+0] + 1 + 1
fib(4) = 3
```

The call tree can be represented as follows

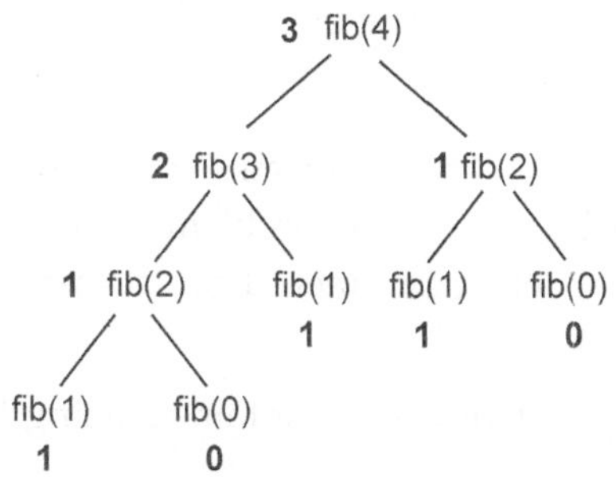

Fig. 5.10.1 Recursive tree

5.10.2.5 Difference between Recursion and Iteration

Sr. No.	Iteration	Recursion
1.	Iteration is a process of executing certain set of instructions repeatedly, without calling the self function.	Recursion is a process of executing certain set of instructions repeatedly by calling the self -function repeatedly.
2.	The iterative functions are implemented with the help of for, while, do-while programming constructs.	Instead of making use of for, while, do-while the repetition in code execution is obtained by calling the same function again and again over some condition.
3.	The iterative methods are more efficient because of better execution speed.	The recursive methods are less efficient.
4.	Memory utilization by iteration is less.	Memory utilization is more in recursive functions.
5.	It is simple to implement.	Recursive methods are complex to implement.
6.	The lines of code is more when we use iteration.	Recursive methods bring compactness in the program.

5.11 Backtracking Algorithmic Strategy

- Backtracking is a method in which
  1. The desired solution is expressible as an n tuple $(x_1, x_2, \ldots x_n)$ where x_i is chosen from some finite set S_i.
  2. The solution maximizes or minimizes or satisfies a criterion function C $(x_1, x_2, \ldots x_n)$.
- The basic idea of backtracking is to build up a **vector,** one component at a time and to test whether the vector being formed has any chance of success.
- The major **advantage** of backtracking algorithm is that we can realize the fact that the partial vector generated does not lead to an optimal solution. In such a situation that vector can be ignored.
- Backtracking algorithm determines the solution by systematically searching the solution space (i.e. set of all feasible solutions) for the given problem.

For example

Example : n-Queen's problem - The n-queen's problem can be stated as follows. " Consider a chessboard of order $n \times n$. The problem is to place n queens on this board such that no two queens can attack each other. That means no two queens can be placed on the same row, column or diagonal. "

The solution to n-queens problem can be obtained using backtracking method.

The solution can be given as below -

		Q	
Q			
			Q
	Q		

⇐ Note that no two queens can attack each other.

5.11.1 Some Terminologies used in Backtracking

Backtracking algorithms determine problem solutions by systematically searching for the solutions using **tree structure.**

For example -

Consider a 4-queen's problem. It could be stated as "there are 4 queens that can be placed on 4×4 chessboard. Then no two queens can attack each other".

Following Fig. 5.11.1 shows tree organization for this problem.

- Each node in the tree is called **a problem state.**

- All paths from the root to other nodes define the **state space of** the problem.
- The solution states are those problem states s for which the path from root to s defines a **tuple** in the solution space.
  In some trees the leaves define the **solution states.**
- **Answer states :** These are the leaf nodes which correspond to an element in the set of solutions, these are the states which satisfy the implicit constraints.

For example- Refer Fig. 5.11.1 (See Fig. 5.11.1 on next page)

- A node which is been generated and all whose children have not yet been generated is called **live node.**
- The live node whose children are currently being expanded is called **E-node.**
- A **dead node** is a generated node which is not to be expanded further or all of whose children have been generated.

5.11.2 The 4 Queen's Problem

Let us take 4-queens and 4 × 4 chessboard.

- Now we start with empty chessboard.

Place queen 1 in the first possible position of its row i.e. on 1st row and 1st column.

Q			

- Then place queen 2 after trying unsuccessful place - 1(1, 2), (2, 1), (2, 2) at (2, 3) i.e. 2nd row and 3rd column.

Q			
		Q	

- This is the dead end because a 3rd queen cannot be placed in next column, as there is no acceptable position for queen 3. Hence algorithm **backtracks** and places the 2nd queen at (2, 4) position.

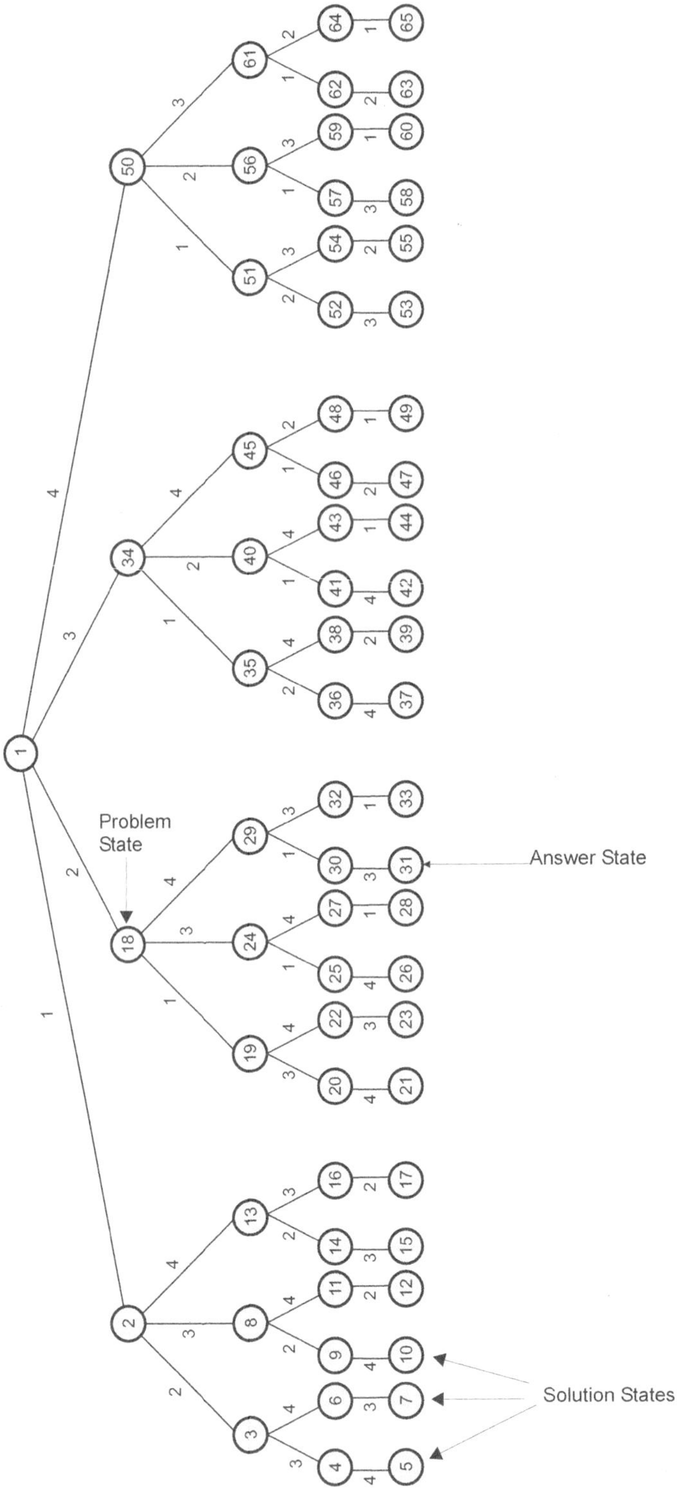

Fig. 5.11.1

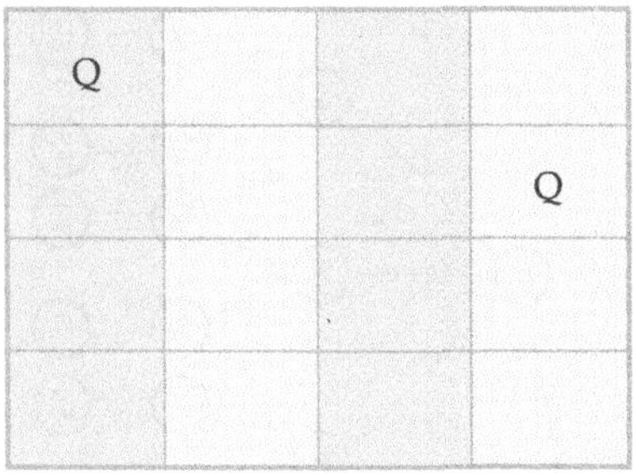

- The place 3rd queen at (3, 2) but it is again another dead end as next queen (4th queen) cannot be placed at permissible position.

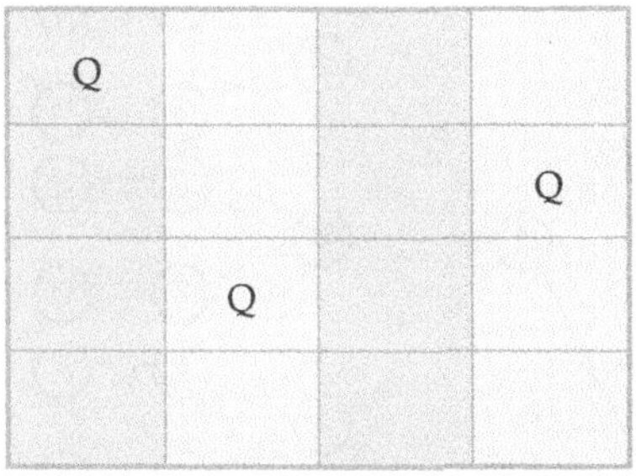

- Hence we need to backtrack all the way upto queen 1 and move it to (1, 2).
- Place queen 1 at (1, 2), queen 2 at (2, 4), queen 3 at (3, 1) and queen 4 at (4, 3).

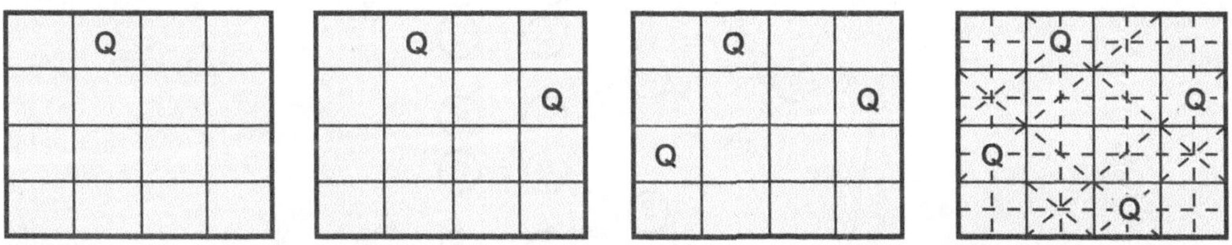

Thus solution is obtained.
(2, 4, 1, 3) in rowwise manner.

The state space tree of 4-queen's problem is shown in Fig. 5.11.2.
(See Fig. 5.11.2 on next page)

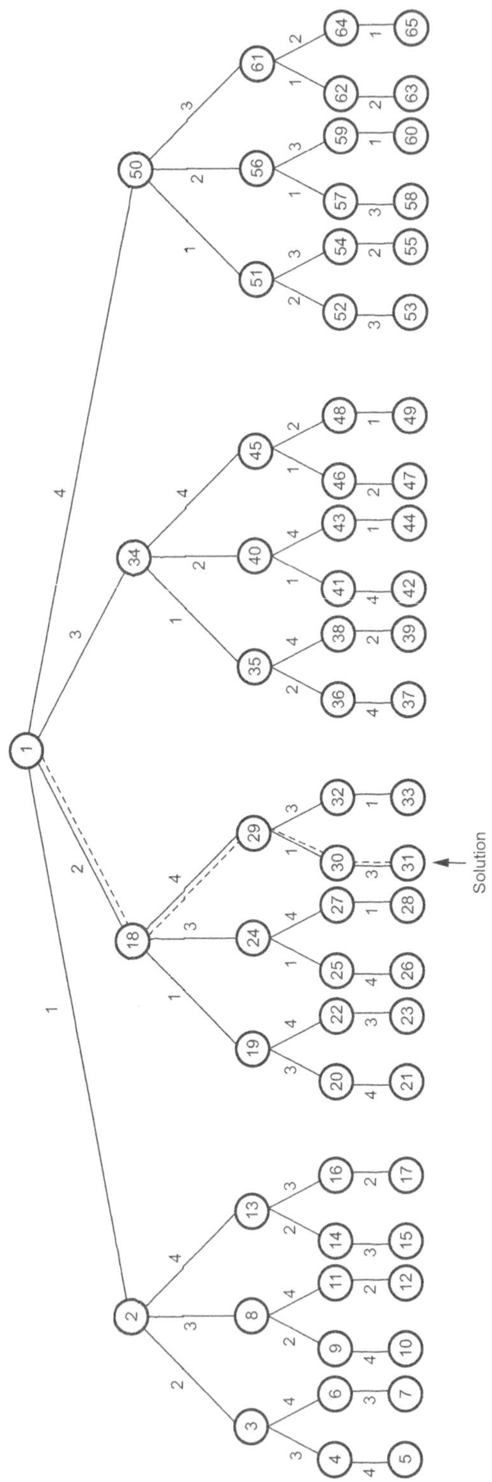

Fig. 5.11.2 State space tree for 4-queen's problem

5.12 Use of Stack in Backtracking

The stack can be used in backtracking to handle the recursive procedures.

Example 5.12.1 *Let us consider, 4 Queen's problem once again to understand the role of stack in backtracking.*

Solution : Step 1 : Place queen 1 on 1st row 1st column push only column number onto the stack.

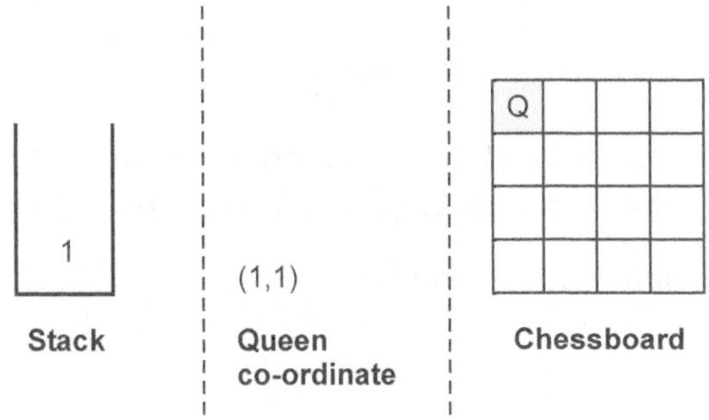

Step 2 : Then place 2 at 2nd row, 3rd column.

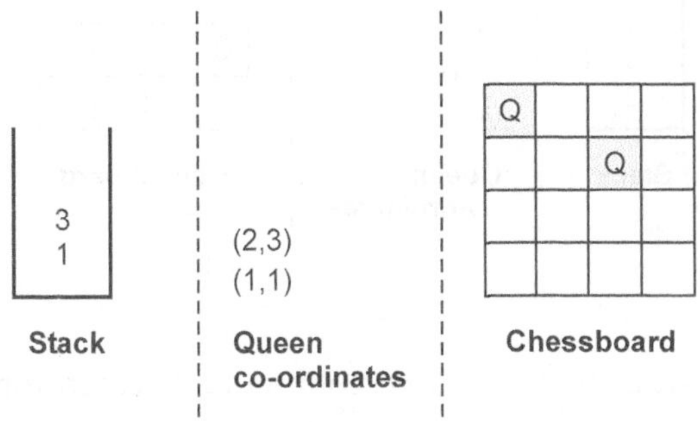

Step 3 : This is dead end, because 3rd queen can not be placed in next column as there is no acceptable poistion for queen 3. Hence algorithm backtrack by popping the 2nd queen's position. Now let us place queen 2 at 4th column.

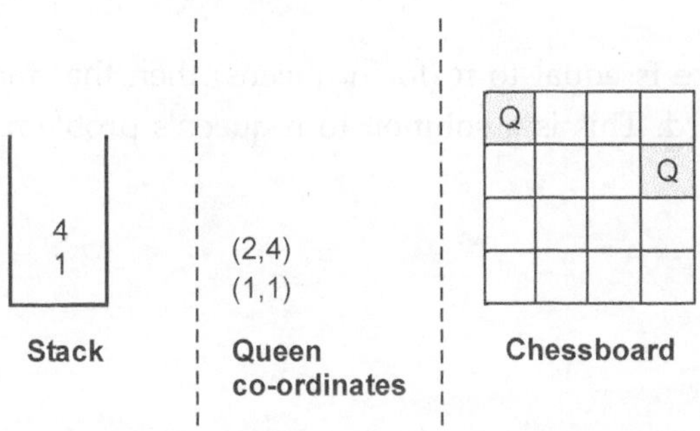

Step 4 : Place 3rd Queen at 2nd column.

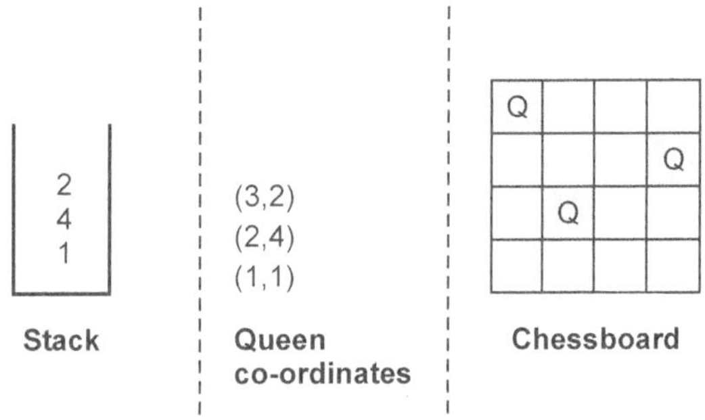

Step 5 : Now, there is no valid place for queen 4. So we needed to backtrack all the moves by popping the column index from the stack to try out other possible places.

Step 6 : Finally the possible solution can be.

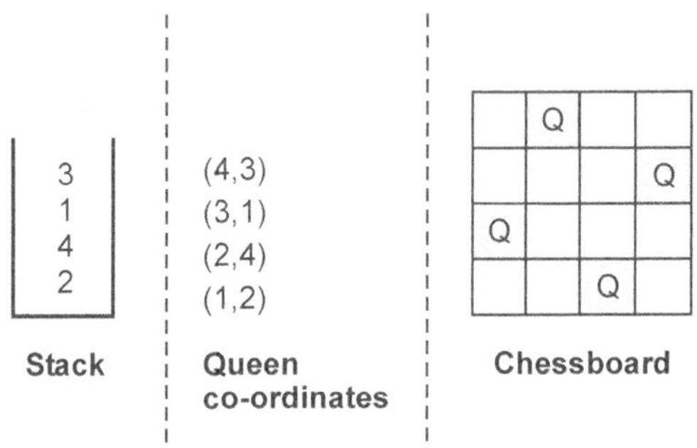

Algorithm :

1. Start with a queen from first row, first column and search for valid position.
2. If we find a valid position in current row, push the position (i.e. Column number) onto the stack. Then start again on next row.
3. If we don't find a valid position in the current row then we backtrack to previous row i.e. POP the column position for previous row from the stack and search for a valid position.
4. When the stack size is equal to n (for n queens) then that means we have placed n queens on the board. This is a solution to n queen's problem.

❑❑❑

Unit - VI

6 Queue

Syllabus

Basic concept, Queue as Abstract Data Type, Representation of Queue using Sequential organization, Queue Operations, Circular Queue and its advantages, Multi-queues, Linked Queue and Operations. Deque-Basic concept, types (Input restricted and Output restricted), Priority Queue- Basic concept, types(Ascending and Descending).

Contents

6.1 Basic Concept

Definition : The queue can be formally defined as ordered collection of elements that has two ends named as **front** and **rear**. From the front end one can delete the elements and from the rear end one can insert the elements.

For example :

The typical example can be a queue of people who are waiting for a city bus at the bus stop. Any new person is joining at one end of the queue, you can call it as the rear end. When the bus arrives the person at the other end first enters in the bus. You can call it as the front end of the queue.

Following Fig. 6.1.1 represents the queue of few elements.

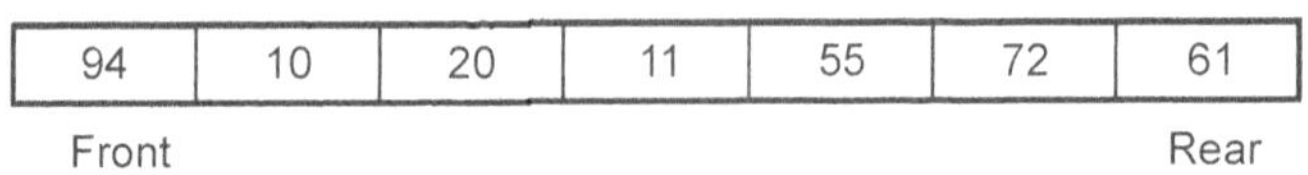

Fig. 6.1.1 Queue

6.1.1 Comparison between Stack and Queue

Sr. No.	Stack	Queue
1.	The stack is a LIFO data structure. That is the element which is inserted last will be removed first from the stack.	The queue is a FIFO data structure. That means the element which is inserted first will be removed first.
2.	The insertion and deletion of the elements in the stack is done from only one end, called top.	The insertion of the element in the queue is done by the end called rear and the deletion of the element from the queue is done by the end called front.

Review Question

1. *Compare stacks and queues.*

6.2 Queue as Abstract Data Type

The ADT for queue is as given below -

AbstractDataType Queue

{

Instances :

Que[MaX] is a finite collection of elements in which insertion of element is by rear end and deletion of element is by front end.

Precondition :

The front and rear should be within the maximum size MAX.

Before insertion operation , whether the queue is full or not is checked.

Before any deletion operation, whether the queue is empty or not is checked.

Operations :

1. Create() - The queue is created by declaring the data structure for it.
2. insert() - The element can be inserted in the queue by rear end.
3. delet() - The element at front end deleted each time.
4. Display() - The elements of queue are displayed from front to rear.

}

Review Question

1. *Explain term : Queue ADT.*

6.3 Representation of Queue using Sequential Organization

- As we have seen, queue is nothing but the collection of items.
- Both the ends of the queue are having their own functionality.
- The Queue is also called as FIFO i.e. a First In First Out data structure. All the elements in the queue are stored sequentially.
- Various operations on the queue are -
  1. Queue overflow.
  2. Insertion of the element into the queue.
  3. Queue underflow.
  4. Deletion of the element from the queue.
  5. Display of the queue.

Let us see each operation one by one

'C++' representation of queue.

```
struct queue
{
    int que [size];
    int front;
    int rear;
} Q;
```

6.4 Queue Operations

1. Insertion of element into the queue

The insertion of any element in the queue will always take place from the rear end.

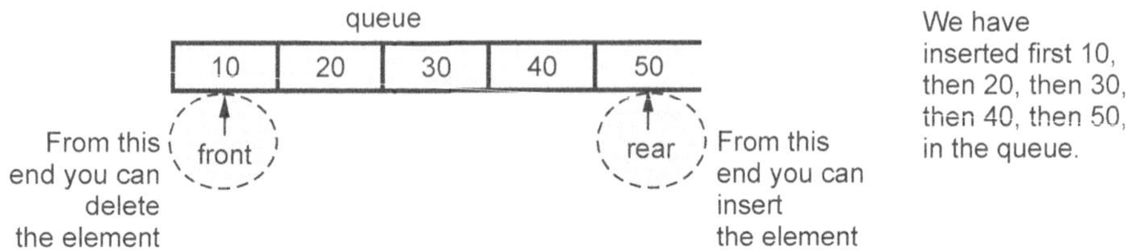

Fig. 6.4.1 Representing the insertion

Before performing insert operation you must check whether the queue is full or not. If the rear pointer is going beyond the maximum size of the queue then the queue overflow occurs.

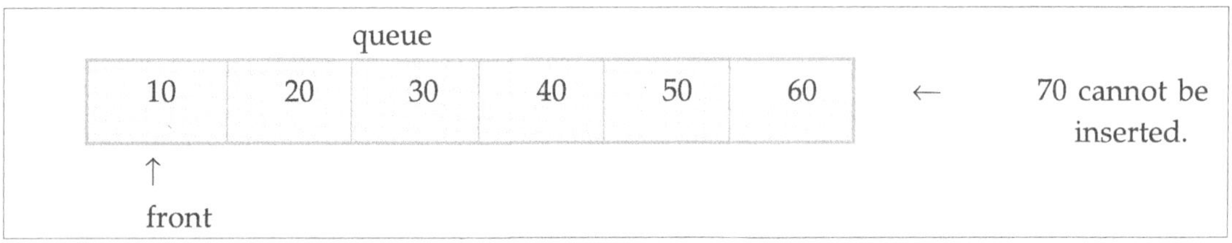

Fig. 6.4.2 Representing the queue overflow

2. Deletion of element from the queue

The deletion of any element in the queue takes place by the front end always.

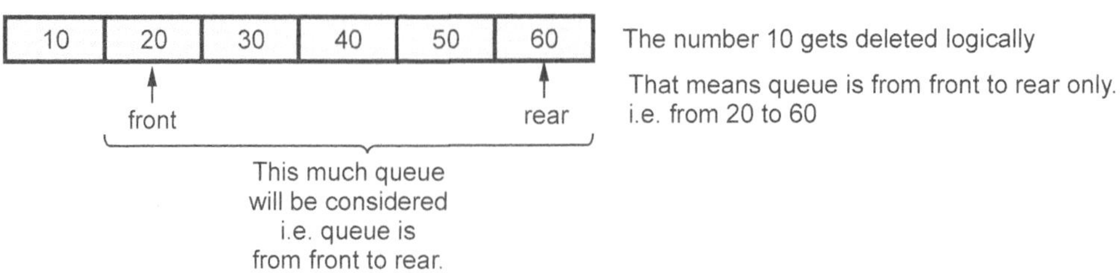

Fig. 6.4.3 Representing the deletion

Before performing any delete operation one must check whether the queue is empty or not. If the queue is empty, you can not perform the deletion. The result of illegal attempt to delete an element from the empty queue is called the queue underflow condition.

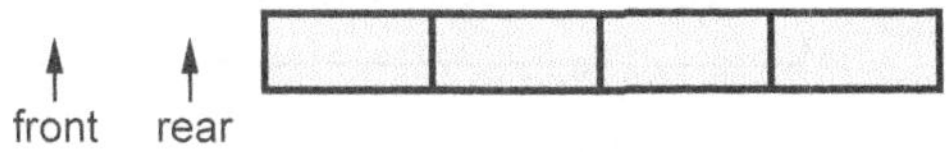

Fig. 6.4.4 Representing the queue underflow

Let us see the C++ implementation of the queue.

C++ Program

```
/*****************************************************************
      Program for implementing the Queue using arrays
*****************************************************************/
#include<iostream.h>
#include<stdlib.h>
#include<conio.h>
#define size 5
class MyQ
{
private:
struct queue
{
 int que[size];
 int front,rear;
}Q;
public:
  MyQ();
  int Qfull();
  int insert(int);
  int Qempty();
  int delet();
  void display();
};
MyQ::MyQ()
{
 Q.front = -1;
 Q.rear  = -1;
}
/*
 The Qfull  Function
 Input:none
```

Queue data structure declared with array que [ ], front and rear

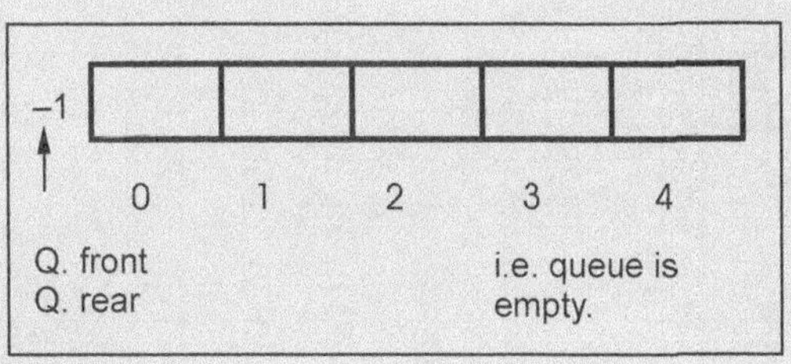

```
 Output:1 or 0 for q full or not
 Called By:main

*/
int MyQ::Qfull()
 {
 if(Q.rear >=size-1)
  return 1;
 else
  return 0;
}
```

If Queue exceeds the maximum size of the array then it returns1 - means queue full is true otherwise 0 means queue full is false

```
/*
 The insert  Function
 Input:item -which is to be inserted in the Q
 Output:rear value
 Called By:main
 Calls:none
*/
int MyQ::insert(int item)
{
  if(Q.front ==-1)
  Q.front++;
  Q.que[++Q.rear] = item;
  return Q.rear;
}
int MyQ::Qempty()
```

This condition will occur initially when queue is empty

Always increment the rear pointer and place the element in the queue.

```
{
 if((Q.front == - 1) || (Q.front > Q.rear))
 return 1;
 else
 return 0;
}
```

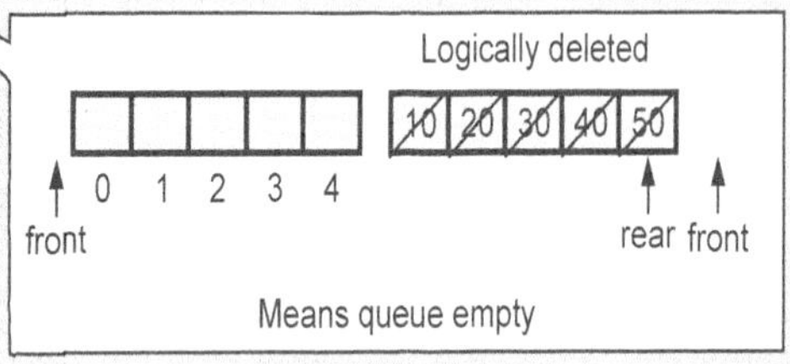


```
/*
 The delete Function
 Input:none
 Output:front value
 Called By:main
 Calls:none
*/
int MyQ::delet()

{
 int item;
```

```
item = Q.que[Q.front];
Q.front++;
cout<<"\n The deleted item is "<<item;
return Q.front;
}
```

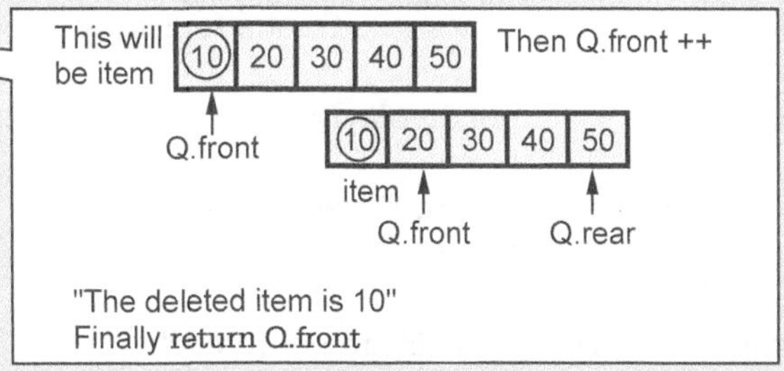


```
/*
 The display Function
 Input:none
 Output:none
 Called By:main
 Calls:none
*/
void MyQ::display()
{
  int i;
  for(i=Q.front;i<=Q.rear;i++)   <------Printing the queue from front to rear
    cout<<" "<<Q.que[i];
}
void main(void)
{
 int choice,item;
 char ans;
 MyQ obj;
 clrscr();
 do
 {
   cout<<"\n Main Menu";
   cout<<"\n1.Insert\n2.Delete\n3.Display";
   cout<<"\n Enter Your Choice: ";
   cin>>choice;
   switch(choice)
        {
        case 1:if(obj.Qfull())       //checking for Queue overflow
                    cout<<"\n Can not insert the element";
               else
               {
                    cout<<"\n Enter The number to be inserted ";
                    cin>>item;
                    obj.insert(item);
               }
               break;
        case 2:if(obj.Qempty())
                    cout<<"\n Queue Underflow!!";
                    else
                    obj.delet();
                    break;
        case 3:if(obj.Qempty())
```

```
                cout<<"\nQueue Is Empty!";
                else
                obj.display();
                break;
        default:cout<<"\n Wrong choice!";
                break;
        }
  cout<<"\n Do You Want to continue?";
  ans =getche();
  }while(ans =='Y'||ans =='y');
}
/********************** End Of Program ***********************/
```

Output

```
 Main Menu
1.Insert
2.Delete
3.Display
 Enter Your Choice: 1

 Enter The number to be inserted 10

 Do You Want to continue?y
 Main Menu
1.Insert
2.Delete
3.Display
 Enter Your Choice: 1

 Enter The number to be inserted 20

 Do You Want to continue?y
 Main Menu
1.Insert
2.Delete
3.Display
 Enter Your Choice: 1

 Enter The number to be inserted 30

 Do You Want to continue?y
 Main Menu
1.Insert
2.Delete
3.Display
 Enter Your Choice: 1
```

```
Enter The number to be inserted 40

Do You Want to continue?y
Main Menu
1.Insert
2.Delete
3.Display
Enter Your Choice: 3
10 20 30 40
Do You Want to continue?y
Main Menu
1.Insert
2.Delete
3.Display
Enter Your Choice: 2

The deleted item is 10
Do You Want to continue?y
Main Menu
1.Insert
2.Delete
3.Display
Enter Your Choice: 2

The deleted item is 20
Do You Want to continue?y
Main Menu
1.Insert
2.Delete
3.Display
Enter Your Choice: 3
30 40
Do You Want to continue?
```

Example 6.4.1 *Show how to implement a queue using two stacks ? Analyse the running time of the queue operations.*

Solution : There are two stacks namely stack1, stack2. Following steps can be performed for **insertq** and **deleteq** operations to implement queue using two stacks.

```
insertq (item)
{
    Step 1 : push everything from stack1 to stack2 while stack1 is not empty.
    Step 2 : push item to stack1.
    Step 3 : Push all elements from stack2 to stack1.
}
deleteq ()
{
```

Step 1 : pop an item from stack1 and return it.
}

Now we will analyze time for queue operations

insertq operation

- Step 1 will require **O(n)** time.
- Step 2 will 'require O(1).
- Step 3 will require O(n).

Thus total O(n) + O(1) + O(n) = O(n) time will be required by insert operation of queue.

deleteq operation : Step 1 will require O(1) time.

Consider elements 10, 20, 30, 40 to be inserted in queue. The steps are as follows -

Step 1 : Insertq(10)

As there is nothing in stack1 initially hence nothing will be pushed to stack1.

push 10 to stack1

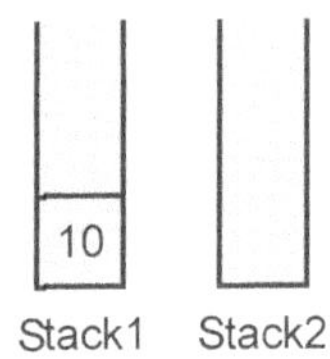

Nothing will be copied to stack1. From stack2 as stack2 is empty. If deleteq operation is to be performed then top element of stack1 will be returned.

Step 2 : Insertq(20)

push everything from stack1 to stack2

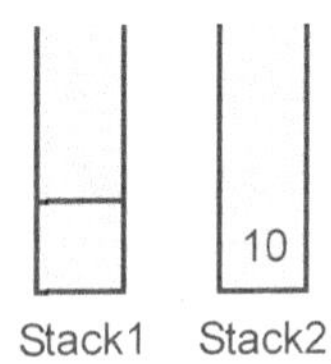

push 20 to stack1

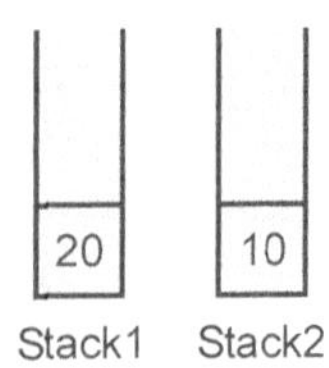

pop everything from stack2 and push it to stack1

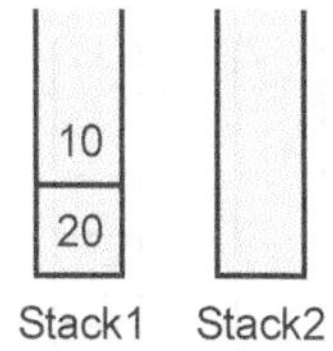

Step 3 : Insertq (30)

push everything from stack1 to stack2

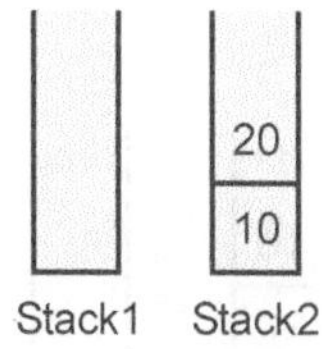

push 30 to stack1.

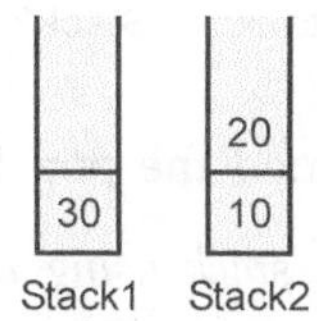

pop from stack2 and push it onto stack1

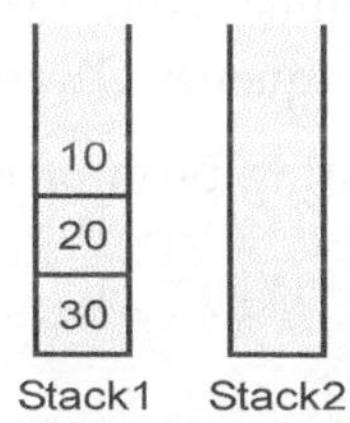

If deleteq operation is to be performed then pop from stack1.

Step 4 : Insertq (40)

push everything from stack1 to stack2

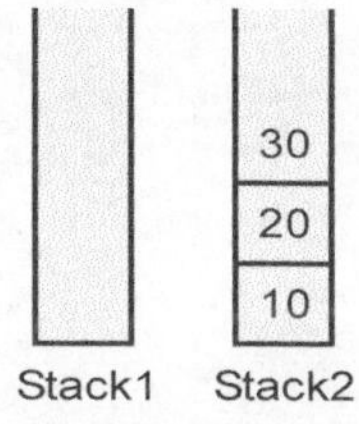

push 40 onto stack1

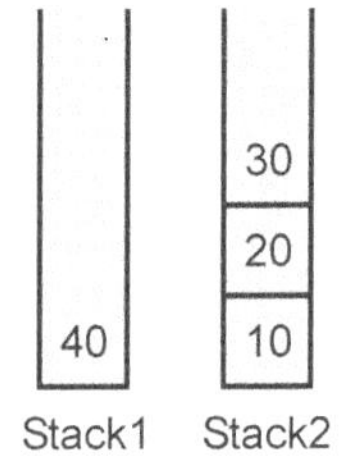

push everything from stack2 to stack1

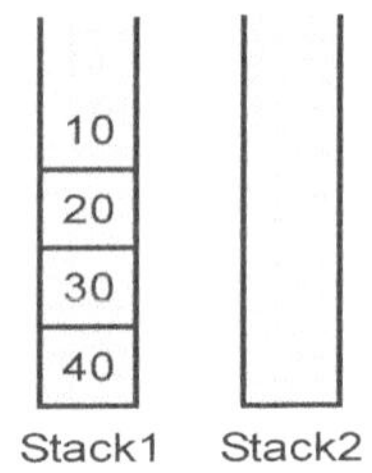

If deleteq operation is to be performed the pop from stack1.

Example 6.4.2 *Show how to implement a stack using two Queues ? Analyse the run time of the stack operations ?*

Solution : We will push the elements 10, 20, 30, 40, 50 onto the stack. During the push operations one can invoke pop at any time. Note that these push and pop operations can be performed only with the help of two queues Q1 and Q2.

Following steps will be followed during push or pop operations.

push (item)
{
Step 1 : Insert **item** in Q2
Step 2 : One by one delete everything from Q1 and insert them to Q2.
Step 3 : Swap names of Q1 and Q2.
That is change name of Q2 as Q1 and Q1 as Q2.
}
pop ( )
{
Delete an item from Q1
and return it.
}

Now let us use above steps.

Step 1 : push 10

Insert 10 to Q2

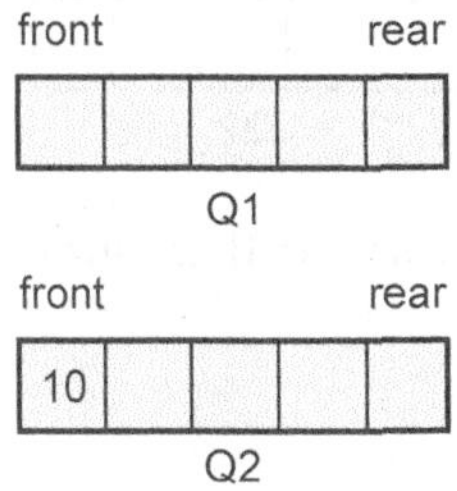

As there is nothing in Q1 no element will be copied to Q2. Now make Q2 as Q1 and Q1 as Q2.

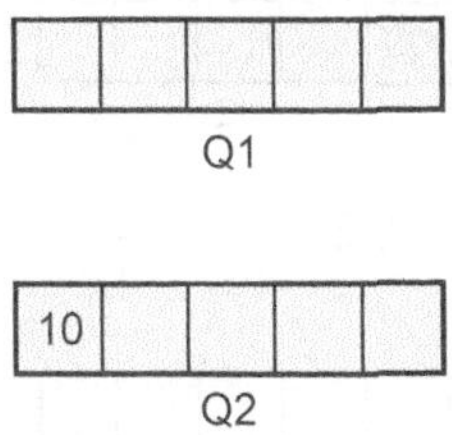

If pop operation needs to be performed then simply delete element from Q1 from front end.

Step 2 : push 20

Insert 20 to Q2.

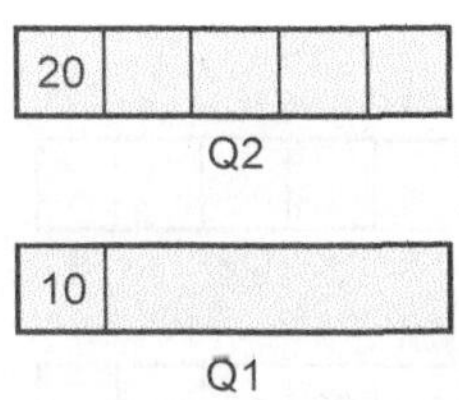

Copy all elements from Q1 to Q2.

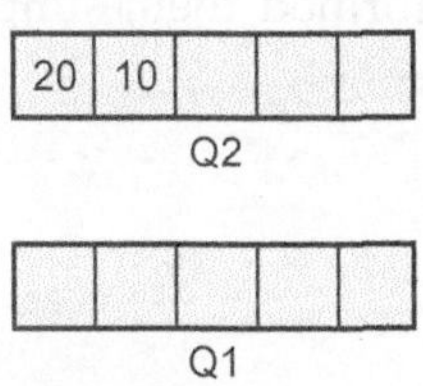

Now make Q2 as Q1 and Q1 as Q2.

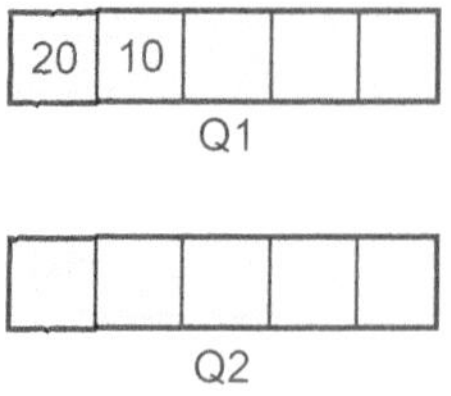

If pop operation needs to be performed then simply delete element from Q1.

Step 3 : push 30.

Insert 30 to Q2.

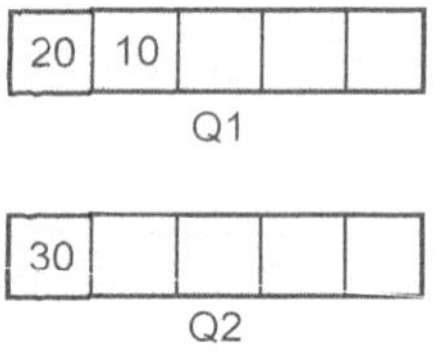

Copy all the elements from Q1 to Q2.

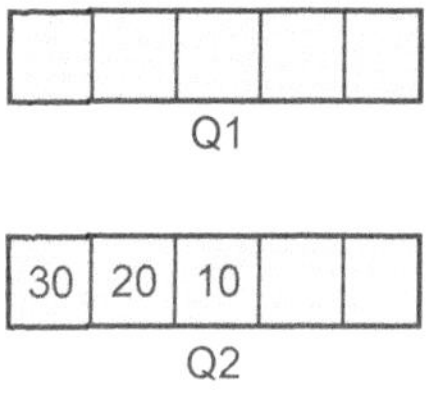

Make Q2 as Q1 and Q1 as Q2.

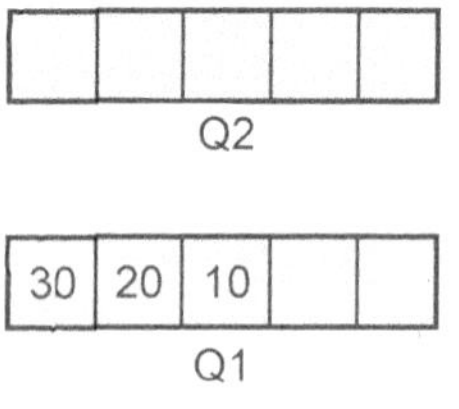

If pop operation needs to be performed then, simply delete element from Q1.

Step 4 : push (40)

Insert 40 to Q2

40				

Q2

30	20	10		

Q1

Copy all the elements from Q1 to Q2

40	30	20	10	

Q2

Q1

Now exchange the names of queues.

40	30	20	10	

Q1

Q2

If pop operation needs to be performed then simply delete element from Q1. In the similar manner if push (50) operation can be implemented and finally -

Q2

50	40	30	20	10

Q1

Review Question

1. *Explain about the operations of queue with an example.*

6.5 Circular Queue

As we have seen, in case of linear queue the elements get deleted logically. This can be shown by following Fig. 6.5.1.

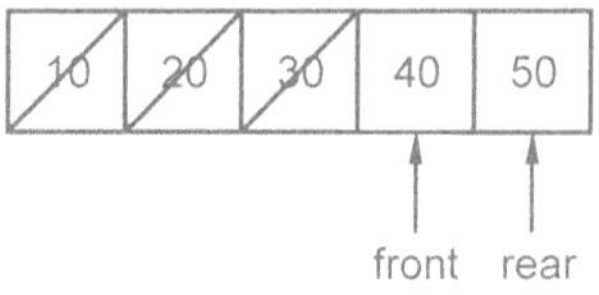

Fig. 6.5.1 Linear queue

We have deleted the elements 10, 20 and 30 means simply the front pointer is shifted ahead. We will consider a queue from front to rear always. And now if we try to insert any more element then it won't be possible as it is going to give "queue full !" message. Although there is a space of elements 10, 20 and 30 (these are deleted elements), we can not utilize them because queue is nothing but a linear array !

Hence there is a concept called circular queue. The main advantage of circular queue is we can utilize the space of the queue fully. The circular queue is shown by following Fig. 6.5.2.

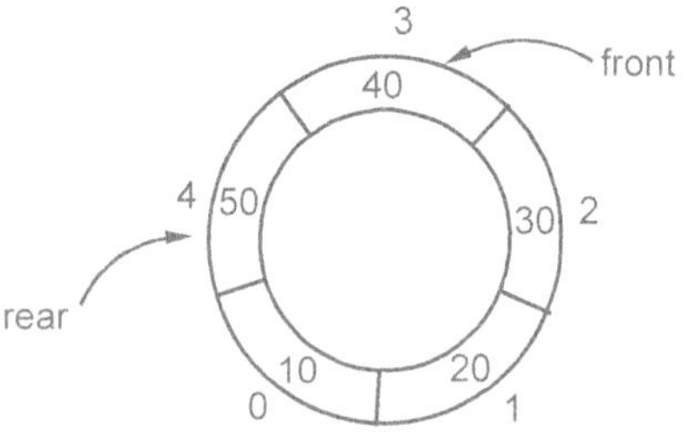

Fig. 6.5.2 Circular queue

Considering that the elements deleted are 10, 20 and 30.

There is a formula which has to be applied for setting the front and rear pointers, for a circular queue.

rear = (rear + 1) % size
front = (front + 1) % size

$$\begin{aligned} \text{rear} &= (\text{rear} + 1)\ \%\ \text{size} \\ &= (4 + 1)\ \%\ 5 \\ \text{rear} &= 0 \end{aligned}$$

So we can store the element 60 at 0th location similarly while deleting the element.

$$\begin{aligned} \text{front} &= (\text{front} + 1)\ \%\ \text{size} \\ &= (3 + 1)\ \%\ 5 \\ \text{front} &= 4 \end{aligned}$$

So delete the element at 4th location i.e. element 50

Let us see the 'C++' program now,

C++ Program

```
#include<iostream.h>
#include<conio.h>
#define MAX 10
class Queue
{
 int Que[MAX];
 int front,rear;
 public:
 Queue()//constructor defined
 {
       front=-1;
       rear=0;
 }
 void init();
 void insert(int ch);
 int delet();
 void display();
};

void Queue::init()
{
 int i;
 for(i=0;i<MAX;i++)
       Que[i]=0;
}
/*
------------------------------------------------------------
insert function
------------------------------------------------------------
*/

void Queue::insert(int item)
{
 if (front==(rear+1)%MAX)
 {
       cout << "Queue is full\n";
 }
 else
 {
       //setting front pointer for a single element in Queue
       if(front==-1)
       front=rear=0;
       else
       rear=(rear+1)%MAX;
```

```
        Que[rear]=item;
  }
 }
 /*
 ------------------------------------------------------------
 delet function
 ------------------------------------------------------------
 */
 int Queue::delet()
 {
  int val;
  if(front==-1)
  {
        cout << "Queue is empty\n";
        return 0; // return null on empty Queue
  }
  val= Que[front];//item to be deleted
  if(front==rear)//when single element is present
  {
        front=rear=-1;
  }
  else
         front=(front+1)%MAX;
  return val;
 }
 /*
 ------------------------------------------------------------
 Display function
 ------------------------------------------------------------
 */
 void Queue::display()
 {
  int i;
  i=front;
  while(i!=rear)
  {
        cout<<Que[i]<<" ";
        i=(i+1)%MAX;
  }
  cout<<Que[i]<<endl;
 }

 /*
 ------------------------------------------------------------
 The main function
 ------------------------------------------------------------
 */
```

```
void main()
{
 int i,choice,item;
 char ans='y';
 clrscr();
 Queue obj;
 obj.init();
 do
 {
        cout<<"   Menu"<<endl;
        cout<<"1.Insert \n 2.Delete \n 3.Display"<<endl;
        cout<<"Enter Your choice"<<endl;
        cin>>choice;
        switch(choice)
        {
         case 1:cout<<"Enter the element"<<endl;
                  cin>item;
                          obj.insert(item);
                          break;
         case 2:cout<<"The element to be deleted is"<<endl;
                  cout<<obj.delet();
                      break;
         case 3:obj.display();
                  break;
        }
        cout<<"Do You Want to Continue?"<<endl;
        ans=getche();
 }while(ans=='Y'||ans=='y');
 getch();
}
```

Output

```
Menu
    1.Insert
    2.Delete
    3.Display
    Enter Your choice: 1

    Enter the element
    10
    Do You Want to Continue?  y
      Menu
    1.Insert
    2.Delete
    3.Display
    Enter Your choice: 1
```

```
Enter the element
20
Do You Want to Continue? y
  Menu
1.Insert
2.Delete
3.Display
Enter Your choice: 1

Enter the element
30
Do You Want to Continue? y
  Menu
1.Insert
2.Delete
3.Display
Enter Your choice: 3
10 20 30
Do You Want to Continue? y
  Menu
1.Insert
2.Delete
3.Display
Enter Your choice: 2
The element to be deleted is
10
Do You Want to Continue? y
  Menu
1.Insert
2.Delete
3.Display
Enter Your choice: 3
20 30
Do You Want to Continue? n
```

Example 6.5.1 *Suppose a queue is maintained by circular array QUEUE with N = 12 memory cells. Find the number of elements in the queue when :*

i) FRONT = 4, REAR = 8, ii) FRONT = 10, REAR = 3

iii) FRONT = 5, REAR = 6, iv) Delete two elements after step (iii)

Solution : The circular queue with 12 Cell is.

i)

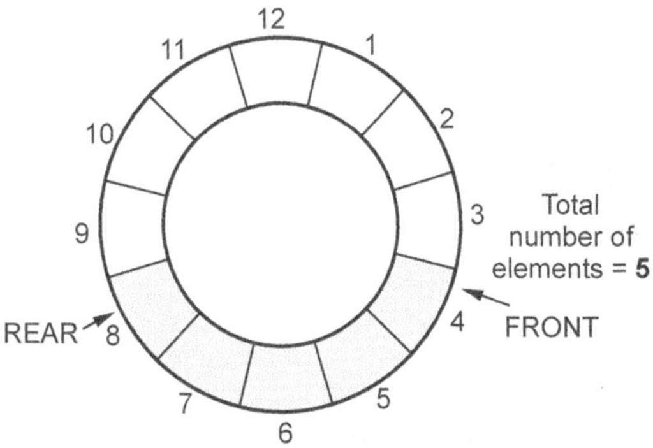

Fig. 6.5.3

ii)

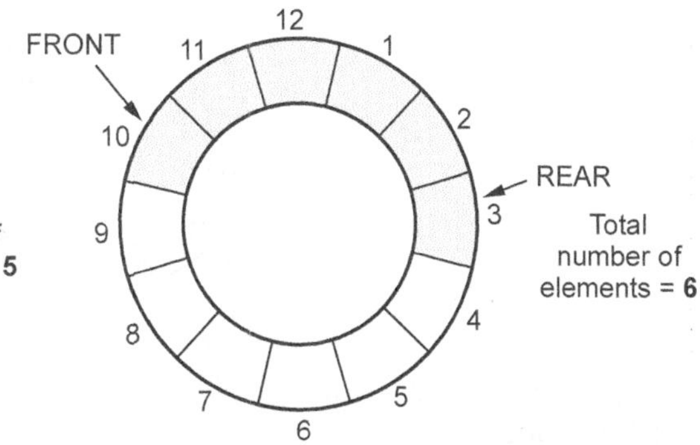

Fig. 6.5.4

iii)

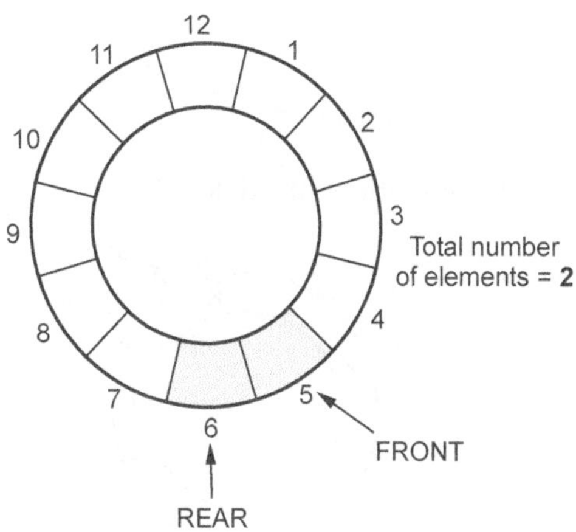

Fig. 6.5.5

iv) The circular queue after deleting 2 elements will be empty.

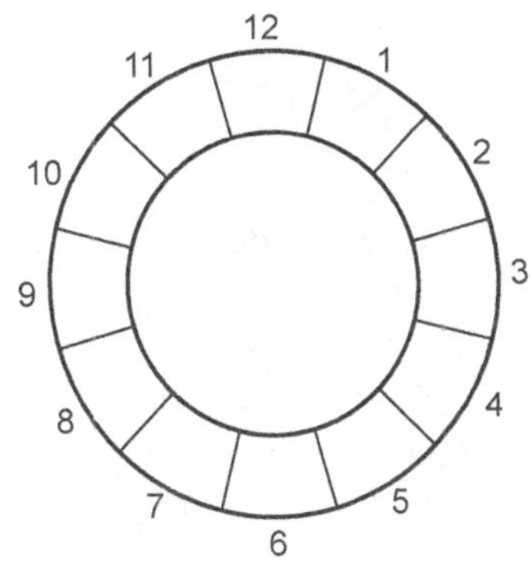

Fig. 6.5.6

Example 6.5.2 *Consider a circular queue of characters and is of size 6. "_" denotes an empty queue location. Show the queue contents as the following opns. take place :*

i) F is added to the queue *ii) Two letters are deleted.*

iii) K, L and M are added to the queue. *iv) Two letters are deleted.*

v) R is added to the queue. *vi) Two letters are deleted*

vii) S is added to the queue. *viii) Two letters are deleted.*

Initial queue configuration is :

FRONT = 2, REAR = 4, Queue : –, A, C, D, –, –

Solution : The initial configuration is,

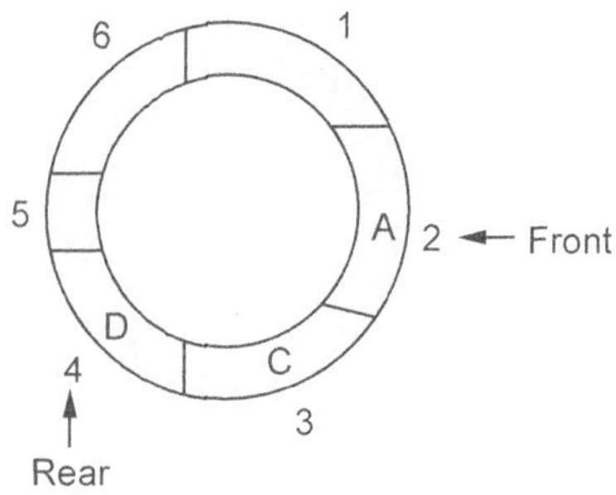

i) F is added

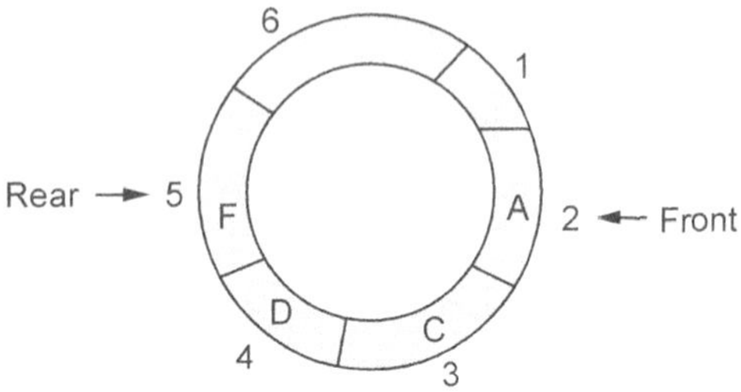

ii) Two letters are deleted

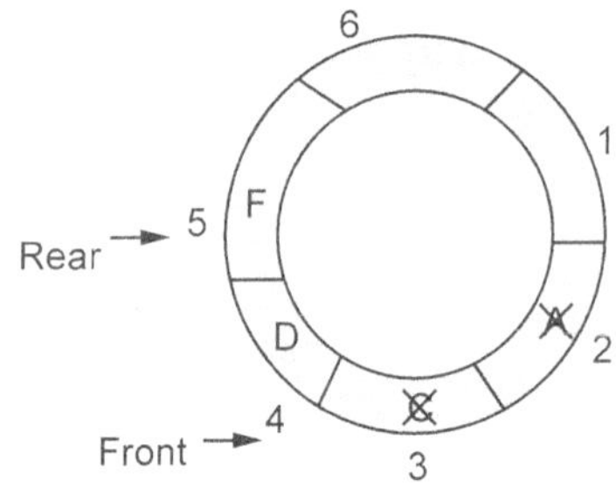

iii) K, L, M are added

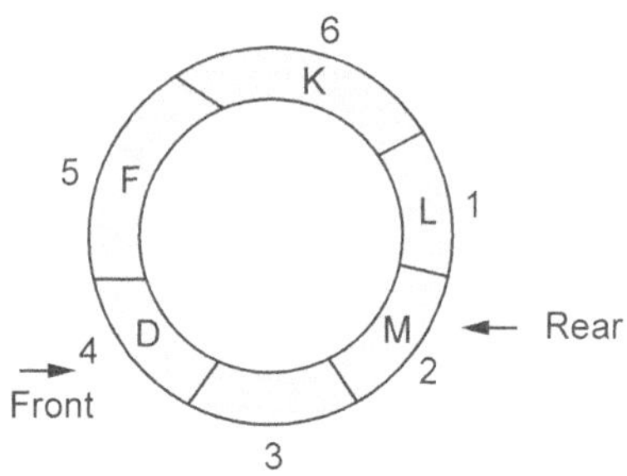

iv) Two letters are deleted

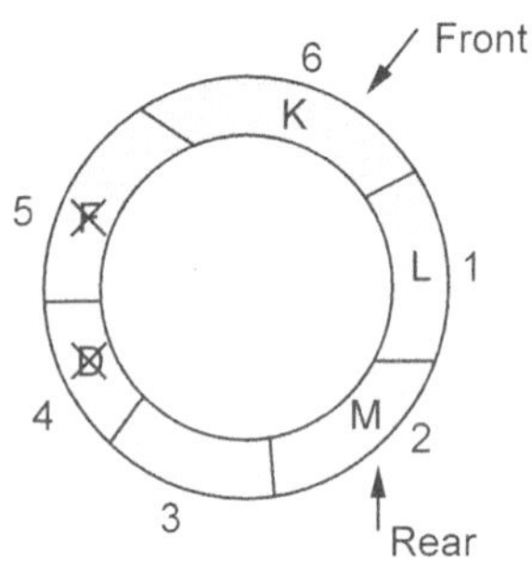

v) R is added

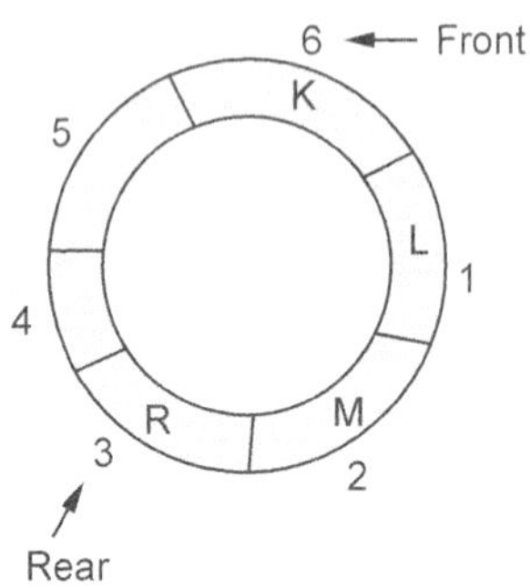

vi) Two letters are deleted

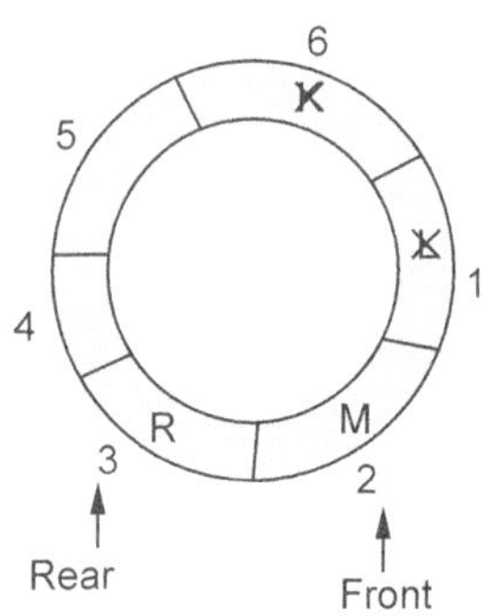

vii) S is added to the queue

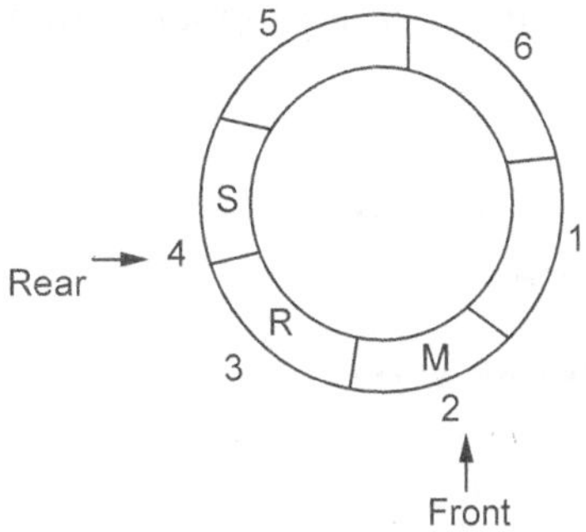

viii) Two letters are deleted

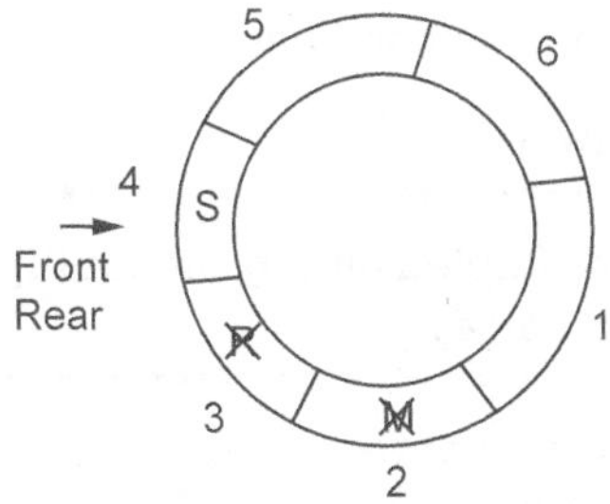

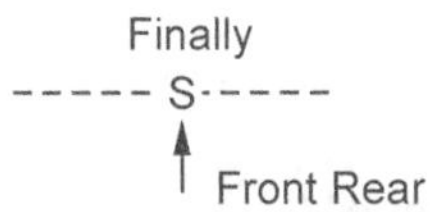

Review Question

1. *What is circular queue ? Implement insert and delete operations.*

6.6 Multi-queues

- One of the application of queues is categorization of data. And multiple queues can be used to store variety of data. We can implement multiple queues using single dimensional arrays.
- In a one dimensional array, multiple queues can be placed. Insertion from its rear end and deletion from its front end can be possible for desired queue. Refer Fig. 6.6.1

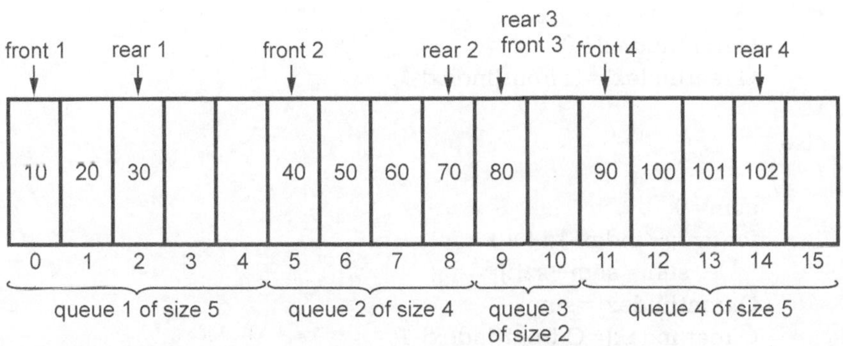

Fig. 6.6.1 Multiple queues using single array

- There are four queues having their own front and rear positioned at appropriate points in a single dimensional array.

- We can perform insertion and deletion of any element for any queue. We can declare the messages "queue full" and "queue empty" at appropriate situations for that particular queue.

C++ Program

```
/************************************************************
Program for implementing the multiple Queues using one
dimensional array.
************************************************************/
#include<iostream>
using namespace std;
#define size 20
class MultiQueue
{
	private:
	/*data structure for multiple queue*/
	struct mult_que {
			int que[size];
			int rear[size],front[size];
		}Q;
	public:
	int sz[size];/*stores sizes of individual queue*/
/*
 The set_que function
Purpose:This function initialises all the front and rear positions of individual queues.
All these queues has to be in a single dimensional array
*/
	void set_que(int index)
	{
		int sum,i;
		if(index==1)
		{
			Q.front[index]=0;
			Q.rear[index]=Q.front[index]-1;
		}
		else
		{
			sum=0;
			for(i=0;i<index-1;i++)
				sum=sum+sz[i];
			Q.front[index]=sum;
			Q.rear[index]=Q.front[index]-1;
	/*computed the rear position based on previous queues*/
		}
	}
/* The Qfull  Function*/
	int Qfull(int index)
```

```
    {
        int sum,i;
        sum=0;
        for(i=0;i<index;i++)
            sum=sum+sz[i];
        if(Q.rear[index]==sum-1)
            return 1;
        else
            return 0;
    }
/* The insert  Function */
    void insert(int item,int index)
    {
        int j;
        j=Q.rear[index];
        Q.que[++j] = item;
        Q.rear[index]=Q.rear[index]+1;
    }

/* The Qempty function */
    int Qempty(int index)
    {
        if(Q.front[index]>Q.rear[index])
            return 1;
        else
            return 0;
    }
/* The delet Function*/
    int delet(int index)
    {
        int item;
        item = Q.que[Q.front[index]];
        Q.que[Q.front[index]]=-1;
        Q.front[index]++;
        return item;
    }
/* The display Function */
    void display(int num)
    {
        int index,i;
        index=1;
        do
        {
            if(Qempty(index))
                cout<<"\n The Queue "<<index<<" is Empty";
            else
            {
```

```
                        cout<<"\n Queue number "<<index<<" is: ";
                        for(i=Q.front[index];i<=Q.rear[index];i++)
                        {
                                if(Q.que[i]!=-1)
                                        cout<<" "<<Q.que[i];
                        }
                }
                index++;
        }while(index<=num);
    }
};
/*  The main function */
int main(void)
{
    int choice,item,num,i,index;
    char ans;
    MultiQueue MQ;
    cout<<"\n\t\t Program For Multiple Queues";
    cout<<"\n How many Queues do you want?";
    cin>>num;
    cout<<"\n Enter The size of queue(Combined size of all Queues is 20)";
    for(i=0;i<num;i++)
        cin>>MQ.sz[i];
    for(index=1;index<=num;index++)
        MQ.set_que(index);/*front and rear values of each queue are set*/
    do
    {
        cout<<"\n Main Menu";
        cout<<"\n1.Insert\n2.Delete\n3.Display";
        cout<<"\n Enter Your Choice: ";
        cin>>choice;
        switch(choice)
        {
            case 1: cout<<"\n Enter in which queue you wish to insert the item? ";
                    cin>>index;
                    if(MQ.Qfull(index))
                    /*checking for Queue overflow*/
                        cout<<"\n Can not insert the element";
                    else
                    {
                        cout<<"\n Enter The number to be inseted: ";
                        cin>>item;
                        MQ.insert(item,index);
                    }
                    break;
            case 2:cout<<"\n Enter From which queue you wish to delete the item?
";
```

```
                    cin>>index;
                    if(MQ.Qempty(index))
                          cout<<"\n Queue Underflow!!";
                    else
                    {
                          item= MQ.delet(index);
                          cout<<"\n The deleted item is: "<<item;
                    }
                    break;
              case 3:MQ.display(num);
                    break;
              default:cout<<"\n Wrong choice!";
                    break;
        }
        cout<<"\n Do You Want to continue?";
        cin>>ans;
        }while(ans =='Y'||ans =='y');
    return(0);
}
```

Output

```
Program For Multiple Queues
How many Queues do you want?4
Enter The size of queue(Combined size of all Queues is 20)
4 6 5 5
    Main Menu
1. Insert
2. Delete
3. Display
    Enter Your Choice 1
 Enter in which queue you wish to  insert the item?3
 Enter The number to be inseted10
 Do You Want to continue?y
  Main Menu
1. Insert
2. Delete
3. Display
 Enter Your Choice1
 Enter in which queue you wish to  insert the item?4
 Enter The number to be inseted20
 Do You Want to continue?y
 Main Menu
1. Insert
2. Delete
3. Display
 Enter Your Choice1
 Enter in which queue you wish to  insert the item?3
 Enter The number to be inseted30
```

```
Do You Want to continue?y
Main Menu
1. Insert
2. Delete
3. Display
Enter Your Choice3
The Queue 1 is Empty
The Queue 2 is Empty
Queue number 3 is: 10 30
Queue number 4 is: 20
Do You Want to continue?y
Main Menu
1. Insert
2. Delete
3. Display
Enter Your Choice2

Enter From which queue you wish to  delete the item?3
The deleted item is 10
Do You Want to continue?y
Main Menu
1. Insert
2. Delete
3. Display
Enter Your Choice3
The Queue 1 is Empty
The Queue 2 is Empty
Queue number 3 is: 30
Queue number 4 is: 20
Do You Want to continue?n
```

6.7 Linked Queue and Operations

As we have seen that the queue can be implemented using arrays, it is possible to implement queues using linked list also. The main **advantage** in linked representation is that we need not have to worry about size of the queue. As in linked organization we can create as many nodes as we want so there will **not be a queue full condition** at all. The queue using linked list will be very much similar to a linked list. The only difference between the two is in queue the left most node is called front node and the right most node is called rear node. And we can not remove any arbitrary node from queue. We have to remove front node always :

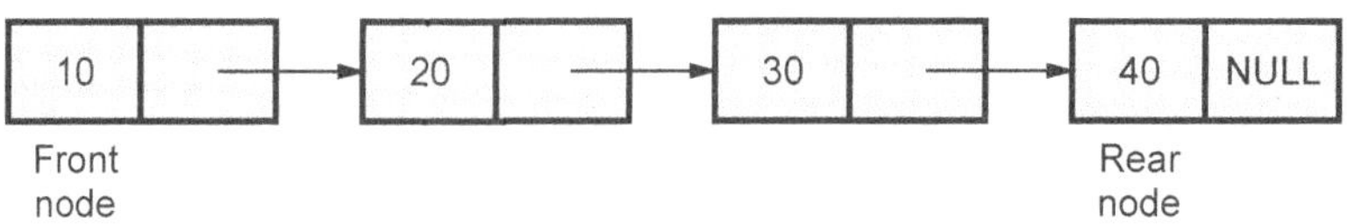

Fig. 6.7.1 Queue using linked list

The typical node structure will be

```
typedef struct node
      {
            int data;
            struct node *next;
      }Q;
```

Let us now see the 'C++' program for it.

C++ Program

```
/****************************************************************
Program For implementing the Queue using the linked list.
The queue full condition will never occur in this program.
****************************************************************/
#include<iostream.h>
#include<stdlib.h>
#include<conio.h>
//Declaration of Linked Queue data structure
class Lqueue
{
 private:
 typedef struct node
 {
  int data;
  struct node *next;
 }Q;
 Q *front,*rear;
 public:
 Lqueue();
 ~Lqueue();
 void create(),remove(),show();
 void insert();
 Q *delet();
 void display(Q *);
};

/*
------------------------------------------------------------
The constructor defined
------------------------------------------------------------*/
Lqueue::Lqueue()
{
 front=NULL;
 rear= NULL;
}
/*
```

```
------------------------------------------------------------
The create function
------------------------------------------------------------*/
void Lqueue::create()
{
insert();
}
/*
------------------------------------------------------------
The remove function
------------------------------------------------------------*/
void Lqueue::remove()
{
 front =delet();
}
/*
------------------------------------------------------------
The show function
------------------------------------------------------------*/
void Lqueue::show()
{
 display(front);
}
/*
------------------------------------------------------------
 The insert Function
------------------------------------------------------------
*/
void Lqueue::insert()
{
 char ch;
 Q *temp;
 clrscr();
 temp =new Q;//allocates memory for temp node
 temp->next=NULL;
 cout<<"\n\n\n\tInsert the element in the Queue\n";
 cin>>temp->data;

 if(front == NULL)//creating first node
 {
  front= temp;
  rear=temp;
  }
  else              //attaching other nodes
  {
      rear->next=temp;
      rear=rear->next;
```

```
        }
}

/*
------------------------------------------------------------
The QEmpty Function
------------------------------------------------------------*/
int Qempty(Q *front)
{
 if(front ==NULL)
  return 1;
 else
  return 0;
}
/*
------------------------------------------------------------
The delet Function
------------------------------------------------------------
*/
Q *Lqueue::delet()
{
  Q *temp;
  temp=front;
  if(Qempty(front))
  {
        cout<<"\n\n\t\tSorry!The Queue Is Empty\n";
        cout<<"\n Can not delete the element";
  }
  else
   {
        cout<<"\n\tThe deleted Element Is  "<<temp->data;
        front=front->next;
        temp->next=NULL;
        delete temp;
   }
 return front;
 }
/*
------------------------------------------------------------
 The display Function
------------------------------------------------------------
*/
void Lqueue::display(Q *front)
{
 if(Qempty(front))
  cout<<"\n The Queue Is Empty\n";
 else
```

```
 {
  cout<<"\n\t The Display Of Queue Is \n ";
  for(;front !=rear->next;front=front->next)
      cout<<"  "<<front->data;
 }
 getch();
}
/*
------------------------------------------------------------------
The destructor defined
------------------------------------------------------------------
*/
Lqueue::~Lqueue()
{
 if((front!=NULL)&&(rear!=NULL))
 {
  front=NULL;
  rear=NULL;
  delete front;
  delete rear;
 }
}

/*
------------------------------------------------------------------
The main Function
Calls:create,remove,show
Called By:O.S.
------------------------------------------------------------------
*/
void main(void)
{
 char ans;
 int choice;
 Lqueue Que;
 do
 {
      clrscr();
      cout<<"\n\tProgram For Queue Using Linked List\n";
      cout<<"\n            Main Menu";
      cout<<"\n1.Insert\n2.Delete \n3.Display";
      cout<<"\n Enter Your Choice";
      cin>>choice;
      switch(choice)
      {
       case 1 :Que.create();
                  break;
```

```
        case 2 :Que.remove();
                    break;
        case 3 :Que.show();
                    break;
        default: cout<<"\nYou have entered Wrong Choice"<<endl;
                    break;
    }
    cout<<"\nDo You Want To See Main Menu?(y/n)"<<endl;
    ans = getch();
  }while(ans == 'y' || ans == 'Y');
  getch();
}
```

Output

```
        Program For Queue Using Linked List
            Main Menu
1.Insert
2.Delete
3.Display
 Enter Your Choice 1

 Insert the element in the Queue
 10

Do You Want To See Main Menu?(y/n)
            Program For Queue Using Linked List
            Main Menu
1.Insert
2.Delete
3.Display
 Enter Your Choice 1

 Insert the element in the Queue
20

Do You Want To See Main Menu?(y/n)
        Program For Queue Using Linked List
            Main Menu
1.Insert
2.Delete
3.Display
 Enter Your Choice 1

 Insert the element in the Queue
30

Do You Want To See Main Menu?(y/n)
        Program For Queue Using Linked List
```

```
            Main Menu
      1.Insert
      2.Delete
      3.Display
       Enter Your Choice 1

       Insert the element in the Queue
      40

      Do You Want To See Main Menu?(y/n)

            Program For Queue Using Linked List

            Main Menu
      1.Insert
      2.Delete
      3.Display
       Enter Your Choice3

            The Display Of Queue Is
        10  20  30  40
      Do You Want To See Main Menu?(y/n)

            Program For Queue Using Linked List

            Main Menu
      1.Insert
      2.Delete
      3.Display
       Enter Your Choice2

            The deleted Element Is  10
      Do You Want To See Main Menu?(y/n)

            Program For Queue Using Linked List

            Main Menu
      1.Insert
      2.Delete
      3.Display
       Enter Your Choice2

            The deleted Element Is  20
      Do You Want To See Main Menu?(y/n)

            Program For Queue Using Linked List
```

```
            Main Menu
    1.Insert
    2.Delete
    3.Display
     Enter Your Choice3

          The Display Of Queue Is
      30  40
    Do You Want To See Main Menu?(y/n)n
```

Program Explanation

In above program we have defined a constructor Lqueue in which front and rear are initialized to 'NULL'.

In insert function

First we will allocate a node called 'temp' with next field assigned with 'Null' value. Suppose we want to insert data 10 then

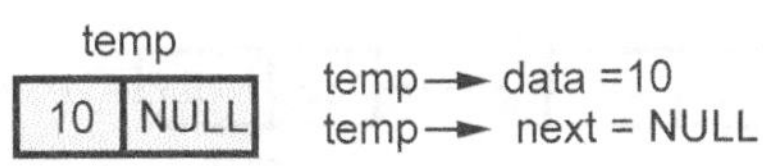

Now mark this node as queue's front and rear

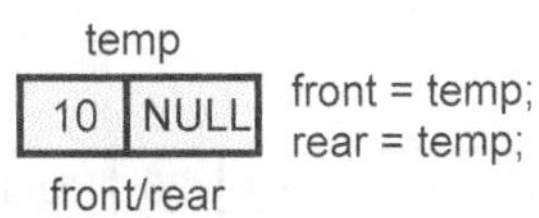

Now next, suppose we want to insert 20 in queue then a new node 'temp' will be created with data 20.

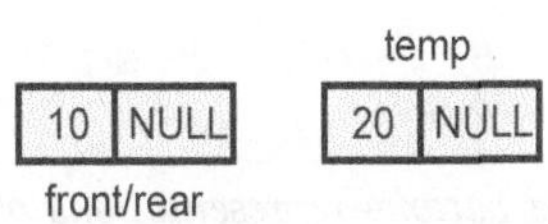

Then, the queue will be formed by setting appropriate front and rear.

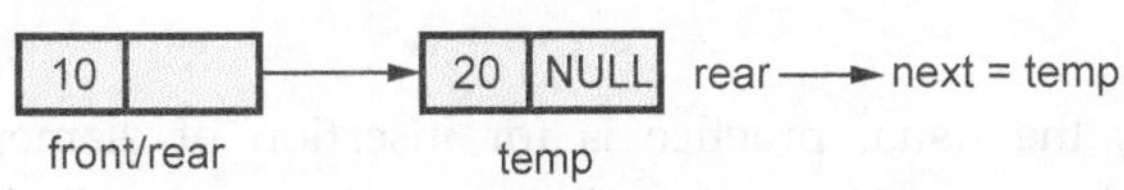

Then

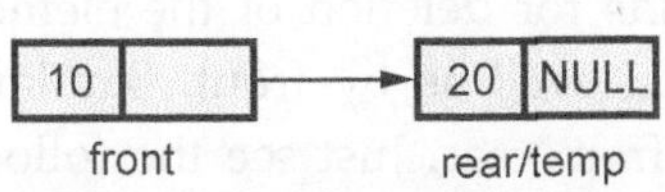

Continuing in this fashion we can create a linked queue.

In delet function

We assume that a queue is created like this -

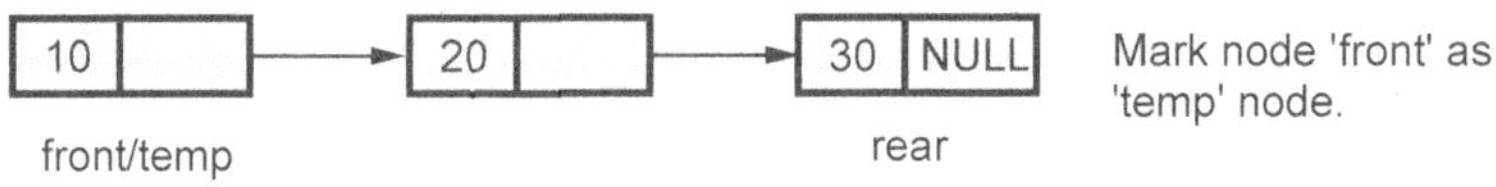

Simply display a message that "The deleted Element is 10" (i.e. temp → data). Then set front as

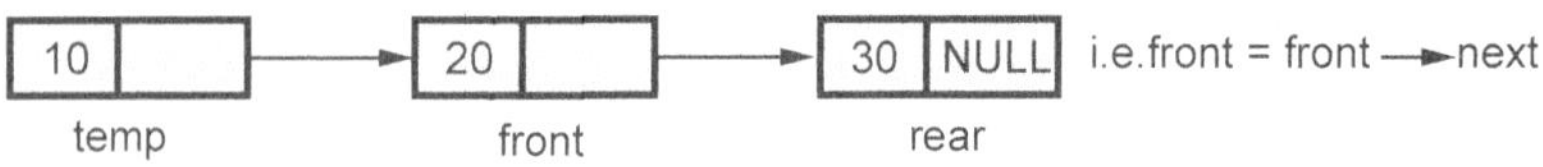

Then

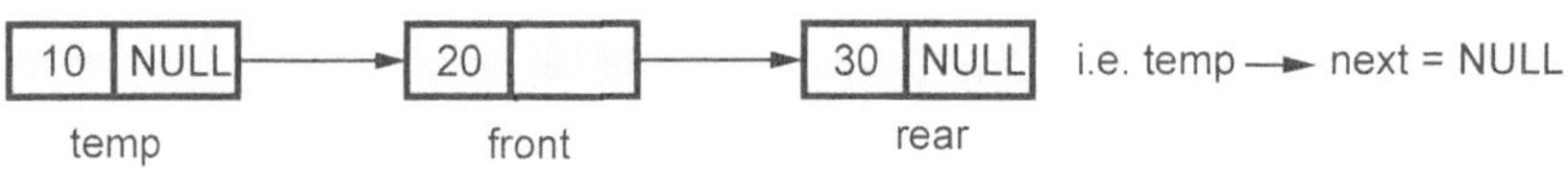

Then,

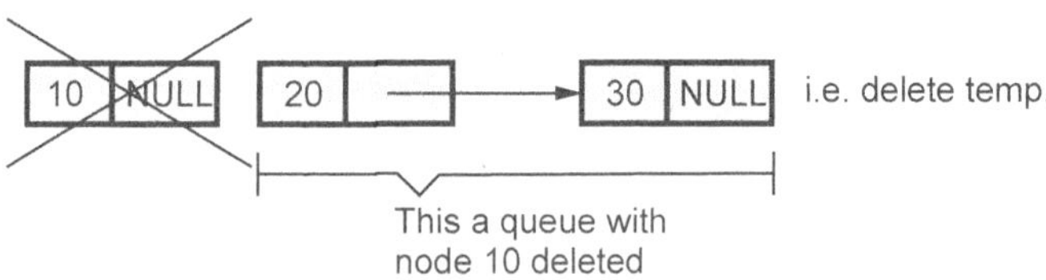

Review Questions

1. *Define queue. Discuss about the various representations of a queue.*
2. *Discuss about various representations of queue.*

6.8 Deque

In a linear queue, the usual practice is for insertion of elements we use one end called rear and for deletion of elements we use another end called as front. But in the doubly ended queue we can make use of both the ends for insertion of the elements as well as we can use both the ends for deletion of the elements. That means it is possible to insert the elements by rear as well as by front. Similarly it is possible to delete the elements from front as well as from rear. Just see the following figure to understand the concept of doubly ended queue i.e. deque.

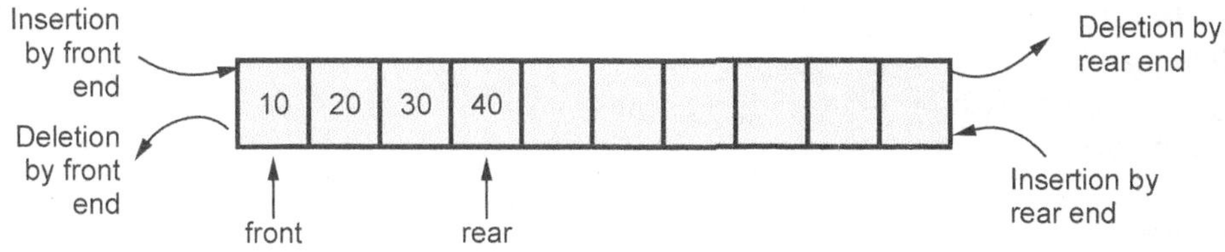

Fig. 6.8.1 Doubly ended queue

As we know, normally we insert the elements by rear end and delete the elements from front end. Let us say we have inserted the elements 10, 20, 30 by rear end.

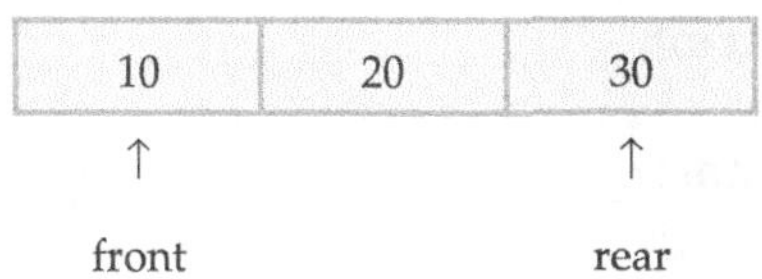

Now if we wish to insert any element from front end then first we have to shift all the elements to the right.

For example if we want to insert 40 by front end then, the deque will be

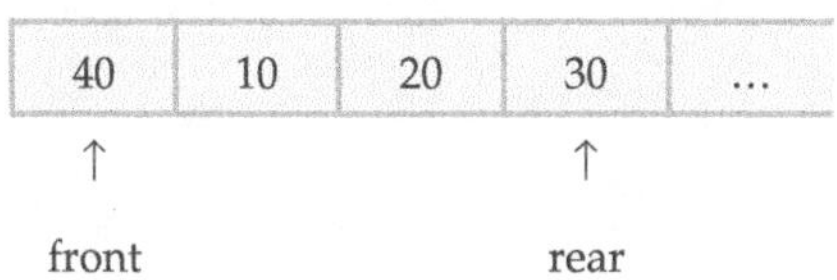

Inserted 40 in the queue by front end

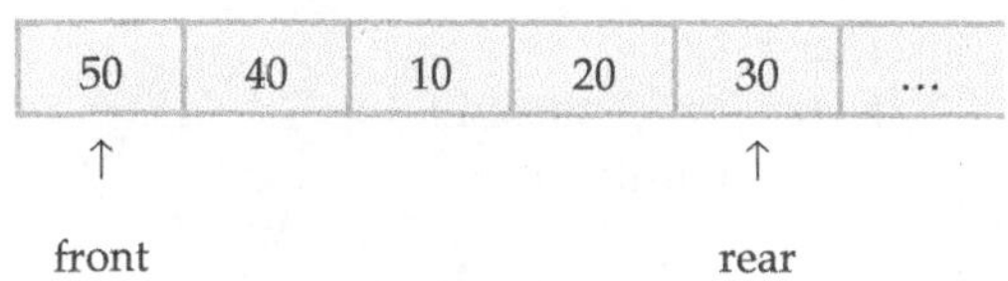

Inserted 50 in the queue by front end

(a) Insertion by front end

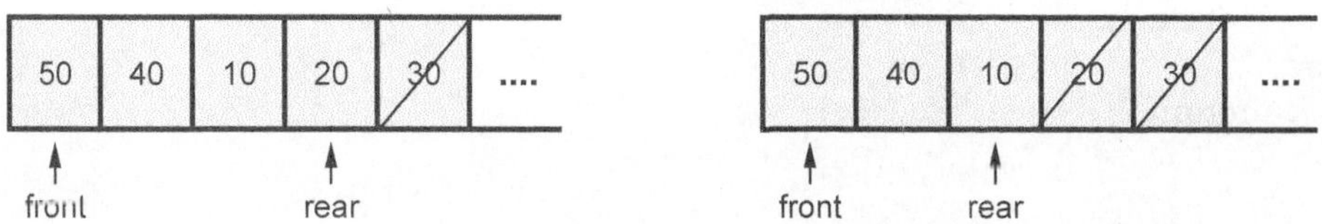

(b) Deletion by rear end

Fig. 6.8.2 Operations on deque

We can place –1 for the element which has to be deleted.

Let us see the implementation of deque using arrays

```
/*************************************************************************
Program To implement Doubly ended queue using arrays
*************************************************************************/
```

```
#include<iostream>
#include<stdlib.h>
#define size 5
using namespace std;
class Dqueue
{
   private:
         int que[size];
   public:
         int front,rear;
         Dqueue();
         int Qfull();
         int Qempty();
         int insert_rear(int item);
         int delete_front();
         int insert_front(int item);
         int delete_rear();
         void display();
};

Dqueue::Dqueue()
{
   front=-1;
   rear=-1;
   for(int i=0;i<size;i++)
         que[i]=-1;
}

int Dqueue::Qfull()
{
   if(rear==size-1)
         return 1;
   else
         return 0;
}

int Dqueue::Qempty()
{
   if((front>rear)||(front==-1&&rear==-1))
         return 1;
  else
         return 0;
}

int Dqueue::insert_rear(int item)
{
```

```
    if(front==-1&&rear==-1)
        front++;
    que[++rear]=item;
    return rear;
}

int Dqueue::delete_front()
{
    int item;
    if(front==-1)
        front++;
    item=que[front];
    que[front]=-1;
    front++;
    return item;
}

int Dqueue::insert_front(int item)
{
    int i,j;
    if(front==-1)
        front++;
    i=front-1;
    while(i>=0)
    {
        que[i+1]=que[i];
     i--;
    }
    j=rear;
    while(j>=front)
    {
        que[j+1]=que[j];
        j--;
     }
     rear++;
     que[front]=item;
     return front;
}
int Dqueue::delete_rear()
{
    int item;
    item=que[rear];
    que[rear]=-1;/*logical deletion*/
    rear--;
    return item;
}
```

```
void Dqueue::display()
{
    int i;
    cout<<"\n Straight Queue is:";
        for(i=front;i<=rear;i++)
    cout<<" "<<que[i];
}

int main()
{
    int choice,item;
    char ans;
    ans='y';
    Dqueue obj;
    cout<<"\n\t\t Program For doubly ended queue using arrays";
    do
    {
    cout<<"\n1.insert by rear\n2.delete by front\n3.insert by front\n4.delete by rear";
        cout<<"\n5.display\n6.exit";
        cout<<"\n Enter Your choice ";
        cin>>choice;
        switch(choice)
        {
         case 1:if(obj.Qfull())
                    cout<<"\n Doubly ended Queue is full";
                else
                {
                cout<<"\n Enter The item to be inserted";
                cin>>item;
                obj.rear=obj.insert_rear(item);
                }
              break;
    case 2:if(obj.Qempty())
              cout<<"\n Doubly ended Queue is Empty";
              else
              {
              item=obj.delete_front();
              cout<<"\n The item deleted from queue is "<<item;
              }
              break;
    case 3:if(obj.Qfull())
              cout<<"\n Doubly ended Queue is full";
              else
              {
              cout<<"\n Enter The item to be inserted";
              cin>>item;
              obj.front=obj.insert_front(item);
```

```
                }
                break;
        case 4:if(obj.Qempty())
                 cout<<"\n Doubly ended Queue is Empty";
                else
                {
                item=obj.delete_rear();
                cout<<"\n The item deleted from queue is "<<item;
                }
                break;
        case 5:obj.display();
                break;
        case 6:exit(0);
  }
  cout<<"\n Do You Want To Continue?";
  cin>>ans;
 }while(ans=='y'||ans=='Y');
 return 0;
}
```

Output

```
          Program For doubly ended queue using arrays
 1.insert by rear
 2.delete by front
 3.insert by front
 4.delete by rear
 5.display
 6.exit
  Enter Your choice 1

  Enter The item to be inserted 10

 Do You Want To Continue?y

1.insert by rear
2.delete by front
3.insert by front
4.delete by rear
5.display
6.exit
 Enter Your choice 1

 Enter The item to be inserted 20

 Do You Want To Continue?y

1.insert by rear
2.delete by front
```

```
3.insert by front
4.delete by rear
5.display
6.exit
 Enter Your choice 1

 Enter The item to be inserted 30
 Do You Want To Continue?y

1.insert by rear
2.delete by front
3.insert by front
4.delete by rear
5.display
6.exit
 Enter Your choice 5

 Straight Queue is:  10  20  30
 Do You Want To Continue?
```

Review Questions

1. *Define dequeue and give its example.*
2. *What is dequeue ? Write pseudo code to perform insertion and deletion of element in a linked implementation of dequeue.*

6.9 Priority Queue

The priority queue is a data structure having a collection of elements which are associated with specific ordering. There are two types of priority queues –

1. Ascending priority queue
2. Descending priority queue

Application of Priority Queue

1. The typical example of priority queue is scheduling the jobs in operating system. Typically operating system allocates priority to jobs. The jobs are placed in the queue and position1 of the job in priority queue determines their priority. In operating system there are three kinds of jobs. These are real time jobs, foreground jobs and background jobs. The operating system always schedules the real time jobs first. If there is no real time job pending then it schedules foreground jobs. Lastly if no real time or foreground jobs are pending then operating system schedules the background jobs.

2. In network communication, to manage limited bandwidth for transmission the priority queue is used.

3. In simulation modeling, to manage the discrete events the priority queue is used.

Types of Priority Queue

The elements in the priority queue have specific ordering. There are two types of priority queues –

1. **Ascending Priority Queue** - It is a collection of items in which the items can be inserted arbitarily but only smallest element can be removed.

2. **Descending Priority Queue** - It is a collection of items in which insertion of items can be in any order but only largest element can be removed.

In priority queue, the elements are arranged in any order and out of which only the smallest or largest element allowed to delete each time.

The implementation of priority queue can be done using arrays or linked list. The data structure heap is used to implement the priority queue effectively.

ADT for Priority Queue

Various operations that can be performed on priority queue are -

1. Insertion 2. Deletion 3. Display

Hence the ADT for priority queue is given as below -

Instances :

P_que[**MaX**] is a finite collection of elements associated with some priority.

Precondition :

The front and rear should be within the maximum size **MAX**.

Before insertion operation , whether the queue is full or not is checked.

Before any deletion operation, whether the queue is empty or not is checked.

Operations :

1. Create() – The queue is created by declaring the data structure for it.
2. insert() – The element can be inserted in the queue
3. delet() – If the priority queue is ascending priority queue then only smallest element is deleted each time. And if the priority queue is descending priority queue then only largest element is deleted each time.
4. Display() – The elements of queue are displayed from front to rear.

The implementation of priority queue using arrays is as given below -

1. Insertion operation

While implementing the priority queue we will apply a simple logic. That is while inserting the element we will insert the element in the array at the proper position. For example if the elements are placed in the queue as -

9	12			
que[0] front	que[1] rear	que[2]	que[3]	que[4]

And now if an element 8 is to be inserted in the queue then it will be at 0th location as -

8	9	12		
que[0] front	que[1]	que[2] rear	que[3]	que[4]

If the next element comes as 11 then the queue will be -

8	9	11	12	
que[0] front	que[1]	que[2]	que[3] rear	que[4]

The C++ function for this operation is as given below -

```
int Pr_Q::insert(int rear,int front)
{
   int item,j;
   cout<<"\nEnter the element: ";
   cin>>item;
   if(front ==-1)
               front++;
   j=rear;
   while(j>=0 && item<que[j])
   {
    que[j+1]=que[j];
    j--;
   }
   que[j+1]=item;
   rear=rear+1;
   return rear;
}
```

2. Deletion operation

In the deletion operation we are simply removing the element at the front.

For example if queue is created like this –

8	9	11	12	
que[0]	que[1]	que[2]	que[3]	que[4]
front			rear	

Then the element at que[0] will be deleted first

8	9	11	12	
que[0]	que[1]	que[2]	que[3]	que[4]
	front		rear	

and then new front will be que[1].

The deletion operation in C++ is as given below -

```
int Pr_Q::delet(int front)
{
        int item;
        item=que[front];
        cout<<"\n The item deleted is  "<<item;
        front++;
        return front;
}
```

The complete implementation of priority queue is as given below -

C++ Program

```
/************************************************************
Program for implementing the ascending priority Queue
*************************************************************/
      /*Header Files*/
      #include<iostream>
      #define SIZE 5
      using namespace std;
      class Pr_Q
      {
       private:
            int que[SIZE];
       public:
            int rear,front;
            Pr_Q();
            int insert(int rear,int front);
```

```
        int Qfull(int rear);
        int delet(int front);
        int Qempty(int rear,int front);
        void display(int rear,int front);
};
Pr_Q::Pr_Q()
{
 front=0;
 rear=-1;
}
int Pr_Q::insert(int rear,int front)
{
 int item,j;
 cout<<"\nEnter the element: ";
 cin>>item;
 if(front ==-1)
        front++;
 j=rear;
 while(j>=0 && item<que[j])
 {
  que[j+1]=que[j];
  j--;
 }
 que[j+1]=item;
 rear=rear+1;
 return rear;
}
int Pr_Q::Qfull(int rear)
{
 if(rear==SIZE-1)
  return 1;
 else
 return 0;
}

int Pr_Q::delet(int front)
{
 int item;
 item=que[front];
 cout<<"\n The item deleted is "<<item;
 front++;
 return front;
}
int Pr_Q::Qempty(int rear,int front)
{
 if((front==-1)||(front>rear))
```

```
  return 1;
  else
  return 0;
 }
 void Pr_Q::display(int rear,int front)
 {
  int i;
  cout<<"\n The queue is: ";
  for(i=front;i<=rear;i++)
  cout<<" "<<que[i];
 }

 int main(void)
 {
  int choice;
  char ans;
  Pr_Q obj;

  do
  {
   cout<<"\n\t\t Priority Queue\n";
   cout<<"\n Main Menu";
   cout<<"\n1.Insert\n2.Delete\n3.Display";
   cout<<"\n Enter Your Choice: ";
   cin>>choice;
   switch(choice)
   {
        case 1:if(obj.Qfull(obj.rear))
                        cout<<"\n Queue IS full";
                else
                    obj.rear=obj.insert(obj.rear,obj.front);
                break;
        case 2:if(obj.Qempty(obj.rear,obj.front))
                    cout<<"\n Cannot delete element";
                else
                    obj.front=obj.delet(obj.front);
                break;
        case 3:if(obj.Qempty(obj.rear,obj.front))
                    cout<<"\n Queue is empty";
                else
                obj.display(obj.rear,obj.front);
                break;
   default:cout<<"\n Wrong choice: ";
          break;
   }
   cout<<"\n Do You Want TO continue?";
```

```
  cin>>ans;
 }while(ans=='Y' ||ans=='y');
 return 0;
}
```

Output

```
            Priority Queue

Main Menu
1.Insert
2.Delete
3.Display
 Enter Your Choice: 1

Enter the element: 20

 Do You Want TO continue?

            Priority Queue

 Main Menu
1.Insert
2.Delete
3.Display
 Enter Your Choice: 1

Enter the element: 30

 Do You Want TO continue?

            Priority Queue
Main Menu
1.Insert
2.Delete
3.Display
 Enter Your Choice: 1

Enter the element: 10

 Do You Want TO continue?

            Priority Queue
 Main Menu
1.Insert
2.Delete
3.Display
 Enter Your Choice: 1
```

```
Enter the element: 40

Do You Want TO continue?

                Priority Queue
Main Menu
1.Insert
2.Delete
3.Display
Enter Your Choice: 3

The queue is:  10 20 30 40
Do You Want TO continue?

                Priority Queue

Main Menu
1.Insert
2.Delete
3.Display
Enter Your Choice: 2

The item deleted is  10
Do You Want TO continue?
```

Example 6.9.1 *Specify which of the following applications would be suitable for a first-in-first-out queue and Justify your answer :*

i) A program is to keep track of patients as they check into a clinic, assigning them to doctors on a first come, first-served basis.

ii) An inventory of parts is to be processed by part number.

iii) A dictionary of words used by spelling checker is to be created.

iv) Customers are to take numbers at a bakery and be served in order when their numbers come-up.

Solution :

i) No, this application will not be suitable for first come first serve queue because sometimes some serious patients may be come and he/she needs doctors in urgent.

ii) Yes, for this application first-in-first-out queue is suitable because here the part number must be stored in specific manner (order).

iii) No, because words can be chosen in random order.

iv) Yes, bakery customers must be served if first come first serve basis.

Review Questions

1. *What are the applications of the data structure priority queue.*
2. *What is priority queue ? What is its use ? Give the function to add an element in priority queue.*
3. *Write a note on priority queues.*
4. *What is priority queue ? Explain insert and delete operations in detail using multidimensional array implementation.*
5. *List down applications of queue.*

❑❑❑

SOLVED MODEL QUESTION PAPER

(As Per 2019 Pattern)

Fundamentals of Data Structures

S.E. (Computer) Sem - I (End Sem)

Time : 2 $\frac{1}{2}$ Hours] [Total Marks : 70

Instructions to the candidates :

1) Answer Q.1 or Q.2, Q.3 or Q.4, Q.5 or Q.6, Q.7 or Q.8.

2) Neat diagrams must be drawn wherever necessary.

3) Figures to the right indicate full marks.

4) Make suitable assumptions if necessary.

Q.1 (a) *Explain sentinel search technique.* **(Refer section 3.2.2)** [6]

(b) *Write a non recursive Python Program to illustrate binary search technique* **(Refer section 3.2.3)** [6]

(c) *Explain selection sort technique with suitable example.* **(Refer section 3.5.3)** [6]

OR

Q.2 (a) *Give the difference between linear search and binary search.* **(Refer section 3.2.3)** [4]

(b) *Explain Fibonacci search technique with suitable example.* **(Refer section 3.2.4)** [6]

(c) *Write a Python program for implementing radix sort technique.* **(Refer section 3.6.1)** [8]

Q.3 (a) *Explain C++ code for insertion of a node in a singly linked list.* **(Refer section 4.6)** [6]

(b) *What is doubly linked list ? Differentiate between singly and doubly linked list.* **(Refer section 4.8)** [6]

(c) *Explain different types of linked list.* **(Refer section 4.7)** [5]

OR

Q.4 (a) *Write a C++ function for addition of two polynomials using linked list.* **(Refer section 4.12)** [7]

(b) *Explain generalized linked list with suitable example.* **(Refer section 4.13)** [6]

(c) *What are applications of linked list ?* **(Refer section 4.11)** [4]

Q.5 (a) *What is stack ? Give an ADT of stack.* **(Refer sections 5.1 and 5.2)** [6]

(b) *Write C++ functions for push and pop operations. Illustrate these operations with suitable example.* **(Refer section 5.4)** [6]

(c) *Write a short note on - Multiple stack.* **(Refer section 5.5)** [6]

OR

Q.6 (a) *Write a C++ code for evaluation of postfix expression.* **(Refer section 5.8)** [6]

(b) *Explain the concept of recursion with suitable example.* **(Refer section 5.10)** [6]

(c) *Write a note on - Backtracking algorithmic strategy.* **(Refer section 5.11)** [6]

Q.7 (a) *What is queue ? Give an ADT of queue.* **(Refer sections 6.1 and 6.2)** [5]

(b) *Explain the concept of circular queue in detail.* **(Refer section 6.5)** [6]

(c) *Write C++ code for performing insert and delete operations in linked queue.* **(Refer section 6.7)** [6]

OR

Q.8 (a) *What is priority queue ? Explain.* **(Refer section 6.9)** [8]

(b) *Write a C++ program for performing various operations on queue. Illustrate these operations with sample input data.* **(Refer section 6.4)** [9]

❑❑❑